בס"ד

ירצוני

Courts and Elites in the Hellenistic Empires

EDINBURGH STUDIES IN ANCIENT PERSIA

Dealing with key aspects of the ancient Persian world from the Achaemenids to the Sasanians: its history, reception, art, archaeology, religion, literary tradition (including oral transmissions), and philology, this series provides an important synergy of the latest scholarly ideas about this formative ancient world civilisation.

SERIES EDITOR

Lloyd Llewellyn-Jones, University of Edinburgh

EDITORIAL ADVISORY BOARD

Touraj Daryaee
Andrew Erskine
Thomas Harrison
Irene Huber
Keith Rutter
Jan Stronk

TITLES AVAILABLE IN THE SERIES

Courts and Elites in the Hellenistic Empires:
The Near East After the Achaemenids, c. 330 to 30 BCE
By Rolf Strootman

FORTHCOMING TITLES

Greek Perspectives of the Achaemenid Empire:
Persia Through the Looking Glass
By Janett Morgan

The Bactrian Mirage:
Iranian and Greek Interaction in Western Central Asia
By Michael Iliakis

Plutarch and the Persica
By Eran Almagor

Visit the Edinburgh Studies in Ancient Persia website at
www.euppublishing.com/series/esap

Courts and Elites in the Hellenistic Empires

The Near East After the Achaemenids, c. 330 to 30 BCE

Rolf Strootman

EDINBURGH
University Press

© Rolf Strootman, 2014

Edinburgh University Press Ltd
22 George Square, Edinburgh EH8 9LF

www.euppublishing.com

Typeset in Sabon
by Norman Tilley Graphics Ltd, Northampton
and printed and bound in the United States of America

A CIP record for this book is available from
the British Library

ISBN 978 0 7486 9126 5 (hardback)
ISBN 978 0 7486 9127 2 (webready PDF)

The right of Rolf Strootman to be identified
as Author of this work has been asserted in
accordance with the Copyright, Designs
and Patents Act 1988, and the Copyright
and Related Rights Regulations 2003
(SI No. 2498).

Contents

List of Illustrations

Acknowledgements

Many people assisted me in the different stages of writing this book. The present text, which grew from my PhD thesis *The Hellenistic Royal Courts*, has benefited from the critical remarks of my erstwhile supervisors, Henk Versnel and Josine Blok. I am obliged, too, to Lloyd Llewellyn-Jones and Andrew Erskine of Edinburgh University for their support, and to my editors at Edinburgh University Press, Jen Daly, Carol MacDonald, and Fiona Sewell. Michel Buijs, Floris van den Eijnde, Hans-Joachim Gehrke, Diana Kretschmann, Amélie Kuhrt, Bert van der Spek, Lina van 't Wout and Sara Wijma read and commented upon parts of the original PhD manuscript; Els Meijer helped me to prepare the bibliography. I of course take full responsibility for any remaining errors, typos and 'Slauerhoffjes'. A travel grant from the Philologisch Studiefonds enabled me to visit Hellenistic sites in Syria, Jordan, Israel and Palestine. Special gratitude is due, as always, to Elise Wiggers, for her support, patience and wisdom.

Abbreviations

Items listed here are periodicals, monographs and works of reference cited in this book. Abbreviations are used for classical authors and works in accordance with the *Oxford Classical Dictionary* (3rd edn, 1996).

AA	*Archäologischer Anzeiger*
AC	*L'Antiquité Classique*
AchHist	H. W. A. M. Sancisi-Weerdenburg et al. (eds), *Achaemenid History* (Leiden 1987–2003)
AJA	*American Journal of Archaeology*
AJPh	*American Journal of Philology*
AncSoc	*Ancient Society*
ANET	J. B. Pritchard (ed.), *Ancient Near Eastern Texts Relating to the Old Testament* (3rd edn, Princeton 1969)
ArchPF	*Archiv für Papyrusforschung*
Austin	M. M. Austin, *The Hellenistic World from Alexander to the Roman Conquest: A Selection of Ancient Sources in Translation* (Cambridge 1981)
AW	*Ancient World*
BCH	*Bulletin de Correspondance Hellénique*
BCHP	R. J. van der Spek and I. L. Finkel, *Babylonian Chronicles of the Hellenistic Period* (forthcoming; preliminary online at www.livius.org)
Berve	H. Berve, *Das Alexanderreich auf prosopografischer Grundlage* (Munich 1926)
BICS	*Bulletin of the Institute of Classical Studies*
BMCR	*Bryn Mawr Classical Review*
CAF	T. Kock, *Comicorum Atticorum Fragmenta* (Leipzig 1880–8)
CAH	*Cambridge Ancient History*
CAT	M. Dietrich, O. Loretz and J. Sanmartín (eds), *The*

	Cuneiform Alphabetic Texts from Ugarit, Ras Ibn Hani and Other Places (Münster 1995)
CE	*Chronique d'Égypte*
CGF	G. Kaibel, *Comicorum Graecorum Fragmentum* (Berlin 1899)
CJ	*Classical Journal*
C Phil.	*Classical Philology*
CQ	*Classical Quarterly*
DHA	*Dialogues d'histoire ancienne*
FGrH	F. Jacoby, *Fragmente der griechischen Historiker* (Leiden 1923–)
FHG	C. Müller, *Fragmenta Historicum Graecorum* (Paris 1841–70)
Fraser	P. M. Fraser, *Ptolemaic Alexandria* (Oxford 1972)
G&R	*Greece and Rome*
Glassner	J.-J. Glassner, *Chroniques mésopotamiens* (Paris 1993)
GRBS	*Greek, Roman and Byzantine Studies*
I.Del.	*Inscriptions de Délos* (Paris 1926–72)
IG	*Inscriptiones Graecae* (Berlin 1873–)
JDAI	*Jahrbücher des deutschen archäologischen Instituts*
JHS	*Journal of Hellenic Studies*
JRS	*Journal of Roman Studies*
OCD	S. Hornblower and A. Spawforth (eds), *Oxford Classical Dictionary* (3rd edn, Oxford 1996)
OGIS	*Orientis Graeci Inscriptiones Selectae*
PF	*Persepolis Fortification Tablet*
RA	*Revue Archéologique*
RBL	*Review of Biblical Literature* (online at www.bookreviews.org)
RE	A. Pauly, G. Wissowa and W. Kroll (eds), *Real-Encyclopädie der klassischen Altertumswissenschaft* (Stuttgart 1893–)
REG	*Revue des Études Grecque*
RIG	C. Michel (ed.), *Recueil d'Inscriptions Grecques* (Brussels 1900)
Sachs-Hunger	A. J. Sachs and H. Hunger, *Astronomical Diaries and Related Texts from Babylonia* (Vienna 1988, 1989, 1996)
SEG	*Supplementum Epigraphicum Graecum* (Leiden and Amsterdam 1923–)
Sel. Pap.	A. S. Hunt, D. L. Page and C. C. Edgar (eds), *Select Papyri* (Cambridge 1932)

Syll.[3] W. Dittenberger (ed.), *Sylloge Inscriptionum Graecarum* (3rd edn, Leipzig 1915–24)

TAPhA *Transactions of the American Philological Association*

Walbank F. W. Walbank, *A Historical Commentary on Polybius* (Oxford 1957, 1967, 1979)

ZPE *Zeitschrift für Papyrologie und Epigraphik*

The Hellenistic Dynasties

All dates are BCE.

279	Meleagros
279	Antipatros II 'Etesias'
279–277	Sosthenes (*stratēgos* only)
277–274	Antigonos II Gonatas
274–272	Pyrrhos of Epeiros, again
272–239	Antigonos II (restored)

THE ANTIGONID DYNASTY

306–301	Antigonos I Monophthalmos
306–287	Demetrios I Poliorketes
287–239	Antigonos II Gonatas
239–229	Demetrios II
229–221	Antigonos III Doson
221–179	Philip V
179–168	Perseus

THE ATTALID DYNASTY

283–263	Philetairos (dynast only)
263–241	Eumenes I (dynast only)
241–197	Attalos I Soter (king in 238/7)
197–159	Eumenes II Philadelphos
159–138	Attalos II Philadelphos
138–133	Attalos III Philometor

THE SELEUKID DYNASTY

312–281	Seleukos I Nikator
281–261	Antiochos I Soter
261–246	Antiochos II Theos
246–226	Seleukos II Kallinikos
226–222	Seleukos III Soter
223/2–187	Antiochos III the Great
187–175	Seleukos IV Philopator
175–164	Antiochos IV Epiphanes
164–162	Antiochos V Eupator
162–150	Demetrios I Soter
150–145	Alexandros I Balas
145–142	Antiochos VI Epiphanes
145–139	Demetrios II Nikator
139–129	Antiochos VII Sidetes

129–125	Demetrios II (restored)
128–122	Alexandros II Zabinas
125–120	Kleopatra I Thea
125	Seleukos V
125–96	Antiochos VIII Grypos
113–95	Antiochos IX Kyzenikos
96–95	Seleukos VI Epiphanes
95–88	Demetrios III Eukairos
95–88	Antiochos X Eusebes
95	Antiochos XI Epiphanes
95–83	Philip I Epiphanes
86–85	Antiochos XII Dionysos
83–69	Kleopatra II Selene (regent)
85–58	Seleukos VII Philometor?
69–64	Antiochos XIII Asiatikos
66–63	Philip II Philorhomaios

THE PTOLEMAIC DYNASTY

323–282	Ptolemy I Soter (king 305)
282–246	Ptolemy II Philadelphos
246–222	Ptolemy III Euergetes
222–204	Ptolemy IV Philopator
204–180	Ptolemy V Epiphanes
180–145	Ptolemy VI Philometor
170–163	Ptolemy VIII Euergetes
145–144	Ptolemy VII Philopator
145–116	Ptolemy VIII (restored)
116–101	Kleopatra III Euergetes
116–107	Ptolemy IX Philometor
107–88	Ptolemy X Alexandros
88–80	Ptolemy IX (restored)
80	Kleopatra Berenike
80	Ptolemy XI Alexandros
80–51	Ptolemy XII Neos Dionysos
58–55	Berenike IV
51–47	Ptolemy XIII Philopator
51–30	Kleopatra VII Philopator
48–47	Arsinoë
47–44	Ptolemy XIV Philopator
36–30	Ptolemy XV Caesar ('Caesarion')

Series Editor's Preface

Edinburgh Studies in Ancient Persia focuses on the world of ancient Persia (pre-Islamic Iran) and its reception. Academic interest and fascination in ancient Persia has burgeoned in recent decades and research on Persian history and culture is now routinely filtered into studies of the Greek and Roman worlds; Biblical scholarship too is now more keenly aware of Persian-period history than ever before, while, most importantly, the study of the history, cultures, languages and societies of ancient Iran is now a well-established discipline in its own right.

Persia was, after all, at the centre of ancient world civilisations. This series explores that centrality throughout several successive 'Persian empires': the Achaemenid dynasty (founded c. 550 BCE) saw Persia rise to its highest level of political and cultural influence, as the Great Kings of Iran fought for, and maintained, an empire which stretched from India to Libya and from Macedonia to Ethiopia. The art and architecture of the period reflect both the diversity of the empire and proclaim a single centrally-constructed theme: a harmonious world-order brought about by a benevolent and beneficent king. Following the conquests of Alexander the Great, the Persian Empire fragmented but maintained some of its infrastructures and ideologies in the new kingdoms established by Alexander's successors, in particular the Seleucid dynasts who occupied the territories of western Iran, Mesopotamia, the Levant and Asia Minor. But even as Greek influence extended into the former territories of the Achaemenid realm, at the heart of Iran a family of nobles, the Parthian Dynasty, rose to threaten the growing imperial power of Rome. Finally, the mighty Sasanian Dynasty ruled Iran and much of the Middle East from the second century CE onwards, proving to be a powerful foe to Late Imperial Rome and Byzantium. The rise of Islam, a new religion in Arabia, brought a sudden end to the Sasanian Dynasty in the mid-600s CE.

These successive Persian dynasties left their record in the historical, linguistic and archaeological materials of the ancient world and *Edinburgh Studies in Ancient Persia* has been conceived to give scholars working in these fields the opportunity to publish original research and explore new methodologies in interpreting the antique past of Iran. This series will see scholars working with bona fide Persian and other Near Eastern materials, giving access to Iranian self-perceptions and the internal workings of Persian society, placed alongside scholars assessing the perceptions of the Persianate world from the outside (predominately through Greek and Roman authors and artefacts). The series will also explore the reception of ancient Persia (in historiography, the arts and politics) in subsequent periods, both within and outwith Iran itself.

Edinburgh Studies in Ancient Persia represents something of a watershed not only in better appreciation and understanding of the rich and complex cultural heritage of Persia, but also of the lasting significance of the Achaemenids, Parthians and Sasanians and the impact that their remarkable civilisations have had on wider Persian, Middle Eastern and world history. Written by established and up-and-coming specialists in the field, this series provides an important synergy of the latest scholarly ideas about this formative ancient world civilisation.

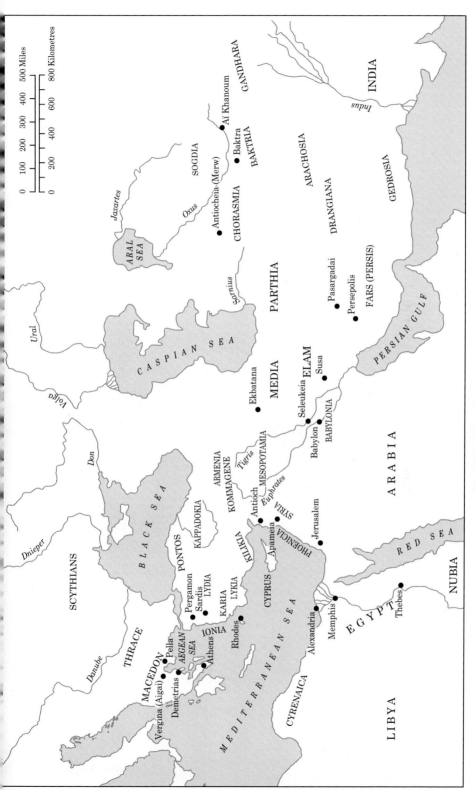

Map 1. The Hellenistic Near East, 330 to 30 BCE.

Introduction:
Court and Empire in the
Hellenistic Near East

After the fall of the Achaemenids in 330 BCE the eastern Mediterranean, Iran and Central Asia were ruled by Macedonian empires, successor states of Alexander the Great's empire. Ending two centuries of relative unity, the former Achaemenid world now became divided between three competing imperial dynasties: the Seleukids, Ptolemies and Antigonids. How far these dynasties (and especially the Seleukids, who controlled territories stretching from the Aegean to present-day Afghanistan) willingly or unwillingly 'Hellenised' the Middle East is difficult to ascertain due to a relative dearth of archaeological evidence from the third and second centuries BCE. What we do know from both literary sources and the archaeological record is that in the course of time, the Seleukids increasingly cooperated and intermarried with noble families with an Iranian and mixed Macedonian-Iranian identity, which resulted in the creation of various small kingdoms and the re-emergence of Iranian culture, particularly in Anatolia, Armenia and Iran – often in the form of a deliberate invention of tradition that may be called 'Persianism'. Still, the Macedonian and Greek element played a pivotal role too, and probably more so than recent scholarship has suggested. Greeks and Macedonians after all did constitute the central elites in the Hellenistic empires. The post-Achaemenid centuries were a time of vigorous cultural encounters in the Middle East and Central Asia.

In the Hellenistic world,[1] dynastic courts were the focus of

---

[1] By 'Hellenistic world' I mean the eastern Mediterranean, Middle East and Central Asia in the period of Macedonian domination, roughly between 330 and 30 BCE. My concern is mainly with the Macedonian empires of this period. I use the word 'Hellenistic' for convenience, *not* to suggest that the period is primarily characterised by the spread of Greek culture and/or the hybridisation of 'western' and 'eastern' culture. We will return to the problem of 'Hellenism in the east' later in this Introduction.

international politics from Greece and Egypt to Baktria. Of course, most peoples inhabiting these areas had for centuries been accustomed to dealing with imperial rulers. The political constellation, however, changed in so far as after Alexander the principal royal dynasties were no longer Iranians, but families of Macedonian stock supported by imperial elites consisting predominantly of Macedonians and Greeks. For the cities in mainland Greece the necessity of dealing with empire increased (though, like the cities in Babylonia, most of these *poleis* remained de facto self-governing, autonomous polities); in Egypt the imperial court was suddenly much closer by, and a more substantial part of the taxes paid by Egyptians was reinvested in Egypt itself; in Asia Minor several competing empires were active in the same areas at the same time. It was for such reasons *and* because of the violent competition between the empires that local polities had perhaps more reason to deal with courts than had been the case in the age of the all-powerful Achaemenids. Because of competition, the empires themselves, too, had to make strong efforts to negotiate with local political units and regional monarchies.

As a result of Greek influence and different political dynamics, novel forms of court culture and political ideology developed in the Hellenistic empires. Hellenistic court culture and ideology would have a profound influence on later monarchies in the Near East and Iran. The Hellenistic kings reshaped their Greek, Macedonian and Persian legacy to create their own form of monarchy which was neither 'western' nor 'eastern'. Appropriated by both Parthian kings and Roman emperors, the culture and ideology of the Hellenistic courts eventually influenced the evolution of royal ideology and court culture in western Europe and the Islamic east.[2]

The aim of this study is to cast new light on the phenomenon of Hellenistic kingship by approaching it from the angle of the court.[3] Ever since the publication of Norbert Elias' *Höfische Gesellschaft* (1969) and Jürgen von Kruedener's *Die Rolle des Hofes im Absolutismus* (1973), historians studying the cultural and political history of Europe after the Middle Ages have understood the im-

[2] For general discussions of Hellenistic kingship and its main problems see Préaux 1978 I: 181–388; Walbank 1984a; Gruen 1996; Virgilio 1999; Ma 2003. Specifically on Ptolemaic kingship: Herz 1992; Hazzard 2000; Hölbl 2001: 77–123 and 160–77. For Hellenistic ruler cult see Chaniotis 2003.
[3] This book grew from my PhD thesis, *The Hellenistic Royal Courts*, written initially for Leiden University, and submitted to the Department of History of the University of Utrecht in 2007. I have tried to take into consideration as many relevant books and articles that became available after I finished the final version of my dissertation in 2006 as possible.

portance of the court for the evolution of the modern European state system, and the number of publications is proportionately substantial. 'Of all the institutions affecting the political, religious and cultural life of early modern Europe,' John Adamson wrote, 'there was probably none more influential than the court.'[4] The study of the early modern court focuses on three basic issues: (1) the court as a socio-political system, (2) the court as the central stage for the monarchy's self-presentation, and (3) the court as the focal point of scientific and cultural developments. I have transferred this three-fold approach to the Hellenistic age.

The present study focuses on the socio-political function of the court. The objects of study are primarily the courts of the Macedonian empires of the Hellenistic period. The great divide between on the one hand a classical or Achaemenid period, and on the other hand a Hellenistic period, can be useful in some contexts – e.g. in the case of the transition from Persian to Macedonian rule in the Middle East – but can also be quite unhelpful in others, particularly in Greek history. I see more political continuity in the Aegean world, and much less continuity in the Middle East, than is usually presumed in current scholarship. I will therefore include among the Hellenistic monarchies the Argead monarchy, the original, localised Macedonian kingdom that became an empire under Philip II and Alexander the Great; the Attalids of Pergamon, though not strictly speaking Macedonians or even Greeks, will play a role, too; and in the third chapter, which is devoted to palaces, I have included a brief discussion of the Hekatomnid dynasts of Karia, who created an Aegean maritime empire in the fourth century, and whose influence on the genesis of early Hellenistic monarchy may have been more significant than that of the Achaemenids or classical Greece. Still, the focus will be on the Ptolemaic, Seleukid and Antigonid empires.

The first of these, the Ptolemaic dynasty, initially controlled a maritime empire striving after hegemony in the Aegean and eastern Mediterranean basin, as well as the Red Sea region. In the second century BCE, after Antiochos III had all but destroyed the Ptolemaic Mediterranean empire, Ptolemaic influence was more or less restricted to Egypt. The Ptolemaic kingdom then became more 'Egyptian' in nature – but the original claims to the whole of Alexander's empire, or indeed universal dominion, were never given up. Imperial ideology, it seems, was hardly adjusted to the new political

---

[4] Adamson 1999b: 7; the modern study of the court, and its relevance for understanding Hellenistic court culture, will be introduced more extensively below.

circumstances and several attempts were made by later Ptolemaic monarchs to make the kingdom a superpower again. Indeed, as late as 34 BCE the last Ptolemaic ruler, Kleopatra VII, still maintained that she had inherited from her (Seleukid *and* Ptolemaic) ancestors an empire stretching from the Aegean to India (see Chapter 10).

The Ptolemies' military antagonists, the Seleukids, were the principal heirs to Alexander's Macedonian empire and the earlier Persian empire of the Achaemenids. The Seleukid state was an archetypal empire: a hegemonic system comprising a huge variety of peoples, religions and polities bound together by the charisma of a 'Great King' – an elaborate (and flexible) network of personal relations rather than a rigidly structured 'state' (see below). The court was the hub of this network. At its greatest extent under Antiochos III, around 195 BCE, Seleukid hegemony stretched from the Pamir Mountains to Thrace. Due to internal strife over the succession, the empire declined after the death of Antiochos IV in 164 BCE. Its existence as a world empire and a superpower was effectively terminated after 140, when the Parthians conquered western Iran, captured the Seleukid centre of gravity, Babylonia, and took over the title of Great King by right of victory. The destruction of the Seleukid field army and the death of its last competent king, Antiochos VII Sidetes, in 129 signified the ultimate collapse of Seleukid power. The dynasty thereafter lingered on for another half century, until finally Pompey abolished the Seleukid monarchy in 64 BCE virtually without a blow. The historical significance of the Seleukids goes well beyond their being merely the transmitters of Achaemenid institutions and ideology to the Parthians and Sasanians. If anything, the Seleukids were the transmitters of *Seleukid* institutions and ideology to the Parthians and Sasanians.[5]

The last, and least successful, of the Macedonian powers was the Antigonid empire: a hegemonic conglomerate based on Macedon that was active in the Balkans, mainland Greece and the wider Aegean between 276 and 168 BCE. The endeavours of Philip V to resurrect his dynasty as a major imperial power were terminated when he was defeated by the Romans in the early second century BCE.

There are three reasons why the court culture of these dynastic empires may be deemed an important subject. First, the court was the apex of political power in the Hellenistic world. Studying it may help us understand Hellenistic kingship and imperialism: the formal

---

[5] Engels 2011 and Strootman 2012.

and social aspects of the court may teach us more about the nature of monarchic rule and the way it functioned vis-à-vis subject peoples and cities; courtly ritual and ceremonial may shed new light on the ideology of Hellenistic kingship because it shows how kings saw themselves or wished to be seen by others. Second, court culture may clarify the nature and significance of 'Hellenism'. Finally, in the Macedonian empires of the Hellenistic age the foundations were laid for the development of the royal court in later history, in both Christian Europe and the Islamic east. In the next section something more will be said about this last aspect.

THE IMPACT OF HELLENISTIC KINGSHIP AND COURT CULTURE

In the Hellenistic age, the eastern Mediterranean and Near East witnessed the emergence of a new and confident imperial culture when Macedonian kings inherited and shaped as their own the legacy of the Achaemenid empire. Later history owes much to these new kingdoms. The Romans initially organised their eastern empire as a system of vassal states (the so-called 'client kingdoms') which was essentially a Seleukid inheritance, as the Romans at first took over Macedonian imperial infrastructure with only minor adjustments. Roman rulers furthermore adopted and adapted the Hellenistic notion of universal empire and other aspects of Hellenistic royal ideology, and accepted and promoted a Hellenistic-style ruler cult in cities in the east. Hellenistic monarchic imagery – the ruler portrait, Dionysos and Herakles as models for rulers, the sun as an image of cosmic rule – influenced the shaping of an image for the Roman emperor as *cosmocrator*. The Romans certainly did not develop their idea of empire from scratch.

The Parthian kings likewise took over much from their Macedonian, particularly Seleukid, predecessors. Centuries later, the Ummayad caliphs, in developing a monarchic ideology for the Islamic world empire, amalgamated a Hellenistic philosophy of kingship with the ideologies of the Sasanians and Byzantines.[6]

The Hellenistic kings of course did not invent 'western' and 'eastern' imperial ideology, but contrary to the prevalent view they did play an important role in its development. This is true especially of the Seleukids, who dominated the Middle East and Iran in the two centuries between Achaemenids and Arsakids. The Seleukids did

---

[6] Al-Azmeh 2001: 11–34.

more than simply transmit eastern traditions of world empire; they further developed that tradition, adding their own refinements and originality. The Parthians, and after them the Sasanian Persians, did not have to reach back all the way to the Achaemenids for inspiration (though the Sasanians for propaganda reasons claimed they did so). It seems that the Parthian monarchy at first presented itself as merely a better version of the Seleukid state. Just as the Seleukids Hellenised ancient Near Eastern imperial ideology, so the later Arsakids and the Sasanians Iranianised the ideology of the Seleukids.[7] But the Iranianising trend of later Hellenistic history had already begun under the Seleukids.

Hellenistic influence is manifest, too, in the court culture of several later kingdoms and empires. Thus, the household of the first Roman emperors was in part modelled on Hellenistic examples. Hellenistic influence included formal aspects such as the institution of imperial *amici*, palace architecture and palace decoration (the Palatine, Nero's Domus Aurea), regalia (the use of purple, and later the diadem, sceptre and perhaps *globus*), and even hairstyle.[8] This influence was not restricted to the formative period of the early Principate; in the age of the Dominate, it may be argued, a kind of 'Hellenistic revival' took place in the field of regalia and ritual (though at that time no one, of course, would have used the word 'Hellenistic' to denote the old Macedonian dynasties of the east). In particular, the development of the ceremony of *adventus* and the use of solar imagery to signify universal power were derived directly from Rome's Hellenistic legacy. Via Rome and Byzantium, aspects of Hellenistic court culture eventually lived on in medieval and Renaissance Europe and in the Ottoman empire.

The reason for the remarkable persistence of Hellenistic royal

---

[7] On Sasanian imperial ideology and its sources see now Shayegan 2011; see also Canepa 2009 on the rival universalistic claim in the late Roman and Sasanian empires, and Canepa 2010, showing how the first Sasanian emperors, Ardashir I and Shapur I, endeavoured to distance themselves from their Parthian and Seleukid predecessors by creating a neo-Persian ideology of empire, and a vision of the past that connected them directly with the Achaemenids.

[8] For the adoption of Hellenistic royal hairstyles by women of the house of Augustus see Kleiner 2005: 242–60, tracing Hellenistic antecedents of the Roman monarchy's self-presentation during the early Principate. Hardie 1986: 85–156 has argued for Hellenistic influence on early Roman imperial ideology as apparent in the theme of gigantomachy in the *Aeneid*. Kosmetatou 2003: 173 makes a strong case for Attalid influence on Roman imperial ideology, although perhaps overestimating the uniqueness of the royal ideology of the Attalids. For the adoption of formal aspects of Hellenistic court society in the Principate see Buraselis 1994: 24–31 with n. 14; Buraselis emphasises the similarities between Hellenistic *philoi* and Roman *amici* but remains undecided regarding the question of influence and continuity; cf. Savalli-Lestrade 1998, showing how in the east pre-existing *philia* networks were preserved by the Roman empire to bind cities to the imperial centre.

culture in the Roman empire and beyond was its typical amalgamation of 'eastern' and 'western' aspects of kingship and empire. The
basics of Hellenistic imperial rule and ideology – forms of taxation
and administration, the ideology of world empire, the centrality and
autocracy of the king – certainly had eastern antecedents, but these
were integrated into the more modest-looking Macedonian tradition
of kingship, as well as their being adapted to Greek morality, philosophy and religion. This resulted in, among other things, a form of
personal monarchy that emphasised the qualities and character of
individual kings and queens. What made Hellenistic kingship an
acceptable model for the developing Roman monarchy is precisely
that: the fact that it was a more or less *Greek*, Mediterranean version
of eastern autocratic rule. Thus, Hellenistic kingship provided a
model of autocratic rule and world empire that was not necessarily,
in the eyes of Greeks and Romans, a form of 'oriental despotism'.
Ancient perceptions of Hellenistic kingship as either 'Asian' or
Hellenic were contextual, and the integration of Hellenistic royal
style into Roman political culture did not of course preclude the
contemporaneous portrayal, in antipathetic Roman propaganda and
historiography, of the Hellenistic kings themselves as despots.

HELLENISM AND IMPERIALISM

The essence of the present approach is to understand the monarchies
of Antigonids, Seleukids, Ptolemies and Attalids as hegemonic
empires: supranational state systems, based on military conquest and
aimed at exacting tribute rather than governing lands and populations. And instead of taking imperial 'rule' for granted, this
approach will conceptualise ancient empires as essentially negotiated
enterprises characterised by diversity.[9] After the initial conquest,
imperial rulers often found it difficult to consolidate their control.
Since military coercion could be used only incidentally and adminis-

---

[9] Going back to the basic notion of Mann 1986 that tributary land empires 'are better
understood as intersecting, often shifting networks of power than as rigidly structural polities'
(Hämäläinen 2008: 441), new approaches to premodern empires emphasise network relations,
negotiation and flexibility. The present definition was based on, among others, those formu-
lated by Sinopoli 1994: 159 ('composed of a diversity of localised communities and ethnic
groups, each contributing its unique history and social, economic, religious, and political traditions'); Barkey 2008: 9 ('a large composite and differentiated polity linked to a central power
by a variety of direct and indirect relations ... These relations are, however, regularly subject
to negotiations over the degree of autonomy of intermediaries in return for military and fiscal
compliance'); and d'Altroy 2001: 125 ('The outstanding feature of preindustrial empires was
the continually metamorphosing nature of relations between the central powers and the
societies drawn under the imperial aegis').

trative capacities and infrastructure made direct rule difficult, empires depended heavily on the cooperation and self-government of civic and provincial elites, who in turn communicated with the population of the hinterland. A further problem confronting imperial rulers was the fact that the imperial aristocracy at the dynastic centre often turned into an opposing force once they had acquired a permanent power base. The integration of local elites within the imperial system was therefore vital for the coherence of the imperial state.

However, the strategies by which empires maintained control over peoples and territories, and managed to create cohesion are still poorly understood. Through what networks were regions and populations integrated into supranational imperial frameworks? How were negotiations between the imperial centre and its subject elites structured? Who acted as brokers? How did political, cultural and religious factors work together to create a sense of belonging to a wider imperial commonwealth among members of disparate communities?

When necessary, the rulers of the Macedonian empires interfered in local politics, or even actively stimulated economic development in order to enhance regular tax and tribute income in certain regions, as the Ptolemies did in some parts of Egypt and the Seleukids perhaps in Babylonia.[10] But generally speaking, subject cities and peoples were relatively autonomous under the umbrella of imperial overlordship. This was most evidently the case in Seleukid Asia but is also true of Ptolemaic and Antigonid rule. Since cooperation with, and only rarely occupation of, autonomous cities, temples or vassal kingdoms was vital to imperial rule, Hellenistic kingship presented itself in multiple forms, adapting itself to multifarious local demands. Particularly in provinces and cities, the manifestation of royal rule was brought to accord with supposed local and regional traditions, which were then manipulated to fit some unifying imperial ideology. Following the example of the Achaemenids, Alexander had done this when he was in Memphis, Babylon, Baktra and Susa. In Egypt, the Ptolemies played the role of pharaoh for the sake of their Egyptian subjects, particularly provincial temple priests. It would be wrong, however, to homogenise Ptolemaic kingship as simply a mix of foreign Greek and indigenous Egyptian elements.

---

[10] Ptolemaic economic *dirigisme* in Egypt: Thompson 2003: 108–11, following the views of Préaux 1939. Aperghis 2004 argued that the Seleukids in Asia showed a comparable concern for economic development, mainly for the sake of increasing tribute in silver coin; cf. Aperghis 2001, with the response by Bringmann 2005 and my review in *BMCR* 2006–06, 40; see also De Callataÿ 2005.

The Ptolemies were pharaohs only in Egypt, not in Cyprus or Palestine, let alone in Ionia or mainland Greece – and, most significantly,
not in Alexandria. There is ample evidence that the Seleukids likewise modified their presentation in accordance with local culture,
presenting themselves for instance as traditional Babylonian kings in
Babylonia, but not elsewhere. Seleukid kingship is certainly more
complex than is suggested by a simplified model of a Macedonian–
Persian or Macedonian–Babylonian cultural blend. Thus we see
Antiochos Epiphanes during his short career being elected as magis-
trate in Athens, enthroned as pharaoh in Memphis, sacrificing to
Yahweh in Jerusalem, taking part in a Syrian new year festival
near Antioch, and performing a ritual of sacred marriage with the
goddess Atargatis at Hierapolis Bambyke. Still, neither Seleukids nor
Ptolemies ever pretended that they really *were* Babylonians, Jews or
Egyptians. They never concealed that they were Macedonians, nor
is there any evidence that they tried to create a fictive genealogy
presenting them as the descendants of the Achaemenid royal house,
as the Seleukids' descendants in Kommagene and Pontos later did to
reinforce their claims to the title of Great King. The Macedonian
aspect also remained of significance even at the Seleukid and
Ptolemaic courts because Hellenistic armies relied to a large degree
on heavy infantry, many of whom can be seen to have cherished a
Macedonian identity.

It would be too rash, however, to characterise the Seleukid empire
as simply a 'multicultural' polity. The multiform cultural roles
played by the monarch are only one of two principal aspects of
Hellenistic and especially Seleukid imperial representation. For
simultaneously an all-embracing, imperial form of monarchy developed, integrating the various local forms of monarchic representation at the highest level, and thereby binding the local elites to the
centre. This unifying royal culture crystallised at the very heart of
empire: the court. As will be argued throughout this book, the imperial high culture that developed at the courts was in essence what
we might now term Greek – or rather 'Hellenistic', since the
Hellenism of the court was a distinct, non-ethnic, supranational
form of culture, tending to smooth the regional differences among
the Greeks and redefine Greek culture in the light of a more cosmopolitan world view. Thus a new, Hellenistic royal style developed, in
part based upon, but eventually replacing, Achaemenid imperial
ideology and imagery.[11] In this culture of empire, non-Greeks could

---

[11] Austin 2003: 127–8.

in principle participate. Just as the kings would play varying cultural roles in accordance with their audience while retaining their Graeco-Macedonian character, so too would local elites who cooperated with the empire adopt to some extent the Hellenism of the court, in order to express their allegiance to the monarchy and be able to participate actively in the imperial system. Hellenism became a kind of 'cultural capital' in Bourdieu's sense,[12] though this specific type of 'class indicator' was perhaps indicative of *acquired* political-economic power rather than its precondition. Indeed, contrary to Bourdieu's original conception of taste as an intrinsic aspect of existing social classes, Hellenistic 'style' could be introduced into a society as a means to challenge the supremacy of the established status groups at the top, as seems to have happened in Jerusalem prior to the Makkabean revolt. Members of civic elite families, non-Greeks as well as 'ethnic' Greeks, can be seen developing a multiple identity that was both local and imperial, e.g. Babylonian-Seleukid, Judaean-Ptolemaic, or Greek-Antigonid. Thus, Hellenism became a means of defining who did and who did not participate in the imperial order of the Hellenistic kings – although this rather simple model of biculturalism, too, may be insufficient to describe the complexity of the wide-ranging acculturation processes that took place in the Hellenistic world and which we are only now starting to comprehend.

Be that as it may, it seems quite certain that through the adoption of Hellenistic culture, members of local elites were bound to the monarchy. 'At home', they could use their (version of) Hellenism as a means to distance themselves from families who did not share in the power and from socially inferior groups. Hellenism presumably structured the progress of vertical interaction between the court and civic elites – between the local and the global – as well as the horizontal interaction between the elites of different cities. The spread and development of Hellenism were a two-way street: Hellenism was promoted top-down (to use a now unpopular term) by the court and was advanced horizontally by various elites who identified themselves with the ruling dynasties.

Thus, 'Hellenism' became a 'reference culture': the high culture of empire facilitating communication between the court and elite groups and creating a sense of commonwealth in states that were characterised by their political, ethnic and cultural heterogeneity.[13] It

---

[12] Bourdieu 1979.
[13] Strootman 2001: 205–6; cf. Strootman 2010a.

was what Bronze Age archaeologists have called an 'international style': a non-national, cosmopolitan form of 'Greekness' with which indigenous ideas and forms could be amalgamated.[14] Court culture could thereby draw upon pan-Hellenic concepts of Greekness that had already been developing before the Hellenistic age.[15]

In written propaganda, public ritual and iconography, Ptolemaic and Seleukid kings cultivated an idealised image of their status as absolute rulers of empires that knew no limits.[16] This may sound paradoxical, given the very real limits of the empires' respective spheres of influence, and the mutual recognition of each other's existence in diplomatic communication. The same apparent ambiguity was recognised by Mario Liverani in his book *Prestige and Interest* as characteristic of the Near Eastern 'concert of nations' in the late Bronze Age, when political power in the eastern Mediterranean was likewise divided up among several competing empires; Liverani brilliantly showed how monarchies developed cognitive strategies to cope with the inconsistency of claims to world power on the one hand and the recognition of the existence of other powers on the other hand.[17] Just as the Greeks were wont to do in matters of religiosity, it was principally a matter of 'avoiding mixing up different contextual registers', as Versnel showed, referring not only to strategies known from cognitive dissonance theory, but also to the concept of 'complementarity', 'meaning that two contradictory predicates or qualities can both be experienced as true and valid.'[18]

Approaching the Hellenistic monarchies as empires can also help us to accept that Hellenistic *basileia* does not accord with modern definitions of 'territorial state' or 'national state'. A territorial state, or 'early state', may be defined, following Claessen, as a form of organisation exercising (legitimate) power over a specified territory.[19] Typical of Hellenistic empires, by contrast, was their *un*specified territory. A national state indeed may be defined as the opposite of an empire: a state pretending or attempting to be a nation-state, that is, 'a state whose people *share* a strong linguistic, religious, and symbolic identity'.[20] In history, national states often suppress minority identities in order to become nation-states, whereas empires can be supranational.

---

[14] Caubet 1998; Feldman 2006; cf. Versluys 2010: 13–15.
[15] Walbank 1985.
[16] Strootman 2011a.
[17] Liverani 1990.
[18] See most recently Versnel 2011: 7 and 8; cf. p. 20 on 'quoting'.
[19] Claessen 1991: 19; cf. Claessen 1978.
[20] Tilly 1990: 2–3 (my emphasis).

Antigonid, Seleukid and Ptolemaic kings never specified on their coins the territory or people over which they ruled. Kingship was personal. *Basileia*, the contemporary *terminus technicus* for the Hellenistic monarchic state, meant 'kingship' rather than 'kingdom'. The Hellenistic Greek term that comes closest to what we would now call an 'empire' was *ta pragmata*, the 'affairs (of the king/dynasty)', or *archē*. The Argeads as well as the later Antigonids used the title 'King of the Macedonians' (*Basileus Makedonōn*, i.e. the people, not the country);[21] but this 'national' Macedonian kingship was rather a component of their overall title of *basileus*, just as a Seleukid *basileus* could be both emperor *and* king of Babylon. The Ptolemies, as the location of their capital shows, saw themselves as the rulers of a maritime empire, an empire of which Egypt was only a part – albeit the most important, and from the early second century the only significant part.[22] Since the 1970s, however, a tendency to reappraise the Ptolemies in the light of postcolonial values has prompted attempts to fit the Ptolemaic empire by force into the model of a modern European colonial state, in which Egypt is considered the motherland and the rest of the empire 'overseas possessions'. It is questionable whether such modernist terminology is helpful in understanding the nature of the Ptolemaic empire in the third century.[23] Rather than considering the Ptolemaic empire an 'Egyptian' empire (or a 'Greek' empire, for that matter), it would be better to think of it as Ptolemaic.

The Seleukids likewise were certainly not 'kings of Syria' – even if by 'Syria' we mean the entire Levant – and Antioch was not their capital. But to say that the Seleukids were first of all rulers of Babylonia and that Seleukeia on the Tigris was their capital, as has now become common, would be missing the point, too. Initially western Asia Minor *and* Syria *and* Babylonia *and* Media *and* Baktria formed the cores (plural) of a fluid imperial geography created and controlled by an itinerant militarised court-cum-army and a vigorous universalist ideology. Even after the treaty of Apameia in 188, the Seleukid empire could boast actual control of the whole of the Levant, Armenia, Mesopotamia, Elam, Persis and Media, and formal suzerainty of a much larger area – a vaster territory than

---

[21] For the evidence see Aymard 1967.

[22] See Winter 2011, listing twenty-eight Ptolemaic settlements in Asia Minor alone, as well as many Aegean cities with Ptolemaic garrisons.

[23] See e.g. Will 1979: 153–208; Briant 1978: 59 and 69, too, describes Argead and Seleukid imperialism as 'European colonization'; for more examples of the equation of Hellenistic imperialism with modern European colonialism see Mairs 2006b: 22–3, to whom I owe this latter reference.

Nebuchadnezzar's Babylonian empire or the empire of the Neo-Assyrian kings. The Seleukids, like the Ptolemies, used the title of *basileus* without any restrictive addition. Particularly in the Seleukid world, the Greek word *basileus* was from the beginning, *mutatis mutandis*, the Hellenistic equivalent of the eastern title of Great King.

THE STATE OF THE QUESTION

In contrast to the Romano-Byzantine courts of late antiquity, Hellenistic courts have in the past been the subject of surprisingly limited scholarship, and have only very recently become a separate category of historical analysis.[24] In the older literature, brief text-book accounts of particular courts can be found, as well as some exceptional attempts at analysis.[25] Most literature dealing with *philoi* has been either institutional history or concered with proso-pographical aspects of court society, including court titulature (which is normally described as more systematised and formalised than will be contended in this book).[26] This did not change with the advent of modern court studies in the 1970s and 1980s. The past decades, however, have seen relatively numerous publications on the Hellenistic court; roughly speaking, these consist of, on the one hand, studies of cultural, particularly literary patronage at the Ptolemaic court, and, on the other hand, studies of the relation between cities and the court. Notable Hellenistic 'court historians' of the period are Gregor Weber, Gabriel Herman and Ivana Savalli-Lestrade. Weber was one of the first to recognise Hellenistic court society as a separate object of study; but although his monograph on

[24] In particular, monarchic ritual in the Roman and Byzantine empires has been the subject of ample research and debate; see e.g. Alföldi 1970; MacCormack 1981; McCormick 1986; see also Maguire 1998; Paterson 2007; Smith 2007.

[25] Bevan 1902 II: 273–4 evokes a decadent 'oriental' court for the (later) Seleukids; the chapter about the Seleukid court in Bickerman 1938 was ahead of its time notwithstanding its rather modernist approach to the formal aspects of the Seleukid court system. Very early attempts at analysis, but lacking theoretical support, are Otto 1927 and Corradi 1929. Ritter 1965 investigates the meaning of the Hellenistic diadem in the context of coronation ritual, claiming Persian origins for both.

[26] Relevant scholarship concentrates on the Argead court under Alexander and the Ptolemaic court. Of importance is notably the work of Mooren (esp. 1975; 1977; 1985). Prosopographical treatments of particular courts, also containing valuable discussions of offices and titles, are Berve; Peremans and Van 't Dack 1968; Heckel 1992. Habicht's contro-versial article on the ethnicity of Seleukid notables (1958) will be discussed in Chapter 5. For the Antigonids in Macedonia see Le Bohec 1985 and 1987, among others; Herman 1980/1 is a pioneering article concerned with the development and meaning of court titles; Strootman 1993, Herman 1997 and Weber 1997 are early attempts to approach Hellenistic court society from Elias' model of the court.

the early Ptolemaic court seems to refer to Elias quite explicitly by using the term *höfische Gesellschaft* in its title, Weber is primarily interested in the place of poets at court rather than with power relations and socio-political developments.[27] His later work is broader in scope.[28] In a renowned article, Gabriel Herman, while concentrating on two cases of factional strife at the Ptolemaic and Seleukid courts, uses Elias but no later literature on courts and court society, and perhaps assumes too much absolutist freedom on the part of the king in conferring titles and honours on *philoi*.[29] Savalli-Lestrade meanwhile concentrated on the function of courtiers as representatives of cities, showing the entanglement of monarchy and city, particularly in western Asia Minor.[30] Palace architecture, too, has only relatively recently acquired its rightful place of honour in the bibliography of Hellenistic archaeology.[31]

Recent approaches to Hellenistic kingship tend to emphasise the differences between the three kingdoms. This has led to important new insights, particularly with regard to the Achaemenid antecedents of Seleukid monarchic ideology and imperial administration (although the historical *significance* of such continuities in itself is often not altogether clear). Regarding Ptolemaic kingship, on the other hand, it has for a long time been customary to emphasise, and perhaps exaggerate, its Egyptian nature, and to view the Ptolemies first of all as pharaohs even in their dealings with the Mediterranean world outside of Egypt (though oddly enough this tendency seems to be stronger among classicists than among Egyptologists).

The present approach developed from the conviction that the Hellenistic royal courts had significant features and structures in common, too, and that the respective courts of these empires showed many more similarities than is commonly assumed.[32] These

[27] Weber 1993. My own application of Elias' court model and post-Elias court theory to the Hellenistic world, in combination with Tilly's then new model for understanding monarchical power in premodern states (Tilly 1990; cf. Chapter 2), was originally put to the test in an unpublished MA dissertation (Strootman 1993), written in Dutch. It is a matter of course that ideas and approaches which then seemed promising and original, and which I continued to develop as a PhD researcher, have in the meantime independently become more widespread in ancient historical scholarship, as is evidenced by the number of recent edited volumes dedicated to ancient courts and utilising Elias, e.g. Brands and Hoepfner 1996, Winterling 1997, Spawforth 2007a, Jacobs and Rollinger 2010, and Erskine and Llewellyn-Jones forthcoming.
[28] See esp. Weber 1997 and 2009.
[29] Elias 1969; Herman 1997; Mooren 1998.
[30] See Savalli-Lestrade 1996 and 1998.
[31] See Chapter 3 for references; for the patronage of poets, scholars and scientists at court see Strootman 2007: 189–250.
[32] Thus Mooren 1975: 2: '[the *philoi* society] is an essential element of Hellenistic monarchy. We are consequently forced to study it in its Hellenistic context. In other words, to take merely the Ptolemaic point of view would be quite meaningless.'

similarities had various causes: (1) a shared Macedonian background that was vigorously expressed by all three dynasties in clothing, among other things; (2) intermarriage and diplomatic contacts; (3) a shared reliance on Aegean Greeks as agents of empire; and (4) an intense, fierce rivalry. All this amounted to a culture of *interaction* rather than segregation. Therefore, believing that Hellenistic court culture was not static but constantly in flux due to changing circumstances within the respective empires *and* a dynamic interplay between the three competing kingdoms, I prefer to approach the courts synoptically for the present purpose, and look for exchanges rather than treat the three of them in isolation, accentuating differences. Only after commonalities have been recognised can the specific peculiarities of the respective monarchies be estimated. Differences between the separate courts, and developments through time, will be noted throughout the text.

STRUCTURE OF THE BOOK

In Part I, theoretical and methodological approaches to the two major functions of the court – the court as a political system and the court as a stage for the theatre of royalty (Chapters 1 and 2) – will be introduced, followed by a discussion of the court's physical setting, the palace (Chapter 3).

Concerning palatial architecture, the focus will be on the symbolism of the architecture and decoration of royal monuments, as well as on the function of royal architecture for facilitating the performance of the 'theatre of kingship'. For not only was the palace an arena for the power games of the court; it was also, more than merely the material backdrop for royal ritual, itself instrumental in the construction and negotiation of power. If anything, Hellenistic palaces and royal monuments were *performative space*. It will furthermore be argued that the architectural forms used in Hellenistic palaces were derived from religious architecture in order to stress the sacral qualities of kingship and distance the ruler and the court society from the socially inferior by presenting the court as in some measure a mysterious and inaccessible place. How such a place may have looked is suggested by a series of wall paintings from a first-century BCE Roman villa at Boscoreale, probably representing a Hellenistic *basileia* or palatial district, most probably that of Alexandria (Fig. I.1). Finally, attention will be given to the fact that the presence of royal palaces belonging to an imperial ruler in formally autonomous cities amounts to a paradox; here it will be

Fig. I.1. First-century BCE fresco from a Roman villa in Boscoreale, probably representing part of a Hellenistic *basileia* or palatial district, c. 50 BCE (Metropolitan Museum of Art, New York/ARTstor).

shown how (sacral) architecture was used to demarcate *and* integrate civic and royal space.

Part II is devoted to court society, concentrating on political and social interaction at the courts, and on the fierce rivalries and conflicts characterising that interaction.

In Chapter 4, the central place of the royal family within the dynastic household will be examined. It will be argued inter alia that although there was no official crown prince in the Hellenistic kingdoms, due to polygamous marriage and perhaps the lack of a concept of primogeniture, Hellenistic kings did use a variety of means to hierarchise their wives and set up a successor in advance. Special attention will furthermore be paid to the place and function of royal women: court women acted as intermediaries at court, as representatives of other dynasties, or were given tremendous power as 'favourites'. The centrality of royal women in dynastic households was to a large degree determined by the Macedonian dynasties' inheritance customs, in which women played a pivotal role.

Chapter 5 deals with the social and ethnic set-up of the group of courtiers who constituted the inner court surrounding the royal family: largely old Macedonian nobility and Greek *philoi*. It will be argued, contrary to a now popular view, that the ethnic identity of the *philoi* was predominantly Greek: whether we like it or not, a better look at the evidence shows that they were either ethnic Greeks from the Aegean – and quite a lot of them so even at the Seleukid and Ptolemaic courts of the second century BCE – or men who identified themselves as ethnic Greeks. Exceptions to this rule were either not *philoi*, or outsiders who served as 'favourites' (see further below). The chapter begins with an analysis of the genesis of Hellenistic court society from the conflicts at Alexander the Great's court. Conflict will remain a leitmotif in other chapters in Part II. The loyalty of the *philoi* was a matter of constant concern for kings. Controlling them was never easy. A distinction is made between Greeks (of various kinds) and ethnic Macedonians, since all the courts contained at their cores small groups of Macedonian aristocrats more closely attached (through kinship and comparable status) to the ruling dynasties than the Greek *philoi*. This is the status group that the king and his family belonged to.

Chapter 6 brings together evidence pertaining to royal pages (*basilikoi paides*) at the dynastic households. Unfortunately, most of what we know about them is connected with the Argead court in the time of Philip and Alexander, though it is clear that the institution persisted at the Antigonid, Seleukid and Ptolemaic courts. From what we do know (e.g. from evidence on the court of Antiochos III preserved in Polybios) it can be deduced that a major benefit of the page system was the creation of a body of loyal *suntrophoi* – men who had grown up with the reigning king and were attached to him through personal ties. Whether the pages served as hostages of sorts guaranteeing their aristocratic fathers' loyalty and subservience, or rather amounted to an institutionalised aristocratic foothold in the dynastic house, will remain an open question. Probably both scenarios were feasible depending on the strength or weakness of the monarchy at a given date. In the later second century BCE the title of *suntrophos* was bestowed also *honoris causa* by the Seleukids and Ptolemies on men not belonging to their personal inner circle of 'boyhood companions'.

Chapters 7 and 8 discuss the social dynamics of court society. It will be shown how relations at court were structured by the Greek moral complex of *philia* (ritualised friendship) and, following a suggestion by Herman, *xenia* (guest-friendship). Ritual, protocol and the practice of ritualised gift-exchange structured social relations. The developing system of court titles hierarchising Hellenistic court society may be termed a formalised informality meant to regulate access to the king – it is *not* evidence of increasing bureaucratisation and a process of 'going out of court'; that is, the physical and formal disconnection of dynastic household and government never took place in any of the Hellenistic empires.[33] Throughout their existence, the Hellenistic courts remained in essence face-to-face societies. This part also contains a section on royal patronage of the arts and sciences, which is understood as part and parcel of the social fabric of the court, court poets like Theokritos and Kallimachos being *philoi* competing with one another for favour and prestige.

The *philoi* served the royal family first of all as military commanders, since there was also no formal disconnection of the household and the armed forces; the standing armies of the empires were attached to the dynasty, not to some impersonal 'state'. The *philoi* furthermore functioned as intermediaries between court and cities. Because they retained bonds with their families and cities of origin, and had at their disposal patronage networks of their own, the king was able to exert influence in cities through his friends; conversely, elite families and cities could exert influence at court through the *philoi*.

Part III brings together four chapters on ritual and ceremonial. Emphasis is on both collective ritual *action* and the symbolic *meaning* of that ritual action.

Chapter 9 considers aspects of etiquette and protocol. The chapter focuses on (1) ceremonial that regulated access to the person of the king, and (2) ceremonial that was instrumental in the creation of group cohesion among the *philoi*. Special attention will be given

---

[33] The exception to the rule seems to be Ptolemaic *Egypt* – but the well-developed system of administration in the Nile Valley was a (varied) regional and not an empire-wide phenomenon imposed from on high; it furthermore continued (varying) pre-existing structures and had the aim of exacting revenue, not introducing 'government'. On the Ptolemaic administration of the Nile Valley see especially Manning 2003, who shows among other things how in Ptolemaic Egypt, in particular the Thebaid, '[t]he rulers negotiated with the local elite and institutions in exchange for revenue. A colonial model that understands Ptolemaic history as the imposition of a uniform political order and without opposition is no longer tenable' (p. 226).

to the 'great events' of the court: the festivities that attracted representatives of local and regional polities to the imperial centre. During festive occasions such as birth and wedding ceremonies, the household temporarily expanded to include an 'outer court' – a ritualised contact zone that facilitated communication and negotiation between centre and periphery, and the (re)distribution of status, power and wealth. The pivotal event of various festivities was the ritual banquet – presumably following sacrifice – which was the focal point for the distribution of honours and status gifts. The collective participation in aulic ceremonial by representatives of local elites furthermore augmented imperial integration. Monumentalised ritual spaces such as the Alexandrian palace district, or the processional way and sanctuaries at Pergamon, facilitated this kind of collective action.

Chapter 10 deals with rituals of inauguration. It will be argued that the fundamental element of Hellenistic king-making – the binding of the diadem – took place behind closed doors (except when the ritual was performed publicly on the battlefield as the founding act of a dynasty, following victory) and was carried out by the ruler himself, there being no higher power on earth than the *basileus*. The king then appeared in public as if (re)born with the diadem already fastened for a ritual of acclamation. This ritual was initially performed by the court society and (household) troops, but could later be repeated in various cities throughout the empires (the Antigonids may again have been exceptional). It will furthermore be shown how the ceremonies of burial and apotheosis of a deceased ruler were closely entwined with the ritual of inauguration of his successor.

Chapter 11 is devoted to rituals of entry. The main question to be addressed is how ritual was used to accommodate imperial monarchy within the values and practices of the city state. It will be argued that Hellenistic rituals of entry – *adventus*, as the Romans would later call their version of that ceremonial – were sometimes modelled on religious rites of divine epiphany, at least in Greek *poleis*. In all cities, independent of their ethno-cultural identity, Hellenistic kings performed a sacrifice, usually in the city's principal sanctuary. By participating in local, civic cults upon entering cities, the king was turned into a citizen. And because within that local cult the king personally performed the crucial act of offering the sacrificial animal on the altar, he became the most highly honoured citizen. So although especially in the Seleukid empire rulers seem merely to have adapted to local 'traditions', the pattern of consistent patronage and manipulation of local religious cults probably actually enhanced integration.

Chapter 12 looks at royal processions taking place at the imperial centre. The focus will be on the symbolic communication of imperial ideology. In capital cities, new monarchical-religious festivals were introduced to create extra opportunities to attract representatives of subject polities to the centre, and to create a unifying image of kingship. It will be argued that the pivotal messages conveyed by the ritual performances enacted during these festivals pertained to the king's heroic, victorious charisma and the ideal of a peaceful and prosperous world empire, and that these two aspects were two sides of the same coin; hence the pivotal role of the image of Dionysos as victorious warrior *and* bringer of good fortune in especially Ptolemaic royal ritual. Attention will also be given to the function of ritual performance as a means to create social cohesion among the participants, namely the *philoi*.

The book ends with a conclusion summarising the main arguments of the respective chapters.

APPROACHES TO THE HELLENISTIC EAST

We will conclude this Introduction with a few words on how the present book relates to the leading approaches to the Hellenistic world, and in particular the Seleukid east.

In the past decades, it has become customary in Hellenistic studies to emphasise the continuity of Near Eastern and Egyptian culture and to question Greek influence beyond Greece.[34] This tendency originated in the late 1970s in reaction to the equally one-sided focus on 'change' (especially in the form of 'Hellenisation' or even the unidirectional spread of Greek culture in the 'east') *and* the traditional conception, in both Assyriology and classical studies, of Near Eastern history after Alexander as essentially a continuation of Greek history.[35] The new approach of the 1980s and 1990s did not in itself create an interest in the so-called 'eastern' side of Alexander's and Seleukos' empires. That interest had always existed: even the works of, say, Edwyn Bevan and William Tarn, though biased, were

---

[34] See the introduction in Kuhrt and Sherwin-White 1993, esp. the opening sentence on p. 1: '[it is] our firmly held view that the Seleukid kingdom was an eastern empire'.

[35] Relatively early studies stressing the continuity of Near Eastern, esp. Babylonian, culture in the Hellenistic period were Oelsner 1978 and Kreissig 1978; in the 1980s and early 1990s continuity became an important focus in studies of 'Hellenism in the east'; see e.g. Van der Spek 1986; Sherwin-White 1987; Kuhrt 1987; Briant 1990; Kuhrt and Sherwin-White 1993; *AchHist* 4.

clearly written from the authors' fascination with the orient, too. The continuity paradigm did result, however, in a positive evaluation of the 'eastern' side of the Macedonian empire in Asia, and a better understanding of the orientalistic stereotype (in Saidic terms) in both ancient and modern historiography. But it perhaps goes a little too far to claim, as e.g. Pierre Briant did as recently as 2010,[36] that 'traditional' scholarship on Alexander and his successors continues to *ignore* non-Greek sources. On the contrary, since at least the 1980s, in the slipstream of the New Achaemenid History, historians of the Hellenistic east have been keen to base their research on cuneiform Babylonian or Egyptian written sources, perhaps even to the detriment of Greek historiography and epigraphy.[37] Indeed, even Bevan in his much despised 1902 monograph on the Seleukid empire keenly used whatever cuneiform sources were available to him – but hardly any non-Greek sources *were* available to him at that time.

This brings us to the second important new development of the past decades: the increased availability for historians of non-Greek, particularly Egyptian and Babylonian, sources for the Hellenistic period – although the impact of these beyond the fields of chronology and local (economic) history should not be overestimated.

The evidence for the culture of the courts of the Ptolemies, Seleukids and Antigonids reveals mostly similarities with the Argead household in fourth-century Macedonia, albeit on a much grander scale and with many 'eastern', chiefly Hekatomnid and Achaemenid, elements integrated into it; the latter especially in the field of ceremonial. I am perfectly aware that in the scholarship of the past three decades Achaemenid and pharaonic influence on respectively the Seleukid and Ptolemaic kingdoms has been favoured over Graeco-Macedonian antecedents. I am not ignoring these views, but instead trying to look ahead. The case for continuity has perhaps been somewhat overdone in the past decades. Pointing out continuities (or discontinuities) by itself has only limited relevance for understanding the functioning of empires or dynastic identity. To appreciate how imperial rulers and imperial elites envisaged their own position in the world, we must look both at how they positioned themselves vis-à-vis their predecessors *explicitly*, and at the interaction with contemporaneous competing imperial elites – in other words, we must try to understand the *meaning* of inter-imperial transfers and to do so both synchronically and

---

[36] In a newly written 'methodological' appendix to the English translation of his 1974 book on Alexander the Great.

[37] On the New Achaemenid History of the 1980s see now Harrison 2011.

diachronically.[38] Similarities between the Hellenistic courts and preceding courts (for instance, the presence of royal pages) may be simply due to this being a typical feature of court culture in general, or to the adoption and appropriation of 'good practice', rather than a meaningful instance of deliberate replication.

The latter may notably be the case with the supposed continuity of the Achaemenid empire, a notion that has become pivotal to modern perceptions of Macedonian imperialism in the Middle East since Briant's famous assertion that Alexander was 'the last Achaemenid'.[39] But the point is that the Achaemenids, Argeads and Seleukids (and later the Arsakids and Sasanians) controlled a type of premodern empire that was essentially a *dynastic* organisation and not an impersonal formal state existing separately from the dynasty (as the, originally republican, Roman empire exceptionally was). Basic continuities of Achaemenid imperial practices under the Seleukids may perhaps not have been so meaningful in terms of contemporary Seleukid self-definition and monarchical representation. For instance, the Achaemenid satrapal system was presumably continued by the Seleukids primarily from practical rather than ideological motives and was, to be sure, actually transformed by them – first by multiplying the number of satrapies, then by gradually replacing satrapal rule with rule through vassal kings. Also, the Seleukids' use of the Royal Road can hardly be thought of as a meaningful act on the part of the Seleukids to show themselves to be, or at least be known as, the heirs of the Achaemenids. The continued use of the former Persian Royal Road and High Road as the main east–west artery of Seleukid imperial rule in the Middle East and Iran was determined strictly by physical geography, not by ideology or conceptions of imperial rule.

Furthermore, it appears that the Seleukids distanced themselves from their predecessors rather than associated themselves with the Achaemenids. The well-attested Seleukid concern for Babylonian civic sanctuaries, often emphasised as a form of continuity and an example of respect for 'tradition' in recent scholarship, was more probably an example of imperial innovation and change, since it can be sharply contrasted with a noticeable lack of Achaemenid concern for Babylonian temples in the preceding centuries. In fact, from one important piece of evidence, the so-called Antiochos Cylinder from Borsippa, it appears that the Seleukids in Babylon rather pretended

---

[38] Cf. the introduction to Aust et al. 2010.
[39] Briant 1974.

to restore the situation that had existed *before* the Achaemenids, erasing the Achaemenids, as it were, from history to initiate a new golden age of Babylonian glory.[40] Moreover, even when the conscious adoption of pre-existing aspects of Achaemenid imperial rule can be proven, it ought to be borne in mind that this is hardly exceptional in the millennia-long sequence of successive empires in the Middle East. To be sure, there are also remarkable similarities between the Hellenistic courts and the courts of the Greek tyrants of the Archaic age, and it is clear that the historical relevance of these similarities is doubtful, too, even if continuity can to some extent be assumed; the point is that the only (and rather vague) reference to archaic Greek tyranny in the ideology of Hellenistic kings themselves was their self-presentation as *destroyers* of tyranny.[41]

The modern image of the Seleukids as 'pseudo-Achaemenids in Macedonian clothing' (see below) is sharply contrasted with the complete absence of any direct or indirect evidence that the Seleukids ever wished to affiliate themselves with the Achaemenids or referred to themselves as the successors of Darius or Xerxes. On the contrary, it rather seems that the Seleukid house, for all its reliance on and intermarriage with *other* Iranian aristocratic families, was keen to steer clear of any association with the Achaemenid dynasty. It is only in the later second and especially first centuries BCE that (former) Seleukid sub-kings like the Persid *fratarakā*, the Parthian *basileis* or the kings of Kommagene begin to mix an invented Achaemenid legacy with Hellenistic forms of monarchy (Fig. I.2). This, of course, is as much reappropriation as it is invention of tradition, but it is all of a rather late date and associated with the transformation of the later Seleukid empire into a system of indirect rule through vassal rulers.[42] Historians in the past have juxtaposed the alleged 'Persian revival' in Persis, Armenia, Parthia and Kommagene with Seleukid rule, but this late Hellenistic Persianism began as a thoroughly Seleukid phenomenon that had but little to do with continuity.

[40] *Pace* Kuhrt and Sherwin-White 1991; cf. Heather Baker's contribution to Stavrianopoulou 2013, also discussing Uruk and Eridu; for the innovative, even manipulative nature of Seleukid patronage of Babylonian religion see now Erickson 2011 and Strootman 2013b. Cyrus and Kambyses may have been exceptional in their concern for Babylonian temples as compared to later Achaemenids. But Cyrus and Kambyses were no Achaemenids. Indeed, as we are dealing with a *dynastic* state, it might be that what we have here are two distinct empires, even if Darius I took over the territory conquered by his two predecessors (but lost no time in replacing Cyrus of Anshan's conquest elite with grandees recruited among Persid grandees and his own family; cf. Sancisi-Weerdenburg 1980: 175).

[41] On this ideological system see Versnel 1978 and 1990.

[42] See Engels 2011; Strootman 2011a.

Fig. I.2. 'Persianistic' head of Zeus-Oromasdes in the late Hellenistic royal
sanctuary on Mount Nemrut, erected c. 50 BCE by Antiochos I of Kommagene,
a Seleukid successor kingdom in the northwest of ancient Syria
(author's photograph).

The search for continuity (and discontinuity) has not yet resulted
in a fundamentally different understanding of Hellenistic kingship
(the partly eastern antecedents of which have always been recognised) and the nature of Macedonian imperialism, precisely because
of its disregard for the Aegean side of Hellenistic imperial culture. As
early as 1996, Oliver Hoover cautioned that, 'while there is no denying the great debt of the Seleukid empire to its predecessors, the
Seleukid kings should therefore not be thought of simply as pseudo-
Achaimenids in Makedonian clothing'.[43] Perhaps more problematic,
the lack of theoretical and methodological backing from the fields of
the social sciences and cultural anthropology, or even the discipline
of history in general – concerning e.g. the functioning of empires,
court society, gift-exchange, culture and cultural interaction – has
precluded the development of a really new approach to the Hellenistic empires. The availability of new, non-Greek sources will lead
to new insights only when these sources are fitted into a sound
theoretical model.

[43] Hoover 1996: 1; comparable doubts have been expressed by Austin 2003.

The tendency to consider Ptolemaic Egypt and Seleukid Asia from a Hellenocentric viewpoint meanwhile has not died out with the ascendancy of these eastern approaches.[44] The idea that the history of the Hellenistic Middle East is not Middle East history, but *Greek* history, persists – but independently, not as a rival approach inspiring fruitful debate. The power of convention is demonstrated by the relatively new Routledge series History of the Ancient World, where the two volumes dedicated to the history of *The Ancient Near East* do not venture beyond Alexander the Great.[45] The addition of a third volume on the Seleukid, Parthian and Sasanian periods would have been really ground-breaking. The conquests of Alexander in the Middle East meanwhile are incorporated into a volume concerned with the history of classical Greece,[46] while subsequent Near Eastern history is incorporated into a book titled *The **Greek** World after Alexander* (my emphasis).[47]

Closely related to the perception of Hellenistic history as a continuation of classical Greek history is the notion prevalent among many modern oriental scholars that the era of Macedonian domination is an anomaly in the history of the Near East, a kind of 'interregnum' between Persians and Parthians that has no place in proper oriental studies. However, the Persian conquerors of Babylonia, Syria and Anatolia were, like the Macedonians, essentially a nation of tribal warriors from a peripheral country on the fringes of urbanised, agricultural civilisation. The Persians, too, both influenced and absorbed local cultures. The same can be said of the later Parthian, Arab and Turkic empire-builders. They too were originally new-comers to the urbanised, agricultural core regions of the Near East. These conquerors, however, have acquired a place of their own in standard narratives of Middle East history while retaining their (partial) Arab or Turkic identity in modern historiography. The Greeks and Macedonians, however, are still mostly perceived as 'western' outsiders, notwithstanding their centuries-long presence in the east and their profound influence on the culture of the east.

---

[44] See for instance Green 2007: esp. 43–63, or the introduction to Ogden 2002, taking 'kingship' as the defining aspect of the age. As late as 2011, Tom Holland in a review in the *Wall Street Journal* described Pierre Briant – whose view of Alexander as 'the last of the Achaemenids' has been the established view since about the early 1980s – as a 'revisionist professor'. Another, crass example is Meißner 2000: 36, describing the Seleukid and Ptolemaic courts as *Höfen im antiken Griechenland* ('courts in ancient greece').

[45] Kuhrt 1995.

[46] Hornblower 2002.

[47] Shipley 2000.

The dissertation on which the present book was based was written from my firmly held view that the study of Hellenistic history and culture is better off without the explanatory framework of an east–west dichotomy and the subsequent accentuation of continuity and change. Instead of emphasising the segregation of the supposedly 'western' Greek civilisation from a huge and amorphous 'eastern' world, I consider Greece as part of a wider Aegean world, and that Aegean world as a part of a wider Near Eastern cultural and economic system. As modern cultural anthropology teaches us, cultures are never self-contained, homogeneous entities that can be distinguished strictly from other 'cultures'. Instead, cultures are usually permeable, flexible and dynamic. This is in opposition to the views of *both* the 'schools' outlined above, since these both tend to separate the Macedonians and Greeks from the neighbouring civilisations that they interacted with.

Rather than to think of a Greek–Egyptian or Greek–'eastern' opposition, either as a contradiction or as the basis of hybridisation, I propose that we view the imperial culture of the Ptolemaic and Seleukid empires as respectively 'Ptolemaic' and 'Seleukid', in the same manner that scholars also speak of, say, Ottoman culture without their being required to evaluate at all times the Ottoman monarchy's multifarious cultural antecedents.

I would therefore like to end with a disclaimer: instead of constantly evaluating whether particular aspects of kingship, court culture or empire are *originally* Greek or non-Greek (Egyptian, Babylonian, Persian, etc.), I have aimed at studying the Hellenistic royal courts *in their own right* – just as the court culture of the Ottoman empire, to stick to that example, is considered by historians worthy of their attention for its own sake, regardless of the evident absorption of elements of Byzantine, Persian and Turkic monarchic culture and ideology.

A NOTE ON THE SOURCES

As recently as the early 1990s there was still much in the literary sources, especially Polybios, that had never been scrutinised from the perspective of court studies, and the royal court had not yet been approached as a socio-political phenomenon with its own particular significance for state formation processes, monarchical politics and the practice of imperialism. The Hellenistic royal court is now no longer a barren field and it has become clear that court studies can indeed provide a new perspective on the old topic of Hellenistic kingship.[48]

Sources, as always when the Hellenistic world is concerned, are uneven and sometimes biased. Epigraphic material provides information concerning Greek *philoi* and early court titles for the third and second centuries BCE, while papyrological documents are an important source illuminating particularly the later Ptolemaic system of aulic titulature. Both have been studied extensively in the past by Savalli-Lestrade and Mooren, among others. For some periods there is relatively good historiographical material. Arrian, Curtius and Diodoros, with the addition of Plutarch, provide detailed information concerning the late Argead court. Polybios was, besides being the most trustworthy of the Hellenistic historians, particularly well informed regarding the Seleukid court of the late third and early second centuries BCE through his membership of the *philia* circles surrounding the Seleukid prince Demetrios (I) in Rome. In addition to Polybios, Diodoros, Appian, Justin and Livy give valuable information. Though relatively late and often biased, much of relevance is to be found too in Plutarch and Athenaios. Behind stereotype descriptions of flattering courtiers or the 'oriental' decadence of Hellenistic kings, found abundantly in Plutarch and especially Athenaios, real aulic practices can often be discerned through comparison with courts in other cultures and periods.[49] Stereotype description is not necessarily a disadvantage. Rather, it is characteristic of outside views of court societies – and not only in the ancient world – and stereotype labels often hide very real practices and institutions of the court. I hope to have been able to 'translate' them well.

---

[48] This approach has now been adopted in Achaemenid studies as well. More recent work on the Persian court includes Brosius 2007, Jacobs and Rollinger 2010, and Llewellyn-Jones 2012; for older approaches see Cook 1985: 225–38, and the relevant sections in Briant 2002.

[49] Strootman 1993.

PART I

Setting the Scene

1 *The Court as an Instrument of Power*

It is difficult to say what exactly a court is. One runs the risk of either excluding too many facets, or defining it too loosely. Most definitions consider the court to be a social space. Thus Elton wrote that '[t]he only definition of the court which makes sense ... is that it comprised all those who at any given time were within "his grace's house"'.[1] Starkey worked from an even narrower definition, excluding from the courtly milieu servants, guards, stablehands and other household personnel.[2] However, such people could in practice be extremely influential since they, too, were part of the 'inner court' which surrounded the king on a regular basis, and thus relatively close to him. The problem, of course, is that in no two periods or states is a court similar. Medieval European courts were often peripatetic. Renaissance and *Ancien Régime* courts, on the other hand, could usually be localised in one or more fixed residences, and consequently modern definitions for this period more often include references to palaces.[3] An interesting alternative definition is provided by Rodríquez-Salgado, who defines the court as the place where the 'sovereign power' of the monarchy resides; this leaves open the possibility that the monarch's 'sovereign authority' can be present even when the monarch himself is absent: 'the monarch's residual authority, not his presence, was the prerequisite of a court'.[4] However, this definition presupposes the existence of a fixed residence or capital – Rodríquez-Salgado was thinking of Philip II's Escorial – so that it is not suitable to describe the courts of the

[1] Elton 1983: 38.
[2] Starkey 1987: 5.
[3] Asch 1991: 9–10.
[4] Rodríquez-Salgado 1991: 207.

31

Argead, Antigonid and Seleukid empires, but may be helpful in understanding Ptolemaic Alexandria.

Considering that in premodern kingdoms the 'political and economic relations' that constituted royal power consisted of networks of *personal* relations, the court can best be approached as essentially a social phenomenon. Following a definition by Adamson, then, I would define the court as the king's immediate social milieu, consisting of (1) the circle of persons ('courtiers') around a ruler; (2) the 'larger matrix of political and economic relations converging in the ruler's household';[5] and (3) the rooms and halls where the king lives, receives guests, and gives audience and banquets, and where the rituals or royalty are performed. It is also important to note that the court is not a place – courts can move.

In more recent literature, a distinction is sometimes made between an 'inner court' – consisting of a core group of people who are permanently part of the king's household, including servants – and a more sizeable 'outer court' – consisting of people less closely connected to the royal family and whose attendance at court is transitory, connected as it is with ceremonial occasions like royal weddings, births, inaugurations and various religious festivals. For instance, according to Josephus, in the late third century the Ptolemaic court farmed out the imperial tax-lease centrally, forcing representatives of civic elites to go to the king and compete for favour: 'Now it happened that at this time all the principal men and rulers went up out of the cities of Syria and Phoenicia, to bid for their taxes; for every year the king sold them to the men of the greatest power in every city.'[6]

As has already been emphasised, court is not a synonym of 'palace'. Kings may maintain several palaces but normally have only one court. Nor is a palace a prerequisite for a court. Many courts in history were peripatetic, not least the Argead, Antigonid and Seleukid courts. This means that a king could also hold court en route in his camp (the natural habitat of Alexander the Great, Pyrrhos, Antiochos III and Philip V, among others), or aboard a ship (the Ptolemies in their floating palace *Thalamegos*; Kleopatra VII at Tarsos). Polybios describes the royal pavilion of the Ptolemaic army camp before the battle of Raphia as if it were a palace, comprising a tent for public audiences.[7] Moreover, crucial court ceremonial such

---

[5] Adamson 1999b: 7.
[6] Jos., *AJ* 12.4.3 (169), trans.Whiston; cf. 12.4.4 and 10 (175 and 224). The court is not necessarily in Memphis: Josephus' protagonist, Joseph, travels to Memphis to meet the king.
[7] Polyb. 5.81.5.

as acclamation rites took place in public spaces in front of large crowds rather than in the confines of a palace.

The modern study of the court began with the pioneering work of Norbert Elias and Jürgen, Freiherr von Kruedener.[8] Both tried to understand the role of the court in the development of absolutism and the national state in early modern Europe. In doing so, both Elias and Kruedener worked from the historical sociology of Max Weber. This accounts for some striking similarities, as Kruedener's model did not develop from Elias' (Kruedener does, however, refer to Elias' civilisation theory of 1936). The point of reference for Elias, whose view of the court as in general a 'golden cage' for the nobility was mainly based on the memoirs of Saint-Simon, was the French court in the later reign of Louis XIV. Kruedener by contrast based his investigations on princely courts in various German states during a much longer period.

Elias argued that the royal court could be an instrument in the hands of the king to pacify the nobility. From the sixteenth to the eighteenth century, Elias maintained, the development of professional standing armies, employed in conflicts fought on an increasingly large scale, gradually led to a military monopoly of the king and the growth of a centralised state apparatus. This eventually forced members of the old nobility – on whose personal military forces the king was now no longer dependent – to leave their ancestral domains and be present near the king in order to obtain offices, military commands and prestige. At court, competition for royal favour and the extensive status expenditures expected from a courtly 'gentleman', in combination with the restrictions and obligations of court etiquette and ceremonial (which the king controlled), resulted in a loss of political and economic autonomy on the part of the old noble families. They changed into a powerless court nobility dependent on an absolutist monarch.

Subsequent scholarship has adjusted or rejected many of Elias' views. To begin with, the absolutism claimed by rulers like Louis XIV was presumably an ideal rather than a reality.[9] Even the very existence of an opposition between king and nobility, on which Elias' model wholly rests, has been disputed.[10] Aloys Winterling was the first to give fundamental criticism of Elias directly, through a case study of the court of the Elector of Cologne, falsifying many of Elias'

---

[8] Elias 1969; Kruedener 1973. Concerning the influence and present applicability of both classic works, Duindam 1994 is essential reading.

[9] See esp. Henshall 1992.

[10] Asch 1991.

generalised assumptions.[11] Jeroen Duindam later nuanced Elias by comparing multifarious sources from the French and the Habsburg court, and by extending the research to the period 1550–1780. Duindam noted that the restrictions and obligations placed upon the nobility by court life also affected the king. For instance, the ethos of obligatory conspicuous consumption that supposedly drained the nobility's resources in fact required the most extensive status expenditures from the ruler himself, he being the person of highest rank. The growth of the apparatus of government that took place in the *Ancien Régime* period did not inevitably result in all power getting into the hands of the king; in other words, if the early modern court really was a golden cage, as Elias maintained, the king was imprisoned in it as well. Duindam moreover argued that presence at court could actually be advantageous for nobles, offering them opportunities to become part of the new central power.[12] Although changes in warfare and political organisation may indeed have forced the nobility to go to court in order to obtain high military office, it is equally true that the nobility succeeded in monopolising these offices, which remained aristocratic prerogatives until the era of revolutionary wars.

The model of the court developed by Kruedener added an extra element to the study of the court. Kruedener also emphasised the court's function in legitimising power and establishing power relations by means of monarchic representation. In Kruedener's model, the court was both a platform for competition with rival monarchies and a stage for visualising the monarchy vis-à-vis the subjects. This basic dimension of the court was conspicuously present in Hellenistic court culture. There even existed a contemporary notion that kings were like actors displaying their *basileia* on a stage – and indeed they often literally did so, as the public pomp and ritual of Hellenistic kingship often took place in theatres, gymnasia or hippodromes.[13]

FIVE FUNCTIONS OF THE COURT

Kruedener's model discerns three principal dimensions or functions of the court. Working from Elias' basic notion that the court could serve as the locus for the (re)distribution of capital, prestige and

[11] Winterling 1986.
[12] Duindam 1994: 79.
[13] Chaniotis 1997: chs3 and 11.

socio-political power (in the form of aulic and military offices), I have added an 'economic' dimension, and a 'symbolic' one:

1. the court as a political arena,
2. the court as administrative centre,
3. the court as symbolic centre,
4. the court as a stage for monarchic representation and
5. the court as the locus for (re)distribution.

The function of the court as a political arena combines its political, economic and social dimensions. The court was the place where the wealth, power and prestige of the dynasty were accumulated and redistributed. This not only made the court an instrument of power in the hands of the ruler, but also had advantages for those who wished to share in the power, wealth and prestige of the dynasty. Acquiring a place of honour in the household of the king was a means for powerful families to exert influence on political matters, even permitting them at times to hold sway against the ruler's desire.[14] In theory, the mechanism structuring power relations at court was the principle of proximity to the throne, or 'favour', i.e. the regulation of access to the person of the king, and the system of honorific titles, court offices and military commands, which developed to give expression to the intangible 'favour'.[15] The public distribution of gifts during banquets and the wearing of specific clothing received from the king, too, served as expressions of status and favour. In practice, however, the ruler was not automatically in full control of the distribution of titles, offices, wealth and status gifts. At the Hellenistic courts, the king shared his power with numerous persons or families, and sometimes was not even their leader. Favour could be the object of negotiation. Attempts by kings to rearrange the social composition of their households to control the distribution of favour better was an important source of conflict at various moment in Macedonian imperial history. Another major source of discord was conflict over the succession. Indeed, internal conflict was a defining characteristic of Hellenistic court culture, but only rarely was it an instrument of control in the hands of the king.

The court was the point of contact between the monarchy and the various ruling classes at the regional and local levels of the kingdoms, the main point from which the Macedonians negotiated

---

[14] Duindam 1994: 95.
[15] Kruedener 1973: 57: 'Abstammung als Quelle sozialer Ehre und als Ordnungsprinzip ... des Ranges [ist] im Prinzip aufgehoben und durch ein anderes Prinzip ersetzt worden: die Nähe zum Thron'. On the dynamics of 'favour' and 'access' see Winterling 2004.

relationships with civic elites and created alliances with regional military leaders.[16] In the Hellenistic world the courtiers (*philoi*) functioned as intermediaries between the court and the cities. They were linked to the king and his family through kinship, ritualised friendship (*philia, xenia, philoxenia*) and other personal bonds. The *philoi* maintained ties with their cities and families of origin, and acted as private benefactors of other cities. They became local magnates because they were royal *philoi*, or vice versa. Thus court society was the epicentre of a complex network of patronage relations. 'The court was an intermediary through which the king controlled his secondary and much wider zone of influence', wrote Gabriel Herman, one of the very few ancient historians to have dealt with Hellenistic court culture analytically in the twentieth century: 'Its tentacles reached into every section of the kingdom, so that the king's power was manifested to his subjects through the members of his court.'[17] The system, I would argue, also worked the other way round, permitting cities and elite families to exert influence at court through royal *philoi*. Moreover, royal courts were not the only source of political power in the Hellenistic world. As long as the monarchy was strong and wealthy, kings were able to attract powerful men to their court and control cities and territory with their aid. But when a monarchy was impoverished or lost charisma – usually the result of military failure – regional leaders turned away from the court or became political rivals. As we will see, the motor that kept the imperial networks of the Macedonian kingdoms going was gift-exchange.

The second dimension is the court as an administrative centre. Since the Hellenistic royal court was essentially the household of the royal family, it was the centre of the (economic) management of the dynastic *oikos*: the exaction of tribute and produce, the financial administration and the chancellery. High ranking office-holders were ultimately responsible, but they were assisted by many lesser officials, servants and local tax-collectors. Most of all, the court was the nerve centre of the kingdom as a military organisation.

In organising a festival and games at Daphne in 166/5 BCE, Antiochos IV Epiphanes

> brought together the most distinguished men from virtually the whole world (*oikoumenē*), adorned all parts of his palace in magnificent fashion, and, having assembled in one spot and, as it were, having put upon a stage

[16] In general: Asch 1991: 4; Duindam 1994: 92.
[17] Herman 1997: 200.

his entire kingship (*basileia*), he revealed everything and left [his enemies] ignorant of nothing ... In putting on these lavish games and stupendous festival Antiochos outdid all earlier rivals.[18]

This revealing fragment from Diodoros sums up the next two dimensions of the court, which are mainly ideological and representational: the court as a symbolic centre and a stage for the theatre of kingship.

The court as a symbolic centre is a separate aspect of neither Kruedener's nor Elias' model, though it does play a significant role particularly in Kruedener's work. I have added this dimension to emphasise that the Seleukids and Ptolemies conceived, styled and propagated the idea of their court as the heart of empire and thus the heart of the entire *oikoumen*. The court was a kind of microcosm where the world empire was exhibited. As the self-declared summit of civilisation, the court was contrasted with the barbaric, even chaotic periphery beyond the king's rule. This ideology enhanced the rulers' self-presentation as world leaders and created a sense of unity in culturally and ethnically heterogeneous empires, at least among the local agents of empire who profited from friendly relations with the centre.

The next dimension, the court as a stage for legitimisation and competition, figures prominently in Kruedener's model. Kruedener distinguishes three closely related aspects of the legitimating function of the court: cultisation, charismatisation and distancing. In the Hellenistic world these were manifested in three clearly distinguishable forms, respectively (1) public rituals in which the superhuman nature of the monarchy, including the king's divinity, was revealed; (2) the presentation of the king as a victorious warrior; and (3) the presentation of the court as sacred and inaccessible, for instance by means of integrating elements of temple architecture into palaces (see Chapter 3). The function of all this was to overawe subjects and enemies alike. The display of wealth, military might and political power – 'höfisches Imponiergehabe', as Kruedener called it – was instrumental in competing with rival kingdoms.[19] Through the display of power symbols, wealth and splendour, the ruler did more than make claims: by putting up a show he could actually gain prestige and thus increase his charisma and power.[20]

The last dimension, the court as a locus for (re)distribution, is an

---

[18] Diod. 31.16.1; Loeb translation with adjustments.
[19] Kruedener 1973: 21–2.
[20] Ibid. 21; cf. Shennon 1974: 475.

economic dimension of sorts. Especially following military victory, the court would become the place where the wealth and land acquired through conquest were distributed among the king's followers. The court furthermore was the place where high offices in the imperial hierarchy could be obtained, as well as the prestige that came with high office, land ownership and association with the dynasty. As an organisation specialising in the gathering of agrarian surpluses, tribute and taxes, the court was an economic powerhouse injecting capital into local economies through the payment of the imperial soldiery and the dealing out of benefactions to cities.

ROYAL COURTS IN THE HELLENISTIC WORLD

'In the court I exist and of the court I speak, but what the court is, God knows, I know not.' With these words the twelfth-century patrician Walter Map began his account of the English court of his own age.[21] Concerning the Hellenistic kingdoms too, the sources do not give the impression that there existed a unanimous notion of exactly what the court was. It may be variously described as either the household of the king or the people belonging to that household as kin, personnel and guest-friends.

To designate a royal household, the words *oikos* or *oikia* could be used. *Oikos* connotes the extended family's house, household, property and interests. By extension it could mean 'kingdom'. Thus, when Polybios contrasts the fortunes of the Antigonid dynasty and the Achaian League, he places the royal *oikia* of the Macedonians on a par with the confederacy of the Achaians, as two 'states'.[22] A more specific term is *aulē*.[23] Athenaios explains that this word (which normally denotes the courtyard of a house or farm) is used for a royal household 'because there are very spacious squares in front of the house of a king'.[24] *Aulē* literally means 'court' in two modern (and apparently also ancient) meanings. Large open courtyards were indeed characteristic of Hellenistic palace architecture, as we will see in Chapter 3. The people surrounding Hellenistic kings were therefore often called 'the people of (or: around) the court' (οἱ περὶ τὴν αὐλήν) or *aulikoi*, literally 'courtiers'.[25] *Aulē*, however, is normally

[21] Cited from Griffiths 1991: 67.
[22] Polyb. 2.37.7 (των Ἀχαιῶν ἔθνους καὶ τῆς Μακεδόςνων οικίας); cf. 2.48.2; 2.50.9.
[23] Diod. 31.15A.1–3; Jos., *AJ* 12.106, 185; 13.368; 16.336; 1 Macc. 2.46; Polyb. 4.42.2; 5.29.3, 40.4. Curt. 10.5.8 translates the term as *vestibulus regis*.
[24] Ath. 189e.
[25] See e.g. Polyb. 4.42.2; 5.29.3, 40.4; 1 Macc. 2.46. Cf. Tamm 1968: 135–242.

not used as a synonym for 'palace', the customary word for which is *basileion* or *basileia*.[26] The Romans took over this usage of 'court' (in Latin: *aula*), and presumably via this route it reached its present use in modern European languages ('cour', 'court', 'Hof').[27]

In addition to *aulikoi* various other terms designating 'courtiers' are used in the sources. A term often encountered in ancient historiography is *therapeia*, meaning 'retinue'. According to Bickerman, *therapeia* was the *terminus technicus* for the (Seleukid) court.[28] However, the word is not used in this meaning in royal correspondence or other primary sources stemming from the courts. Moreover, when used in the context of monarchy, *therapeia* can refer to the king's personal attendants or his bodyguard, and the difference is often unclear.[29] For instance, it is not clear at all whether Alexandros, επὶ τῆς θεραπείας at the court of Philip V, was the king's major-domo (or *maître de l'hôtel*), a functionary in charge of the access to the (inner) court, *or* captain of the bodyguard, *or both*, as the Achaemenid *hazarpat* and his Macedonian counterpart, the chiliarch, perhaps had been.[30]

There remains, however, one contemporary term for 'courtiers' which figures in both historiography and official documents, and this is simply 'the friends of the king' (οἱ φιλοὶ του βασιλέως). On civic decrees, the standard formula 'the king, his friends (*philoi*), and his military forces (*dynameis*)' is recurrently used,[31] an unholy trinity neatly summing up the basic constituents of Hellenistic imperialism. In ancient historiography, too, *philoi* is used most often to denote Hellenistic court society.[32]

We may conclude then, that although there was no 'official' *terminus technicus*, a contemporary notion of a royal court did exist, conceiving the court as a distinct form of household. Terminology was not consistent, but the most widely used Greek term to indicate

---

[26] Polyb. 10.27.9, 31.5; Diod. 19.18.1; Plut., *Luc.* 29.8; Ath. 654b; Jos., *AJ* 13.136; 14.16, 59; 17.90; Strabo 508 and 524.

[27] Tamm 1968.

[28] Bickerman 1938: 36.

[29] *Therapeia* as royal retinue: Polyb. 5.39.1, 50.3, 56.7–8. As bodyguard: Diod. 33.4a. Cf. Polyb. 7.12.1; 5.50.1; 15.32.8; Diod. 31.17c; 18.27.1. An interesting variant is αὐλὰς θεραπεύειν (Ath. 189e). In place of *therapeia*, *therapontes* is also used in e.g. Polyb. 5.39.1. Before the Hellenistic age, Greek writers used *therapeia* to indicate the retinue of Persian kings; see e.g. Hdt. 1.199; 5.21; 7.184; Xen., *Cyr.* 4.6.1; 7.5.65.

[30] Polyb. 4.87.5; *pace* Walbank I: 536.

[31] See Musti 1984: 179.

[32] See Chapter 5. The Latin word for a Hellenistic courtier is *purpuratus*, because of the purple dye used to colour the clothing that was given to *philoi* as status marker; e.g. Liv. 30.42.6; 32.39.8; 37.23.7; 37.59.5; 42.51.2; Cic., *Cat.* 4.12; *Tusc.* 1.102; Curt. 3.2.10; 3.13.13; 5.1.37; Vitr. 2 *pr.* 1. Quint. 8.5.24.

Hellenistic court society was royal *philoi*. The evidence normally does not differentiate between the court as a household and as a social group, and in this sense the court is indeed not unlike the *oikos*. There is also a marked difference from the modern terminology: *philos* could indicate both a courtier (someone who was *at court*, i.e. part of the king's immediate social milieu) and someone who strictly speaking was not *at* court but was linked to the king by means of *philia*.

HISTORICAL DEVELOPMENT

At first glance, Hellenistic court culture was essentially Greek and Macedonian elite culture imported to Egypt and the Near East. As I will expound in Chapter 5, non-Greeks were present at the Macedonian courts (especially Iranians at the dynastic centre of the Seleukids) – only they did not belong to the '*philoi* society' because they were tied to the king by other bonds than (Greek) *philia*. Iranians were important at the very beginning of Hellenistic history, in the later reign of Alexander, and in the second century BCE when political change in the empire was accompanied by a transformation of the composition of the Seleukid ruling class.[33] After 200 BCE, the Ptolemies, too, increasingly allied themselves with (and perhaps helped create) indigenous (Egyptian) elites, especially in Upper Egypt. More research will be needed to assess how far these provincial nobles, who often received aulic titles of honour from the king, actually gained access to the court and the person of the ruler. Because in the Seleukid empire alliances with Iranian princes were often cemented by dynastic marriages, a strong Iranian presence at court is very likely.

The historical development of the Hellenistic court may be roughly divided into four main phases:

1. The period of imperialist expansion under Philip II and Alexander the Great, in which growing royal autocracy led to conflicts with the Macedonian high nobility (350–323 BCE). Greek (i.e. non-Macedonian) courtiers turn up as early as the reign of Philip, mainly as 'favourites'; Alexander favoured Macedonians from the lesser nobility, and later Iranians, to balance the power of the Macedonian grandees who had risen to power in his father's reign.

---

[33] Strootman 2011a.

2. The age of the Diadochs, when new courts were set up by Alexander's Successors (323–c. 225). In this period, Greeks began to dominate the courts, although there always remained a super-elite of ethnic Macedonians surrounding the king; non-Hellenic aristocrats, however, retreated from the dynastic centres to their power bases in the periphery. To mark the transition from a chiefly Macedonian court to a court dominated by Greeks from *poleis* bound to the king by means of *philia*, the Macedonian term *hetairoi tou basile s* was replaced by *philoi tou basile s* as the prevalent designation for 'courtiers'.

3. A longer period in which the institutions of the court developed and became more complex and hierarchised, and the Antigonid, Ptolemaic and Seleukid households became increasingly distinct from each other. The possibilities for the king to manipulate the composition of court society decreased as an established class of land-holding nobles came into being; kings tried to check the growing power of the *philoi* by patronising (non-Greek) favourites, by cooperating more with local (Egyptian, Iranian) nobles in the provinces, and by introducing a more complex system of aulic titulature meant to control access to the person of the king, a system which after c. 200 spread from the Seleukid to the Ptolemaic court (c. 225–150 BCE).

4. The period of the decline and fall of the Macedonian dynasties; their court culture and ideology were adopted by the dynasties emerging in their wake in Judaea, Kommagene, Armenia and Pontos, among others. Hellenistic court culture became more localised and was more extensively mixed with elements from various native cultures, although the supposed 'Achaemenid' aspects of the Pontic and especially Kommagenian royal style were to a large degree a matter of invention of tradition. Hellenistic royal ritual and iconography furthermore influenced the self-presentation of Roman and Parthian rulers in this period (c. 150 BCE–50 CE).

2 *The Theatre of Royalty*

In their outward show of majesty, they were like actors on a stage.

Plutarch, *Life of Demetrios* 41.3

Whenever a Seleukid or Ptolemaic king appeared in public he appeared both as man and as the incarnation of royalty, with all the appropriate signs of power and authority. Clothing, weapons, objects and iconography represented aspects of kingship. Kings were furthermore permanently accompanied by a retinue of *philoi*, guardsmen and other members of the royal entourage.[1] Plutarch describes, as a negative mirror image of the sober Roman rulership he favoured, how in the Hellenistic kingdoms it was quintessentially royal to be surrounded 'by a profusion of purple robes and mantles, [and] a throng of messengers and door-keepers'.[2] When the Athenians welcomed Demetrios Poliorketes, they sang how 'his friends surround him like stars around the sun' (see below). The number of *philoi* gathering around the king, each with his own status and reputation, was a sign of how much a ruler was held in esteem by great men; conversely, the prestige of the king reflected on those who stood by his side.

The presence of a large crowd surrounding the ruler to strike awe into visitors is a typical facet of the monarchical rituals at many courts in history. Grand viziers of the Ottoman sultans received foreign ambassadors on Fridays, when the palace personnel received their salary and the central court of Topkapı Palace was crowded with people. In 1526 an ambassador of the Habsburg emperor wrote of the court of Vassili III: 'The presence of so many people on such a day arises from two causes: so that foreigners may note the size of the crowd and the mightiness of its lord and also that vassals may

---

[1] Inseparability of king and *philoi* in public: Polyb. 5.20.8, 43.3; 7.21.1; 8.20.8; Diod. 29.29.1; Liv. 32.39.8; 36.11; 42.15.10, 51.2; Plut., *Pyrrh.* 16.10; Ath. 253b.
[2] Plut., *Cleom.* 13.1–2.

note the respect in which their master is held.'[3] Ancient sources, too, sometimes acknowledge that the pomp and ostentation surrounding a Hellenistic king were intended to intimidate guests.[4] When Perseus of Macedon set out to negotiate with Roman commanders during the Third Macedonian War, 'a large crowd of friends and body-guards [was] thronging about him' – a retinue so large that the Roman delegation feared for its own reputation (rather than its safety). They demanded that the king came accompanied by only three *philoi*, but this was perceived as insulting and provocative by the king, who refused to come even though he himself had requested the talks. Tension built up quickly and it took a long time before an agreement on the proper protocol was finally reached.[5]

The behaviour of *philoi* at court was to some extent regulated. There were both the unwritten rules of 'courtly conduct' and the more or less prescribed forms of social conduct for symposia and hunting, and especially ritual. Internally, social conduct was instrumental in the creation of group coherence, and the negotiation of status and hierarchy within the *philoi* group. In his seminal article on the symbolism of monarchical ritual, 'Centers, kings, and charisma', Clifford Geertz rightly stated that: '[n]o matter ... how deeply divided among themselves [the members of the elite] may be (usually much more than outsiders imagine), they justify their existence and order their actions in terms of a collection of stories, ceremonies, insignia, formalities, and appurtenances that they have either inherited or ... invented'.[6] As a consequence, it is often difficult to assess whether public court ceremonial is an expression of the norms and values of its participants, its audience or both. Moreover, shared values are no necessary preconditions for a Durkheimian creation of group solidarity, since, as David Kertzer asserted, '[t]he common reading of Durkheim, that he identified solidarity with value consensus in his interpretation of ritual, misses the strength of his argument. His genius lies in having recognized that ritual builds solidarity *without* requiring the sharing of beliefs. Solidarity is

---

[3] Picard 1969: 61–2.
[4] See e.g. Plut., *Luc.* 21.6.
[5] Liv. 42.39.2–7. Cf. Diod. 31.17c, where a Ptolemaic king is deposed in 163 'by taking from him his royal retinue' (θεραπείαν τὴν βασιλικὴν); so also Diod. 33.4a, where Diodotos (Tryphon) makes Antiochos, the son of Alexander Balas, king: 'Binding a diadem about his head and providing him with the retinue (θεραπεία) appropriate to a king, he restored the child to his father's kingship' (145). For some further examples see Diod. 32.15.6–7 and 33.5a.
[6] Geertz 1977: 152.

produced by people acting together, not by people thinking together.'[7]

Externally, collective ritual action emphasised the unity of the court by conveying images of harmony and solidarity among the *philoi*, and a strong bond between the *philoi* and the king. But at the same time, collective ritual behaviour functioned as a means to control access to the court society and keep away outsiders.[8]

THE SIGNIFICANCE OF ROYAL RITUAL

Scholarly discussions of ritual often start by quoting Edmund Leach's maxim that there is 'the widest possible disagreement as to how the word ritual should be understood'.[9] Definitions of 'ritual' vary from Roy Rappaport's claim that ritual is '*the* basic social act' to Frits Staal's assertion that ritual is 'pure activity, without meaning or goal'.[10] For the social scientist David Kertzer (political) ritual is essentially a way of understanding the world, and political reality is in part created by symbolic means: 'political rites are important in all societies, because political power relations are everywhere expressed and modified through symbolic means of communication'.[11] In what follows, I will not distinguish between 'secular' (political) and 'sacral' (magico-religious) ritual, since I believe such a distinction is not historical.

Why is royal ritual so important for monarchy? In *Ritual, Politics and Power*, David Kertzer summarises the importance of court ritual and ceremonial thus:

> Where the gap between rulers and ruled is greatest, rites of rulers are most highly developed. The logical outcome of the sacralisation of power is the divinisation of the ruler, who reigns not by force, still less by illusion, but by supernatural powers vested in him. Such an ideology cannot take hold without a powerful ritual through which the ruler's supernatural power is made visible to the population.[12]

According to David Cannadine, there are two basic questions

---

[7] Kertzer 1988: 76; cf. Shils and Young 1953, and Geertz 1964, claiming that an (ideal) image *of* social relations can become a model *for* (real) social relations.

[8] Ragotzky and Wenzel 1990: 7–8, defining *höfische Repräsentation* as 'Formen der Darstellung, die rituellen Charakter haben und durch die Herstellung bzw. Bestätigung von Gruppenidentität integrierend nach ihnen und abgrenzend nach aussen wirken.'

[9] Leach 1968: 521.

[10] Rappaport 1979: 174; Staal 1975: 9.

[11] Kertzer 1988: 9; cf. Kertzer 1974. For a critical discussion of the history of the scholarship devoted to ritual see Bell 1992: 19–66. Especially in the 1970s and 1980s, sociologists perceived political ritual as *secular* ritual; see e.g. Goodin 1978; Lane 1981; Wilentz 1985.

[12] Kertzer 1988: 52.

historians and anthropologists should ask when studying political ritual: 'what is the connection between divine and terrestrial order?' and 'what is the relationship between power and pomp?'[13] These questions betray the influence of Edward Shils and Clifford Geertz.

In their classic analysis of the modern British coronation ritual, Shils and Young conclude that public monarchical ritual is instrumental in holding a society together by reaffirming the 'sacred' moral standards which constitute it as a society: 'In an inchoate, dimly perceived and seldom explicit manner, the central authority of an orderly society, whether it be secular or ecclesiastical, is acknowledged to be the avenue of communication with the realm of the sacred values.'[14] This interpretation of the coronation as an act of communion is based, as Shils and Young are prone to emphasise, on Durkheim's belief that (religious) ritual is a means of expressing and dramatising the 'system of ideas with which the individuals represent to themselves the society of which they are members'.[15] This still holds good – though only as long as one does not undervalue the religious dimensions of royal ritual.

In 'Centers, kings, and charisma', Geertz reconsidered the Weberian concept of charisma by stressing the connection between the *symbolic* persona of the individual charismatic ruler and the shared values of the society he heads. Thus, charisma is understood as an integral part of the social order. In Geertz's view, charisma can only exist 'in the point or points in a society where its leading ideas come together with its leading institutions to create an arena in which the events which most vitally affects its members' lives take place … It is a sign, not of popular appeal or inventive craziness, but of being near the heart of things.'[16] Thus, Geertz challenges the conventional claim that political ideology functions as a means to conceal the 'actual' (unequal and exploitative) realities of power. In fact, Geertz turns this notion upside down: ritual brings together the real word (or 'world view') and the imagined world ('ethos'). In monarchy-related terms this means that the 'theatrical' performances of king and court in ritual contexts aim to bring together the ideology of kingship and the real world, so that the actual king will become the same as the imagined king.

Geertz has been criticised for making the ritual act itself

[13] Cannadine 1987: 6.
[14] Shils and Young 1953: 80.
[15] Ibid. 67; Durkheim 1915: 225; cf. Lukes 1975: 292.
[16] Geertz 1977: 151; cf. Geertz 1980, with its famous suggestion that public monarchical pomp was not in the service of power, but power was in the service of pomp.

secondary to its implicit message.[17] Such criticism is certainly justified, but fundamental understanding of ritual as a symbolic act remains useful: royal ritual and court ceremonial went beyond simply propagating or explaining ideology: it turned the ideal of kingship into tangible reality for both spectators and participants, or, as Geertz puts it: 'In ritual, the world as lived and the world as imagined ... turn out to be the same world.'[18] This viewpoint, combined with the Durkheimian understanding of ritual as an instrument of social integration and hierarchisation, will form the basis of the present discussion of Hellenistic royal ritual.

The emphasis on the shared values of 'society' in the work of Shils, Geertz and Kertzer seems to render this approach less appropriate for imperial states: empires by definition are composed of various societies that are often very different from one another in terms of culture, language, and social and political system. Throughout this chapter, however, I will argue that (1) Hellenistic kings both adopted (and modified) *local* symbolism and ritual forms when approaching a city (for instance, Alexander's and the Seleukids' entries into Babylon); and (2) in both the Ptolemaic and Seleukid empires there developed simultaneously a form of *central* monarchical ritual that created a supranational ideology of monarchy aimed at the integration of various local elites within the imperial system. For instance, in the symbolism of the Grand Procession of Ptolemy Philadelphos, cultural forms from various sources were integrated into an imperial semantic system that contemporaries presumably did not understand as a 'mixture' of 'Greek' and 'Egyptian' cultural elements with static semantic values.[19] This means that in what follows I do not aim to untangle the varying degrees of 'Greekness' or, say, 'Egyptianness' in a given ritual.

THE MONARCHY ON STAGE

An aspect of the exercise of power was the public display of power. Palace architecture, public spectacle, luxurious ostentation, solemn ritual, ruler portraits and court poetry – it all added up to the presentation of power as something tangible. The grandeur, wealth and

---

[17] Vries 1995.
[18] Geertz 1973: 112. Kertzer 1988: 101 states that: 'Successful [political] ritual ... creates an emotional state that makes the message uncontestable because it is framed in such a way as to be seen as inherent in the way things are. It presents a picture of the world that is so emotionally compelling that it is beyond debate.'
[19] Versluys 2010: 19–23; cf. Hölscher 1987.

beauty of the court gave the impression that it was desirable and beneficial to be part of the imperial system.

The court as the stage for the theatre of kingship is one of the principal functions in Jürgen von Kruedener's model for the study of the court.[20] This function primarily served competition with rival courts. We will look at that aspect more closely in Part III, in which courtly pomp and pageantry will be discussed.

In the Hellenistic age, the similarity of royal ceremonial and theatrical performance was explicitly recognised.[21] It is difficult to see why there should have been among contemporaries 'widespread aversion to [the kings'] theatrical excess, which in the eyes of the spectator, was associated with overblown pretence and inauthenticity', as one modern scholar claimed there was.[22] More probably the contrary was true. Writing about early modern kings playing themselves in dramatical performances, Wikander observed that 'playing the king and being the king are not essentially different activities, for the thing itself is as much an imagined construct as any part a playwright might sketch out for an actor. The king is a type.'[23] When Antiochos IV celebrated a festival at Daphne in Syria (in 166 or 165 BCE), a Hellenistic source, Diodoros, comments that:

> Antiochos brought together the most distinguished men from virtually the whole world, adorned all parts of his palace in magnificent fashion, and having assembled it in one spot, as it were, put his entire kingdom upon a stage.[24]

The equation of Hellenistic royal representation with theatrical performance was still a common motif when, centuries later, Plutarch wrote his account of the assumption of the diadem by the Successors, which

> did not mean the mere addition of a name or a change of fashion, but it stirred the spirit of the men, lifted their thoughts high, and introduced into their lives and dealings with others pomposity and ostentation, just as tragic actors adapt to their costume their gait, voice, posture at table, and manner of addressing others.[25]

---

[20] Kruedener 1973: 21–5.

[21] Although the *locus classicus*, Plut., *Demetr.* 41.3, is not in itself Hellenistic: '[The Diadochs] imitated Alexander in the pomp and outward show of majesty, like actors on a stage.' See Hesberg 1999 for more examples of Greek tyrants and Hellenistic kings performing as actors in and outside the theatre. On the widespread Hellenistic notion that public ritual was somehow similar to drama see Chaniotis 1997.

[22] Hesberg 1999: 70.

[23] Wikander 1993: 4; in modern anthropology the compelling analogy between drama and ritual is also recognised; see Gilbert 1994: 119 n. 2 with further literature.

[24] Diod. 31.16.1.

[25] Plut., *Demetr.* 18.3.

Fig. 2.1. The theatre of Dionysos in Athens, seen from the south
(author's photograph).

Moreover, kingship was also most literally put on a stage, as the
public appearances of kings frequently took place in theatres. For
instance, in 297, Demetrios Poliorketes addressed the Athenians
from the stage of the theatre of Dionysos (Fig. 2.1):

> He ordered all the citizens to assemble in the theatre. He surrounded the rear
> and sides with troops and lined up his personal guard at the back of the
> stage. Then he himself, like a tragic actor, made his appearance down one of
> the stairways at the side.[26]

Of course, the main stage for the theatre of royalty was the palace.
Theatres and other structures where crowds could assemble (gymnasia, stadia) were often built near or adjacent to royal palaces – for
instance, the integration of *basileia* and theatre in Pergamon or
Aigai, or the gymnasion in Alexandria. During major festivities
whole cities became the stage for the theatre of kingship, as processions passed by the principal sanctuaries and monuments, and
guests of honour watched from temporarily erected tribunes.[27] The

---

[26] Ibid. 34.3.
[27] For the temporary platform (βῆμα) see Nielsen 1994: 18 and 131.

chain of monarchy-related religious structures along the processional route winding up the akropolis at Pergamon, discussed
in Chapter 3, could thus serve as the monumental backdrop for
religious royal ritual such as the Attalid Nikephoria.

POLITICAL RITUAL AND THE IDEOLOGY OF EMPIRE

The purpose of monarchical representation is usually taken to be
legitimisation of royal power. The pivotal question then must be:
what was the relationship between royal representation and royal
power – in other words, between image and reality?[28] To answer this
question, we must first define what power is, since '[t]o discuss
the ideological basis of power, one first should tackle the question
what power is and what it does ... Any analysis of the relationship
between image and power has to include a definition of power.
Common sense will not do.'[29]

According to Max Weber's classic definition, power ('Macht') is
any possibility for one actor within a social relationship to impose
his will on others, even despite resistance, and regardless of the
means by which it is done.[30] Naked power may become legitimate
power, or authority ('Herrschaft'), when it is voluntarily accepted by
the subjects because they regard it as rightful and advantageous.[31]
This definition has often been questioned and modified. One important variation is given by Michael Mann, who, in the context of the
political power of states, defined power as control of the means for
attaining whatever goals one wants to achieve.[32] Thus Mann shifts
the emphasis away from the *exercise* of power – Weber's rather
indeterminate imposition of one's 'Wille' or 'Befehl bestimmten
Inhalts' – to the more concrete organisational *sources* of power,
that is, the strategies to gain routine access to human and material
resources. Recently Olivier Hekster and Richard Fowler refined
Mann's terminology by defining royal power in the ancient world as
the sum of the monarchy's legitimacy, military force, administrative

---

[28] Strootman 1993: 7–8.
[29] Carlos Noreña in *BMCR* 2006–07, 06.
[30] Weber 1964: 38: 'Macht bedeutet jede Chance, innerhalb einer sozialen Beziehung den
eigenen Willen auch gegen Widerstreben durchzusetzen, gleichviel worauf diese Chance
beruht.'
[31] Weber 1968: 215: 'Herrschaft soll heiszen die Chance für einen Befehl bestimmten
Inhalts bei angebbaren Personen Gehorsam zu finden.' Cf. Weber 1964: 122.
[32] Mann 1986: 6, based on the definition by Parsons 1968: 263.

competence and capacity to extract surpluses.[33] This certainly leads
us further, although the connection between the named elements is
not explicated.

If we accept Mann's understanding of political power as the
control of resources needed to attain a political goal, two new
questions arise: by what means did Hellenistic rulers obtain that
control, and with what goals?

The Hellenistic empires, like any empires, were based on conquest
and ultimately were founded on the use of force. The power of a
given dynasty at a given time was the sum of that dynasty's control
of military resources and its willingness to use violence. To understand the significance of war and coercion for Hellenistic kingship, I
have made use of Charles Tilly's model of state formation, which in
turn is an elaboration of Norbert Elias' ideas pertaining to the same.

Tilly basically offers a synthesis of Weber's notion of power as the
enforcement of one's will and Mann's notion of power as the control
of resources.[34] The model was developed to explain the genesis of the
European national states, so much of it is irrelevant for ancient
history. What is relevant, however, is the central presumption that
monarchical states are competitive and violent by nature. For Tilly,
the 'means of coercion' with which to impose one's will even on
reluctant others is simply military force. Conflicts arise when in a
particular territory there are several actors who dispose of coercive
means: kings, noblemen, chieftains, warlords. As a rule, such men
will attempt to monopolise the control of resources – manpower,
metals, agrarian surplus – in that territory. As Tilly puts it: 'Men
who controlled means of coercion ... ordinarily tried to use them
to extend the range of population and resources over which they
wielded power. When they encountered no one with comparable
control of coercion, they conquered; when they met rivals, they
made war.'[35] Peace occurs only when the resources of the competitors become exhausted or when one of them is victorious. Thereafter the competition continues on a vaster scale in a larger territory.
The dynamics of this competition are beyond the participants' grasp,
and no more are they able to withdraw lest they be conquered by
their rivals. Hence the endemic warfare among the Hellenistic kingdoms. Control of resources (Tilly uses the term 'capital') is essential
for acquiring military means. Hellenistic kings preferred taxes in
silver to tribute in kind, for in the Hellenistic age money was, as

[33] Hekster and Fowler 2005: 24–6.
[34] Tilly 1990; Elias 1936.
[35] Tilly 1990: 17; cf. Elias 1969: 142–57.

Plutarch says, 'the sinews of war'.[36] Diodoros knew that too: 'In warfare a ready supply of money is indeed, as the familiar proverb has it, the companion of success, since he who is well provided with money never lacks men able to fight.'[37] Marcus Crassus allegedly exclaimed that no man could be called wealthy unless he could afford to pay for a legion.[38]

The one who controls the largest population and extracts the most surpluses has at his disposal the strongest army, which in turn enables him to control even larger populations and extract more surpluses. In Tilly's words: 'Some conquerors managed to exert stable control over the population in substantial territories, and to gain routine access to part of the goods and services produced in the territory; they became rulers.'[39] Monarchical states, and especially empires, are thus in several respects the products of warfare: permanent armies come into existence, the administration of taxes and tribute is professionalised, opponents are eliminated, and an ideology of kingship develops in which the triumphant monarchy acquires, to use Elias' term, a monopoly of 'legitimate violence' within the territory it controls. 'Why did wars occur at all?', Tilly asks. 'The central, tragic fact is simple: coercion *works*.'[40]

Still, it all takes place largely unplanned and even unintentionally. Elias himself asserted that the process of monopolisation of violence comes about 'als Ganzes ungeplant; aber sie vollzieht sich dennoch nicht ohne eine eigentümliche Ordnung'.[41] It goes without saying that until the nineteenth century, no government (and surely not the Hellenistic kingdoms) ever really succeeded in completely monopolising the legitimate use of violence.

Imperial projects based on repression and intimidation alone are doomed to fail. Therefore cooperation was as important as coercion, particularly cooperation with cities. Cities commanded the infrastructure and formed the loci where surpluses were collected. Only rarely did rulers lay siege to cities actually to coerce them into submission; to do so in an area as large as the Hellenistic world would be impossible. Normally a deal was struck: the ruler promised to protect the city against its enemies and guaranteed the city's autonomy, in return for which the cities voluntarily succumbed to

---

[36] Plut., *Cleom.* 27.1.
[37] Diod. 29.6.1.
[38] Plut., *Crass.* 2; Cic., *Off.* 1.25; Plin., *NH* 33.134.
[39] Tilly 1990: 14.
[40] Ibid. 15.
[41] Elias 1969: 13.

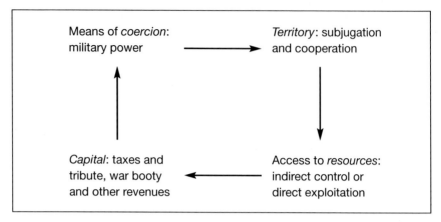

Fig. 2.2. Charles Tilly's model of the entanglement of city and state in the monarchies of premodern states.

the ruler and promised to pay him tribute, or to provide military aid.[42] Hence the self-presentation of Hellenistic rulers as liberators and saviours of cities. The Seleukids furthermore formed coalitions with lesser rulers at the imperial fringe – the Black Sea region, Armenia, Arabia, Iran – who obtained independence in return for acknowledging Seleukid overlordship. As far as the Seleukids were concerned, such rulers were vassals. Put into a simple diagram the model adapted from Tilly can be summarised as shown in Figure 2.2.

The question that follows is: how did all this relate to royal ideology as expressed in court ceremonial and monarchic ritual? As we will see especially in Chapters 11 and 12 kings in their official representation were far from concealing that violence formed the foundation of their power. On the contrary, they presented military prowess as the principal legitimisation of their rule. They did so by celebrating their personal abilities as warriors, their victories and their success as conquerors; by displaying their wealth and military strength; and by showing themselves *with their armies* to subject populations. Even seemingly peaceful aspects of the self-presentation of rulers – as liberators of cities, god-like peace-makers, sumptuous benefactors – were ultimately derivatives of the monarchy's military foundation. Thus it could be argued that the ideology of kingship

---

[42] Tilly 1994; Millar 1987: 29 defined the Seleukid state as 'primarily a system for extracting taxes and forming armies'. The normal policy of Hellenistic kings was to divide and rule; by supporting certain aristocratic families or factions within a city or region against their competitors, dependent and thus relatively loyal oligarchic regimes could be created; cf. Strootman 2011b.

Fig. 2.3. Silver tetradrachm of Demetrios Poliorketes celebrating a naval victory:
on the obverse the goddess Nike is standing on the prow of a warship while
on the reverse Neptune is thrusting his trident and holding a *chlamus*,
a Macedonian mantle (courtesy of the Numismatic Association, Inc.).

was *in agreement with* the reality of kingship.[43] Acquiring legitimacy
meant convincing others that one was a more successful warrior, and
thus a better protector, than one's rivals (Fig. 2.3). In a world accustomed to monarchic rule for many centuries there was no need to
justify the existence of kingship as such. A ruler needed to assert that
he, and only he, was the *rightful* king or emperor. This compelled
kings to be victorious warriors in actuality (another explanation for
the continuous warfare in Hellenistic history), to be generous and
benevolent, and most of all to be *visible* in as large a territory as
possible – not only in 'documentary' form (portraits on coins,
statues, inscriptions) but also physically on the battlefield, in
ceremonial entries into cities and in court

---

[43] As opposed to the more common, originally Marxist understanding of political ideology
as a means to cover up or legitimise inequality or exploitation; see e.g. Liverani 1979: 298:
'Ideology has the aim of bringing about the exploitation of man by man, by providing the
motivation to receive the situation of inequality as "right", as based on qualitative differences,
as entrusted to the "right" people for the good of all.'

3 The Royal Palace: A Stage for Royal Rituals

The sacred is a fine hiding-place for the profane: they are always so similar.
David Mitchell, *Cloud Atlas*

Not much has been preserved of Hellenistic palaces. Often we can only identify their (approximate) location, and sometimes not even that. The proverbial exceptions are Pella and Vergina in Macedonia, Pergamon, and the Hasmonean and Herodean palaces in Judaea. This lack of material is the result of sites being built over or otherwise lost, but also of archaeological habit. The exceptions mentioned above demonstrate what can be realised if a real effort is made (recent work in Messene on the Peloponnese is another example of how a shift of focus can have spectacular results).

Most Hellenistic palaces we know of were located inside, or adjacent to, cities. This is indicative of the importance that cities held for the empires. There was also a logistical reason: only at civic markets could enough surplus food be accumulated to feed the king's household and army, as well as fodder for horses and pack animals. Logistical requirements were presumably an additional reason for the nomadic behaviour of the Seleukid court and army. The Ptolemies, on the other hand, were able to provide their court with a more or less permanent base because their principal city, Alexandria, could be easily supplied from Egypt by river transport.

The location of imperial palaces in cities amounts to a paradox. Cities, especially when governed by an assembly, council and magistrates, normally cherish their autonomy. In the Macedonian empires, most cities were de jure and de facto self-governing, independent states. The monarch was in principle a foreign 'state'. The epigraphical record shows that a city's dealings with a king were a form of foreign diplomacy, although mostly conducted through the informal instrumentality of guest-friendship relations known as *philia* (or *philoxenia*; see Chapter 7). Even Alexandria, Antioch and Pergamon in all probability had a council and magistrates at their disposal.[1] Cities in Antigonid Macedonia normally had an *ekklēsia*, a *boulē* and civic magistrates too.[2] Royal palaces in cities were alien entities in what was essentially civic space. On the other hand, city and palace had a symbiotic relationship: the palace needed the city for reasons of prestige as well as for logistical reasons; conversely, the city would benefit from the presence of a palace and might actually grow when the palace grew, as presumably happened with Pella, Alexandria and Aï Khanoum.

The Seleukid court was mobile. Lacking within their realm a traditional place of origin and thus a symbolic, ritual centre like Persepolis, the Seleukid kings were arguably more nomadic than their Achaemenid predecessors had been. Besides the well-known residences of Seleukeia on the Tigris and Antiocheia on the Orontes (Antioch), the Seleukid empire had various 'capitals', including Baktra, Merw, Ekbatana, Susa, Seleukeia in Pieria (except between 245 and 219), Sardis, perhaps Aï Khanoum, and even (for a short time) Lysimacheia in Thrace. They furthermore maintained palaces in Babylon, Apameia, Tarsos, Mopsuestia and Tambrax, among others. The Antigonids of Macedon were wandering kings, too, though on a much smaller geographical scale than the Seleukids. The dynasty's principal residences were Pella, Aigai and Demetrias. Only the Ptolemies had at their disposal a real imperial centre, Alexandria, although they also maintained palaces in Memphis and Pelousion.[3]

To designate a palace, Greek historians most often use the word *basileion*.[4] Although usage is not consistent, *aulē*, 'courtyard', can by extension mean 'palace', too.[5] Hellenistic palace architecture is connected with the wider tendency in Hellenistic architecture to link together the most important buildings in an ordered fashion according to a preconceived design. Thus, rather than being a single

[1] For the 'democratic machinery' of Ptolemaic Alexandria see Fraser I:93–115. The existence of a *boulē* in Alexandria is disputed; for a discussion of the issue see Cohen 2006: 368–71.

[2] Hatzopoulos 2001: 190–1; Hammond and Walbank 1988: 475–6; for the evidence see Hatzopoulos 1996a I: 1270–65 and II: 54–110.

[3] After c. 200 the Ptolemaic court may perhaps have migrated seasonally from Alexandria to Memphis and vice versa; cf. Jos., *AJ* 12.4.3 (170).

[4] E.g. Ath. 654; Diod. 34.15; Plut., *Luc.* 29.8, Jos., *AJ* 13.36; cf. Polyb. 10.31.5; 1 Macc. 11.45; Strabo 17.1.9. Roman historians translate *basileion* as *regia*.

[5] Diod. 31.15A.1–3; Jos., *AJ* 12.106, 185; 13.368; 16.336; 1 Macc. 2.46; Polyb. 4.42.2; 5.29.3, 40.4. Curt. 10.5.8 translates *aulē* as *vestibulus regis*.

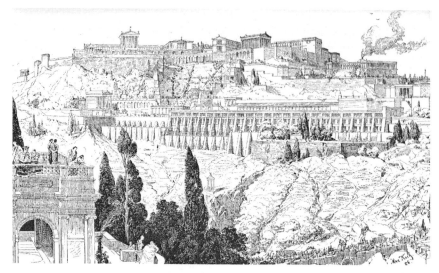

Fig. 3.1. 'Theatrical' reconstruction of the royal akropolis of Pergamon as it may
have looked in Roman times. Nineteenth-century drawing showing on the right
the Great Altar and in the centre the sanctuary of Athena. Behind the sacral
architecture the living quarters of the royal household were hidden.

building, a *basileion* consisted of numerous structures of which
the king's private house was only one.[6] The huge royal district in
Alexandria was known as the *basileia*, 'the palaces' or 'the royal
buildings' (see below). Since some of these monuments, notably
temples, had a public or semi-public nature, one would expect
some concept, visible in the architecture, that set the two 'antitheti-
cal societies'[7] of court and city apart and made visible the king's
otherness. Another conspicuous characteristic of Hellenistic palaces
was that royal space was in large part ceremonial space, where the
(religious) ritual performances connected with kingship and empire
could be performed – hence the noticeable preference for temples
and other religious structures (e.g. the Great Altar of Pergamon or
the Sema at Alexandria) in the heart of the palace district (Fig. 3.1).

How were royal palaces incorporated into cities? By what (architectural) means were civic and royal space distinguished and how
connected? Most importantly: what can the use of space tell us
about the relationship between the royal and the civic in Hellenistic
cities? In what follows, an overview will be given of the principal
imperial residences of the Hellenistic world. It will be shown how

[6] Lauter 1986: 85–8; Nielsen 1994: 25–6. But see Morgan in Erskine and Llewellyn-Jones
forthcoming.
[7] Nielsen 1994: 208.

the otherness of the monarchy was made visible by a careful choice of site and by architectural means. The main hypothesis is that through the use of architectural elements adapted from religious structural design, the palace precinct was shaped as a sacred *temenos* of sorts. Thus the sacredness of kingship was accentuated, and a mode was created of separating *and* connecting royal and civic space.

MACEDON

Drawing inspiration from Macedonian, Anatolian and Achaemenid examples, the evolution of Hellenistic palace building was associated with the early Hellenistic tradition of royal city founding.[8] The planning of new cities enabled kings to select sites deliberately to become military and civic centres and to think about the place and form of the palaces within the new cities. The main rationale determining the foundations was the wish to control roads and territory, and warrant a steady accumulation of surpluses. Strategic considerations prevailed over economic ones in the choice of sites. Thus, Demetrios Poliorketes relocated Sikyon on a more defensible but consequently less accessible site; Antioch was sited to defend a strategic stone bridge over the Orontes predating the city's foundation by Seleukos Nikator.[9] Controlling the main roads was a prerequisite of imperial rule. In the Seleukid empire, rulers did not attempt to control vast tracts of land in the way that modern historical atlases suggest they did. Nor did they try to establish clear boundary lines or defensible borders. Instead, the Seleukids tried to gain access to the military resources of the Middle East by controlling the cities and military colonies that guarded mountain passes and river crossings, creating a strategic network which commanded particularly the Royal Road between Babylonia and the Aegean, and the High Road into Iran and Central Asia.

The origins of Hellenistic palace architecture can be traced back to a variety of Greek, Macedonian, Anatolian, Mesopotamian and Iranian sources. Eastern influences were strongest in the Seleukid empire and least strong in the kingdom of the Antigonids.[10]

---

[8] Much new work on Hellenistic palaces has been published in the past decades; of relevance are Heerman 1986; Brands and Hoepfner 1996; Nielsen 1994; Kutbay 1998; Netzer 1999 and 2008; Hatzopoulos 2001; Morgan and Kopsachaeili in Erskine and Llewellyn-Jones forthcoming. Specifically for eastern influences on Hellenistic palace architecture see Nielsen 1996 and Held 2002.

[9] Lawrence 1979: 114 and 41.

[10] For the various precedents consult Nielsen 1994: 27–80; cf. Etienne 1998 and Tomlison 1983.

Royal palaces in pre-Hellenistic Macedonia probably resembled the fortified farmsteads in which the Macedonian landed aristocracy dwelled.[11] One characteristic of these structures that we see returning in Hellenistic palaces is the integration of military and domestic architecture, in particular the form of *tetrapyrgion*, a rectangular structure around an open courtyard with four corner towers, a form also known from pre-Hellenistic Asia Minor and Syria.[12] This model, combined with other Aegean examples (especially from Asia Minor), was the basis of the palaces at Demetrias (for which there is archaeological evidence; see below) and Antioch (Jos., *AJ* 13.36), among others. Through the addition of arcades and loggias, palaces, though fortified, were given an 'open' outlook on the outside.

HALIKARNASSOS

Among the fourth-century palaces preceding Hellenistic developments, the palace of the Karian ruler Mausolos at Halikarnassos stands out. Because of some striking similarities, it seems that Mausolos' work informed particularly Alexander's plans for a palace at Alexandria.

From at least 367 BCE, Halikarnassos had been the residence and principal naval base of the satrap-king Mausolos. The Karian ruler had rebuilt and enlarged the original Greek city. Because of its huge size, rectangular Hippodamian outline and character as a royal city, Halikarnassos may be regarded a proto-Hellenistic city, a model for the city foundations of subsequent kings.[13] The short-lived Aegean empire that Mausolos ruled from Halikarnassos may furthermore have been a model for the maritime empire of the Ptolemies.

Mausolos' residence was situated on Zephyrion, a promontory directly adjoining the harbour. It was built next to a fortress guarding this harbour.[14] Its architectural style presumably combined Hellenic and Karian elements. All we know about it, however, is that the outer walls of the palace were covered in gleaming marble and beautifully decorated.[15] Mausolos' tomb, the famed Mausoleum, was located elsewhere. It stood on an artificial terrace of gigantic proportions in the heart of the city, along the main road connecting the eastern and western gates. The huge terrace supported several

---

[11] Nielsen 1994: 93, with n. 197; cf. 81 nn. 176 and 177.
[12] Ibid. 65 and 115.
[13] Lauter 1986: 85; Hoepfner and Schwandner 1994: 226.
[14] Nielsen 1994: 63; cf. Hoepfner and Schwandner 1994: 228.
[15] Vitr. 2.8.10; Plin., *NH* 36.47.

other structures as well, including a hippodrome or stadion.[16] The tomb of Mausolos prefigures the Hellenistic practice of burying kings in a monumental tomb (*heroon*) in a city as *heros ktistēs*, deified city founder (Mausolos had refounded Halikarnassos). For example, there was a *heroon* of Alexander in Alexandria, of Demetrios Poliorketes in Demetrias, and of Seleukos Nikator in Seleukeia in Pieria.

Alexander laid siege to Halikarnassos in 334. Though the city fell quickly, the Macedonian forces were not able to take the fortified palace on the Zephyrion peninsula. It is presumably no coincidence that Alexander founded one of his own capitals, Alexandreia-by-Egypt (Alexandria), on a site closely resembling that of Halikarnassos, and ordered a palace to be built on the Lochias promontory next to the military harbour. (The same concept returned late in the Hellenistic period in Herod's Caesarea-by-the-Sea.)

Three features of Mausolos' building programme can be seen again in Hellenistic residences: first, the fact that the palace was set apart from the rest of the city (here by its location on a peninsula); second, the fact that the palace was fortified and positioned adjacent to a fortress; and third, the nearby presence of a structure to accommodate large crowds, e.g. a stadion, hippodrome or theatre.

ANTIGONID PALACES

The Antigonids of Macedon maintained residences at Pella, Aigai, Demetrias, Thessalonike, Kassandreia, Pydna and Miëza. No more than a damaged temple of Sarapis remains of Hellenistic Thessalonike.[17] The location of ancient Miëza, one of the royal cities of Macedon, is unknown; it is often identified with modern Lefkadia, where a monumental tomb was found but no palace.[18] The palaces at Pella, Aigai (Vergina) and Demetrias have been excavated. The last was an Antigonid foundation, while the first two were early Hellenistic rebuildings of former Argead palaces. The cities of Antigonid Macedon were mostly independent political entities with civic institutions combining Greek and Macedonian traditions. Royal palaces, therefore, could be connected with, but not incorporated into, these *poleis*.

---

[16] Pedersen 1991; Waywell 1988.
[17] Müller 1989b.
[18] Ibid. 392.

Palace

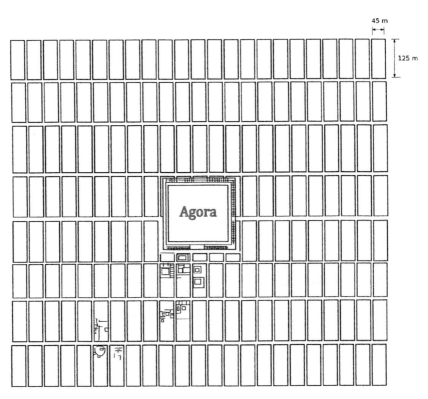

Agora

Fig. 3.2. Plan of ancient Pella showing the relative positions of the city and the akropolis with the royal palace (from Siganidou and Lilimpaki-Akamati 2003).

The best-known Antigonid palace is that of Pella.[19] Lying on one of the main roads of Macedon, Pella had been a royal residence at least since the reign of Archelaos (413–399).[20] Under the Antigonid dynasty the importance of Pella increased. The palace of Pella was situated on a hill some distance from the actual city (Fig. 3.2).

[19] Nielsen 1994: 89–93; Siganidou 1996; Hatzopoulos 2001; Siganidou and Lilimpaki-Akamati 2003.
[20] Hatzopoulos 2001: 189; Siganidou 1996.

Excavations have revealed a large complex with exceptionally massive outer walls. Most of this complex was constructed in the second half of the fourth century BCE; the most active builders seem to have been Philip II and Demetrios I.[21] The interior of the palace consisted of multiple rooms and halls for residence, reception, dining, administration, service and storage, grouped around open courtyards. The palace was clearly divided into an 'official', ceremonial section and perhaps a residential section at the back of the complex. The two parts were separated by means of a portico. The ceremonial part of the complex was located at the front of the palace, behind a monumental façade on a high terrace, facing the city. From the city a broad ramp ran up to the main entrance and vestibule. Public audiences were perhaps held on the palace's threshold in the propylon gatehouse in the main façade, as was the case in Alexandria (see below). Besides *andrones* for ritual feasting, the official section contained two rounded rooms that may have served as sanctuaries. In the residential wing, heated apartments and a bathhouse with swimming-pool have been excavated. In 1957 Greek archaeologists uncovered in the villas in the city of Pella several figurative floor mosaics, representing a lion hunt, a pair of centaurs, a griffin attacking a stag, and Dionysos on a panther's back. The mosaics probably date to the Diadoch period and are illustrative of the palace's former grandeur and the subjects preferred at court; in 1961 three more mosaics were uncovered, representing a stag hunt, an Amazonomachy and the kidnapping of Helen by Theseus (Fig. 3.3).[22] Perhaps the western wing of the palace formed yet a third section, set apart for administration, service and storage.[23] Livy, drawing on Polybios, suggests that there were separate quarters for different princes and mentions such elements as a *vestibulum* (*aulē*), *triclinium* (ceremonial dining room, *andr n*) and *ambulatio* (covered portico).[24] Plutarch furthermore mentions the presence of a library and a royal treasury.[25]

Nearby, on the slope of the hill below the palace, was a theatre dating to the fourth century BCE.[26] In the Hellenistic kingdoms, theatres were the principal stages for the enactment of royal rituals.

---

[21] Nielsen 1994: 89–93; Siganidou 1996; Hammond and Walbank 1988: 479; Hatzopoulos 2001: 191 and 194.
[22] Petsas 1978: 83–111. Two mosaics are signed by the otherwise unknown artist Gnosis.
[23] Nielsen 1994: 92–3.
[24] Liv. 40.6.1–16–3; Hatzopoulos 2001: 193.
[25] Plut., *Aem.* 18.6 and 23.3.
[26] Lauter 1986: 86; Nielsen 1994: 88.

Fig. 3.3. Deer hunt mosaic from Pella, signed by the artist Gnosis
(after Sakellariou 1983, 183).

In the city proper, smaller palaces were excavated, presumably
belonging to high-ranking Antigonid courtiers.[27] A game park
(*paradeisos*) was located in the vicinity of the palace.[28]

Where the *philoi* lived is never easy to ascertain, as the residential
quarters of Hellenistic palaces are usually too small to house large
groups of friends and their households.[29] The *philoi* may have had
mansions of their own near palaces and at their estates. Members of
the inner court may have lived in the king's house. Concerning
mansions in the classical Greek cities, Nevett writes that

> as well as a core nuclear family, individual households are most likely to
> have housed a number of other individuals, including long-term guests, and
> that friends and neighbors are also likely to have been an important part of
> domestic life. It remains to be explored how far these individuals were able
> to move freely about the house, and in what way the basic categories of
> outsider and family member ... need to be modified in order to accommo-
> date them

[27] Nielsen 1994: 84.
[28] Polyb. 31.29.1–8.
[29] Weber 1997: 40 n. 51.

Fig. 3.4. The so-called House of Dionysos in Pella, one of the *philoi* residences in the lower city (author's photograph).

in order to understand what an *oikos* is.[30] In Pella, rich private mansions have been excavated in the city, near the central agora (Fig. 3.4).

The palace at Aigai, present-day Vergina, resembled the palace at Pella but was of more modest size.[31] Aigai was a sacred site, the place where the kings of the Argead line were buried.[32] The site of Aigai had been inhabited since c. 1000 BCE; it was connected with traditional Macedonian royalty from the beginning of the Macedonian monarchy around 700 BCE.[33] A votive inscription of Queen Laodike, the Seleukid wife of King Perseus, shows that Aigai remained a royal centre until the end of the Antigonid kingdom.[34] The excavated Antigonid palace was situated halfway between the

---

[30] Nevett 1999: 174.

[31] Andronikos and Mpakalakis 1960, 1964, 1969; Andronikos 1984; Saatsoglou-Paliadeli 2001; Hatzopoulos 2001. For the identification of Vergina with Aigai see Hammond 1970 and Hatzopoulos 1996b.

[32] The identity of the persons buried in the various tombs found at Vergina is extremely controversial; see among others Andronikos 1987 and 1994; Borza 1982 and 1987; Green 1982. For the architecture and decoration of Macedonian tombs see Miller 1982.

[33] Hatzopoulos 2001: 189 with n. 6 at p. 195; Saatsoglou-Paliadeli 2001: 207.

[34] Saatsoglou-Paliadeli 2000.

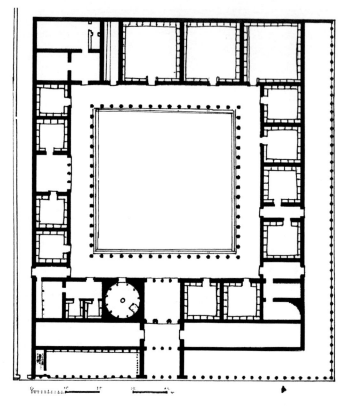

Fig. 3.5. Reconstruction by John Travlos of the floor plan of the palace at Vergina
(Aigai), showing banqueting rooms arranged around a central courtyard. Note
the round sanctuary to the left of the entrance (from Andronikos 1984;
courtesy of the Hellenic Ministry of Culture).

city and the akropolis. Both Kassandros and Antigonos Gonatas
built there; the latter restored the palace after the Celts had sacked it
in 279.[35] At Aigai, too, the palace was approached via a broad ramp
leading up to a monumental façade on a large artificial terrace. A
second terrace around the corner of the outer wall commanded a
superb view over the plain and the city. Between palace and city was
again a theatre.[36]

The palace proper was a rather basic version of the common
arrangement of palaces in the western Hellenistic world: a rectangular peristyle courtyard surrounded by banqueting rooms (Fig. 3.5).
The courtyard was reached through a propylon gatehouse in the
middle of the palace's monumental façade. The courtyard was on the

[35] Nielsen 1994: 81; Hammond and Walbank 1988: 477.
[36] Nielsen 1994: 81–2.

first floor, surrounded by rooms for ritualised feasting: three pillared ceremonial chambers and nine smaller *androne*.[37] Directly adjacent to the innermost vestibule of the propylon entrance was a conspicuous round hall, the function of which remains unexplained. Its interior was clad in marble, and in it were found an inscription dedicated to Herakles and a large base with two steps. This *tholos* has been variously identified as a throne room (for inauguration rituals), an audience hall or a sanctuary.[38] The chambers on the second storey may have been bedrooms.

A third important Antigonid residence that is relatively well known from archaeological excavations was located in the city of Demetrias in southern Thessaly, one of the three Fetters of Greece.[39] The city was founded by Demetrios Poliorketes shortly after he had gained control of Macedon in 294; he was buried there in 283.[40] Due to the city's favourable location on the bay of Iolkos, as well as the commercial privileges granted to its *politai*, Demetrias soon became an *urbs valida et ad omnia opportuna*, its population rising to approximately 25,000 in the third century BCE.[41] There was a strong element of non-Greeks among the population, in particular Phoenicians.[42] Demetrias was the Antigonids' principal naval base in the Aegean until 168.[43] There were two natural harbours, serving as commercial and military harbour respectively. The city was easily defensible, with steep approaches on virtually all sides.[44] The particularly massive defences were constructed by Demetrios, Philip V and finally Antiochos III, who held the city briefly in 192/1.[45] The city was protected by a wall over 8 kilometres long and strengthened with artillery towers and defensive outworks. There were three fortresses: two on the akropolis in the west and one in the south adjoining the royal palace.[46]

The royal palace lay on an eminence within the perimeter of the city walls. Excavations have revealed a large structure around a central peristyle courtyard.[47] Its main entrance, a monumental

[37] Andronikos 1984: 42; Hammond and Walbank 1988: 477; Nielsen 1994: 81–4. On the development of palatial banqueting rooms see Hoepfner 1996b: 1–43; Nielsen 1998.
[38] Nielsen 1994: 82–3; Saatsoglou-Paliadeli 2001: 202–4.
[39] Kramolisch 1989; Stähelin et al. 1934; Marzolff 1996.
[40] Plut., *Demetr.* 53.3.
[41] Kramolisch 1989; Marzolff 1994; the phrase is from Liv. 39.23.12.
[42] Fabricius 1999.
[43] For the history of Demetrias consult Stähelin 1924: 69–70.
[44] Strabo 9.5.1; Diod. 20.102. See Winter 1971: 114.
[45] Winter 1971: 277 with n. 31.
[46] On the fortifications see Stähelin 1924: 72–3; Winter 1971: 178 with fig. 172; Hammond and Walbank 1988: 480.
[47] Mpatziou-Efstathiou 1991, 1996, 1997, 2008.

propylon gateway in the western façade, was positioned on an artificial terrace overlooking the city. This structure, which was defended by thick outer walls and corner towers, was the heart of a larger royal area.[48] Adjoining the palace was a citadel of considerable size. Below the palace was an open square, which according to an inscription found there was known as the *hiera agora*, 'sacred square'. This square was the heart of a ceremonial and cultic area between the palace and the *polis* proper, comprising various (religious) buildings.[49] The square apparently functioned as a transitional area between the *basileion* and the city. As in Halikarnassos, the city's *heroon* – here the tomb of Demetrios Poliorketes – was not connected to the *basileion* but located at some distance, at the summit of a steep hill at the west of the city; on the slope of this hill was a theatre which was probably also used for monarchic representation.[50]

SELEUKID PALACES

The vastness of their empire and their warlike nature induced the Seleukids to travel around continuously, and hence to maintain numerous residences. Seleukos I Nikator initially established his base at Babylon but added more and more 'capitals' as his territorial control expanded. In Babylon he possessed the three palaces originally built by Nebuchadrezzar II (c. 604–562) and later extended by the Achaemenids. In the centre of his empire, the former Achaemenid palaces of Ekbatana and Susa were at his disposal, and in the west Sardis. But Seleukos was the most energetic founder of cities of all the Macedonian kings, including Alexander. According to Appian (*Syr.* 57), Seleukos built sixteen cities named Antiocheia after his father, five Laodikeia after his mother, nine Seleukeia after himself, and four after his wives, namely three Apameias and one Stratonikeia.[51] In Mesopotamia he founded Seleukeia on the Tigris, in Syria Antioch, Seleukeia in Pieria, Laodikeia on the Sea, and Apameia. In all these cities were palaces. In the second century BCE, when the Seleukids had lost control of Asia Minor and were gradually losing Iran, the residences of the dynasty were restricted to Mesopotamia and the Levant. After c. 120, only Syria remained.

---

[48] Winter 1971: 277; Nielsen 1994: 93.
[49] Lauter 1986: 86; cf. 99–113; Kramolisch 1989: 191.
[50] Lauter 1986: 86.
[51] On the foundations of Seleukos Nikator see Grainger 1990; Kuhrt and Sherwin-White 1993: 20–1; Cohen 2006.

In this period Antioch and Damascus were left as (competing) operation bases for the by then hopelessly divided dynasty.

Modern historians have fruitlessly discussed the question of where the Seleukid capital was located. In the past, historians as a rule identified Antioch in Syria as the capital. Later historians preferred Seleukeia on the Tigris. Downey claimed that initially Seleukeia in Pieria was the Seleukid capital until Antiochos I 'shifted the capital to Antioch'.[52] Bickerman maintained that Seleukeia in Pieria was no more than a port for the 'capital' Antioch; he criticises Seleukos Nikator for 'shifting' his capital from Babylonia to Syria and thereby weakening his position in the east.[53] However, a 'capital', i.e. a central seat of central government, did not exist in this empire. The search for the Seleukid capital presupposes a completed process of 'going out of court', i.e. the disconnection of the state administration from the royal household as it took place in early modern Europe, but not in the Hellenistic world. Several cities held a special position for the dynasty, including Miletos, Sardis, Seleukeia in Pieria, Antioch, Seleukeia on the Tigris, Babylon, Susa, Ekbatana, Merw and Baktra.

The largest city in the Seleukid empire, until its loss to the Parthians in the 140s, was Seleukeia on the Tigris.[54] Seleukeia was founded by Seleukos Nikator in the heart of Babylonia at a crossing of the Tigris where the roads from northern Iran, Syria and the Red Sea area met, and was connected to the Euphrates by means of an artificial canal. Seleukeia controlled the principal mountain pass through the Zagros Mountains and commanded the rich agricultural fields of Babylonia, the empire's richest heartlands. Two later imperial dynasties, the Arsakids and the Abbasids, built capital cities in this vicinity too: Ktesiphon and Baghdad. Seleukeia was larger than Antioch and had a mixed Macedonian, Greek and Babylonian population.[55] The so-called 'administrative block' may have been part of a palace complex or connected with the palace.[56] Finds of terracotta figurines and some bronze statues, as well as a vast number of seals, show both local and Greek cultural influences.

---

[52] Downey 1961: 54 and 87. See further, among others, Seyrig 1970; Marinoni 1972; Will 1990.

[53] Bickerman 1983: 4–5.

[54] See generally Kuhrt and Sherwin-White 1993: 135; further Streck 1917; Wagner 1976; Hadley 1978; Invernizzi 1993.

[55] Van der Spek 1986: 177.

[56] Nielsen 1994: 112. On the 'administrative block' see the preliminary report of seasons 1969 and 1970 in *Mesopotamia* 5/6 (1970/1) 9–104; for the excavations see further Waterman 1931 and 1933.

Fig. 3.6. The akropolis of Seleukeia in Pieria from the south
(author's photograph).

In northern Syria, another area that was of central importance for
Seleukid imperialism, Seleukos Nikator founded a cluster of fortified
cities: Antiocheia on the Orontes (Antioch), Laodikeia on the Sea,
Seleukeia in Pieria and Apameia. They were constructed from c. 300
onward on a concerted plan, involving the same architects, and
resembled each other in their design.[57] They were therefore known
as 'sister cities' and the region in which they were founded was called
the Seleukis.[58]

As the name indicates, Seleukeia was initially the most important
of the four cities.[59] It was meant to become the main port of the
Levant and a base of operations for Seleukos' Mediterranean
aspirations. In 281 Seleukos was buried there, presumably according
to his own wish, in a famous *heroon* known as the Nikatoreion.[60]
The city's splendid architecture and strong defences are vaguely

---

[57] Downey 1961: 54; Grainger 1990: 67–87.
[58] Strabo 16.2.4.
[59] See generally Downey 1961: 54 and Nielsen 1994: 112. The evidence for the foundation
of Seleukeia is collected in Downey 1963: 29 n. 8. See further Seyrig 1970 and Will 1990.
[60] App., *Syr.* 63. In Seleukeia, Antiochos I not only introduced a cult for his father but also
established a cult of Apollo Soter (his grandfather), to commemorate his own victories over
the Celts in Asia Minor and emphasise his descent from the god (Strootman 2005a: 115–17).

described by Polybios (5.59.3–11). The city, now a Turkish village at the foot of the former akropolis called Çevlik, has not been systematically excavated (Fig. 3.6). The outlines of the Seleukid naval harbour have been preserved. Some remaining structures outside the ancient city date from the Roman period. As the burial place of the dynasty's founder, Seleukeia in Pieria held pivotal ideological significance for the Seleukids. Seleukid prestige was badly shaken when in 245 the city was taken by Ptolemy III in the Third Syrian War.[61] Antiochos III made the reconquest of this hallowed city a key objective at the beginning of his rule, in part for reasons of his family's public honour. He recaptured the city in 219 during the Fourth Syrian War.

Because Antioch became such a large and important city *after* the Seleukid period, especially in the later Roman empire, its history is relatively well known from written sources.[62] Thus it is interesting to hear that the foundation of Antioch in 300 was accompanied by a grotesque symbolic act at the expense of Antigonos Monophthalmos, Seleukos' arch-enemy, whom he had vanquished the previous year at Ipsos. For Seleukos not only transferred to his new city the inhabitants of nearby Antigoneia, the prestigious city foundation of Monophthalmos, but demolished Antigoneia completely, using the salvaged materials to build his own residence.[63]

Outside the city, across the Orontes river, Seleukos moreover set up a remarkable statue on a place that was known from that time as Hippokephalos, 'Horse's Head'. The statue represented the head of a horse with a gilded helmet lying beside it. The horse was said to be symbolic of Seleukos' flight to Egypt when Antigonos Monophthalmos drove him from Babylonia, while the helmet symbolised Seleukos' final victory at Ipsos. The group bore the inscription: 'On this Seleukos escaped from Antigonos, and was saved; and returning and defeating him, he destroyed him.' A horned horse's head

---

[61] On the war in general see Ager 2003: 44–5 and Beyer-Rotthoff 1993: 17–67; for the capture of Seleukeia consult Jähne 1974; Piejko 1990; Muccioli 1997. Laodikeia on the Sea, too, was temporarily lost to the Ptolemies.

[62] For the history of Antioch see Downey 1961 and 1963; Hoepfner 2004. The literary and epigraphical evidence for Antioch under the Seleukids is collected and discussed in Downey 1961: 24–45. For the excavations in and around Antioch (present-day Antakya in the Hatay, Turkey), see the reports published from 1960 onward by the University of Chicago as *Excavations in the Plain of Antioch* and the series *Antioch-on-the-Orontes* edited by Elderkin et al. 1934–72. Lib., *Ant.* 72–7, 87, 250, ascribed the original initiative to found a city at this site to Alexander the Great, probably in an attempt to give his home city greater prestige; see Downey 1963: 27–8 with n. 2.

[63] Downey 1961: 57.

appeared on some of Seleukos' coins.[64] Despite all this, a town called
Antigoneia still existed in Syria as late as 53 CE.[65]

Antioch commanded a junction of roads linking Asia Minor,
Mesopotamia and Koile Syria. It had access to the Mediterranean
via the Orontes and the port of Seleukeia in Pieria. The city was
formally autonomous and was fitted out with the institutions of a
genuine Greek *polis*. As in Ptolemaic Alexandria, the inhabitants
of Antioch were organised in citizen bodies, *politeumata*, based on
ethnicity and each living in its own district.[66] Libanius says that the
city Seleukos built was so beautiful that even the gods were eager to
dwell there.[67] One category of gods actually did so: from literary
sources it can be established that the Seleukid kings maintained one
their principal palaces in Antioch, though perhaps not earlier than
the reign of Seleukos II or even Antiochos IV.[68] The most active
builder in Antioch was Antiochos IV, who re-founded Antioch and
may have wished to be buried there as *heros ktistēs*. He added a new
quarter and a second agora and erected a gigantic statue of himself
on a hill overlooking the city.[69] The enlargement of Antioch was
connected with Antiochos' attempts to turn the shrine of Apollo and
Daphne at nearby Daphne into a pan-Hellenic sanctuary and a
Seleukid cult place of central importance (see below). In all probability the present image of Antioch as the Seleukids' main capital is
based only on the city's increased status in Antiochos IV's reign and
its importance in Roman times; in the third century, Antioch was a
residence of secondary importance.

The palace of Antioch was located on an island in the Orontes,
where the remains of a hippodrome, a Roman governor's palace and
surrounding fortifications were excavated.[70] This river island was
still called Regia in the time of Malalas (sixth century CE). Of the
Seleukid palace little is known. Written sources attest that the royal
area consisted of numerous buildings; that the main palace had a

---

[64] On Antigoneia see Billows 1990: 152, 242 and 297; cf. Downey 1963: 29 with n. 7.

[65] Dio 40.39.1–2.

[66] Strabo 16.2.4; Downey 1941; Lauter 1986: 78.

[67] Lib., *Ant.* 109. For Seleukos Nikator's building activities in Antioch see Downey 1963:
31–4 and 27–44. For rhetorical reasons, Libanius contrasted the glory of Seleukid Antioch
with the city in his own time (Wiemer 2003). Next to nothing remains of the Hellenistic city,
although the street grid of the centre of present-day Antakya is still based on the original
Hippodamian outline of Seleukid Antioch (Demir 2004).

[68] Apart from numerous sources attesting that the Seleukids resided at Antioch, Diod. 33.4,
Jos., *AJ* 13.129–142, Strabo 16.2.5 and 1 Macc. 11.45 mention a palace specifically.

[69] Downey 1961: 95–6, 99–107; Mittag 2006: 145–9.

[70] Nielsen 1994: 112–13. Roman palace: Downey 1961: 643–7 and 1963: 117–18. Hippodrome: Campbell 1934. The island no longer exists, but its former shape can be determined
from traces in the ground (Downey 1961: 27).

monumental *propylon* entrance; that it was fortified; that it was a renowned centre of royal patronage and housed a famous library; and that it comprised a fortress with military barracks and arsenals.[71]

About 8 kilometres outside Antioch was the sacred grove of Daphne. This sanctuary of Apollo and Artemis was revered by the Seleukids from the days of Seleukos Nikator,[72] albeit initially not more strongly than other important holy places such as Didyma, Borsippa or Hierapolis in Mesopotamia. The site, known only by its Greek name, was presumably a sacred site before the Hellenistic age. Strabo mentions an 'asylum precinct' (*asulon temenos*) containing a temple consecrated to Apollo, tutelary deity and ancestor of the royal family, and Artemis. The sanctuary's focus was the laurel tree into which the maiden Daphne had been transformed when Apollo pursued her.[73] The valley of Daphne (modern Harbiye and still today a place of exceptional beauty) was a renowned *paradeisos* in Hellenistic and Roman times. The shades of the laurel trees and an abundance of clear water coming from streams and springs provided coolness in the heat of summer. The water was said to originate in the Kastalian springs at Delphi in Greece, flowing all the way to Syria via an underground waterway, suggesting a link between the Apollo worshipped at Daphne and the Pythian Apollo of Delphi: in the murmur of the water oracles were heard.[74] The inhabitants of Antioch celebrated a yearly festival there.[75] The importance of Daphne increased when Antiochos IV transformed the festival into an international event (see below, Chapter 12) and made the sanctuary a central shrine of his dynasty. The grove at Daphne in Hellenistic times further consisted of a theatre, a stadion and a fortified royal palace.[76]

It is unknown whether there was a palace at the port of Laodikeia on the Sea, present-day Latakia in Syria (and still a naval base). As in Antioch and Seleukeia in Pieria, the outline of the city is all that

---

[71] Nielsen 1994: 113; cf. Bevan 1902 II: 223–6; Downey 1961: 641. Library: Downey 1963: 47–8. Antioch also harboured a royal treasury and a royal mint. For the Seleukid patronage of the arts at Antioch see Balty 2004.

[72] Strabo 16.2.6; Lib., *Or.* 11.94–; cf. Downey 1961: 83.

[73] Myths relating to Syrian Daphne have been collected in Downey 1963: 41–4 and Porteous 1928: 75–6.

[74] Strabo 16.2.4–5.

[75] Ibid. 16.2.6.

[76] Downey 1963: 44; cf. Downey 1961: 642–3; Nielsen 1994: 115. A fortified palace existed here from at least 246 BCE, when during the Laodikean War its outnumbered defenders withstood a siege (Just. 27.1.4–7, App., *Syr.* 65; Val. Max. 9.10 ext. 1; Polyaen. 8.50; Hieron., *In Dan.* 11.5).

remains of Seleukos' foundation.[77] There was a palace, though, in the Seleukids' main military base in the Seleukis region. Apameia with its broad plains served as a base of operations against the Ptolemies in southern Syria. Strabo (16.2.10) mentions a 'war office' (λογιστήριον τὸ στρατιωτικὸν), a stud farm (ἱπποτρόφιον) with 300 stallions and more than 30,000 mares, and instructors in phalanx warfare.[78] The palace, where the peace conference after Antiochos' III war with the Romans took place (188), has not been excavated; presumably it was located on or near the fortified akropolis, now a Syrian village, where the remains of a theatre have been found.[79] As a military and royal centre, the city also accommodated a mint.

Sardis, the western terminus of the Royal Road, was the Seleukids' main stronghold in western Asia Minor.[80] On a terrace on the northern slope of the reputedly impregnable citadel hill there once stood the palace of Kroisos and later an Achaemenid palace.[81] In the third century the Seleukids transformed Sardis into a semi-Hellenic *polis*, both architecturally and institutionally. Kuhrt and Sherwin-White call Sardis 'perhaps the best example [of] deliberate hellenisation' in Asia Minor.[82] The process of Hellenisation took place especially after Sardis had been depopulated by Antiochos III as punishment for the city's role in the revolt of Achaios (220–213 BCE); it was later repopulated by Antiochos' governor Zeuxis, who resided at Sardis.[83] Correspondence between Sardis and Antiochos III reveals that the city had a *boulē*, passing regular decrees.[84] Architectural innovations included an agora, a theatre and a stadion.[85] The Seleukids enlarged the citadel's defences and rebuilt the palace. The new Hellenistic *basileion* served as a royal palace when the king was present and as a governor's palace in his absence.[86] This palace area harboured a royal treasury, a royal mint and royal archives.[87]

Of the former Achaemenid palaces further east, the Seleukids, like Alexander, used Susa in Susiana and Ekbatana in Media as royal

[77] Sauvaget 1934.
[78] For the history of the city see El-Zein 1972; for the (archaeology of) the city in Roman times see Ball 2000: 159–62 and Sartre 2005: 192–4.
[79] Balty 1969 and 1972.
[80] Bickerman 1938: 53–5; Hanfmann et al. 1983.
[81] Polyb. 7.15.2; Hdt. 1.154. Winter 1971: 324–5; Hanfmann 1977; Nielsen 1994: 63.
[82] Kuhrt and Sherwin-White 1993: 180.
[83] Hanfmann et al. 1983: 109.
[84] Ibid. 113.
[85] For Sardis as a *polis* see Kuhrt and Sherwin-White 1993: 181–2 and 135; for the Hellenistic architecture see Foss and Hanfmann 1975: 29–30.
[86] Winter 1971: 318–24; Hanfmann et al. 1983: 113.
[87] Hanfmann et al. 1983: 113.

residences. The two pre-existing palaces at Susa had been built by Darius I and Artaxerxes II; the Seleukids rebuilt them using elements of Achaemenid architectural style.[88] Ekbatana was strategically located at the eastern end of the pass through the Zagros Mountains that connected Media with Babylonia. It had been the residence of Median kings until conquered by Cyrus the Great.[89] Polybios (10.31.12-13) says that at the start of his *anabasis* in 210/11 Antiochos acquired nearly 4,000 talents by stripping off presumably Achaemenid-era decorations from the palace in order to coin money for his troops, indicating the continued importance of Ekbatana as a store of wealth to support royal campaigns. Ekbatana was the principal Seleukid stronghold in Media, controlling both road and plain. The region was also vital because of the horses being bred there, which the Seleukids needed for their heavy cavalry. The site now lies beneath the modern city of Hamadan.

The Hellenistic palace excavated in the ancient city at the foot of the mountain of Aï Khanoum in northern Afghanistan may have been built originally by the Seleukids, perhaps by Antiochos I when he was co-ruler and consolidated the eastern provinces.[90] The city may be perhaps be identified as Alexandria on the Oxus. It was built on a Hippodamian grid, and had a gymnasion and a theatre. Around 150 BCE, when Baktria and Sogdia had become fully independent from the empire, the palace was enlarged to serve as residence for an unknown ruler. The palace in its final form was enormous, the whole area being some 87,500 m². Its architecture combined Greek-Macedonian and Iranian elements.[91] The palace enclosure was

---

[88] Susa as a Seleukid residence: Strabo 15.3.5; see Kuhrt and Sherwin-White 1993: 135; Nielsen 1994: 35. Seleukid building activities: Boucharlat 1990. See also Le Rider 1965 and Martinez-Sève 2002.

[89] Ekbatana as residence of the Median kings: Kuhrt 1995 II: 654, 657–8; as a Seleukid residence: Polyb. 10.31.4–13; Strabo 11.13.5; 2 Macc. 9.3.

[90] The results of the excavations by the Délégation Archéologique Française en Afghanistan (DAFA), led by Paul Bernard, have been published in the eight volumes of *Fouilles d'Aï Khanoum*. Discovered only in 1961, excavations at Aï Khanoum came to a standstill with the Soviet invasion of Afghanistan in 1979; see Bernard 2001. In 2004 the site was stripped of much of its remaining archaeological treasure by treasure-hunters.

[91] Karttunen 1997; Colledge 1987: 143; Bernard 1967 and 1982: 129. Holt 1989: 5, dismissing both the 'western bias' of Tarn 1938 and the 'eastern bias' of Narain 1957, stated that the discovery of Aï Khanoum 'has clearly demonstrated the active cross-current of eastern and western cultures [in Hellenistic Baktria] in ways that Tarn and Narain could scarcely imagine ... Ai Khanoum ... provides a clear picture of Greek and Oriental features side by side.' According to Kuhrt and Sherwin-White 1993: 178–9, on the other hand, the palace was 'eastern' and not Greek; see Nielsen 1994: 127–8. Its huge size in itself, however, is hardly an indication of the palace's 'ethnicity' – with a total surface area of over 80,000 m², the palace at Aï Khanoum may indeed 'dwarf' the 'by comparison miniscule' c. 10,000 m² of the palace at Aigai, as Kuhrt and Sherwin-White claim (1993: 136), but hardly the 60,000 m² of the palace at Pella, and certainly not the even larger *basileia* of Alexandria, both of which they do not mention.

reached from the city through a monumental *propylon*, giving access to a broad avenue leading up to the palace proper. After passing a mausoleum the avenue terminated at a forecourt in front of the peristyle entrance to the main palace. The latter was divided into an official and ceremonial and a residential wing, separated by a wide corridor. The central element of the ceremonial part was a hall resembling the Great Apadana at Persepolis. Behind this lay the residential part, comprising apartments, decorated reception halls and dining rooms.[92] As in other Hellenistic royal cities, a theatre was built on the slope of the akropolis at the divide of royal and civic space.

PTOLEMAIC PALACES

Unlike the Seleukids or Antigonids, the Ptolemies ruled mainly from a single city. Alexandria was not the capital of Egypt (the civic centres of Lower and Upper Egypt were Memphis and Thebes respectively) but the central city of the Ptolemaic Mediterranean empire. Still, Alexandria was not the only place where the Ptolemies resided or owned palaces. Several Ptolemaic kings travelled, moving their court for the ad hoc reasons of war and diplomacy, marriage and accession. In the second and first centuries BCE, when Egypt grew in importance as the result of a shrinking empire, the Ptolemies visited the Egyptian countryside on a more regular basis. They maintained palaces in Memphis, Siwah and Pelousion.[93]

The port of Alexandreia-by-Egypt (Alexandria) was the symbolic and actual heart of the Ptolemaic seaborne empire.[94] It was the home of a polyglot population of Greeks, Egyptians, Levantines and others.[95] Initially, Greeks were dominant; with the reign of Ptolemy VIII (145–116) as watershed, a certain degree of 'Egyptianisation' set in.[96] Egypt with its agricultural abundance was around the corner, and via the seas the Ptolemies had relatively quick access to all parts of the eastern Mediterranean: under normal weather conditions it was e.g. a mere 4.5 days sailing to Ephesos and only 2.5 days to Cyprus.[97] In a later age, Dio Chrysostomos commented that

[92] Nielsen 1994: 125–6.
[93] Ibid. 130 n. 235.
[94] The most extensive study of Alexandria remains Fraser. See further Bernard 1966; Hinske 1981; Grimal et al. 1998; Grimm 1998; Pfrommer 1999; Harris and Ruffini 2004.
[95] For the population see Fraser I: 5–7; Cavenaile 1972 ; Jähne 1981: 68–72.
[96] Fraser I: 115–31; Hoepfner and Schwandner 1994: 242. On the multiethnic but divided population see Delia 1996.
[97] Alexandria–Ephesos: Ach. Tat. 5.15.1, 17.1; Alexandria–Cyprus: Lucian, *Nav.* 7.

Alexandria 'is situated, as it were, at the uniting centre of the whole earth, of even its most far away nations, as if the whole city is an *agora*, bringing together all men into one place, displaying them to one another and, as far as possible, making them one people.'[98]

Alexandria was the first city founded by Alexander the Great. All sources claim that the plan of building Alexandria was conceived when Alexander was in Egypt, where he noticed a most favourable site at Lake Mareotis, near the western delta, with unique possibilities for trade with both the Mediterranean and the Egyptian hinterland. But Alexander normally planned his actions well in advance. The foundation is usually dated after the king's return from Siwa in 331. Alexander supervised the demarcation of the city's outline himself, and ordered his architect Deinokrates of Rhodes to build on a rectangular grid five city districts, containing about forty residential blocks each, i.e. enough to accommodate a total population of 75,000–100,000 people. Attracting many new settlers from greater Greece, the city later perhaps reached a population of 300,000 or even 500,000 in the third century BCE.[99] When Ptolemy Soter buried Alexander here as *heros ktistēs*, Alexandria also became the most hallowed of Alexander's foundations. The city had the institutions of an autonomous *polis*.[100]

As long as Ptolemy was satrap of Egypt, he resided in Memphis. After having gained control of the Levant following his defeat of Perdikkas' troops in 320, Ptolemy left Egypt and set up court in Alexandria – a clear sign of his more far-reaching ambitions.[101] There, waiting for him to take possession, was the royal palace that Alexander had ordered to be built.

Archaeologically, this most renowned palace of the Hellenistic world remains something of a mystery, despite efforts to find remains under water.[102] The lack of remains is counterbalanced, however, by relatively extensive literary evidence provided by Polybios, Strabo and others. Of the original palace commissioned by Alexander to be built on the peninsula of Lochias, no more is known than that it was a large and rich complex; interestingly, the same

[98] Dio. Chrys. 32.36.
[99] On the foundation: Arr., *Anab.* 3.1.5–2; 7.23.7; Diod. 17.52.1–2; Plut., *Alex.* 26.2; see Bosworth 1993: 247. Population numbers: Diod. 17.52.6 (300,000); Hoepfner and Schwandner 1994: 237 and 241 (500,000).
[100] Fraser I: 93–115.
[101] Ibid. II: 11–12 n. 28. On Ptolemy's far-reaching ambitions see the contributions by Meeus, Strootman and Hauben in Hauben and Meeus forthcoming.
[102] For an overview and evaluation of the finds at Alexandria until the end of the twentieth century consult Bagnall 2001: 229–31; see further Goddio et al. 1998; Empereur 1998 and 1999; Yoyotte 1999. For pictures see Grimm 1998 and Foreman 1999.

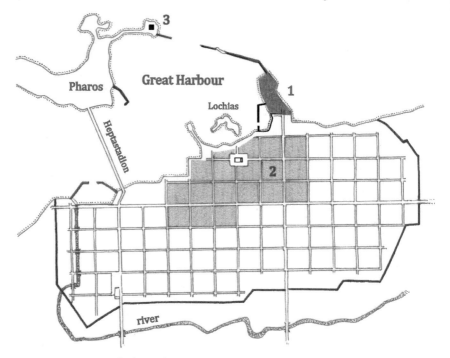

Fig. 3.7. Map of Alexandria in the Hellenistic period, showing the relative
position of (1) the inner palaces, (2) the *basileia* and (3) the lighthouse
on Pharos Island (reconstruction drawing by the author).

source adds that Alexander did not conceive the palace as an integral
part of the city, but as an additional element.[103] The later Ptolemaic
palace was much larger, comprising not only Lochias but also a vast
area on the mainland. Strabo visited Alexandria in the late first
century BCE and describes this royal district in some detail (Fig. 3.7):

> And the city has beautiful public sanctuaries and the *basileia*, which occupies
> a quarter or even a third of the entire enclosure. For each of the kings added
> some adornment to the public structures and each one also added further
> buildings to those already existing, so that, as the poet says, 'from others
> others grow'. But all stand near each other, between the harbour and what
> lies beyond them.[104]

Pliny claimed that the Alexandrian *basileia* covered only one fifth of
the city – but that still brings the total area to about 1 square kilo-
metre, against 2 square kilometres in Strabo's estimation.[105]

---

[103] Diod. 17.52.4.
[104] Strabo 17.1.9 (793).
[105] Plin., *NH* 5.2.62; cf. Hoepfner and Schwandner 1994: 243; Nielsen 1994: 131–3; Fraser
I: 11–37.

The royal district according to Strabo consisted of two parts: first, the *basileia* proper: a large semi-public, ceremonial area with temples, tombs and other monuments; and second the so-called inner palaces, the residential palace complex on Lochias.[106] There also was a smaller residential palace on the island of Antirrhodos, close to Lochias, with a small harbour.[107] Lochias resembled Zephyrion peninsula at Halikarnassos, where Mausolos built his palace. The long, narrow peninsula had its own enclosed harbour, giving the Ptolemies direct access to the Mediterranean. Polybios describes the inner palaces in some detail.[108] The complex was entered through the monumental Gate of Audience.[109] Inside were residential rooms, offices and a variety of peristyle reception halls, including a central 'Great Peristyle'. In a park on the landward side of Lochias were pavilions for feasting, as well as guesthouses.[110] On the northern tip of the peninsula there was a citadel (*akra*), containing a prison.[111]

In 279 or 278 Ptolemy II entertained his household and guests in the gardens on the occasion of the first celebration of the Ptolemaia festival and the posthumous apotheosis of his parents, Ptolemy I and Berenike I. A huge banqueting pavilion was erected for this occasion, described in detail by Kallixeinos of Rhodes, whom Athenaios cites extensively.[112] The pavilion could hold 130 couches along its sides. It was entirely covered with a canopy coloured with expensive scarlet-purple dye. The canopy rested on wooden pillars shaped like palm trees. The side curtains were dyed purple, too, and decorated with myrtle and laurel branches and the pelts of exotic animals. On the interior, the pavilion was decorated with marble portrait statues of the royal family and painted panels depicting symposia and mythic scenes. Along the sides, beautifully elaborate military cloaks, armour and shields were hung. The ceiling was adorned with large golden images of eagles. The floor was covered with 'Persian' carpets on which various kinds of flowers were strewn. All the tableware was made of gold and silver, worth more than 10,000 talents in total, to

---

[106] Fraser I: 22–3; II: 60–3; Hoepfner and Schwandner 1994: 238 and 242; Nielsen 1994: 131.

[107] Strabo 17.1.9; cf. Fraser II: 63 n. 147.

[108] Polyb. 15.25–34; cf. Fraser II: 61–2 nn. 144–5.

[109] Polyb. 15.31.2: τὸ χρηματιστικὸν πυλῶνα. Compare the Bab-üs Saadet, the Gate of Felicity, in front of the private Third Court of Topkapı Sarayı, where the Ottoman *padishah* sat on his emerald throne to receive homage from his subjects and officials.

[110] Nielsen 1994: 130–1.

[111] Polyb. 5.39.3; Plut., *Cleom.* 37.5; Ath. 196 A. Cf. Fraser I: 29, II: 99 n. 228.

[112] Kallixeinos, *FHG* III 58 *ap.* Ath. 196a–197c. For reconstructions of this pavilion see Calandra 2011.

be distributed among the guests when the festivities had ended.[113]

Some idea of what the inner palaces of Alexandria may have looked like on the inside has been indirectly preserved in Athenaios' description of the *Thalamegos*, the ceremonial river-boat of Ptolemy IV Philopator.[114] Philopator and his successors used the *Thalamegos* to travel up and down the Nile in order to make sacrifices at the temples alongside the river, show themselves to the populace, and demarcate the extent of Ptolemaic sovereignty. The *Thalamegos* had three floors outfitted with 'all conveniences of pleasant living', including bedrooms, banqueting rooms and even sanctuaries. The first two floors were surrounded with colonnaded promenades, while the upper floor was shaped as a concealed peristyle with walls and windows. It had separate women's quarters. Athenaios particularises especially the wealth of decorations inside this floating palace. It is worth quoting this part in full since it is a unique description of a Ptolemaic palace. The citation is moreover interesting because Athenaios' account was presumably based on an official report publicised by the Ptolemaic chancellery to impress and astonish the world.

> As one came on board from the stern there was an open vestibule with columns against its sides; at the side facing the bow there was a peristyle fore-gate made of ivory and exquisite wood. Opposite the main gate, at the other side of a kind of over-roofed proscenium, was a portal with four doors leading into a second vestibule. Beyond this was the main hall. It had columns all around and there was space for twenty couches. Most of it was made of Syrian cedar and Milesian cypress; the surrounding doors, twenty in total, had panels made of fragrant cedar wood and were adorned with ivory ornaments and handles of red copper which had been gilded in fire. The shafts of the columns were made of cypress wood, their capitals in the Corinthian style were decorated with gold and ivory. The entire entablature was inlaid with gold, supporting a frieze with remarkable ivory figures, more than one and a half foot high, of rather mediocre workmanship, to be honest, but of extraordinary profusion. The ceiling consisted of panels made of cypress wood, beautifully decorated with gilded sculptured ornamentation. Adjacent to this banqueting-hall were seven sleeping apartments, behind which was a narrow passageway dividing off the women's quarters. The latter contained a dining-hall with nine couches, similar to the main hall in its magnificence, and five sleeping apartments.[115]

The second storey contained more banqueting rooms, a peristyle hall

---

[113] Jos., *AJ* 12.2.14 (116): after the banquet, Philadelphos distributes the tableware among his guests.

[114] Ath. V 204d–206c. Cf. Grimm 1998: figs 54a–d at pp. 54–5 and fig. 70 at p. 69 (reconstructions).

[115] Ath. V 204f–205d, trans. C. B. Gulick (Loeb).

with columns of Indian marble, apartments, and a circular sanctuary (ναὸς θολοειδής) with a marble statue of Aphrodite. There also was a dining room in Egyptian style with columns decorated with floral motifs. These rooms, too, were richly decorated:

> Near the bow one came upon a chamber devoted to Dionysos; it contained thirteen couches and was surrounded by a row of columns. It had a cornice which was gilded as far as the surrounding architrave; the ceiling was decorated in accordance with the spirit of the god. In this room, on the right-hand side, a recess was built, which was entirely covered with real gold and precious stones so that it looked like a stone wall. Enshrined in it were portrait statues of the royal family made of Parian marble.[116]

The semi-public part of the Alexandrian *basileia* dominated the centre of the city, lying between the inner palaces and the city as a kind of transitional area. It was a performative area. Here the rituals of both the city and the monarchy took place. It was, in other words, a contact zone. It consisted of a variety of buildings and monuments. Strabo, who was amazed by their magnificence and size, names several of them. Close by the inner palaces were a theatre and a stadium,[117] where the king could show himself to the public. For this purpose the gymnasion too was used. Strabo further mentions a huge temple of Poseidon at the harbour, a temple of Dionysos, law courts, a precinct for the ruler's dynastic cult,[118] and a precinct containing the tombs of Alexander and the Ptolemies, known as the Sema.[119] The buildings belonging to the Museum (*mouseion*) were also in the *basileia* area, as was the library. The *basileia* furthermore consisted of parks and gardens harbouring collections of exotic animals and plants.[120] The Ptolemies looted the

[116] Ath. V 205d–206c.

[117] Bernard 1966: 140–1; Fraser I: 23, 31, II: 64 n. 149, 99–100 n. 231; Hoepfner and Schwandner 1994: 245.

[118] In Strabo's time, the former Ptolemaic *temenos* for the ruler cult was consecrated to the worship of Augustus and was called σεβαστὴ ἀγορά (cf. the *hiera agora* at Demetrias); cf. Fraser I: 98 n. 220; the focus of this new sanctuary was a temple called the *Sebasteion*; the building of this temple was begun by Kleopatra VII but was finished under Augustus; see Hoepfner and Schwandner 1994: 237 and 245; Bernard 1966: 134–6; Fraser I: 24–5, II: 68–9 n. 155–8.

[119] Strabo 793–4; cf. Plut., *Ant.* 86. Other writers mentioning Alexander's tomb include Suet., *Aug.* 18; Dio 51.16.3–5; Hdn. 4.8.9. For an extensive discussion of the sources see Fraser I: 31–6 nn. 79–84; cf. Bernard 1966: 229–37. The location of Alexander's grave has puzzled scholars and laymen for the last two centuries, but there is little chance it will be found. Ach. Tat. 5.1 and Zenob. 3.94 vaguely locate the Sema 'in the middle of the city'; cf. Fraser II: 36–41 nn. 85–8. For the history of the search for Alexander's tomb see Saunders 2006. The Ptolemies were buried in the same enclosure as Alexander (Fraser II: 34–5 n. 82) but probably not in the same monument. Kleopatra VII built separate mausoleums for Antony and herself (Dio 51.8.6; Plut., *Ant.* 74; Suet., *Aug.* 17.4), perhaps in a separate precinct (Fraser II: 33–4 n. 81).

[120] Ath. 654b–c.

Fig. 3.8. The Nile mosaic from Palestrina, perhaps based on a fresco from
a Ptolemaic palace, presumably giving some idea of the splendorous
decorations adorning the Ptolemaic palace.

Egyptian countryside for monuments to adorn their capital. Obelisks
and sphinxes from especially the New Kingdom and Saite periods
were transported from Egypt to Alexandria.[121] Rather than being
evidence of the dominance of Egyptian culture in Alexandria, the
presence of these antiquated monuments expressed Ptolemaic dominance in Egypt, their foremost and most stable source of income –
a fascination comparable to the depiction of Egypt on the famous
Nile mosaic from Palestrina, if that was indeed based on Ptolemaic
court art (Fig. 3.8).[122] Of course, this does not make Alexandria
automatically a *Greek* city, either. We will probably never understand the culture of Ptolemaic Alexandria as long as we continue
claiming that it was either 'Greek' or 'Egyptian', or a fusion of Greek
and Egyptian – as if Greek and Egyptian cultures were monolithic

[121] Bagnall 2001: 229–30.
[122] On the mosaic see Versluys 2002.

and unchanging entities.[123] This is what Versluys described as 'static ethnic interpretation', writing that '[i]t seems of little use to value material culture in terms of relative degrees of "Greekness" or "Egyptianness" and relate the outcome to the social make-up of society'.[124]

The only Ptolemaic residence of real significance apart from Alexandria was Memphis. Here the Ptolemies were enthroned as pharaohs and here delegations from the Egyptian temples would gather to meet the king.[125] In the course of the second century BCE, the Ptolemies increasingly used Memphis as a second capital. The later Ptolemies presumably celebrated their anniversaries as pharaoh and their military victories there. At these occasions representatives of the gods of Egypt would assemble to express their loyalty to, and negotiate with, the monarchy.

Memphis was already about 3,000 years old when Ptolemy the son of Lagos took possession of it in his capacity as satrap of Egypt in 323. Strategically located between the Delta and the Nile valley, and at the terminus of the land routes to both Asia and Cyrenaica, Memphis had always been the principal economic, military and administrative centre of Lower Egypt.[126] The central position of Memphis is reflected in an earlier name given to the place: *Ankh-tawy*, 'The Balance of the Lands'. Strabo (17.1.31) says that Memphis lay 'near Babylon', i.e. that it was the gateway from Asia to Egypt. Foreign invaders of Egypt always headed for Memphis first.[127]

Memphis had been a royal residence since the Early Dynastic Period but flourished especially during the New Kingdom and under the pharaohs of the Saite period (664–525). After 525 Memphis became the residence of the Persian and subsequently Macedonian governors.[128] In Ptolemaic times Memphis had a mixed population of Greeks, Egyptians and Idumaeans, organised in *politeumata*.[129] The monuments of Memphis were built by various pharaohs, and

---

[123] See the valuable remarks by Versluys 2010, including that '[w]hen we want to understand the use of ... "Egypt as a cultural concept" there is an additional complicating factor in the Hellenistic and Roman periods: the presence of foreign rulers *in* Egypt coming from *outside* Egypt. How should we regard it if they use Egyptian styles, symbols or motives *in* Egypt ... And for how long and when, exactly, is "foreign" seen, felt and perceived as *foreign?*' (p. 9). A *cultural concept* is 'a semantic system in which specific themes and styles were used to evoke specific associations' (Versluys 2010: 19, summarising Hölscher 1987).

[124] Versluys 2010: 23.

[125] On the Ptolemies and Memphis see Thompson et al. 1980; Thompson 1988; Huss 1994.

[126] Thompson 1988: 3.

[127] Kuhrt 1995 II: 499, 634 and 662; Thompson 1988: 4.

[128] Kuhrt 1995 II: 640 and 690.

[129] Thompson 1988: 82–105; cf. 107–8.

the Ptolemies too were eager to leave their mark on city and temple.[130] The temple of Ptah was surrounded by several dependencies, including the stables and court of the Apis bull and the mother of Apis, built by Psammetichus II (595–589), and the Apis bull-embalming house of Soshenq I (945–924). A colossal statue of Ramesses II (c. 1290–1224), who added more structures to the temple of Ptah than any other king, stood outside the enclosure gates (in the twentieth century the statue was taken to Cairo, but was later returned). Other builders at Memphis were Amenemhet III, Tuthmosis IV, Amenophis III and Merneptah. Ptolemy II presented the priests of Ptah with a statue of his deified sister-wife Arsinoë, who was consequently known as the consort of Ptah.[131] Philadelphos' grandson, Ptolemy IV, set up statues of himself and added a ceremonial *propylon* in Egyptian style to the temple, presumably to be used for audiences.[132] Kleopatra VII, too, added monuments to the temple area.[133]

The Egyptian element was dominant, and the temple priests constituted the city's ruling elite.[134] Strabo says that the palace district and the temple district formed the two most noteworthy features of Memphis.[135] The Ptolemaic palace lay on a height in the northern part of the city, but all that Strabo says about it is that it included a citadel (*akra*) and a large park with a lake. Memphis is a relatively under-excavated site and remains of the Hellenistic palace have not been found yet; it already lay lay in ruins when Strabo visited Memphis in the later first century BCE. For ceremonial purposes, the Ptolemies also maintained the pre-existing Egyptian palace buildings, located in a spacious enclosure to the northeast. The largest of these was the palace built by the pharaoh Apries of the Saite dynasty (589–570), the only palatial structure in Memphis that has been explored by archaeologists to some extent.[136] This palace was later used by the Achaemenid satraps, by Alexander when he stayed at Memphis in 332 and 331, and by Alexander's representative Kleomenes, whom Ptolemy replaced in 323. Close by the Saite palace was an ancient temple precinct where Ptah was worshipped.

Memphis was a sacred site. It was the home of the creator god

---

[130] Ibid. 18.
[131] Ibid. 126–7; for the relationship between the Ptolemies and Ptah see further Thompson 1980.
[132] Thompson 1988: 17.
[133] Ibid. 125.
[134] For Egyptian priestly elites in the Ptolemaic period see Lloyd 2002: 117–36.
[135] Strabo 17.1.31–2.
[136] Thompson 1988: 15; Nielsen 1994: 27. Cf. Petrie and Walker 1909; Kemp 1977.

Ptah and housed his physical manifestation, the Apis bull. The cult of Ptah at Memphis goes back to the Early Dynastic Period. Ptah was a symbol of the unity of Egypt and thus of special importance for pharaonic kingship. In the *Theology of Memphis*, an ancient text explaining the connection between Ptah and the pharaoh, Ptah is himself hailed as the king of the union of Upper and Lower Egypt.[137] Alexander, too, paid homage to the Apis bull when he visited Memphis.[138] It was in the large ceremonial hall of the Ptah temple that the Ptolemies were enthroned as pharaohs of the Two Lands according to Egyptian custom.

THE PALACE OF PERGAMON

The best-preserved palace district of the Hellenistic world was built not by one of the three great imperial monarchies, but by the Attalids of Pergamon. Monarchic architecture in Pergamon reveals the same basic structure as in other royal cities. Particularly, the archaeology of the Pergamene *basileia* is reminiscent of the *basileia* of Alexandria as described by Strabo.[139] As in Alexandria, it is possible to distinguish between an inner palace – the heavily fortified private house of the king and his family – and a semi-public outer area filled with monuments celebrating kingship and victory. Both were on the akropolis (Fig. 3.9).

The Attalid building programme on the akropolis was initiated by Attalos I after he had assumed the diadem in 238 or 237. Attalos' assumption of the diadem together with the title of *sōtēr*, whereby he formally repudiated Seleukid sovereignty, was legitimised by his victory over a Celtic force. This enabled him to pose as the protector of the Greek cities, a role normally played by the Seleukid emperor (who, however, failed to deal with this barbarian menace). Although both Attalos I and his successor Eumenes fought other enemies as well – Bithynia, Pontos, Rhodes, the Seleukids – recurrent victories over the archetypal barbaric Celts conferred upon the Attalids an aura of being the very saviours of civilisation, and the theme of the king as barbarian-slayer subsequently became pivotal to Attalid image-building.[140] Attalos rededicated the ancient *temenos*

---

[137] *ANET* 4–6; Kuhrt 1995 I: 145–6, II: 631 and 637; for the cult of Apis under the Ptolemies see Thompson 1988: 190–211.

[138] Arr., *Anab.* 3.1.4; Diod. 17.49.1; Curt. 4.7.5.

[139] For the archaeology of Pergamon see Koester 1998 and Radt 1999.

[140] For the Attalid wars in Asia Minor see Habicht 1956; Hansen 1972: 28–33; Allen 1983: 195–9; Chamoux 1988. 'Celtic' propaganda in the Hellenistic world: Strobel 1994; Strootman 2005a; Koehn 2007: 89–127.

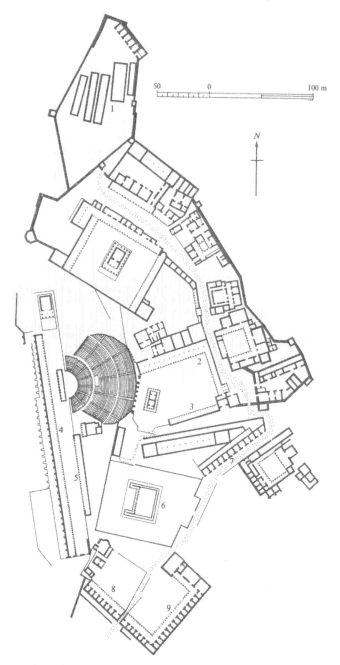

Fig. 3.9. Plan of the citadel of Pergamon showing *i.a.* the akra (1), Athena
Sanctuary (2 and 3) and Great Altar (6). The Attalid 'inner palaces' are along
the north-western wall (from *The Architectural Development of the Greek
Stoa* by Coulton, 1976; by permission of Oxford University Press.

of Athena Polias, Pergamon's main deity, to Athena Nikephoros and introduced a cult of Zeus Soter on the Pergamene akropolis.[141] Because Athena and Zeus, the deities most closely associated with *akropoleis*, were the saviours of cities and bestowers of victory par excellence, they provided good paradigms for Attalid kingship; it was not uncommon for Zeus and Athena to be worshipped jointly, sharing the same cult epithets.[142] Just outside the city walls, Attalos constructed a second sanctuary dedicated to the war goddess Athena Nikephoros, the Nikephorion.[143] Attalos' sons and successors Eumenes II (197–159) and Attalos II (159–138) transformed the akropolis and its slopes into a coherent royal domain.[144] The themes of victory and deliverance (*sōtēria*) were central to the monarchical representation in Attalid domestic architecture.

The physical transition from civic to royal space was gradual. It was structured by means of the processional road leading from the Nikephorion to the sanctuary of Athena Nikephoros on the akropolis. The road went past various sanctuaries and other religious monuments directly or indirectly connected with the monarchy. This was presumably also the route taken by the *pompē* of the triennial pan-Hellenic Nikephoria festival, founded in 180 by Eumenes II to commemorate a victory over the Celts of Galatia.[145] The first landmark the road passed was the agora, the symbolic heart of the *polis* of Pergamon. After passing several public building associated with civic life, the road led through a gate and went on up the southern slope of the akropolis until it reached a large peristyle court behind a gate decorated with a statue of Nike. Here were an altar and a temple dedicated to Zeus Soter, and later an equestrian statue of Attalos III. This square – inaccurately called the Upper Agora in modern literature – marked the definite transition from civic to royal space (numbers 8 and 9 in Fig. 3.9). Behind it, on the akropolis, were three interrelated precincts that together formed the representative heart of the Pergamene *basileia*: the terrace supporting the Great Altar, dedicated to Zeus; the *temenos* with the tombs of the Attalids; and the sanctuary of Athena Nikephoros.

The Great Altar deserves a somewhat more extensive discussion

---

[141] Allen 1983: 121–2; Hansen 1972: 447–50; cf. *OGIS* 302.
[142] Neils 2001: 224–6.
[143] Radt 1999: 242–3; Schalles 1985: 145–6. The Nikephorion was rebuilt by Eumenes II after the troops of Philip V had demolished it in 201 (Polyb. 16.1; App., *Mac.* 4; see Hansen 1972: 55–7). In 155 the sanctuary was again razed, this time by Prousias II, who carried the cult statue off to Bithynia.
[144] Strabo 13.4.2; cf. Hansen 1972: 234–98.
[145] Segre 1948; Hansen 1972: 449–50; Jones 1974; Allen 1983: 123–9.

Fig. 3.10. Detail of the gigantomachy frieze showing Athena defeating
the Titan Alkyoneus.

here because of its significance for the Attalids' representation. It
was clearly a victory monument. The reliefs on the altar's outer walls
depicted a gigantomachy, the war between the Olympian gods –
representatives of *kosmos* – and the giants – representatives of
chaos – being an allegory of the Attalids' military prestige.[146] Athena
Nikephoros and Zeus figure most prominently among the gods
(Fig. 3.10); but the central figure is Herakles, the mortal whose help
was crucial in defeating the barbaric giants and whose reward was

---

[146] For the Great Altar see Callaghan 1981; Hoepfner 1996a: 115–34; Dreyfus and Schraudolph 1996; Stewart 2000; Queyrel 2005.

his transformation into an Olympian god after his death. Inside the altar, the Telephos frieze stressed the Attalids' descent from Herakles; it also showed how Telephos' mother, Auge, introduced the cult of Athena on the akropolis of Pergamon.[147] The *heroon* of Pergamon's *heros ktistēs*, Telephos, the son of Herakles and ancestor of the Attalids, was presumably located in the same precinct where the Attalids too were buried; the sacred precinct with the royal tombs was directly opposite the *temenos* with the Great Altar. Exactly when the Great Altar was built, and which victory it commemorated, remain a matter of controversy. Perhaps it was no specific victory at all. The imagery of the Great Altar was part of a wider iconographic programme which (though probably not planned all at once in advance) consistently disseminated an image of the Attalids as victorious saviour-kings and god-like protectors of cities.[148] Especially, they posed as the guardians of the cities of Asia Minor against the Galatians, whom the Attalids, like other Hellenistic kings, consciously presented as the archetypal enemies of civilisation. This in turn legitimised the Attalids' independence from, and violent competition with, the Seleukid empire. For in contrast to the widespread belief that the Attalid monarchy was relatively peace-loving, or the more reasonable notion that at least the Attalids themselves preferred to emphasise in their propaganda their altruism rather than their victoriousness,[149] the 'messages' conveyed by the various monuments that they built in Pergamon were predominantly concerned with the theme of creating peace by crushing enemies. This is especially true of the final destination of the Nikephoria procession: the sanctuary of Athena the Bestower of Victory.

The sacred *temenos* of Athena Nikephoros was reached through a propylon entrance decorated with images of Athena's owl and Zeus' eagle. The focal point of the sanctuary was a small pre-Hellenistic temple, originally dedicated to a goddess known in Greek sources as Athena. In this temple, Attalos I or Eumenes II placed a cult statue of Athena with a golden victory wreath held above her head. The precinct further harboured huge statues of Athena Promachos and Attalos Soter standing side by side, and various votive offerings commemorating Attalid successes in war. The surrounding porticos were decorated with sculptured and painted images of trophies, in particular Celtic and Macedonian (that is, Seleukid) armour and

[147] For the Telephos frieze see Kertész 1982; Andreae 1996: 121–6; Heilmeyer 1997.
[148] Strootman 2005a: 124–34.
[149] Koehn 2007: 89–127.

weapons; the northern portico gave access to a *tropaion* where the captured weapons offered to Athena Nikephoros were stored.[150]

Behind the *temenē* triad the residential quarters of the Attalid family were hidden. They consisted of five houses with peristyle courtyards and beautifully decorated reception rooms, classified by the excavators as Palaces I–V; in addition to these houses there were storage rooms, workshops and offices.[151] The area was heavily fortified.[152] A strong fortress with arsenals and barracks was part of the Pergamene 'inner palace' area.[153] In spite of the rather extensive fortifications, especially on the northern and eastern sides of the akropolis, the palace showed an 'open' face towards the city. On the slope of the hill between palace and police was a huge theatre where the Attalid royals could present themselves to the people.

CONCLUSION: THE ROYAL PRECINCT

In Hellenistic residences such as Antioch, Alexandria or Pella, the royal palace formed the heart of the city. Yet at the same time palaces were cut off from the cities in which they stood so sharply that the city became divided into clearly discernible civic and royal spaces.[154] Both choice of site and architectural means were employed to set palaces apart from their urban surroundings. The dividing line was delimited by walls, by water, by differences in altitude, or by a combination of these. Palaces could be built on a promontory (Halikarnassos, Alexandria, Herod's Caesarea, to some extent Aï Khanoum), an island (Antioch) or, more commonly, a hill (Aigai, Demetrias, Pergamon, Sardis, Apameia).

Bertelli wrote about the palaces of the Italian Renaissance: 'The spaces, external and internal, in which the court is situated, are the visible measure of its sacred quality; its ideal separateness is accentuated by physical separation from the town in which it stands.'[155] In the Hellenistic age, too, 'sacred quality' and 'ideal

---

[150] For the finds in the Athena precinct see Fraenkel 1890 and Radt 1999: 159–68. Interpretations and theories regarding the so-called 'dying Gauls' associated with this sanctuary: Künzl 1971; Wenning 1978; Schalles 1985: 80–149; Stewart 2005.

[151] Kawerau and Wieland 1930; see Salzmann 1995 for the decorations.

[152] Kohl 2004; cf. Hoepfner 1996b: 17: 'von einer eigenen Wehrmauer umgeben und deutlich von der Wohnstadt abgesetzt'.

[153] Radt 1999: 63–81. The service and storage rooms were located on the site where in Roman times the Traianaeum was erected.

[154] Jos., *AJ* 14.59: 'the palace and the city of Jerusalem' (πόλις καὶ βασίλεια); cf. 13.36, where we read that Demetrios II shut himself up in a palace 'near Antioch', though evidently the *basileion* on the Orontes island *in* Antioch is meant.

[155] Bertelli 1986: 17.

separateness' were made visible and substantiated by architectural means. Monumental façades on high terraces, to be approached by broad avenues and ramps, enhanced the image of the palace as an elevated, mysterious place. Visitors to the archaeological remains of Pergamon can still experience how height was employed to elevate kingship literally; the *Rough Guide to Turkey* comments that 'the acropolis is readily accessible on foot – though this is one attraction you may want to reach by taxi, at least on the way up'.[156]

Thus, royal space and civic space were separated in a way that could not be misunderstood. The separation could be reinforced by the use of strong defensive outer walls, towers and bulwarks, and the incorporation of a fortress. The perception of akropolis and citadel as royal space – in non-residential cities royal garrisons could also be stationed on the *akropoleis* – emphasised the military nature of the monarchy. It indicated the king's role as protector of cities. In Hellenistic town planning it was customary to incorporate the citadel into the defensive walls surrounding the city as a whole,[157] as expressed in Kallimachos' encomiastic *Hymn to Zeus*: 'From Zeus come kings ... You gave them cities to protect. And you yourself are seated in the citadels of the cities to judge those who rule their people badly, and those who rule well.'[158] The use of *akropoleis* meant that kings appropriated not only the city's main military focus but also, at least according to Hellenic tradition, the city's principal *sacred* area. In Greek *poleis*, and many eastern cities too, the citadel hill was the abode of the principal city deities: Zeus and Athena, Baal, Yahweh. These were the gods who were expected to protect a city from its enemies – precisely the responsibility that Hellenistic kings too promised to take on themselves. Cities in turn sometimes offered cult to their royal protectors and benefactors, precisely as they offered cult to their divine *sōtēres*. When Demetrios Poliorketes visited Athens in 304, he stayed on the akropolis in the *opisthodomos* of the Parthenon as the *xenos* of Athena Polias.[159] By incorporating elements of religious architecture – enclosure walls, *propylaia*, forecourts, theatres, temples and *tholoi* – the palace district was consciously fashioned to resemble a sacred *temenos*,

---

[156] *Rough Guide to Turkey* (3rd edn; London 1997) 251. Compare the recommendations in the 1996 *Lonely Planet* guide for Israel and the Palestinian Territories regarding the (in)accessibility of the Herodean residence of Masada: 'The steep and long "Snake Path" ... is hard going and, depending on how fit you are, the stagger to the top takes anything from 30 minutes to over an hour ... Top up with water before you start out, even though there is water available at the summit.'

[157] Lawrence 1979: 131.

[158] *Hymn* 1, ll. 78–88.

[159] Plut., *Demetr.* 23–4; cf. 26.3 and Diod. 20.100.5–6.

with the 'closed' and somewhat hidden 'inner palace' where the king dwelled resembling a temple or *naos*.

The incorporation of sacral architecture into palaces is known too from pre-Hellenistic Mesopotamia and Egypt, and these examples may have influenced Hellenistic palace architecture to some extent. Unlike in Mesopotamian or Egyptian palace architecture, however, the boundaries between royal and civic space in Hellenistic cities were not rigorously demarcated. Palaces were not entirely isolated from their surroundings. On the contrary, 'royal space' was the scene of lively interaction between *basileus, philoi, politai* and foreign ambassadors. In most residences we find a transitional area between *polis* and palace, such as the *basileia* in Alexandria, the *hiera agora* in front of the palace at Demetrias, or the sequence of *temenē* along the processional road in Pergamon that began at the victory temple outside the gate, becoming increasingly connected with the Attalid monarchy as it neared the palaces at the top of the akropolis. The public representational area between the residential quarters and the city proper belonged both to the palace and to the *polis*. At least in Alexandria and in Pergamon, this is where the city's main public (religious) buildings were located. In the stadia, hippodromes and theatres that were built there, public rituals of royalty were performed in which monarchs presented themselves to the populace. This representational intermediary section was the more or less public area where king and citizens met.

PART II

The Court as a Socio-Political System

4 *The Royal Household*

Viewed from the outside, the royal household presented an image of unity and harmony. Courtiers found it advantageous to keep up a façade of mutual agreement and of their compliance with the king's absolute power. In practice, however, the unity of the court was often disarrayed as a result of polygamous marriage and competition among the courtiers. At the Argead court, the core of the household was divided into sub-families centred on the respective queens and their children, all with their own followers and personal attendants. The Ptolemaic court was often broken into segments centred on various candidates for the throne, both male and female. As a result, conflict over the succession frequently broke out, often with disastrous effects. In the Seleukid empire, there could be two or three courts at the same time in various places within the gigantic realm: always one around the king, often one around his heir and co-ruler (who also carried the title of *basileus*), and sometimes one around the principal queen and mother of the heir. Relations between the *philoi* and the king, and among *philoi*, were not always harmonious. The reigning king was not automatically the most powerful individual. Conflicts among courtiers were common. In order to remain masters of their own houses, kings often employed 'favourites' to counterbalance the power of the *philoi*.

Hellenistic court societies were social units characterised by straightforward, face-to-face relations. The chapters in Part II of this book are concerned with these relations. They deal with the persons constituting the courts and with the social interactions between them, especially conflicts. We will first take a look at the royal family, the nucleus of the court. Hellenistic *basileia* was not an impersonal office within the structure of a 'state'. It was a heritable personal possession; the driving forces behind royal politics were the interests and honour of the dynasty and its adherents rather than *raisons d'état*. The first Macedonian kings after Alexander had been charismatic warlords deriving prestige from military success and the distribution of land and wealth acquired through successful warfare. Their successors remained true in ideology, and often in practice, to the original foundation of imperial rule.

In reaction to the thesis of Daniel Ogden that succession strife was endemic in the Hellenistic courts because there were no fixed principles regulating succession in the Macedonian kingdoms, it will be argued that Macedonian kings potentially had at their diposal various means to appoint a 'crown prince'. Thus, co-rulership of father and son was a successful strategy for arranging the succession in advance, but there were other strategies as well. The inter-dynastic conflicts that broke up the Seleukid and Ptolemaic empires in the second century BCE must have had other roots, 'amphimetric disputes' (see below) being the result rather than the cause of decline.[1]

Following the section on the crown prince and succession, two explanations will be proposed for the extraordinarily powerful position of royal women at the Hellenistic courts. One is the pivotal role that Macedonian noblewomen traditionally had in transferring inheritance; this means that the ancestral title of *basileus* could be passed on in the matriline as well as in the patriline – hence the claims of e.g. the kings of Pontos and Kommagene to be the Seleukids' successors as Great Kings. Indeed, the main rationale behind Ptolemaic full-sibling marriage may have been the wish to combine the two lines of inheritance. The second explanation will be that royal women were the ideal 'favourites' to whom kings could delegate power; precisely because Macedonian monarchs were polygamous, and favour could be transferred to another queen (and her offspring), favoured queens were loyal and thus reliable associates. It will be hypothesised that the title of *basilissa* was employed to designate a 'first queen', both as another means to hierarchise royal women and prearrange the succession, and as a means to transform a queen's sub-court into a most loyal segment of the dynastic house-hold. Particularly in the Seleukid empire, women who married into the imperial dynasty probably had an important role to play in maintaining networks of contact with, and securing the loyalty of,

---

[1] See now also Wright 2011, who contends that during the dynastic war that broke up the Seleukid empire, 'succession by primogeniture was respected within each patrilineal branch of the Seleukidae. No two claimants of the Epiphanaic line emerged simultaneously, nor until the mid-90s BC did any other branch see more than a single king contemporaneously. The problem was that once an individual was accepted as a king, his eldest living son evidently saw himself as eligible to succeed, even if there were already qualified successors of previous rulers waiting in the wings' (p. 46).

various (Iranian) royal families ruling the vassal kingdoms in the empire's periphery.

THE SOCIAL STRUCTURE OF THE ROYAL HOUSEHOLD

The extended family of the king consisted of relatives and non-kin friends, as well as servants and guards. The most visible segment of court society is the group constituted by the so-called *philoi tou basileōs*, the 'friends of the king'. They were mainly Hellenes who were related to the royal family through aristocratic guest-friendship and sometimes fictive kinship. The problem, for the modern historian, is that the *philoi* system in all kingdoms was informal and personal. Even though a system of honorific and other court titles developed in the second century in the Ptolemaic and Seleukid kingdoms, Hellenistic court societies remained at root face-to-face societies. Personalised networks rather than institutions held the empires together.[2] What is more, *philia* relations were not restricted to people who were part of the king's entourage – there were also royal *philoi* outside of the court – and not all people in the king's entourage were technically *philoi*, that is, attached to the king by means of *philia* (slaves, royal wives and concubines, and kinfolk, for instance, were not). In short, not all *philoi* were courtiers and not all courtiers were *philoi*.

As far as it is possible to distinguish between courtiers who were near the king on a daily basis and those who were not, it appears that in the first group, Macedonians were overrepresented even at the Ptolemaic and Seleukid courts, while in the latter group Greeks constituted the majority. Servants and slaves are almost completely absent from the sources. Relatively difficult to see, too, are the constituents of the so-called outer court: the civic ambassadors, provincial aristocrats, local priests and others who attended court only on a temporary basis. Notably in the Seleukid empire with its great variety of semi-autonomous cities, tribes, temple states, aristocratic dynasties and vassal kingdoms, representatives of local polities must have flocked to the court in substantial numbers for 'great events' like weddings, birth celebrations and inaugurations. Sporadically we hear that indeed they did so. Generally speaking, however, they do not figure prominently in the sources. The same applies to the personal entourage and family of the (predominantly

[2] So also Mueller 2006.

Iranian) wives of the Seleukids: they too are certain to have been there but are not easily seen in the (Greek and Roman) sources. This might in part be a matter of epigraphic habit, too: unlike Greek civic patricians, Iranian aristocrats did not publicise the privileges or honours they had obtained at court in stone inscriptions set up in public places.

THE ROYAL FAMILY

The nucleus of the court was the royal family: the king, his consort(s), offspring and other relatives. In a Greek context, the male head of the family or *kyrios* was in charge of the *oikos*.[3] He was also responsible for his family's relations with the outside world. However, in both the Ptolemaic and Seleukid kingdoms these responsibilities were also carried out by queens and adult princes. They were not necessarily together in the same place at all times. On the contrary, potential heirs to the throne were often kept away from their father's household, notably in the Seleukid empire. A queen could stay in a central place to deal with ambassadors while the king was on campaign (the best-known example being Laodike, the wife of Antiochos III). In that case the court was, as it were, doubled. Even when together 'at court', adult, married princes could be at the head of households of their own.

Hellenistic monarchy was a family affair. The political activities of Hellenistic kings were prompted by family interests, the need to defend honour and obtain new glory, obligations to kinsmen, affiliates, friends and allies, and competition with other dynasties. In Greek sources this was summarised as the king's *pragmata*, the affairs or interests of the king. Kingship, *basileia*, was personal and charismatic and it is impossible to distinguish between the king as a private person and as *basileus*, between court and household, between state and dynasty. *Basileia* was not a public office but a hereditary privilege, a family possession like landed estates and other material property, or like ancestral prestige.

In particular the continuity from father to son was stressed. Brothers of the king, however, rarely held positions at court or in the army, or figured prominently in royal propaganda, and neither did

---

[3] Pomeroy 1997: 23 and 28, perhaps overestimating the absolute authority of the male head of the family over all aspects of his household, including over his wife and children. The meaning of the word *oikos* remains evasive; it could denote 'household' as well as 'family', and was not even in classical Athens a legal term (MacDowell 1989). For the various Greek notions of 'family' and 'household' see Patterson 1998: 1–4, and Pomeroy 1997: 19.

other male agnates in the patriline. They were potential claimants to the throne. This was not the case, however, with the king's sons. The unity of father and son was the primary dyad in the royal family. The moral subordination of a son to his father guaranteed that the latter was in practice senior to the former.

Family was the main source of identity. The *genos* ('kin') provided the individual with prestige, protection, economic security and social networks. The association of the ruling monarch with his family and ancestors is a recurrent theme in court poetry, honorary inscriptions and texts related to ruler cult.[4] Sculptured group portraits of kings and their families formed a popular subgenre of 'royal art'.[5] Hellenistic kings did not affiliate themselves with native *poleis* or tribes as the origin of their identity, as most Greeks did,[6] or with the countries they ruled. Ethnic denominations are absent from royal coins, as well as from royal letters and decrees.[7] Conquered territory could be considered a personal possession, or was seen as land favoured and protected by the king. But territory was never a defining aspect of monarchy. Hellenistic kingship was not confined by geographical or cultural boundaries.

An exception to this pattern is the self-presentation of kings and their families as 'Macedonian'. The Argead kings had been '*basileus* of the Makedones', though the title of *basileus* is absent from coins before Alexander's reign. Philip II added to this the title of *hēgemōn* of the Greeks; Alexander added to it the title 'king of Asia', the Greek rendering of the Persian title 'King of Kings' or 'Great King'. The Seleukids inherited the title 'king of Asia' from Alexander; the Antigonids appropriated the prestigious title βασιλεὺς Μακεδόνων, king of the Macedonians. The Antigonids used this title vis-à-vis ethnic Macedonians in Macedonia; in addition they carried the title of *basileus* in its own right – a title with a broader scope, connoting claims of hegemony over diverse peoples and territories.[8] Still, the Seleukids and Ptolemies were Macedonian kings, too. They had Macedonian personal names. Macedonian culture prevailed in the kings' clothing and armour. Vis-à-vis non-Macedonian subject

---

[4] See e.g. Theocr. 17.114–15; *OGIS* 219 = Austin 139. For more examples and references consult Roy 1998: 112.

[5] Hintzen-Bohlen 1990.

[6] Hansen 1996.

[7] Hammond 1989: 69 claims that kings did not even use patronymics, as these do not appear on coins; patronymics, however, were used regularly in royal letters and decrees.

[8] The vast pretensions of *basileia* were noted as early as Macurdy 1932b: 258: 'The word βασιλεία with almost no exception in Diodorus and elsewhere means royal power, *not* the country ruled over' (e.g. Diod. 18.2.2; 20.20.2–3; 20.28.1).

peoples too kings might present themselves as Macedonians. On the Borsippa Cylinder, a Seleukid propaganda text from 268 BCE, written in cuneiform Akkadian for the sake of the Babylonians, Antiochos I Soter is presented as a traditional Babylonian king who justifies his rule by calling on the Babylonian gods. Still, it is stressed that the king is a 'Macedonian'.[9]

This might seem strange at first sight: the descendants of Ptolemy Soter and Seleukos Nikator never set foot on Macedonian soil; they ruled over territories where even Greeks were a minority, to say nothing of Macedonians; and cultural life at court was predominantly Greek, not Macedonian. But the ethnic did not refer to the country of Macedonia. The Macedonian aspect of Hellenistic kingship was important because even the Seleukid and Ptolemaic dynasties depended on a Macedonian court elite for their rule, and on Macedonian infantry as the core element of their armies.

DYNASTIC CONTINUITY

Descent was an important factor in the identity of individual Hellenistic kings. The dynasty was supposed to be permanent, but its members were not. Descent determined a king's personal charisma and legitimised his rule, for prestige (and disgrace) was hereditary.[10] Hellenistic kings were heirs to the (military) reputation of their forefathers, in particular the founders of the respective kingdoms: Ptolemy Soter, Seleukos Nikator, Antigonos Monophthalmos and Demetrios Poliorketes. Alexander did not figure prominently in propaganda until late in the second century BCE. Kings considered themselves to be the heirs of these men for generations, laying claim to territory that had once belonged to the legendary founders as if it were their own *doriktētos chōra*, or 'spear-won land'. For instance, in 219, Antiochos the Great laid claim to southern Syria because, according to him, it had been part of the spoils awarded to Seleukos Nikator after the battle of Ipsos a century earlier, even though the Seleukids had never actually possessed that area.[11] In 196, the same king legitimised his conquest of Thrace by referring to the victory of Seleukos Nikator over Lysimachos in the battle of Kouropedion in 281.[12]

[9] *ANET* 317; Austin 189. For references to the Seleukids as Macedonians in literary sources consult Edson 1958.
[10] In classical Athens it was even believed that a son inherited the character of his father (Cox 1998: 84).
[11] Polyb. 5.67.
[12] Polyb. 18.50; Liv. 33.38.

Continuity from father to son was a central claim in royal propaganda. It is striking that Alexander the Great – supposedly the role-model for all Hellenistic kings – is absent from royal genealogies, although these even contained gods and demigods, until the first century BCE. Also absent from the official genealogies is the parentage predating the foundation of the kingdoms by the Diadochs. Ptolemy Soter may have been known as the son of Lagos, or claimed that he was the son of Philip II,[13] but under his successors, when the Ptolemaic kingship was firmly established, Lagos and Philip no longer played a role in Ptolemaic propaganda. On the contrary, 'Lagos' does not turn up as a name in the Ptolemaic family tree, as if he had been erased from history – as if history had begun anew with the reign of Ptolemy Soter.

The Hellenistic dynasties claimed divine ancestry. Like the Argeads before them, the Ptolemies and Attalids were the offspring of Herakles – a hero who was well suited to be an icon of kingship because of his stature as invincible warrior and saviour, and his posthumous deification as an Olympian god. This example was later followed by, among others, the kings of Pontos, Kommagene and even Numidia.[14] The Antigonids descended from Perseus, yet another semi-divine conqueror and saviour. The kings of the Molossians in Epeiros descended from Achilles and, from the time of the reign of Pyrrhos, from Herakles too. The Seleukids went farther, creating the myth (perhaps in the reign of Antiochos I) that Seleukos Nikator had been the actual son of Apollo (and thus a grandson of Zeus himself), modifying the earlier, but too drastic, attempt of Alexander to be recognised as the immediate son of Zeus-Ammon.[15] The claim that a new epoch had begun was emphasised by the introduction of a new year reckoning, the Seleukid era, probably under Antiochos I. Like the Jewish, Christian or Islamic systems of year reckoning, which were later derived from it, the Seleukid era counted the years from the (re)beginning of time: Seleukos' first performance as king in Babylonia in 312.

The traditional custom of naming sons after their grandfathers was practised by the Antigonid dynasty, where the names Antigonos and Demetrios alternated, with Philip being the most popular name for second or third sons. Among the Seleukids the names Seleukos and Antiochos were given to the first two sons but seemingly

---

[13] Collins 1997.
[14] Herakles as ancestor: Huttner 1997: esp. pp. 65–85, 153–62 and 175–90.
[15] Just. 15.4.2–10. Cf. Grainger 1990: 2–3. For the association of Seleukos and Apollo see Hoover 1996.

without any order; from the mid-second century onward the names Demetrios and Philip became popular too. Seleukid princesses were invariably called Laodike, Stratonike, Antiochis or Apama. The Attalid kings were alternatingly named Attalos and Eumenes. Minor Hellenised dynasties in the east also had repeating (throne) names: Nikomedes and Prousias in Bithynia; Mithradates and Pharnakes in Pontos; Ariarathes in Kappadokia; Yannai (Jonathan) in the Hasmonean kingdom; Herod in the Herodean dynasty. These were indigenous names, but the method of name-giving seems to have been copied from the Macedonian dynasties – compare the varying throne names in the Achaemenid, Arsakid and Sassanian dynasties, or the names of Assyrian and Babylonian kings.

In the Ptolemaic kingdom the use of dynastic names was radical. From the time when Ptolemy Soter had by coincidence been succeeded by another 'Ptolemaios', the Ptolemaic kings gave this name to all their firstborn sons. In due course, Ptolemy became a throne name, assumed at the accession if a king was not named so at birth. When two, or even three, full brothers successively became king, they were all called 'Ptolemy'; given the high rate of child mortality even among elite families, it is inconceivable that all firstborn sons survived. As a result, the name Ptolemy came to refer not only to the legendary forefather Ptolemy Soter, but to literally all Ptolemaic kings, and thus to the dynasty itself. During the third century the Ptolemies' firstborn daughters were still given names in the customary manner, that is, after their parental grandmothers – alternately Arsinoë and Berenike – and sometimes Ptolemaïs after their fathers and grandfathers. After c. 200 nearly all reigning queens were named Kleopatra, after the Seleukid wife of Ptolemy V.[16] As a consequence, the Ptolemaic realm was for a period of 150 years continuously ruled by a royal couple called Ptolemy and Kleopatra. This cannot but have emphasised the dynasty's eternal continuity.

The family's unity and continuity could furthermore be stressed in epithets: Philopator ('he who loves his father'), Eupator ('son of a noble father', but with divine connotations), Philometor ('he who loves his mother') and Philadelphos ('he who loves his brother'). Such dynastic epithets suggested that the succession from father to son or from brother to brother had been harmonious and legitimate, even when in reality this had not been the case. More than half of all

---

[16] There is one instance of three such queens who were full sisters: Kleopatra IV, Kleopatra Selene and Kleopatra Tryphaina, who were all daughters of Ptolemy VIII and Kleopatra III.

the Ptolemaic kings had dynastic epithets, of which Philopator turns up most often.[17] Among the Seleukids ten out of twenty-six kings had dynastic epithets, mainly Philopator and Philadelphos. Of the four ruling Attalid monarchs, three had dynastic epithets added to their names. The unity and continuity of the family were confirmed on coins, where the son was always made to resemble the father as much as possible. Specific physical features were presented on portraits through several generations, especially if such features could be conceived as signs of vigour and strength (in particular the typical Ptolemaic 'strong chin' and the bull's neck of the early Seleukids). In the third century, kings were generally portrayed as forceful, strong-willed warriors. Later, the softer features of gods were assimilated into the portraits so that images were created which showed both human aspects and divine descent. Fleischer, who noted this development, argued that in the second and first centuries BCE competition between various lines in the Seleukid house compelled both kings and pretenders to emphasise their descent, i.e. legitimacy, more strongly, but at the same time needed to distinguish themselves from their rivals; the (perhaps illegitimate) Alexandros Balas struck posthumous coins of Antiochos Epiphanes, whose son he claimed to be, on which the features of Antiochos were altered to look like those of Balas, rather than the other way round. Similarly, coin portraits of queens were made to resemble the sons in whose names they reigned; on double portraits the features of king and queen were often manipulated to resemble each other even when they were not actually kin.[18]

INHERITANCE AND SUCCESSION

Hellenistic kings articulated their legitimacy in terms of inheritance. The household was, ideally speaking, permanent, hereditary and indivisible. The ideal household was furthermore hierarchical, with one male head who was vested with absolute authority over the other members of the household, and having only one heir to succeed him as head of the family. This son would become the new *basileus*. Thus, in theory, the kingdom was indivisible.

When a king died, the inheritance was divided according to the prevalent Greek custom, but probably retaining the Macedonian

---

[17] Two Ptolemaic kings even had two such epithets: Ptolemy XII Philopator Philadelphos and Ptolemy XV Philopator Philometor. I have also included Kleopatra VII Thea Philopator in my count.

[18] Fleischer 1990.

practice of awarding a more prominent place to the deceased's female offspring.[19] This means, first, that only agnates in the patriline could be heirs, and not affines (i.e. wives and their blood relatives); second, that the royal dynasties practised partial inheritance. Apparently, the inheritance was not bequeathed to all children in equal portions. Only one son would be heir to the title of *basileus* and receive the main part of the household's possessions. The other sons either stayed in the household together with their wives, children and possessions, so that the family's property remained intact, or left the household to found an *oikos* of their own. Partitioning of wealth and, above all, privately owned landed estates is potentially dangerous for a monarchy.[20] Such partitioning, leading to fragmentation and the creation of power bases for pretenders, may well have contributed to the eventual fragmentation of power in the Seleukid and Ptolemaic kingdoms. Even full brothers of the king were therefore usually kept away from the court. In the histories of the Hellenistic kingdoms, brothers of the king seldom held significant positions at court or in the army. For instance, this becomes clear from the group of powerful confidants surrounding Antiochos the Great, a king strong enough to determine the composition of his royal council personally. Polybios provides detailed information about the composition of Antiochos' court at various moments during his reign; but beside his own sons, who successively turn up as designated successors, no relatives are recorded to have held positions of honour and responsibility.

Female offspring could potentially threaten the unity of the household. Upon marriage a woman would take her dowry into another family, and thus take away a portion of her own family's possession (goods or estates). This could, however, be countered by means of a marriage the other way round in the next generation, i.e. a daughter of the princess who had been married off was sent to her mother's native *oikos* as a bride, bringing back a dowry of equal value. This mechanism can be discerned in all royal family trees. For instance the Argeads exchanged princesses with the kings of Epeiros, among others. Philip II's wife Olympias was a daughter of the Epeirote king

---

[19] See Strootman 2007: 108–10, with n. 43 on p. 109, for a discussion of, and bibliographical references to, the perhaps underlying Aegean customs.

[20] Royal *oikiai* possessed landed estates called *chōra basilikē* in Greek sources. This was private property comparable to land owned by private persons, cities or temples, and should be distinguished from the monarchy's more ideological claim to political sovereignty over countries and peoples. Documents from Seleukid Babylonia show that *chōra basilikē* was not indivisible, since portions of it could change hands through sale or donation; see Van der Spek 1986: 14–17 and 171–2.

Neoptolemos I; Olympias' daughter Kleopatra was then married to Alexandros the Molossian, the son and successor of Neoptolemos I. The Seleukids married Antigonid and Ptolemaic princesses, and vice versa, but preferably exchanged women and dowries with the lesser dynasties of Asia, in particular the royal house of Pontos. The effect was that, generation after generation, bonds were forged and lines of communication established between the Seleukid royal house and its vassal kingdoms. Sometimes kings married women from the elite families of Greek *poleis*, as for example Antiochos III, Philip V and Mithradates VI did. Thus, polygamous marriages created not merely threats to the internal harmony of the monarchies, but also political opportunities.

If a king had only one wife, the eldest son from this marriage would normally have the right of primogeniture, although this was no iron-clad rule.[21] Many Hellenistic kings, however, were polygamous and the existence of several wives complicated the succession. Daniel Ogden has contended that Macedonian royal polygamy was unhierarchised and that the resulting 'amphimetric disputes' – conflicts between royal wives and between paternal half-brothers – structurally destabilised the three major Hellenistic dynasties, and that this was the principal cause of their decline and ultimate collapse:

> They failed to establish any consistent method of hierarchising their wives and the sons that were born of them ... Their various wives were therefore in fierce competition with each other to ensure both their own status and the succession of their sons, phenomena which were intimately linked ... The corollary was that rival wives hated each other [and that] the various groups of paternal half-siblings hated each other.[22]

But the fact that there were no *consistent* rules for the succession does not mean that kings did not have at their disposal methods to secure the accession of a chosen heir. Hellenistic kings had various strategies for hierarchising their wives and children, and even for designating a more or less official 'crown prince'. Other factors were of importance, too. Thus Gehrke has argued that in the second and first centuries BCE the Ptolemaic monarchic system was much more stable than is normally admitted, due in particular to the

---

[21] Mitchell 2007, arguing that at the Argead court succession depended more on social relationships than on the accident of birth.

[22] Ogden 1999: ix–xi; see the table on p. xiii showing all, certain and uncertain, instances of amphimetric dispute; the practice of polygamy seems to have been Macedonian; see Greenwalt 1989; for evidence of some rare instances of bigamous marriages outside Macedonian dynasties, see Pomeroy 1997: 201 n. 36.

unwavering loyalty of the population of Alexandria to the dynasty.[23]
The Ptolemaic practice of brother–sister marriage was one strategy
for preventing amphimetric dispute: as blood relative of the king, the
sister-wife obviously had a higher status than non-kin wives, and
the firstborn from this marriage would naturally have the best title
to the inheritance. Amphimetric problems for the Ptolemies began
only when *two* sisters vied for the throne. The wish to keep the
inheritance undivided and secure the succession was arguably the
principal reason for the Ptolemaic practice of full-sibling marriage.[24]

    There were other, less extraordinary means to preclude succession
strife. A common strategy was the elevation of one son above his
(half-)brothers by giving him far-reaching responsibilities, honours
and authority. A public sign of such an elevation to the status of
'crown prince' was the assignment to the command of the cavalry
on the left flank in battle; this place of honour was traditionally
reserved for the man who was second only to the king, who himself
commanded the right flank. Thus, in the great battles of Alexander
the Great this position was the prerogative of Parmenion. Examples
of 'crown princes' commanding the left flank include Alexander at
the battle of Chaironeia, Antiochos (I) the son of Seleukos Nikator
at Ipsos,[25] Antiochos the son of Antiochos the Great at Panion, and
Seleukos (IV), another son of Antiochos the Great, at Magnesia.[26]
All these men later indeed succeeded to their fathers' thrones, with
the exception of Antiochos the son of Antiochos, who died before
his father did.[27] Other princes could at the same time be kept away
from the court (and the possibility of their being recalled secured the
crown prince's loyalty). A more solid variant was association with
the throne by granting the designated heir the title of *basileus*, with
corresponding responsibilities and authority during the father's
lifetime.[28] There is no indication that the kingship of the son was

[23] Gehrke 2005.
[24] The inspiration and motivation of royal brother–sister marriage are still debated; the conventional explanation follows Diod. 1.27, who claims that it was a pharaonic tradition; e.g. Turner 1984: 136–8. However, the only possible examples of brother–sister marriage before the Ptolemaic period date to the eighteenth century BCE, more than a millennium earlier; see Huebner 2007: 21–4; the sibling marriage practised by the Hekatomnid rulers of Karia is a far more plausible source inspiration; cf. Carney 2005. Ogden 1999 explained it as an attempt to annul the danger of amphimetric dispute, Hazzard 2000 as an attempt on the part of Ptolemy Philadelphos to reunify around himself the family descended from the Theoi Soteres, Ptolemy I and Berenike.
[25] Plut., *Demetr.* 29.3.
[26] Liv. 37.41.1.
[27] Compare the practice in the later Roman empire of presenting the designated heir to the public by letting him ride with the emperor in one chariot during an imperial *adventus* (Castritius 1971).
[28] For co-regency as a means to designate an heir see also Billows 1995; cf. Habicht 2005.

inferior to that of the father. Father and son shared the same *basileia*, stressing its continuity and preparing the succession. For the attainment of hierarchy the intrinsic seniority of the father over the son was presumably enough. The well-known story about Seleukos I giving his young bride Stratonike, the daughter of Demetrios Poliorketes, to his love-sick son Antiochos (I)[29] is connected with this; the marriage happened in reality and the tale may well have emanated from Seleukid propaganda meant to legitimise this experiment in dynastic continuity.[30]

The best-known examples of such diarchy are the earliest instances: the joint kingship of Antigonos Monophthalmos and Demetrios Poliorketes, of Seleukos Nikator and Antiochos Soter, and of Ptolemy Soter and Ptolemy Philadelphos. The last, significantly, counted his regnal years from his elevation to the position of *basileus* next to his father, not from the time that he became sole ruler, some two years later.[31] This practice is reflected in cuneiform documents from Babylonia that call Seleukid co-rulers *dumu lugal* or *mar šarri*, terms designating a 'crown prince', 'heir apparent'. That of course is no evidence of the existence of a dauphin, but merely shows the Babylonian understanding, and Akkadian rendering, of the Macedonian diarchy. By moving one son into a position of power and making him *basileus*, it was made difficult for other sons to stand up against him after their father's death. The point was, in other words, that the 'crown prince' *was* already king – beside the obvious advantage of there being two courts, and double opportunities for 'live' monarchic representation. The junior co-ruler would already have been accepted by the armed forces and known the population. The drawback of this system was that it was difficult for the reigning king to remove a co-*basileus* from power if he changed his mind, and in some such cases kings found that killing their own son was the only solution.

When a king died before one of his sons had come of age, it was possible for a brother to rule as regent. By the uncle's marrying the queen mother and adopting the minor heir apparent, the possibility could be precluded that the regent would refuse to hand over power to his nephew. This latter mechanism worked well in the case of Antigonos III Doson and Attalos II, but not in the case of Antiochos IV.

---

[29] App., *Syr.* 59–61; *Suda* s.v. 'Seleukos'.
[30] On the marriage see Breebaart 1967; Broderson 1985.
[31] Hölbl 2001: 35 with n. 2; for the co-regency of Philadelphos see Gygax 2002.

There was also an informal mechanism at work to hierarchise wives and offspring, namely the respective queens' own 'Hausmacht', i.e. the relative power and status of their own families. Royal women retained strong bonds of loyalty to the families they came from. As a member of the Molossian royal house, Olympias' senior position within the Argead household was never seriously challenged by Philip's various marriages to the daughters of Illyrians and Thracian tribal rulers; amphimetric conflict broke out only when Philip married Kleopatra the daughter of Attalos, a powerful and wealthy baron from Upper Macedon. Brother–sister marriage prevented to a certain degree the infiltration of other royal families into the Ptolemaic household. The Seleukids, on the other hand, always had to reckon with the presence of 'foreign', specifically Pontic and Ptolemaic, entourages accompanying brides, a phenomenon that is known in court studies as the 'doubling' of the court. There is, however, no evidence that Hellenistic palaces were physically divided into male and female parts.[32] Still, there is some scattered evidence that queens had their own servants and dignitaries. The later Seleukid court knew an office of Chamberlain of the Queen (or Lord of the Queen's Bedchamber, as Bevan translates).[33] Other members of the queen's own household may have been relatives of hers or men from her father's entourage. The official responsible for the upbringing of the pages at the court of Philip II was a kinsman of queen Olympias.[34] Queen Berenike, the wife of Antiochos II, had a personal bodyguard of Galatian swordsmen put at her disposal by her father, the Ptolemaic king.[35] Presumably, a queen's children grew up under her custody. Upon reaching the age of *paides*, her sons would become royal pages, serving the king. There is evidence that at the Ptolemaic court in the late third century princesses of the same age class, i.e. between their thirteenth and eighteenth years, likewise served the queen as ladies in waiting together with the daughters of *philoi*.[36] Although more research is

---

[32] To be sure, nor is there conclusive proof that the private houses of Greek elite families had separate women's quarters (Jameson 1990; Nevett 1999: 155; cf. Cohen 1991: 133), although that was the official ideology and is still the modern consensus (see e.g. Pomeroy 1997: 29: 'the fundamental division of private space was between male and female', and Just 1989).

[33] *RIG* 1158: κοιτῶνος τῆς βασιλίσσης (c. 100 BCE). Bevan 1902 II: 283. The same man also bore the title of chief physician of the queen (ἀρχίατρος τῆς βασιλίσσης).

[34] Plut., *Alex.* 5.

[35] Just. 27.1.4–7; App., *Syr.* 65; Val. Max. 9.10 *ext.* 1; Polyaen. 8.50 (246 BCE).

[36] Polyb. 15.33.11, mentioning female *suntrophoi*, 'foster-sisters', of a Ptolemaic queen. On *basilikoi paides* and *suntrophoi* see further Chapter 6.

needed, it at least seems that royal women after marriage could act as the representatives of their native households.[37]

ROYAL WOMEN AND FEMALE POWER

In the kingdoms of the Argeads, Seleukids and Ptolemies, queens played such leading roles that female power can be considered a defining aspect of Hellenistic monarchy.[38] As an indication of this, there emerged after Alexander's death, perhaps around the 'Year of the Kings' 306/5, a new title for the queen, *basilissa*, a 'female king'; Argead royal wives apparently had no official title.[39] This new title could function as an instrument establishing hierarchy among the royal women, too, since no more than one wife would be given the title of *basilissa* by her husband and thereby be proclaimed 'first queen'.[40] Five wives of Demetrios Poliorketes are known, but for only one, Phila, has the title of *basilissa* been attested – the first attestation of that title, which may have been an Antigonid invention.[41] Among the Ptolemies, the queen gradually became more or less the equal of her brother-husband,[42] until finally Kleopatra VII for some time ruled alone: not as regent but as queen in her own right. Among the later Argeads and in the Seleukid dynasty, the importance of women is conspicuous, too. Macurdy has hypothesised that the prominence of royal women at the Hellenistic courts was rooted in a supposed relative equality between man and woman in the culture of pre-Hellenistic Macedon.[43] Of perhaps greater significance was the relative importance of Macedonian women in the transmission of the royal inheritance.[44] When the Seleukid line became extinct, the right to the Seleukid diadem passed to the nearest kin in the female line, at that time to be found in the Ptolemaic family. In 34 BCE, at the public ceremony known as the Donations of Alexandria,

---

[37] Strootman 2007: 110–11; cf. Strootman 2011a for the diplomatic agency of women in the creation and maintenance of the Seleukid vassal state system.

[38] The only comprehensive study of female power at the Hellenistic courts remains Macurdy 1932a. Biographies of individual queens can be found in e.g. Whitehorne 1994 and Pfrommer 2002. On Argead queens and princesses see, among others, Carney 1994, 2000a, 2003b, 2006; Miron 2000. See further Meyer 1992/3; O'Neil 2002; Nourse 2002. For the function of role-model that Hellenistic queens supposedly had for Greek upper-class women see Bielman Sanchez 2003.

[39] Carney 1991.

[40] Polyb. 5.43.4; Plut., *Luc.* 18.3; Nikolaos of Damascus, *FHG* III 414 *ap*. Ath. 593a. See also the section on royal weddings in Chapter 9.

[41] Carney 1991.

[42] Hazzard 2000.

[43] Macurdy 1932a; cf. Macurdy 1927.

[44] Miron 2000; Strootman 2002.

Kleopatra VII claimed the Seleukid royal title for herself and her children: Kleopatra was an immediate descendant of Antiochos the Great, whose daughter Kleopatra (I) had married Ptolemy V Epiphanes in 193; more significantly, of the last twelve Seleukid kings, ten had Ptolemaic mothers.[45] Similarly, Antiochos IV in 170/69 had claimed tutelage of the minor Ptolemaic king Ptolemy VI, his sister's son.[46] And later kings of Pontos and even Kommagene could claim the title of Great King because of their descent from the Seleukids through the matriline (through they added to their genealogy a fictitious patrilineal descent from Darius the Great just to be sure).[47]

Although 'eastern' influences may have been at work here too, as has often been argued, this rather seems to have been founded first of all on a pre-Hellenistic Macedonian custom. The problem is that our richest source for female power in pre-Hellenistic Anatolia and the Near East, Herodotos' *Histories*, may give a biased image. Josine Blok has shown how in the *Histories* women are essential indicators of the Greek view of normality when transgressing the borders between the feminine and the masculine in an oriental court setting.[48] This does not imply, of course, that women at the Achaemenid court were *un*important, as indeed there is evidence that Persian royal women, too, participated in royal gift-exchange, receiving landed property and economic privileges from the king,[49] and perhaps played a crucial role in the dynastic transmission of kingship, as was argued by Tourraix.[50] But in the Hellenistic as well as in the Achaemenid empires, it is often impossible to say whether an individual royal woman is powerful and influential because her son is the crown prince, or a particular son of the king becomes crown prince because his mother is powerful and influential.[51] Still, when all is said and done, the fact remains that compared to Hellenistic queens and princesses, Achaemenid royal women are near-invisible in the official propaganda of the dynasty.[52]

Another reason why royal women played such prominent roles is the fact that as a result of Macedonian royal polygamy women were ideal 'favourites'. This means that for various reasons queens were

---

[45] On the Donations of Alexandria see below, Chapter 11.
[46] Mørkholm 1966: 68.
[47] Strootman 2010b.
[48] Blok 2000.
[49] Sancisi-Weerdenburg 1988; cf. Bigwood 1995; Stolper 1985: 63–4; Cardascia 1991.
[50] Tourraix 1976: 369–86.
[51] *Pace* Sancisi-Weerdenburg 1983.
[52] The evidence for Achaemenid queens is collected and discussed by Brosius 1996.

considered the most trustworthy persons to whom power could be delegated, especially when a king was on campaign far from the geographical centre of his kingdom.[53] For instance, when Antiochos III was campaigning in the Aegean, having his eldest son with him, his consort Laodike represented him as monarch elsewhere, maintaining diplomatic contacts with the cities of Asia Minor on his behalf and having authority over the royal treasury:

> Queen Laodike to the council and people of Iasos, greetings. Having often heard my brother recall the help he constantly provides to his friends and allies, and how when he recovered your city which had been afflicted by unexpected natural disasters, he restored to you your freedom and your laws, and for the rest he intends to increase the citizen body and bring it to a better condition; and since it is my policy to act in accordance with his zeal and eagerness and because of this to confer a benefaction on those citizens who are destitute, which would be of general advantage to the entire people; I have written to Strouthion, the financial official (*dioikētēs*), to have brought to the city every year for ten years 1,000 Attic medimnoi of corn to be delivered to the people's representatives ... If you continue to be (well) disposed towards my brother and in general towards our house as is fitting, [and] gratefully remember all our benefactions, I will try to help in securing in every way the other benefits I intend to confer, acting in accordance with the wishes of my brother. For I know that [he] is very eager to bring about the restoration [of the] city. Farewell.[54]

The queen is here acting as a typical favourite, a defensive 'screen' between the king and those seeking to contact him.[55] In Laodike's letter to Iasos, the bond between the king and his principal consort is emphasised by the queen's designation of her husband as 'brother' – an expression of fictive kinship related to the actual kinship between king and queen in the Ptolemaic family.[56] Just as a king's son could be appointed heir apparent by being awarded a central place in the government and the army, and the title of *basileus*, so the *basilissa* was raised to power by being granted a central place in royal cult, court ceremonial or panegyric.[57] Therefore, when a king died (or was taken prisoner, as in the case of Demetrios II Nikator) leaving only sons who were minors, the principal wife was

---

[53] Strootman 2002.

[54] Austin 156; *SEG* 26, 1226 (c. 195): 'natural disasters' probably refers to an earthquake.

[55] On this function of royal women see Strootman forthcoming (b).

[56] In his correspondence from the field, Antiochos III likewise emphasised that Laodike was his other self by calling her 'our sister and queen'; cf. Austin 151 and 158.

[57] Wikander 1996. Ptolemaic queens figure quite notably in the poetry of Kallimachos, e.g. fr. 392 (on the marriage of Philadelphos and Arsinoë, but dedicated to the latter), fr. 228 (on Arsinoë's apotheosis), *Epigram* 51 (in which Berenike I is compared with Charis), as well as the *Coma Berenices* and *Victoria Berenices*.

frequently able to step into the breach, drawing on her husband's prestige and her own status as mother of the successor.

Rivalry between queens and their factions was endemic at the Macedonian courts, as Ogden has argued, but it is not always easy to decide whether succession strife was due to a 'failure' on the part of the king 'to establish a consistent method of hierarchising his wives and the sons that were born of them',[58] or such conflicts resulted from a deliberate policy of the ruling monarch to keep the court divided. Kings may have benefited from a structurally divided court. As was argued above, kings had at their disposal various mechanisms to hierarchise royal women and secure the enthronement of a favoured successor. Indeed, the position of a 'crown prince' could be so secure that kings in some cases took to executing their own sons after a change of mind. The failure to employ such strategies consistently and successfully may therefore have been for other reasons.

[58] Ogden 1999: ix.

5 Court Society

This chapter begins with a brief discussion of the genesis of Hellenistic courts in the reigns of Philip and Alexander. Thereafter, the *philoi tou basileōs*, 'the friends of the king', will be discussed. Who were these courtiers? What were their (ethnic) origins, how were they attracted to court and what was their relationship with the royal family? After a general introduction of the *philoi* as a socio-political group, special attention will be given to them as a political factor in the Hellenistic empires. It will argued that in the Hellenistic world the court hardly served as the 'golden cage' hypothesised by Norbert Elias, that is, an instrument of power to suppress aristocratic resistance to absolutism and centralisation. When employed as an instrument of power to the king's own benefit, the Hellenistic court could in rare circumstances facilitate the creation of a *new* elite connected with the court – e.g. the creation of the first *philoi* societies in the decades after Alexander's death, or the transformation of the Seleukid empire from a centralised system of direct rule to a decentralised system of indirect rule through local vassal dynasties in the reign of Antiochos III – rather than a means to pacify unruly existing noble households with strong provincial power bases by forcing them to stay at the centre. However, new elites could easily turn into established aristocracies defending their own interests rather than those of the dynasty, and indeed the Hellenistic court could be a place where power and status could be obtained by established elites at the expense of the king.

The constantly shifting social mechanisms regulating the ritual dance around the altar of power – fictive kinship, guest-friendship, gift-exchange, aulic titulature, favour and disgrace – will be further examined in Chapter 8. This chapter ends with a reconsideration of the ethnicity of the *philoi*. Contrary to the now established view, it will be shown that the *philoi* were overwhelmingly of Greek origin, the reason being that, at least initially, they were first and foremost instrumental in maintaining relations between the imperial centre and Greek or Hellenised cities. Indeed, it will be argued that the promotion of non-Greeks to prominent positions by the Macedonian rulers – Iranians in the Seleukid empire and Egyptians in the Ptolemaic kingdom – was a *reaction* to the ethnic and social homogeneity of powerful established groups of *philoi*.

THE GENESIS OF HELLENISTIC COURT SOCIETY UNDER PHILIP AND ALEXANDER

Hellenistic court culture originated in Macedon in the fourth century. The social composition of the Argead household changed drastically as the power of the monarchy increased. Before the age of Philip and Alexander, when Macedonia was still a Persian satellite state of sorts, Argead monarchy and court underwent Achaemenid influences.[1] In the second half of the fourth century the earlier sub-Achaemenid empire of the Hekatomnids perhaps provided a model for the Macedonian expansion. But it was most of all Alexander who appropriated aspects of Achaemenid court culture in order to transform his household into a court more befitting his status as world ruler. The subsequent ruthless, violent conflict between factions of the old aristocracy and the king and his supporters over the absolutism of the monarchy broke up the Argead court so that a new form of court society could come into being.

In pre-Hellenistic Macedon the king shared his power with local barons. These so-called *hetairoi,* or companions of the king, dominated with their retainers the armed forces of the Macedonian kingdom until the reign of Philip, who reorganised and expanded the kingdom.[2] In principle, the king was the ultimate war leader of the united tribes of Macedon. Although official ideology presented him as an absolute ruler, he was in practice *primus inter pares* among the members of the high nobility. The Argead family dominated the coastal plain around the Thermaic Gulf and initially was merely the most powerful of several powerful clans.[3] The male heads of the mightiest noble families were called the king's *sungeneis*, 'relatives'. They were often connected to the royal family by marriage ties, had the right to greet the king with a kiss, and together constituted a

---

[1] Kienast 1971; Olbrycht 2010.
[2] Hammond 1989: 141 estimates that in 334 BCE the total number of companions was about 2,800; cf. Weber 2009.
[3] Hammond 1989: 141–2.

council advising the king.[4] From the mid-fourth century on the monarchy endeavoured to monopolise political power. Philip II took the first step in breaking the military dominance of the *hetairoi* by relying on heavy infantry recruited from the common Makedones. These *pezhetairoi*, foot companions, constituted the phalanx and were directly answerable to the king.[5] However, in the reign of Alexander the regular infantry was still organised according to tribal principles,[6] and thus presumably commanded by local lords – an indication that Philip did not succeed in creating real absolute autocracy. Only the royal infantry guard was, at least in Alexander's time, not recruited on an ethnic basis.[7]

Despite the continuing ethnic organisation of the army, and notwithstanding the fact that the nobility continued to supply the army's heavy cavalry and to derive political power from that, the common Makedones serving in the royal phalanx acquired some political influence to counterbalance the power of the *hetairoi*.[8] The new Macedonian royal army furthermore enabled Philip to pursue a foreign policy of his own, particularly in Greece. The creation of an infantry army and the expansion of the Macedonian kingdom outside Macedon subsequently gave the king the opportunity to control the nobility by monopolising the selection of officers and officials, and to promote to important positions his own personal followers and friends, whom he recruited not only among the Macedonian nobility but also among Thessalians and other Greeks.

Theopompos, quoted by Athenaios, expresses in a revealing passage how in his view the old nobles felt when confronted with the upsurge of favourites at court and in the army: 'From the entire Greek and barbarian world men of debauched, villainous and servile character flocked to Macedon and obtained the title companion of

---

[4] Arr., *Anab.* 7.11.9; Diod. 17.77.5. *Hetairos* is slippery term. It is suggestive of a dependence on the monarchy which may not have been very strong in reality, and it is used with various meanings in written sources, referring to the Macedonian nobility as a whole, to the heavy cavalry riding with the king in war, or to the small group of privileged intimates surrounding the king at court; see Hammond 1989: 53–8 and 140–8.

[5] Hammond 1989: 148–50; Walbank 1940: 1–2. For Philip's pursuit of absolutism see Errington 1990: 220–2.

[6] Rzepa 2008: 41–3.

[7] Ibid. 41; cf. Bosworth 1988: 261; Hammond 1989: 24–5.

[8] The power of the assembly was informal since there existed no (codified) Macedonian constitution (Errington 1978: 77–133; cf. Errington 1983: 89–101); the assembly acclaimed new kings and played a part in trials for treason against the king, sometimes acting (with the king) against the interests of the nobility (Arr., *Anab.* 3.26; 4.14.3; Plut., *Alex.*, 55.3; Curt. 6.8.25; cf. Polyb. 5.27.5, 29.6; Plut., *Eum.* 8.3; *Demetr.* 18; Diod. 18.37.2; 19.51.1; App., *Syr.* 54).

Philip.'[9] Athenaios adds that Philip consulted such men in even the most weighty matters, and cites as an astonishing example the case of the 'flatterer' Agathokles, the son of a Thessalian serf, who was given the command of an army and sent to the kingdom's northern marches with full administrative mandate.[10] Another passage in Athenaios suggests that Philip's predecessor Perdikkas III had already attempted to bypass the Macedonian nobility by promoting a favourite, a Greek called Euphraios, who became so powerful at court 'that Parmenion, as soon as Philip had become king, seized Euphraios and killed him'.[11] The same Parmenion, exponent of the independent Macedonian nobleman par excellence – but at the beginning of his career clearly 'Philip's man', as this passage suggests – would become the leader of the aristocratic opposition against Alexander's pursuit of absolutism.

Parmenion the son of Philotas came from a leading family of Upper Macedon and had been Philip's most trusted commander. At the beginning of Alexander's reign, Parmenion was still in the centre of power. Alexander, however, continued his father's policy of bestowing favours upon his personal friends, partly outsiders and lesser nobles, and to eliminate his opponents at court in cooperation with these favourites. His reign is characterised by a succession of increasingly harsh conflicts with the Macedonian nobility.[12] Carney argues that the image of Parmenion as Alexander's principal opponent at court in the extant sources was taken from Kallisthenes and thus ultimately derives from Alexander's own propaganda justifying the killing of Parmenion; this may be so, but that does not rule out the possibility that Parmenion was an opposition figure in historical

---

[9] Theopompos, *FGrH* 115 F 225a; cf. Polyb. 8.9.6–10.11; and Aesch., *Letter* 12.8, writing that two Athenian friends of Philip were given land and 'very comely wives'. For a different interpretation see O'Neil 2003: 510–11, explaining the presence of Greeks at Philip's court as an 'error' in the sources, which confused Philip's court with the later Hellenistic ones, where Greeks formed the majority of the *philoi*.

[10] Ath. 167b. Cf. Plut., *Alex.* 9. 'Son of a Thessalian πενέστης' is an allegation that is often used to discredit someone who has crossed a social boundary; Athenaios (260a) says the same of Lysimachos; cf. Lund 1992: 2, accepting that Lysimachos' father Agathokles was Thessalian; Paus. 1.9.5 claims that Lysimachos was a Macedonian, and this is also the conclusion of Merker 1979 and Tataki 1998 (both cited after O'Neill 2003: 510 n. 5). Polybios (8.10.5–6) claims in response to Theopompos' view that Philip's non-Macedonian friends instead of being flatterers were selected by the king for their competence as officers and administrators.

[11] Carystius, *FHG* IV 357 *ap*. Ath. 508e.

[12] The conflicts at Alexander's court are exhaustively discussed by Müller 2003. See also Badian 2000: 50–95, arguing that Alexander systematically exploited tensions at his court in order to suppress opposition. Weber 2009 examines the conflicts at the court of Alexander in the light of his adoption of Achaemenid court culture.

reality (after all, he and his sons *were* killed by Alexander).[13] During the campaign in Asia, Alexander systematically manipulated the composition of the court and thus the command structure of the army. This enabled him to enforce his own decisions without the consent or even against the wishes of the nobility. Various anecdotes containing verbal exchanges between Alexander and Parmenion bear witness to this process. The most illustrative of these is the dialogue recorded by both Plutarch and Arrian after Darius' peace proposal following the battle of Issos: 'If I were Alexander, I would accept these terms,' Parmenion said. 'So would I,' Alexander replied, 'if I were Parmenion.'[14]

Alexander's initial strategy was to advance to prominent positions certain young men who had been royal pages with him. The most important of these held the position of *sōmatophulax*, Royal Bodyguard. *Sōmatophulax* is perhaps the oldest Macedonian court title, and the title persisted well into the Hellenistic period in the Antigonid and Seleukid kingdoms (see below). At the Argead court there were seven *sōmatophulakes*. They were drawn from the nobility and of about the same age as the ruling monarch. They were responsible for the king's safety and personal well-being. They accompanied the king wherever he went and guarded the entrance to his bedchamber or pavilion together with the royal pages.[15] The *sōmatophulakes* were not allowed to hold other offices.[16] Alexander broke with this tradition and promoted his *sōmatophulakes* to important positions in the army. In 325 he even broke with the traditional number of seven bodyguards by creating an eighth post for the officer of the infantry guard, Peukestas. This was officially legitimised by the fact that Peukestas had saved Alexander's life in a battle with the Mallians. It is surely no coincidence that Peukestas became the most fervent supporter of Alexander's introduction of Achaemenid court ceremonial.[17] With the assistance of such

[13] Carney 2000b; cf. Baynham 1988, arguing that Curtius' description of Alexander's absolutism is based on the topical discussion of *regnum*, *libertas* and *tyrannus* by writers of the Principate, in particular Tacitus.

[14] Plut., *Alex.* 29.4; cf. Arr., *Anab.* 2.25.2. See also Arr., *Anab.* 3.10; Plut., *Alex.* 31.5–7.

[15] Arr., *Anab.* 4.13.7; Curt. 3.12.6; 8.6.22; 9.6.4; 1 Macc. 1.6. See Berve I: 25–6, also identifying as *sōmatophulakes* the *custos corporis* mentioned in Curt. 4.13.19 and 6.11.8; but here probably are meant the royal pages, who served as bodyguards of the king under the supervision of the *sōmatophulakes* (see Chapter 6). After Alexander's death, new *sōmatophulakes* were appointed for Alexandros IV and Philip III, two of whom are known by name (Burstein 1977).

[16] Berve I: 28.

[17] Arr., *Anab.* 6.28.3–4; 6.13.2; Diod. 17.99.4; cf. Schachermeyr 1970: 16 n. 13; Berve II: no. 634. Although Grainger 1990: 46 presumably goes too far in claiming that Peukestas was a non-noble and 'one of the very few Macedonians ever to rise from among the common people to a position of power', he may have come from a family of lesser nobles.

favourites as Peukestas, Ptolemy, Peithon, Perdikkas, Leonnatos and notably Hephaistion, Alexander was able gradually to remove the leaders of the old nobility and the members of the former entourage of Philip II from senior positions at court and in the army, to be replaced by Alexander's own protégés, men of his own age group. For instance, Kleitos and Hephaistion became commanders of the companion cavalry, a position previously held by Philotas, and the hypaspists (royal infantry guard) came under the command of Neoptolemos, a Molossian relative of his mother's.[18] Alexander divided up power between a larger number of people than had previously been the case; he also profited from, and probably encouraged, rivalry between his friends, notably between Krateros and Hephaistion.[19]

The process of elimination started with the execution of two brothers from the noble house of Lynkestis in 336, followed two years later by the killing of a third brother, Alexandros, a son-in-law of Parmenion, on the accusation of treason, and culminated in the elimination of Parmenion and his sons in the winter of 330.[20] In the case of Parmenion's eldest son Philotas, too, the official accusation was treason, so that the infantry assembly could be employed to authorise the death sentence and forestall aristocratic resistance to the verdict.[21] Once these examples were given, other men could be more easily demoted. After Gaugamela (331), Alexander also promoted Persians to senior positions, most famously Darius III's brother Oxyathres and Mazaios, who became satrap of Babylonia. They were allowed to call themselves the *sungeneis*, 'relatives', of the king, an honorific title also in use at the Achaemenid court,[22] giving them the right to greet the king with a kiss. Of course, Alexander initially would not have been able to remove all Iranian nobles from their positions even if he had wanted to, but in this case the king in all probability benefited from the presence of these powerful outsiders at his court, as indeed the irritated reactions of several Macedonian aristocrats reveal.[23] A similar hostile reaction to a favourite by the old elite has been described for the Achaemenid

[18] Plut., *Eum.* 1; cf. Arr., *Anab.* 2.27.6; Berve II: no. 548.
[19] Bosworth 1988: 104.
[20] Arr., *Anab.* 1.25.1; 3.27; Plut., *Alex.* 49; Curt. 7.1.5–9, 2.11–35. Heckel 2003: 210–25 argues that there were surprisingly few conspiracies against Alexander; cf. Badian 2000; Heckel 1997.
[21] Curt. 6.8.1, 11.9–10; Plut., *Alex.* 49.8–10.
[22] Arr., *Anab.* 1.15.7; 3.11.5; 7.11.1 and 6; Ath. 48e; Curt. 3.3.14 (*cognati regis*); Diod. 20.1–3.
[23] See e.g. Arr., *Anab.* 7.11.6; Plut., *Alex.* 43; Diod. 17.61.3, 77.4; Curt. 6.2.10.

court about a century earlier: when a Greek called Entimos was given the right to have breakfast in the presence of the king, Artaxerxes II, the Persian high nobility (likewise called *sungeneis* in Greek sources) 'were offended because they found that the honour was depreciated'.[24]

Various Achaemenid officials who had initially been left in office were removed upon Alexander's return from the east, to be replaced by Macedonians from Alexander's inner circle. For instance, Orxines, the satrap of Persis, was accused of maladministration and summarily executed to make way for Peukestas, while in Baktria the elderly Artabazos was dislodged from his satrapy and replaced by Kleitos on the pretext that the former had become too old. Other powerful non-Macedonian favourites at Alexander's court were the eunuch Bagoas, the Cretan Nearchos and Eumenes of Kardia, a Greek, whose loyalty to Alexander was proverbial even after the death of the king.[25] Anson argued that ethnicity was not a crucial political factor at the Macedonian court and that Eumenes was an outsider primarily because he lacked family ties with the Argeads and other noble families of Macedon; the net result, however, was the same, and familial allegiances can of course contribute to the construction of someone's ethnic identity.

So successful were Alexander's rearrangements that these 'new men', particularly the *sōmatophulakes*, although internally divided, were in complete control of the court at his death, opposed only by the 'old men' Antipatros and Antigonos, both of whom operated from power bases far removed from the imperial centre.

THE FRIENDS OF THE KING

Philip and Alexander had endeavoured to create a court in which not ancestry but the favour of the king determined who would rise to prominence. Apparently, Alexander was relatively successful at this. This was made possible by the enormous scale of his conquests, which allowed him to redistribute vast quantities of wealth and power among his followers. His successors inherited both the scale and, at first, the social flexibility of Alexander's court. Antigonos, Seleukos and Ptolemy were empire-builders, too, reaping the benefits of conquest. They too tried to select their courtiers personally on the basis of loyalty and merit. Although in their case it is more difficult

[24] Ath. 48f.
[25] Anson 2004.

to ascertain from the sources whether they succeeded in controlling the social composition of their courts, it seems that at least they had good opportunities to do so.

The transition from pre-Hellenistic Macedonian court society to the Hellenistic court societies was marked by the replacement of 'companion of the king' by 'friend of the king' as the genuine Greek term for someone belonging socially to a royal circle. From an informal designation that was much like the indefinite 'companion' (*hetairos*), the word 'friend' (*philos*) in due time acquired a somewhat more formal gist in some contexts. However, up until the end of the Hellenistic period the principal friends were, like the companions, attached to the royal household by means of ritualised friendship; and contrary to a common modern perception, this was not a degenerate, bureaucratic form of *philia*, as I will argue below.

Who were the *philoi tou basileōs*? Where did they come from and how did they relate to each other and to the king? In what manner were power, status and wealth distributed among them? To answer these questions, we will first look at the general characteristics of the society of friends as a social group. We will then look at their origins and ethnicity, and finally at their association with the royal family through *xenia* and *philia*. Finally, hierarchy and conflicts will be briefly discussed.

FRIENDS OR OFFICIALS?

In the Macedonian empires, all political power ideally was in the hands of the ruler. But even god-like kings could not rule alone. In order to retain, increase and exploit monarchic power, kings had to distribute wealth and power among others. 'Monarchs make many hands and ears and feet their own,' Aristotle wrote, 'for they appoint persons who are friends of their rule and of themselves as their fellow-rulers.'[26] Whether kings were really free to select fellow-rulers according to their own designs is questionable.

The 'fellow-rulers' of the Hellenistic kings were the so-called *philoi tou basileōs*, the 'friends of the king'. The terms φίλος and φίλος τοῦ βασιλέως are commonly found in both contemporary epigraphic texts and secondary sources (Polybios, Diodoros, Appian, Josephus, Plutarch, Athenaios); the equivalent of *philos* in Latin writings is *purpuratus*, which is, among other things, Livy's standard

---

[26] Arist., *Pol.* 1287b.

translation of Polybios' *philos*.[27] Other terms for 'courtiers' in the literary sources are θεραπεία, 'retinue',[28] and οἱ περὶ τὴν αὐλὴν, 'people of (or: around) the court'.[29] Finally, αὐλικοὶ is an interesting literal synonym of 'courtiers', but it is only rarely found;[30] an interesting variant of the latter is οἱ περὶ τὴν Ἄτταλον, 'the people of Attalos'.[31] Apparently these different denominations did not have distinct meanings – *pace* Bickerman, who is too strictly formalistic in assuming that περὶ τὴν αὐλὴν is the umbrella term for friends and household together, and that *therapeia* is only the Seleukid king's personal household or inner court as opposed to the *philoi*: 'Atour de roi se placent les "gens de la cour", *hoi perì tên aulên*, comme le langage hellénistique les appelait. Nous pouvons distinguer parmi ces "courtisans" deux groupes: "la maison du roi" et les "amis."'[32] There is, however, no evidence to support the claim that there existed such formalised distinctions in any of the kingdoms, especially because these terms feature mainly in secondary literary sources. Moreover, *philoi* seems to have been the umbrella term rather than περὶ τὴν αὐλὴν, if we give credence to Polybios (5.40), who says that Theodotos, governor of Koile-Syria for Ptolemy IV, 'loathed the king ... and was wary of the περὶ τὴν αὐλὴν', by which is meant those *philoi* who were present at the court, i.e. in the king's presence (as opposed to those *philoi* who were not at court, like Theodotos himself). Polybios elsewhere distinguishes between the *philoi* at court (οἱ περὶ τὴν αὐλὴν), *philoi* administrating the province of Egypt (οἱ τὰ κατὰ τὴν Αἴγυπτον χειρίζοντες), and *philoi* responsible for the Mediterranean Ptolemaic empire (οἱ ἐπὶ τῶν ἔζω πραγμάτων διατάγμενοι).[33]

Members of the status groups forming the supreme elites of the kingdoms were called *philos*. It was also a broader term, indicating any friendly relationship between the king and a private person, including those not present at court. The *philoi* were of varied ethnic origin, though they were primarily Hellenes, as we will see below. With the exception perhaps of those *philoi* who were actually at court, they did not constitute a single social group. The *philoi* first

[27] E.g. Liv. 30.42.6; Cic., *Cat.* 4.12; Curt. 3.2.10; Vitr. 2 *pr.* 1; Quint. 8.5.24.
[28] Polyb. 4.87.5; 5.56.7; 5.69.6; cf. Bickerman 1938: 36.
[29] E.g. Polyb. 4.87.7; 5.26.13, 34.4, 36.1, 40.2, 41.3, 50.14, 56.5; 16.21.8; 18.55.3; App., *Syr.* 45; Jos., *AJ* 12.125; 13.54; 17.125; 18.54.
[30] Polyb. 16.22.8; Plut., *Mor.* 778b; *Demetr.* 17.
[31] Diod. 29.22.
[32] Bickerman 1938: 36.
[33] Modern literature on *philoi* society is still not very substantial; for general discussions see Mooren 1975; Herman 1980/1 and 1997; Le Bohec 1985; Weber 1997; Savalli-Lestrade 1998.

of all created and maintained bonds between the dynasty and cities; furthermore, they were the advisors of the king in all his undertakings, the accountants of the royal finances, the functionaries and tax-collectors who administered the provinces, the king's representatives in cities and his ambassadors at foreign courts, and most of all the generals and admirals who commanded troops and ships. The close ties between the king, his friends and the armed forces is expressed in the standard phrase 'the king (and his family), the *philoi*, and the armed forces (δυνάμεις)' on civic decrees from Seleukid contexts.[34] They were not employees of the king; they did not receive a regular salary. Born in elite families, many *philoi* in the king's service did not depend on the court for their income, even though they could be rewarded for their services with rich gifts and land grants, take their share of the plunder in war, and through their own networks participate in international trade. Instead, the *philoi* were linked to the person of the monarch in a subtle, hierarchical system of ritualised personal ties, being attached to the king's *oikos* as guest-friends.[35] In other words, they were neither servants nor officials, and it is with reason that these men were known as the *friends* of the king.

Approximately how many *philoi* there were at the various courts at different moments in Hellenistic history can only be guessed at. It is difficult, too, to say where they lived. Some may have been lodged as guest-friends in the king's house. In Pella, several villas dating to the Hellenistic period have been uncovered, which may have belonged to *philoi*. No such evidence has been found in the Seleukid and Ptolemaic empires. It is quite likely that in royal capital cities like Alexandria, Seleukeia on the Tigris or Antioch, wealthy courtiers had their own little palaces. The wife and children of the Seleukid courtier Hermeias (late third century BCE) lived in Apameia while their husband and father was on campaign with the king.[36]

There were various means by which kings tried to hierarchise and thus control their *philoi*. One was the distribution of honorific titles, court offices and military commissions. The upper stratum of the *philoi* at court had a seat in the royal council, or *sunedrion*,

---

[34] Kern 1900: 86.15; Habicht 1958: 4; Hermann 1965. *Philoi* as ambassadors: Olshausen 1974; Mooren 1979.

[35] Nevett 1999: 174–5 on the Greek *oikos*: 'Recent work has shown that as well as a core nuclear family, individual households are likely to have housed a number of other individuals, including long-term guests, and that friends and neighbours are also likely to have been an important part of domestic life.'

[36] Polyb. 5.56.15. We may furthermore assume the existence of houses belonging to the families of *philoi* in their cities of origin, as well as villas on their landed estates.

granting them access to the person of the king on a regular basis, and hence influence on political matters. Especially at the Argead, Antigonid and Seleukid courts, the members of the council were military commanders before anything else. In all accounts of the informal meetings of the royal council at Alexander's court,[37] its members invariably discussed military matters. Writing about the court of Philip V, Polybios calls the same *philoi* alternately 'courtiers', 'commanders' and 'co-generals' of the king.[38]

Below the circle of council members there were various other levels of courtiers, also often called *philoi*, not all of whom were military men. In the Ptolemaic kingdom in the second century BCE a wide variety of court titles is attested, suggesting that 'friend' in the course of time also became a marker of more formal rank, of 'officials'. The Hellenistic system of court titulature, however, was not principally a Ptolemaic invention. It grew from Argead and Achaemenid antecedents, and presumably developed first at the Seleukid court. Because we know very little about the exact meaning and function of Hellenistic court titles, it would be rash to conclude, from the fact that the system apparently became more complex in the second and first centuries, that it became formal, static and bureaucratic. A formalised bureaucracy may indeed have developed at the middle and lower levels of the administration, particularly in the context of the administration of Ptolemaic Egypt, but this tells us nothing about what happened at the core of Ptolemaic court society.[39]

THE PARADOX OF POWER

Another priority of rulers was securing the allegiance of military leaders, both centrally appointed officials and localised aristocrats, including, as in the case of the Seleukids, vassals and client kings. This required substantial rewards for success, such as land grants,

---

[37] All instances are collected in Hammond 1989: 143–4.

[38] Polyb. 4.87.7 (περί τὴν αὐλήν); 5.4.13 (ἐγεμόναι); 4.87.8 (συστρατευομένων); cf. Plut., *Mor.* 183b; Diod. 33.22; *pace* Herman 1997: 214, who distinguishes men with power in the army from the courtiers proper; and Ehling 1998: 97–106, assuming a strict separation of 'civil' and 'military' office-holders in the *sunedrion* of Antiochos III.

[39] In the past, only Rostovtzeff was wary of what Spawforth later called 'the modernist attempts to define the formal or even legal basis of the relationship of king and courtier' (Spawforth 2007a: 1); Rostovtzeff 1928: 116 writes that '[the king's] chief assistants in the task of administration are for the most part literally the members of his own household with whom again are closely connected their own households and their agents'.

booty and honours.[40] This explains why many empires remain focused on conquest and military success (the Antigonid and Seleukid kingdoms are two notable cases in point) and why so many empires decline when expansion stagnates.

By sharing power with others, kings inevitably risked losing power to others. This is the eternal dilemma of all despotic, personal forms of rulership throughout the centuries. As Duindam explicates:

> It appears to be a universal principle that handing out favours is temporarily effective as an instrument of power, but eventually burdens the dispenser with newly-established interest-groups ... Favourites could turn into rebels with remarkable speed ... Power delegated, titles and privileges granted, places sold or given away would initially create a group loyal to the king, who usually, however, eventually turned into quick-tempered defenders of their own privilege.[41]

Kings first of all needed helpers they could trust. Ideally, they chose as their closest collaborators men who could not themselves claim positions of importance by right of birth or otherwise, as such men were least difficult to remove from high office and thus more loyal. In other words, kings tended to select their courtiers as much on personal grounds as for their military or other professional capabilities. In practice, however, kings rarely really controlled the social composition of their courts completely. Even Alexander for years was not able to remove Parmenion from his key position of power at the Argead court.[42] The first generation of Diadochs may have had exceptional opportunities to 'hand-pick' their friends, but not even they had at their disposal such absolute power as to be able to appoint men of their own choosing to all crucial posts at court and in the army, and to manipulate the distribution of honours, titles and offices at their own discretion. This is a recurrent characteristic of courts in history. As Kaiser and Pečar put it in the opening lines of a volume dedicated to favourites in early modern Europe: 'Politische Herrschaftsgewalt war zu keiner Zeit in der Hand einer Person konzentriert. Stets waren mehrere Personen und Personengruppen involviert, wenn politische Entscheidungen beraten, getroffen und umgesetzt werden sollten. Die Monarchien und Fürstenherrschaften des Ancien Régime sind da keine Ausnahme.'[43] The loyalty of the *philoi* therefore remained a matter of constant concern for kings. The principal danger was not revolt. Rebellion against the legitimate

---

[40] Sinopoli 1994: 167.
[41] Duindam 1994: 50–1.
[42] See Arr., *Anab.* 6.27.1, on satraps 'who neglected [Alexander's] orders'.
[43] Kaiser and Pečar 2003: 9.

monarch was difficult to conceive and furthermore hazardous, since the armed forces were normally loyal to the dynasty. In the east there are examples of non-dynastic rebels from within trying to replace the (Seleukid) dynasty with their own *basileia*, most notoriously Molon and Diodotos Tryphon. They all failed. Malcontent courtiers, furthermore, could unite with a dynastically legitimate claimant to the throne or join a rival court, taking their personal satellites, influence and even troops with them (for instance, the powerful Theodotos the Aitolian, who shifted his allegiance from Ptolemy IV to Antiochos III). Still, most threatening for kings was the situation in which powerful men remained devoted adherents of the dynasty but acted completely at their own discretion, without the king's consent or even against the king's wishes. Kings could regain control by replacing those at the top levels of the empire with new men of lesser status and power, but needed considerable military success to be able to reward and bind them. The combination of territorial expansion and the re-organisation of the court characterises the reigns of Philip II and Alexander the Great, and of Philip V and Antiochos III around 200 BCE.

Thus, paradoxically, the ideal *philos* should on the one hand be subordinate to the king and on the other hand stalwart and able enough to command armies independently, administer provinces, and frankly advise the king on important matters. Demetrios of Phaleron once advised Ptolemy Soter to read books about rulership because, he said, 'those things which the king's friends are not bold enough to recommend to him are written in the books'.[44] This anecdote presents Demetrios as an ideal courtier, one who does *not* mind mincing his words. Many are the passages in the sources portraying *philoi* as either sycophantic and designing profiteers or a fearful lot who can only flatter and dare not speak their minds in the presence of the king, let alone argue with him. When kings listen to flatterers, there are always disastrous consequences.[45] Although the motif of a king being corrupted by wicked advisors – presented as amusing anecdote by Athenaios, as moral example by Plutarch, and as political theory by Polybios – is a *topos*, at least it recognises, as Polybios says, that 'the decisive importance for young kings, as leading either to their misfortune or to the firm establishment of their rule, is the judicious choice of the friends who attend on them'.[46]

[44] Plut., *Mor.* 189d.
[45] See for instance Diod. 28.2; Polyb. 8.22.1–3; 9.23.9; 15.34.4; Plut., *Demetr.* 17.2; Theopompos, *FGrH* 115 fr. 225 *ap.* Polyb. 8.9.5.
[46] Polyb. 7.14.6, adding that most young kings fail to make such a choice.

THE ETHNIC BACKGROUND OF THE *PHILOI*

In an influential article on the elite of the Seleukid monarchy, Christian Habicht calculated that in the third century a mere 2.5 per cent of the empire's ruling class consisted of non-Greeks. He based his conclusion on a sample of about 250 leading men in the empire. Unlike Tables 5.1–5.4 below, Habicht accepted personal names as ethnic indicators.[47] Frank Walbank comments that 'The exclusion of non-Greeks from this circle probably reflected the prejudices of the Greeks and Macedonians rather than any incapacity or reluctance to serve on the part of the indigenous population. Racial prejudice was characteristic of the Graeco-Macedonian caste within the kingdoms at least throughout the late fourth and third centuries.'[48] In the past decades Habicht's view of the Seleukid elite as a more or less homogeneous social group, and the implicit allegation of imperialist exploitation it entailed, has become an object of controversy. Historiography of the 1980s and 1990s has revived the idea of substantial non-Greek influences in the Seleukid empire, while the image of the Ptolemaic empire as essentially an Egyptian national state even in the third century has never been anything *but* the prevailing view. Although probably no one would deny that the Seleukid empire was an eastern empire in a strictly geographical sense, it is questionable whether the dichotomy of 'western' Greek intruders and 'indigenous' orientals is really helpful in understanding historical conditions in the Hellenistic Middle East. To put it differently: it would have been rather surprising if at the top of the Seleukid empire there had *not* been a dominant ethno-class, to use the term coined by Pierre Briant to designate the imperial elite of the Achaemenid empire, whose ethnic identity was a mixture of cultural construct and descent.[49]

The principal arguments against Habicht's calculation have been collected by Kuhrt and Sherwin-White in *From Samarkhand to Sardis*. Apart from several methodological objections – notably that the sample is 'statistically worthless since the evidence then was (and still is) so incomplete and random geographically and chronologically' – the central argument is that personal names are unreliable as ethnic indicators, since non-Greeks in the Seleukid kingdom, as is well known, often assumed Greek names. Kuhrt and Sherwin-White conclude that:

[47] Habicht 1958; cf. Herman 1997: 201.
[48] Walbank 1984a: 68.
[49] Briant 1988a.

What we should visualize is a small exclusive court group, close to the king and dependent on his favour, occupying the top positions in the satrapies and armies, whose male members, in the third century, *generally* had Greco-Macedonian names. How and to what degree they were interlinked with members of the various indigenous populations remains unclear at present, although some recruitment into their ranks is likely. Below that were regional élites (Greek and non-Greek) running local affairs and representing and governing the ethnically variegated mass of farmers, soldiers, artisans, herders, cult personnel, traders and slaves.[50]

Although the main thrust of the argument is certainly correct – the self-evident existence of autochthonous elites running regional and local affairs – the suggestion that in the third century non-Greeks gained admission to the highest imperial ranks on a regular basis raises questions. The fact that behind Greek names 'ethnic' non-Greeks *may* be hidden does not, of course, help identify them as such. More importantly, ethnic identity is not a matter of genealogy only; it is *also* a cultural construct, and a complex one to boot.[51] If non-Greeks who gained access to court indeed assumed a double identity, e.g. Babylonian-Hellenic, Judaean-Hellenic or Egyptian-Hellenic,[52] this may not have turned them into ethnic 'Greeks' entirely, but at least it does testify to the dominance of Graeco-Macedonian culture at court – or rather, of a supranational Hellenistic culture of empire, which, like Austrian or Ottoman court cultures of later ages, offered a means to express allegiance to the empire and to distance oneself from rivals excluded from power.[53] Thus the empire was united at its highest level through a shared elite culture. The royal household served as a point of contact for otherwise unconnected elites. The upper stratum of the court societies,

[50] Kuhrt and Sherwin-White 1993: 124–5; cf. 150–1. Carsana 1996 supports this view. McKenzie 1994 goes further by arguing that, because the Seleukid administration combined Persian and Macedonian elements, an infrastructure was created that welcomed non-Macedonians, which in turn encouraged the creation of a shared culture. For a comparable view see Shipley 2000: 222. In defence of Habicht's view see Weber 1997: 40–1 and Herman 1997: 208. Herman 1987 explained the preponderance of Greeks at the Macedonian courts as coming from the use of *xenia* networks to attract them (see below).

[51] See Jones 1997: 13–14, defining ethnic identity as self-definition through the subjective and situational identification with a group on the basis of *perceived* (my emphasis) cultural differences and/or common descent (cited after Mairs 2006a: 8). For a full overview of the complexity of matters of ethnic identity and cultural interaction see now Burke 2009. On Greek identity as a cultural construct see especially Hall 1997 and Malkin 2001. See also Davies 2001, showing that among the Greeks personal names were indicative of the cohesion and cultural continuity of specific communities. Thompson 2001b has argued that in Ptolemaic Egypt native Egyptians, and not ethnic Greeks, were the pre-eminent conveyors of the Hellenic culture that the Ptolemaic rulers favoured. See Mairs 2008 on ethnic identity in Hellenistic Central Asia.

[52] See, among others, Van der Spek 2005 on the (double) identity of the Babylonian elite.

[53] Strootman 2001, 2006, 2010a.

however, consisted predominantly of ethnic Greeks and Macedonians. Finally, as I will expound later on, the rare non-Greek courtiers who do turn up in the sources unconcealed were favourites, rising to prominence precisely because they were outsiders. First, however, we will take a closer look at the geographical and ethnic origins of the *philoi*.

THE ORIGINS OF THE *PHILOI*

As we have seen, the *philoi* community originated in the Argead kingdom during the reigns of Philip and Alexander. Here the courtiers were called *hetairoi tou basileōs*, the companions of the king. The title of ἑταῖρος, although originally designating a member of the hereditary rural nobility of Macedon, has similar connotations to φίλος in Greek. When Philip was trying to counterbalance the power of these mighty barons by placing in key positions at court men of his own choosing (see above), he took to awarding the name of *hetairos* at his own discretion, which from then on became an honorific as well a hereditary title for a relatively closed social group. After the division of Alexander's empire by the Successors, separate courts developed in each of the new kingdoms. The demand for capable commanders and administrators increased accordingly and became too great for the Macedonian nobility alone to meet. It was mainly Greeks that now moved in to fill the gap. Scions of indigenous, i.e. Iranian, aristocracies sometimes rose to high office, too. Iranians had already been present at Alexander's court. They are later found in the entourages of Seleukos Nikator and notably Antigonos Monophthalmos. One generation later, when the kingdoms had been firmly established, non-Greek courtiers have all but disappeared from the sources. Instead, after c. 300 BCE a new imperial elite emerged throughout the eastern Mediterranean and Near East, consisting almost entirely of Greeks and Macedonians. The earliest reference to *philos* as meaning, *mutatis mutandis*, 'courtier' dates to 285 BCE.[54] Plutarch uses *hetairos* as a technical term to denote a member of the Macedonian nobility in his *Life of Alexander*, but uses *philos* in the biographies of Demetrios, Agis, Flamininus and Aemilius Paullus; Diodoros on the other hand uses *philos* for both Alexander's and later Hellenistic courtiers.[55]

The courts of the new kingdoms offered rare opportunities to

---

[54] Welles 1934: no. 6; cf. Walbank 1984a: 69; *pace* Konstan 1997: 96.
[55] Herman 1980/1: 13.

obtain prestige, influence and wealth. At the same time presence at court became a prerequisite for obtaining power and status. As a consequence, in the early Hellenistic period high birth was no longer the principal source for one's position at court. Instead, status was fixed by even less tangible determinants such as 'proximity to the throne' or 'favour', while differences in rank and status were expressed through court titles, etiquette, dress and ceremonial.[56] Elias Bickerman even stated that the basis of the early Macedonian states in the Near East was the mutual goodwill (*eunoia*) between king and *philoi*: 'Macedonians, Thessalians, other Greeks and various non-native elements were partners in exploiting the Orient and were as isolated in the immense alien country as the king himself. They all had to sink or to swim together. This was the real meaning of the mutual "good will" of which we have just spoken.'[57] Flavius Philostratos described the early Ptolemaic court as 'a dining table in Egypt to which the most distinguished men in the world were invited'.[58] This is not poetic licence: Hellenistic courtiers really came from all over the Mediterranean, inducing Gabriel Herman to call the court in the Hellenistic world a 'kosmopolis'.[59] This said, it is also noticeable that within the open and cosmopolitan social framework of the Hellenistic courts, a minority of Macedonian nobles continued to dominate the highest stratum of court society. This was of course the case in the Macedonian kingdom of the Antigonids, but also in the Seleukid and Ptolemaic empires (see below).

The general developments outlined above can be exemplified by looking at the social composition of the court of Antigonos Monophthalmos. In an appendix to his book on the one-eyed king, Richard Billows has listed the names of all the friends of Monophthalmos mentioned in the sources as having been in his entourage at any time of his career after Alexander's death. This comprehensive prosopography contains 149 entries, and in the case of 82 individuals the ethnicity or birthplace is known.[60] The largest group is constituted by ethnic Macedonians, of whom there are 30, including the king's son and grandson. This number is typical of the transition in the years following Alexander's death: 30 Macedonians out of a total of 82 courtiers constitutes a strikingly lower percentage than

---

[56] Strootman 1993: 33; Weber 1993: 40; cf. Kruedener 1973: 58; Duindam 1994: 28–30.

[57] Bickerman 1983: 7–8.

[58] Philostratos 1.22.524. Theopompos (*FHG* I 320 = Ath. 167b) sneers that the confidants of Philip II were 'men who had rushed to his side from very many quarters'.

[59] Herman 1997: 208. Cf. Le Bohec 1985.

[60] Billows 1997: 361–452. The remaining 67 individuals for the greatest part carry Greek personal names.

the number of Macedonians at Alexander's court, but it is also strikingly higher than the percentage of Macedonians at the Ptolemaic and Seleukid courts some generations later. Three more friends of Antigonos came from the Balkans: two men from Epeiros (one of them Pyrrhos, the later Molossian king, who as a youth served Antigonos for some time) and a man called Olkias, who was presumably an Illyrian. Remarkable too is the relatively high number of non-Greeks: four Iranians, a Lydian and a Bithynian. The remainder can be confidently identified as Greeks.

In the third century BCE, the number of Macedonians decreased even in the Antigonid kingdom. The majority of *philoi* were citizens of Greek *poleis*. They were drawn into the orbit of the court from an immense area, coming even from cities beyond the kingdoms' respective spheres of influence. For instance, at the court of Antiochos the Great, of a total of 41 friends mentioned by Polybios and Livy whose place of origin is known, no fewer than 21 came from cities outside the actual Seleukid sphere of influence (Table 5.1).[61]

Table 5.1. Courtiers of Antiochos III, 223/2–187 BCE

Origin	Number
Macedonians	9
Mainland Greece	10
Aegean islands	9
Asia Minor	6
Syria	4
Non-Greeks	3
Total	41

Sources: After Liv. 35.18.1; 36.5.3, 11.6, 12.4; 37.13.9, 34.1, 45.17; Polyb. 5.40.1, 41.2, 45.6, 70.11; 5.79; 7.15.2; 10.29.6; 11.39.12; 20.3.7; 21.17.7; 56.1.

In this sample there are nine Macedonians at the top of Antiochos' court (including the king's two eldest sons) and no more than three non-Greeks. To the latter belongs Hannibal, who had found refuge at the Seleukid court after the Second Punic War. Polybios (5.79.7–8) moreover mentions a 'Mede' called Aspasianos and an Arab prince called Zabdibelos as commanders of allied troops at the battle of Raphia, but these vassal princes seem to have been present

---

[61] The tables in this section were compiled for the international congress on 'The Post-Classical City' (held in Groningen, 2003) and were earlier used in Strootman 2005b; when compiling these tables I could not benefit from O'Neil 2003 and 2006, presenting similar figures, based on partly overlapping samples.

only for the duration of the Raphia campaign. The remainder are Greeks. The number of Macedonians may seem small. Their relative importance, however, was not: in c. 200 BCE three of the five most influential Seleukid *philoi* were Macedonians.[62]

Tables 5.2–5.4 shows the origins of Ptolemaic, Seleukid and Attalid *philoi* through longer periods of time. In the case of the Ptolemies and Seleukids two periods are distinguished, the second being the time when the empires declined. The tables are based on the prosopographies of Mooren and Savalli-Lestrade, neither of which is exhaustive, with some additions. Again, I have discarded *philoi* whose place of origin or ethnic is unknown.

Table 5.2. Origins of Ptolemaic *philoi*, 305–30 BCE

Origin	305–180 BCE	180–30 BCE
Macedonians	3	7
Alexandria	6	8
Cyrenaica	0	4
Egypt	0	4
Aegean islands	3	3
Mainland Greece	8	10
Asia Minor	4	3
Syria and Kilikia	0	3
Cyprus	0	1
Total	24	43

Source: After Mooren 1975.

Of the four courtiers from Egypt in Table 5.2, only one was an ethnic Egyptian. This was Petosarapis, a favourite (i.e. a manifest outsider) at the court of Ptolemy VI. In this table it is interesting to see that between the years 300 and 180, of the total number of the *philoi* whose place of origin is known about a quarter came from Alexandria, but none from Cyrenaica and Egypt proper. In the second period, 8 of 43 came from Egypt and Cyrenaica. The increased number of North African Greeks may reflect the development of a settled ruling class with landed estates in Cyrenaica and the Egyptian interior. At the Ptolemaic court, relatively many courtiers apparently took pride in presenting themselves as Macedonians. How Greeks and Macedonians thought about each other

[62] O'Neil 2003 formulates a similar conclusion with respect to the later Antigonids: the number of Greeks at the Antigonid court increases but Macedonians continue to dominate the most important positions.

after Alexander is difficult to assess; it appears, however, that being a Macedonian was prestigious in court circles.[63]

Table 5.3. Origins of Seleukid *philoi*, 312–64 BCE

Origin	312–187 BCE	187–64 BCE
Macedonians	6	0
Mainland Greece	6	7
Aegean islands	7	4
Asia Minor	15	13
Syria and Kilikia	7	10
Cyprus	2	0
Crete	4	0
Other	2	0
Total	49	34

The sample does not include sons of kings. To avoid imbalance, the Greeks who sought refuge at the Seleukid court after Antiochos III's defeat by the Romans in Greece in 192 are excluded; they are included in Table 5.1 for the court of Antiochos III.
Sources: After Savalli-Lestrade 1998, with the addition of Liv. 36.5.3; 37.13.9; Polyb. 5.40.1; 41.2, 45.6, 70.11, 79.7, 8, 10, 12; 7.15.2; 10.29.6; 11.39.12; 30.3.7.

The Seleukids relied heavily on Greeks from Asia Minor (Table 5.3). The percentage of *philoi* known to have come from Asia Minor remains unchanged even after they had lost their Anatolian empire in the Roman–Seleukid War (192–188 BCE). The number of Greeks from the Aegean and the Greek mainland likewise remained stable after 188.

Table 5.4. Origins of Attalid courtiers, 241–133 BCE

Origin	241–133 BCE
Pergamon	18
Asia Minor	12
Aegean islands	4
Greek mainland	2
Magna Graeca	2
Total	38

Source: After Savalli-Lestrade 1998.

Attalid *philoi* (Table 5.4) came predominantly from the city of

[63] For the mutual perceptions of Greeks and Macedonians up until the death of Alexander see Badian 1982.

Pergamon and surrounding regions on the Aegean coast of Asia Minor, as well as the Aegean islands. Only two of the Attalid *philoi* came from beyond the Aegean.[64]

NON-GREEKS AT THE MACEDONIAN COURTS

In the empires of Alexander, Antigonos and Seleukos, members of the Achaemenid ruling class initially retained positions of influence and power, particularly as provincial grandees in Anatolia, Iran and the provinces further east. These Iranians evidently retained a pronounced Iranian identity based on perceived traditions and increasingly invention of tradition (as is evident from the Neo-Achaemenid imagery of Nemrut Dağı). Because Macedonian rule was not yet firmly established, Alexander and his immediate successors needed to collaborate with the pre-existing elites of the former Achaemenid empire in order to pacify and govern the conquered territories. Alexander's policy was to come to terms with the Iranian elites rather than to try to subdue and replace them at all cost. Many Iranian magnates retained, or were newly appointed to, positions as satraps and commanders. Some were awarded places of honour at the Macedonian court.[65] The most prominent examples are Oxyathres, a brother of Darius III, who became a member of Alexander's entourage and received the title of companion of the king; and the eunuch Bagoas, a former favourite of Darius, whose influence with Alexander is stressed twice by Curtius.[66] Iranians, however, were normally assigned to, or affirmed in, posts in the provinces rather than at court. These could still be important positions. Mazaios, the able commander of the Achaemenid army in the Gaugamela campaign, became satrap of Babylonia in 331.[67] Artabazos, another prominent figure at the court of Darius III, became satrap of Baktria in 329.[68] Apparently, Alexander wished to bring into his orbit men whose families possessed authority and prestige among the Iranians, but at the same time tried to keep them away from the centre of power.[69]

[64] On Attalid *philoi* see also Tarn 1913: 233; Allen 1983: 129–35.
[65] Borza 1992: 21.
[66] Oxyathres: Curt. 6.2.11; Berve II: no. 586. Bagoas: Curt. 6.5.23; 10.1.22–38; Berve II: no. 195.
[67] Berve II: no. 484; Mazaios' son became satrap in Syria (Curt. 5.13.11); when Mazaios died of old age he was replaced by another Iranian called Stamenes (Arr., *Anab.* 4.18.13) or Ditamenes (Curt. 8.3.17; cf. Berve II: no. 718).
[68] Berve II: no 152.
[69] *Pace* Hammond 1997, arguing that there was complete equality between Macedonians and Persians at Alexander's court (pp. 134, 143–4, 159, 190, 201); see the objections to this view by C.A. La'da in *Mnemosyne* 52 (1999) 757–61, esp. 759.

Even in Alexander's reign, particularly after his return from Baktria and India, efforts were made to remove Iranians from the most crucial positions. Shortly after Alexander's death, his generals planned a rearrangement of the empire in which many of the remaining Iranian satraps lost their positions.[70] The indigenous elites reacted to their exclusion by retreating to their provincial power bases.[71] In relatively inaccessible regions such as northern Anatolia, Armenia or Persis, non-Greek states would eventually spring up to challenge Macedonian domination.

In Egypt, Egyptian provincial nomarchs remained in office after the Macedonian conquest. Alexander placed them under the supervision of two Egyptians, Doloaspis and Peteisis. Their authority was limited, however, by the fact that apparently they had no military responsibilities. The armed forces in Egypt were under the command of two Macedonians, Balakros and Peukestas. The ultimate responsibility for the whole satrapy was given to Kleomenes, a native of Naukratis.[72] Ptolemy Soter employed Egyptian functionaries, too. He gave an Egyptian military responsibilities in one recorded case, which probably did not stand alone – but apparently he tried to keep them all at arm's length from the inner court.[73] Egyptian functionaries in the *chōra* are known from hieroglyphic grave epitaphs, but the meaning of their honorific titles is unclear; the sarcophagus of the Egyptian nomarch Nektanebo boasts the title of 'the great first-ranking officer of the army for his majesty'.[74] Shipley quotes several epitaphs of Egyptian elite persons bearing Egyptian-language Ptolemaic honorific titles. These men were apparently very influential in the province of Egypt, especially in the Thebaid. By means of aulic titulature and, we may presume, the accompanying gifts of clothing and other status markers, local Egyptian officials were connected *with* the court though they were not necessarily *at* court.[75] The important relations between the Ptolemaic court and Egyptian temples and priests are of course well known. Far more difficult is to establish how far representatives of the Egyptian priesthood were structurally present in inner court circles, having direct access to

---

[70] On the decisions made at Babylon in 323 BCE see Bosworth 2002b.

[71] For Iranian dynasts in Hellenistic Asia Minor see Briant 1985; Sullivan 1990.

[72] Arr., *Anab.* 3.5; cf. Hölbl 2001: 12 with nn. 11–12.

[73] Hölbl 2001: 27 with n. 89.

[74] Hölbl 2001: 27 n. 90; cf. Turner 1984: 126. On ethnicity in Ptolemaic Egypt see further Bagnall 1988; Goudriaan 1988; Bilde et al. 1992; Clarysse 1995; Ducat 1995. For the social and economic privileges of Macedonians and Greeks under the Ptolemies see Thompson 2001b.

[75] Shipley 2000: 222.

the person of the king or the queen. With the reign of Ptolemy Philadelphos, Egyptians all but disappear from the upper ranks of Ptolemaic hierarchy, being mainly employed as provincial and local administrators. They reappear as favourites in the second century BCE.

In the eastern and northern parts of the former Achaemenid empire local barons maintained regional control of mountainous regions. Although it would in any event have been hard (and presumably unnecessary) to remove them, there was also a more positive reason for Alexander, Antigonos and Seleukos to court the Iranian ruling caste actively, and that was its military potential. The intense and constant warfare among the Diadochs had divided the Macedonian armed forces into various smaller armies. In the ensuing demand for troops, the Iranian nobility was the key to the military resources and manpower of Asia. Notably, Iranian cavalry – heavily armed and armoured nobles, the forerunners of the Seleukid kataphrakts, together with their retainers – could be decisive on the battlefield. Persian aristocrats were reputedly the best horsemen in Asia. The Achaemenid noble cavalry was known in Old Persian as *huvaka*, 'kinsmen' of the king (*sungeneis* in Greek sources); they were the most prominent courtiers of the emperor and formed the core of the Achaemenid army, not unlike Alexander's elite cavalry, the companions.[76] They were said to find it a disgrace to be seen on foot.[77] Alexander had 1,000 Iranian horsemen at his disposal at the battle of the Hydaspes in 326. Large numbers of eastern troops, Iranian horsemen foremost, formed part of several Diadoch armies. In the battle of Gabiene (317 BCE), Eumenes and the eastern satraps fielded about 5,000 Iranian horse supported by huge numbers of diverse Asian light infantry (Diod. 28.1–8); on the opposing side, Antigonos Monophthalmos had at least 1,000 Iranian heavy cavalry, 1,000 cavalry from Anatolia, and more than 10,000 'Asian' and Anatolian light infantry at his disposal – of a total number of 36,500 men.[78] Antigonos' Iranian horsemen had Iranian commanders.[79] At the battle of Ipsos (302) both Antigonos and Seleukos fielded about 10,000 horsemen,[80] an enormous number reminiscent of the armies of the Persian Great Kings. The military

---

[76] See e.g. Arr., *Anab.* 4.12.1; Diod. 17.59.2. On Persian noble cavalry in the Achaemenid empire see Briant 1999: 108–11.

[77] Xen., *Cyr.* 4.3.22; cf. Hdt. 136.2: 'The Persians teach their sons between the ages of five and twenty only three things: to ride, use a bow, and speak the truth.'

[78] Diod. 19.29.1–7.

[79] Grainger 1990: 47.

[80] Diod. 20.13.4; cf. Plut., *Demetr.* 28.3.

success of Seleukos Nikator in the east between 312 and 303 was presumably to a large degree due to his good relations with the Iranian nobility, in which the family ties of his Baktrian wife Apama may have played a crucial role. The successors of Seleukos Nikator, too, relied on Iranian cavalry for their armies, and maintained bonds with Iranian royalty through systematic intermarriage.

GREEK *PHILOI* AND NON-GREEK NON-*PHILOI*?

The fact that royal *philoi* and their kinsmen acted as the agents of empire in the world of the *poleis* accounts for the predominance of Greeks and 'Hellenised people' in the Seleukid and Ptolemaic *philoi* societies, and for their domination, together with Macedonian aristocrats, of the highest imperial offices. It does not explain, however, the noticeable *absence* in both literary and epigraphic documentation of non-Greek courtiers. The exceptional appearance of non-Hellenes as favourites among the *philoi* only underlines their absence. Perhaps we are looking for them in the wrong place.

There can be no doubt that many people unconnected with *poleis* were present at the royal courts, too. Because Egypt was the principal source of wealth of the Ptolemaic empire, representatives of Egyptian temples, and perhaps of local aristocracies as well, must have been attached to the court even in Alexandria for special festive occasions, or when the court was at Memphis or at other places in Egypt.[81] At the Seleukid court, the presence of Iranians must have been notable. The huge numbers of (heavy) cavalry, sometimes even specified as being Iranian, in Seleukid armies suggests that the Seleukids maintained good relations with the Iranian aristocracies controlling the countryside in the Upper Satrapies from the beginning. Contrary to the once-popular view that from the coming of Alexander to the disappearance of the Seleukids there was a virulent Persian resistance to Macedonian rule, the Iranian east was in fact conspicuously loyal to the Seleukid house.[82] From the wedding of Seleukos and Apama at Susa on, the Seleukid house through regular marital exchanges had become connected in an increasingly complex manner with various, especially Iranian (vassal) dynasties; royal women acted as mediators because they retained links with their

---

[81] For Egyptian priests attending the Ptolemaic court see Thompson in Erskine and Llewellyn-Jones forthcoming.

[82] See Kuhrt and Sherwin-White 1993: *passim*. The modernist view of Iranian 'indigenous' resistance to 'foreign' occupation was popularised especially by Eddy 1961.

original households. The Seleukids were not exceptional in this respect. The prominence of various Balkan troops in the later Antigonid armies, too, is indicative of a wide network of Antigonid social relations outside the Greek-speaking world.

After the death of Alexander the Great, Iranian aristocracies had retreated to the peripheries of the Hellenistic world in reaction to the upsurge of Greek *philoi* at the imperial centre and their own subsequent exclusion from it. From c. 200 BCE they returned. The importance of local rulers increased following the imperial re-organisations of Antiochos III, and that may well be connected with Antiochos' difficulties in curtailing the power of the *philoi*. Representatives of dynastic households from Bithynia, Kappadokia, Pontos, Armenia, Kommagene and Baktria must at any rate have been present in the Seleukid household at various moments in time; likewise, in the broad stretches of the outer court during the grand events of the court (weddings, inaugurations, anniversaries, festivals), there must have been delegates of many dynasts and kings unconnected through kinship with the imperial family. Such people, I would tentatively suggest, helped secure the loyalty of provincial aristocracies and were the key to the Seleukids' access to the military resources of the Middle East, whereas the *philoi*, as a *civic* social group, secured the loyalty of cities and access to *capital*. Analysis of Seleukid relations with provincial aristocracies and dynasties in relation to the empire's military apparatus may lead, I would suggest, to a better understanding of the Seleukid empire and its place in Near Eastern history than would a new investigation of the formal 'institutions' of the Seleukid 'state', or yet another study focusing in continuities and discontinuities from the Achaemenid to the Hellenistic period.

In sum: the *philoi* may have been predominantly Greek and Hellenised *polis*-people after all – *not* because people of other ethnic affiliations were absent from the courts, but because non-Greek, non-civic courtiers were attached to the royal households by other means than *philia*.

6 Royal Pages

A remarkable group of people at the royal household, attested for the courts of all the Macedonian kingdoms, are the royal pages (*basilikoi paides*). They formed an age group consisting of youths between about their fourteenth and eighteenth years, recruited among the sons of nobles, including the king's own sons. The common Greek term is βασιλικοὶ (δὲ) παῖδες or simply παῖδες; Curtius and Livy translate literally as *regii pueri*.[1] Because it was their duty to guard the king, Alexander's pages are sometimes referred to as 'bodyguards'.[2]

The royal pages were educated and trained at court, where they had the task of waiting on the king and guarding him. It was originally an Argead institution, continued in the kingdoms of the Antigonids, Seleukids and Ptolemies.[3] Berve, with characteristic disdain for the 'oriental' nature of the Hellenistic kingdoms, disputes the continuation of the institution because 'es scheint [nicht] glaublich, dass diese eng makedonische, durchaus philippische Institution unverändert, gleichsam als Fremdkörper, in die neue Herrschaft übernommen ward';[4] but the distinct Macedonian character, I would argue, makes this all the more plausible. There is some evidence that a similar institution existed for girls at the Ptolemaic court – Polybios mentions 'some young girls who had been the σύντροφοι (i.e. who had grown up together) of Arsinoë',

---

[1] Alternative designations are *puerorum regia cohors* (Curt. 10.7.16) and *nobiles pueri* (10.5.8).

[2] Diod. 17.65.1: σωματοφυλακιαι; Curt. 5.1.42: *custodia corporis*.

[3] Curt. 8.6.6. Evidence for continuation under the Diadochs: among others, Curt. 10.8.3; Diod. 28.3, 29.5; 19.91.4; Plut., *Eum.* 3.5; cf. Billows 1997: 246–50. At the Ptolemaic court: Polyb. 15.33.11; cf. Mooren 1975: 2–7 and 52–80; Fraser I: 101–2; Herman 1980/1: 103–49. At the Seleukid court: Polyb. 5.82.13; 30.25.17; 31.21.2; 2 Macc. 9.29; cf. Bevan 1902: 283–4; Bickerman 1938: 38; Habicht 1958. At the Antigonid court: Polyb. 15.33.11; Liv. 44.43.5; 45.6.7–8. Mithradatic court: Plut., *Pomp.* 36.4.

[4] Berve I: 39; Kienast 1971, too, assumed that the institution was copied from the Achaemenids.

and the Grand Procession of Ptolemy Philadelphos included 500 παιδίσκαι ('young girls') dressed in purple *chitons* with gold girdles.[5]

Although the institution of *basilikoi paides* had its roots in pre-Hellenistic Macedon, the education of these youths, whose age corresponds to that of ephebes in Hellenistic Greek cities, was also in keeping with current Greek educational practices, namely *paideia* and *ephēbeia*. The age of *paides* and ephebes varied from place to place. In late classical Athens, *paides* were roughly between 12 and 17 years old and ephebes between c. 18 and 20. In the course of the Hellenistic age a more distinct distinction between primary and secondary education evolved, civilian *paides* being usually under 14 years old, and ephebes between 14 and 18. Intellectual education for girls, too, became more common among civic elites. Ex-ephebes were called *neoi*, '(young) adults', and a corresponding aulic title, *neaniskos*, is attested for the Ptolemaic courtier and poet Kallimachos, a scion of a leading family of Kyrene, who made his literary debut when he was a νεανίσκος τες αυλες,[6] unless of course that means that Kallimachos was a 'debutant' at the Ptolemaic court.

Pages were important for the court for three reasons: because, as hostages, their presence at court was a means to control the nobility; because at court they could be brought up as loyal adherents of the dynasty; and because kings often recruited their principal collaborators among the men with whom they themselves had been trained as pages – their boyhood friends, so to speak (see Chapter 6).

RECRUITMENT AND ORGANISATION

At the Argead court, especially under Alexander, *basilikoi paides* were young aristocrats of the Macedonian *hetairoi* class, who possessed horses and whose prerogative it was to carry weapons.[7] In the Macedonian kingdoms that came after Alexander, *basilikoi paides* were present at the courts, but we know very little about them. All that is certain is that the king's own children, too, were *basilikoi paides* during their adolescence. It is not known on what grounds other boys were recruited into the pages' corps. Were they only the sons of powerful courtiers in the entourage of the king, or did they also come from leading families in the provinces and

[5] Polyb. 15.33.11; Ath. 200e. For the Grand Procession see below, Chapter 8.
[6] Cameron 1995: 3–5.
[7] Curt. 5.1.42; 8.6.2–3; 10.5.8, 8.4; Arr., *Anab.* 4.13.1, 16.6; Diod. 17.65.1; 19.27.3, 29.5; Val. Max. 3.3 *ext.* 1. cf. Diod. 17.79.5.

families of foreign *xenoi*? Nor is it possible to determine whether non-Macedonian and non-Greek magnates sent their sons to court, as one would expect particularly in the Seleukid empire. It would have been an excellent way to create bonds between indigenous princely dynasties and the Seleukid house, and given the widespread practice of dispatching sons as hostages it seems most likely that it happened. One isolated attestation concerns Mithradates, the son of Ariobarzanes, an Iranian prince in the entourage of Antigonos Monophthalmos. He had been a 'youth companion' (i.e. a royal page) of the king's son Demetrios.[8]

In 331 the pages' corps that was with the king consisted of 200 youths, a number analogous to that of the *ilai* (units of 200 men) and of the companion cavalry; they were subdivided into four units of fifty youths each.[9] When in 331 a fresh levy was sent from Macedon to Alexander in Babylon, the pages marched eastward in a squadron of fifty.[10] Hammond argued (against the opinion of Berve) that this was the first time that pages arrived in Alexander's army camp; however, the royal pages were as a rule educated at court, and Alexander's army camp *was* the court.[11]

In 322, shortly after Alexander's death, Eumenes of Kardia had 200 pages with him, and at the battle of Paraitakene in 317 he fielded them subdivided into two squadrons of fifty pages each, against his opponent Antigonos Monophthalmos' three such units; both commanders kept the pages close to their own persons as guards of honour.[12] In the Grand Procession of Ptolemy Philadelphos marched 1,600 *paides*, dressed in white *chitons* and adorned with *stephanoi* made of ivy and pine.[13] Much later, in the military parade staged by Antiochos IV at Daphne in c. 165 BCE, 600 royal pages were present.[14]

DUTIES AND RESPONSIBILITIES

Detailed information concerning the pages' duties is readily available, but only for the court of Alexander the Great. Because of the so-called Pages' Conspiracy, an attempt to murder Alexander in

---

[8] Plut., *Demetr.* 4.1: παῖς ἑταῖρος. This Mithradates, an ancestor of Mithradates Eupator, later founded the royal dynasty of Pontos; cf. Bosworth and Wheatley 1998.
[9] Diod. 19.28.3 and 19.29.5. See Hammond 1989: 56 with n. 24.
[10] Diod. 17.65.1; Curt. 5.1.42.
[11] Hammond 1990: 265–6; *contra* Berve I: 37.
[12] Diod. 19.27.3 and 29.5.
[13] Ath. 5.200a.
[14] Polyb. 30.25.17; cf. Walbank III: 611.

327 BCE, the institution of *basilikoi paides* at the later Argead court has received ample treatment by Alexander's biographers, particularly Arrian and Curtius.[15] The classic text is Curtius 8.6.2–6:

> It was the custom for the Macedonian nobility to entrust their grown-up sons to the kings for the performance of duties comparable to the services of slaves. They took turns keeping watch at night at the door of the king's bedchamber, and let in his women through an entrance other than that watched by the armed guards. They also took the king's horses from the grooms and presented them for the king to mount; they accompanied him in the hunt and in battle; and they were educated in all aspects of the liberal arts. They regarded it as a great honour that they were allowed to wait on the king at his table.[16] No one had the right to flog them save the king. This fellowship formed, as it were, a training school for the commanders and officials of the Macedonians, and from it came the kings whose descendants many generations later lost all their power to the Romans.[17]

Arrian says that it was Philip II who first created a pages' corps:

> [Philip] was the first who ordered that the sons of Macedonian nobles who had reached the age of *paides* should be sent to the royal court; and besides general attendance on his person, the duty of guarding him when he was asleep had been entrusted to them.[18]

On the basis of this passage, modern historians have assumed that Philip copied the practice from the Achaemenid court, where according to Xenophon a similar institution existed.[19] However, as Bevan noted, such an institution might easily have started in any monarchic state.[20] Indeed, there is evidence for the presence of pages in pre-Hellenistic Macedon dating back to the late fifth century BCE.[21] Hammond explains Arrian's claim by suggesting that Philip established 'the final form for the school' but that it was 'invented' much earlier. This surely makes sense. It remains questionable, however,

---

[15] Evidence for royal pages at the Argead court is collected in Hammond 1990; cf. Hammond 1994: 40–4; Heckel 1992: 237–98. For the Pages' Conspiracy see Bosworth 1993: 118. I was not able to consult Carney 2008.

[16] *Praecipuus honor habebatur quod licebat sedentibus*, literally 'were allowed to sit'; see, however, Cameron 1995: 83 n. 82: 'But the King and his Friends *reclined*. The point is that pages *sat* while their elders reclined. Only adult males were allowed to recline.' See Errington 1983: 92: 'It may indeed be correct that it was normal Macedonian practice that youths sat at table until they had proved themselves in the fashion approved by their society (*viz.* killing a boar without a net): also in other parts of the Greek world, it seems, it was normal practice for the sons and women of the house to sit at meals while the men reclined'; cf. Xen., *Symp.* 1.8; Lucian, *Symp.* 13; *Asinus* 2.

[17] Curt. 8.6.1–6; cf. 5.1.42; 8.6.4; 10.8.4; Arr., *Anab.* 4.13.1; Liv. 44.43.5.

[18] Arr., *Anab.* 4.13.1; cf. Curt. 8.6.2.

[19] Xen., *Cyr.* 8.6.10 and *Anab.* 4.13.1; references to modern literature in Hammond 1990: 261 n. 2.

[20] Bevan 1902 I: 123; see the additional arguments advanced by Briant 1994: 298–302.

[21] Collected in Hammond 1990: 261–4; cf. Hammond 1989: 56 with nn. 22 and 23.

whether the institution was ever wilfully invented at all. It is more likely that it developed from a traditional form of fosterage that gradually became institutionalised, although of course it never became a 'school' in the modern sense.[22]

Royal pages had military duties, too. At Alexander's court they served as the king's bodyguards and safeguarded his personal belongings.[23] When on guard duty, the pages were under the command of one of the seven *sōmatophulakes*.[24] They rode with the king in battle and during the hunt, thereby acquiring military experience.[25]

EDUCATION

The king's sons and the other pages received an education under the supervision of a court dignitary usually called *tropheus*, 'foster-father', at the Seleukid and Ptolemaic courts. The office of *tropheus* was already a position of great honour at the court of Philip II.[26] After their accession to the throne, kings normally held their former *tropheus* in high esteem, addressing him as 'father' in official correspondence.[27] An interesting case is that of the eunuch Krateros, a courtier of the Seleukid king Antiochos IX. Krateros had been the king's *tropheus* and was honoured by his former pupil with an impressive series of aulic offices and honorific titles. The base of a statue of Krateros found in Delos, perhaps his native city, honours him as 'foster-father of Antiochos Philopator; first friend of King Antiochos; chief physician and chamberlain of the queen'.[28] The *paides* who were brought up with the king were afterwards honoured as the king's *suntrophoi*, or foster-brothers, and they addressed one another as 'brother'.

The *tropheus* was the leader, not the teacher, of the pages. Learned

---

[22] Hammond 1989: 56: 'The School resembled in many ways the traditional "public boarding school", as it was in England and Scotland in 1850–1930.' Cf. Berve I: 38, claiming that the public flogging of Hermolaos demonstrated Alexander's 'erzieherisches Verständniss für den jugendlichen Sinn'.

[23] Curt. 8.6.21; 10.8.3; Arr., *Anab.* 4.13.1–4; Diod. 17.65.1, 79.5.

[24] Curt. 8.6.22; Arr., *Anab.* 4.13.7.

[25] Arr., *Anab.* 4.13.1–2, 16.6; Curt. 5.1.42; 8.8.3; Diod. 16.93.4; 19.27.3, 29.5. Cf. Chankowski 2004, stressing the effective military role played by aristocratic ephebes in the defence of cities and on the battlefield.

[26] Plut., *Alex.* 5.

[27] Polyb. 31.20.3; Plut., *Ant.* 5.31; *OGIS* 148, 256; 1 Macc. 11.1, 11.31–2; Jos., *AJ* 12.127, 12.148, 13.126–7, 148; Diod. 33.4.1. Cf. Hammond 1989: 57; Berve I: 38; Bevan 1902 II: 283, 302; Bevan 1927: 236.

[28] τροφεὺς Ἀντιόχου Φιλοπάτρος τῶν πρώτων φίλων βασιλέως Ἀντιόχου καὶ ἀρχίατρος καὶ ἐπὶ τοῦ κοιτῶνος τῆς βασιλίσσησ (*RIG* no. 1158); Krateros is mentioned also by App., *Syr.* 68; Jos., *AJ* 13.271; Eus. 1.257; Porphyrios, *FGrH* 260 F20.

men and other skilled professionals were appointed as tutors to train
the pages in multifarious skills. The education was both physical and
intellectual. The royal princes and young nobles were prepared for
their later tasks as military commanders, as well as trained in all the
liberal arts.[29] This was already the case at the Argead court.[30] The
noticeable progress of educational practices for the children of elite
families in Hellenistic Greek cities may have been influenced by
developments at the courts; in the Hellenistic cities, Greek *paideia*
was regarded as the essential badge of Greekness, and educational
institutions, in particular the gymnasion, were thought necessary to
maintain, or assert, Greek identity.[31] The curriculum known to have
been taught to elite children in the cities included philosophy, literature, writing, recitation and sometimes music and the writing of
verse, as well as various forms of athletic activities. The best-known
example of such a teacher is of course Aristotle, who was invited to
the court of Philip II when Alexander had reached the age of thirteen
and his education with the other pages began. Aristotle taught the
pages mainly philosophy and politics.[32] Aristotle was not a *tropheus*,
nor was he Alexander's only teacher, and his influence on Alexander
should not be overestimated. Alexander's foster-father was Leonidas,
a kinsman of his mother Olympias.[33] It was not exceptional that
Alexander was educated by a tutor of such standing as Aristotle,
or that as an adult Alexander appeared as a man of learning who
enjoyed the works of poets like Telestos and Philoxenos, discussed
atomic theory with Anaxarchos, and quoted Homer.[34] Kassandros,
the son of Antipatros, who had been a page with Alexander, knew
the *Iliad* by heart too.[35] Later kings, too, did their best to attract
intellectuals of renown to their courts to tutor the princes and
other pages. Thus, Alexander himself appointed Aristotle's pupil
Kallisthenes as the tutor of the pages at his own court. Ptolemaic
pages received their intellectual education from the scholars who
worked in the Museum of Alexandria, and this may well have been
the principal reason why this institution, and similar institutions
in the other kingdoms, was founded.[36] The pages at the court of
Ptolemy Soter were educated by, among others, Strato, and at the

[29] Carney 2003a; Clarke 1971; Cribiore 2001.
[30] Curt. 5.1.42 and 8.6.4.
[31] OCD p. 508.
[32] Plut., *Alex.* 7.
[33] Plut., *Alex.* 5.
[34] Poetry: Plut., *Alex.* 8. Atomism: Diog. Laert. 9.60–3; cf. Plut., *Alex.* 28.
[35] Ath. 620.
[36] *P.Oxy* 1241; cf. Fraser I: 330–3; Green 1990: 86 with nn. 27 and 28.

court of Ptolemy Philadelphos by Aristarchos, Apollonios and perhaps Kallimachos.[37] Antigonos Gonatas brought the Stoic philosopher Persaios to his court to tutor his children and the pages too. Moreover, prominent representatives of major philosophical schools, including Aristotle, Zeno and Kleanthes, wrote treatises on the art of kingship for the benefit of kings' sons. Some sons of kings were even sent abroad for higher education after their training as a page had ended, although this was also a means to keep them away from court when a brother had been selected for the succession. Thus, Antigonos Gonatas was educated by Zeno in Athens; Antiochos Grypos, too, studied in Athens as a youth; the Attalids perhaps sent their sons to Rhodes for further study.[38]

FOSTER-BROTHERS OF THE KING

Even if royal pages really were 'quasi-hostages for their fathers' good behaviour',[39] it will have been an honour above anything else to have one's son educated at the royal household, where he would be a personal valet of the present king, and perhaps become a foster-brother and companion of the future king. Conversely, it was prestigious for a king, too, to be served and guarded not by mere servants and soldiers, but by the sons of nobles. Pages furthermore revealed the magnitude of a king's power, since by putting their sons under the care of the king the fathers implicitly acknowledged his sovereignty.

Bringing up the children of powerful men at court, under the custody of the king, cut off from their families, was a means to create a loyal elite and to shape noble identity.[40] Loyalty was an obligation of honour not easily broken. The pages, together with their commanding *sōmatophulax*, were entrusted with guarding Alexander's bedchamber when he was asleep, and this may be precisely why the conspiracy of the pages (and only some of them) at the court of Alexander was considered such a grave misdeed. After the catastrophic defeat of Perseus in the battle of Pydna, the pages were the last to remain loyal to the king.[41]

Kings therefore often promoted as their closest collaborators their

[37] Meillier 1979: 9–21.
[38] App., *Syr.* 68; Polyb. 31.31.
[39] Grainger 1992: 6.
[40] Duindam 1994: 30; see more generally Brown 2000: 309–56, contending that group membership is perhaps the most important source of an individual's social identity.
[41] Liv. 45.6.7–8.

former fellow-pages. Conversely, it was natural for nobles to support the candidate for the throne coming from their own peer group. As *suntrophoi*, 'foster-brothers', they were bound to each other by strong mutual moral obligations for life. The dependence of Alexander on Hephaistion was proverbial.[42] An identical friendship existed between Antiochos the Great and his trusted youth companion Antipatros, a Macedonian *suntrophos* of his who was one of the most powerful members of the Seleukid court during Antiochos' entire reign.[43] His career is an interesting one, as one of the few Hellenistic courtiers whose history we can follow to some extent. Antipatros commanded the prestigious right flank in the battles of Raphia[44] and, almost thirty years later, Magnesia (together with the young crown prince Seleukos).[45] This bears witness to the exceptional trust the king put in him: it is notable that Antiochos III continuously reshuffled the power relations at his court.[46] Antipatros was also present as a cavalry commander at the battle of Panion in 200.[47] In 217 he led an embassy to Ptolemy IV to negotiate peace after the Seleukid defeat at Raphia.[48] In 190 he was sent with Zeuxis to Sardis to negotiate peace with the Romans, with a mandate to accept terms in the name of the king,[49] and later led an embassy to Rome to ratify the treaty of Apameia.[50] Livy's claim that Antipatros was 'the son of Antiochos' brother' (Seleukos III) is a mistranslation of Polybios' *adelphos*, a form of fictive kinship and an honorific title.[51] This of course does not *exclude* the possibility that Antipatros and Antiochos were related; the name Antipatros is after all suggestive of Macedonian ethnicity. But the assumption that Antipatros was a son of Antiochos' older brother and predecessor as king is highly implausible: that would have given Antipatros a better title to the throne than Antiochos himself had – not exactly the man whom the king would have made second-in-command of the army. The fact that Polybios nowhere in book 5 recounts how Antipatros became a member of the court (as he does for all other leading friends of Antiochos), and the long time span of Antipatros' collaboration with

---

[42] Hephaistion grew up with Alexander (Curt. 3.12.16; cf. Ps.-Kallisthenes 1.18; Jul. Valer. 1.10) and was of about the same age (Curt 3.12.16).

[43] Polyb. 5.79.12: βασιλέως ἀδελφοὺς, and 5.87.1: ἀδελφοὺς.

[44] Polyb. 5.79.12; cf. 5.82.9.

[45] Liv. 37.41.1.

[46] For the development of the court of Antiochos the Great see Strootman 2011a.

[47] Polyb. 16.18.7.

[48] Polyb. 5.87.1.

[49] Polyb. 21.7.9, 16.4; Liv. 37.45.5–6.

[50] Liv. 37.51.10, 55.3; 56.8.

[51] Liv. 37.41.1; 37.55.3; *pace* Bevan 1902 II: 109 and 111.

Antiochos, leave little room for doubt that he was of the same age as the king and thus presumably had been a page with him, as the designation *adelphos* also implies. Antipatros may therefore have been among the group of friends of the king who plotted with him against Hermeias.[52]

On the other hand, the institution of the corps of *basilikoi paides* may also have endangered the personal domination of the king over his court. If the *paides* were indeed (in part) the sons of *philoi*, the page system was tantamount to the emergence of a hereditary aristocracy at the royal courts, and thus may have gradually undermined the kings' freedom in choosing their friends. In the next chapter the restraints on, and threats to, the king's absolute power at court will be further discussed, as well as the instruments used by kings to try and keep court society under control.

[52] Polyb. 5.56.13.

7 *Social Dynamics*

Political leaders must follow their followers ... History and theory suggest that followers create leaders rather than the converse.

Murray Edelman, *Constructing the Political Spectacle*

In this chapter the significance of *philia* (ritualised friendship) and *xenia* ('guest-friendship') for court society will be examined. It will be argued that gift-exchange was the principal mechanism underlying social relations at court. It will furthermore be argued that the bestowment of honorific titles and aulic offices on *philoi* was part of this same complex of conspicuous gift-exchange. The main thrust of the argument is that kings never had absolute power over their courts at their disposal, and that their control in the course of time even decreased; kings therefore constantly needed to develop new instruments of power to control their courts and thereby their kingdoms.

GUEST-FRIENDSHIP (*XENIA*) AND THE COURT

As we have seen, royal *philoi* had their origins in a wide range of Greek cities. They often came even from beyond the empires' boundaries. An explanation of this perhaps remarkable fact has been offered by Gabriel Herman by expounding the interrelation of *philia* and *xenia*.[1] According to Herman, the Greek tradition of *xenia* (or *philoxenia*) – a form of ritualised personal relationships with traits of fictive kinship, usually translated as 'guest-friendship' – constituted supranational, 'horizontal' elite networks linking men of approximately equal social status but of separate social units, i.e. *poleis*, thus uniting the Greek world at its highest level. It was an

---

[1] Herman 1987.

aristocratic ideal, an archaic legacy.[2] Through participation in a
social sphere outside the city, civic elites distanced themselves from
their inferiors. With the renewal of class distinctions in the Hellenistic *poleis*, the significance of *xenia* increased. It is worth quoting
the summary of Herman's argument in full, as it also sheds light on
the preponderance of Greek culture at the courts of the Ptolemies,
Seleukids and Antigonids:

> Many of the courtiers ... were recruited through the instrumentality of
> *xenia*, an ancient form of fictive kinship ... The Hellenistic rulers ... availed
> themselves of pre-existing *xenia* networks to draw new allies into their orbit.
> These networks account not only for the preponderance of Greeks among
> the newly recruited Hellenistic court members, but also for the increasing
> similarities between the three courts. The Hellenistic court societies, then,
> did not operate *in vacuo*. Instead, they were part of a wider, interactive,
> international society of ritualized friends. This society had since time imme-
> morial constituted a world of its own, binding together the social elites of the
> Greek world through upper-class ideals ... As a first step towards under-
> standing Hellenistic 'court politics', one should therefore explore the relation
> between court societies and friendship networks.[3]

A king's personal or inherited paternal *xenia* network provided him
with means to attract from outside settled court circles *philoi* who
did not yet possess a power base at the court, but whose families
were influential within their own cities. This had an additional
advantage, since the *philoi* normally retained links with their
families and cities of origin, presumably through several generations.[4] 'Having turned royal officials, these members of governing
élites are often found to be acting as mediators between the kings
and their own communities of origin, deriving substantial benefits
from both systems.'[5] Two interesting examples of the geographical
range of aristocratic *xenia* in the Hellenistic age are provided by the
third-century Spartan kings Leonidas and Kleomenes. Leonidas had
lived 'in the palaces of satraps' and was married to the daughter of
a Seleukid *philos*.[6] Kleomenes, after having been driven from Sparta,
went to Alexandria with his followers and stayed at the court of

---

[2] Φιλοξενία as an aristocratic ideal goes back to the world of Homer, and is prominent
especially in the *Odyssey*; see Scott 1982; Van Wees 1992: 44–8.
[3] Herman 1997: 208.
[4] Savalli-Lestrade 1996; Muccioli 2001. In cities we find both honorific decrees for kings
dedicated by *philoi* (e.g. *OGIS* 128, 171 and 255) and decrees in honor of *philoi* dedicated by
the king (e.g. *Syll.*[3] 462; Welles 1934: no. 45; *OGIS* 317; cf. Buraselis 1994: 20; Habicht 1958:
11–12). For a different view see O'Neil 2006: 20: 'We cannot assume that all these men had
an active connection with their home cities.'
[5] Herman 1996: 613. On *philoi* as mediators between king and cities see also Bringmann
1993: 7–24 and Savalli-Lestrade 1996.
[6] Plut., *Agis* 10; cf. 3.

Ptolemy III, who gave him an annual pension of twenty-four talents; Kleomenes used that money largely to distribute gifts among his own clients.[7]

This web of relations bound the empires together, as the Greek *poleis*, being de jure and normally also de facto autonomous states within the imperial framework, were the cornerstones of imperial rule. Kings could influence civic politics through their *philoi*. Their families or adherents in the cities benefited indirectly from royal favour; this gave them an advantage over other families' factions in the internal political struggles of the cities.[8] Thus, the *philoi* were able to represent the interests of the cities at court, and the interests of the court in the cities.

PHILIA

Courtiers were called 'friends of the king', or simply 'friends', because that is precisely what they were.[9] Various forms of dependence tied the courtiers to the king and vice versa, but the principal arrangement underlying the relationship was *philia*, the Greek moral complex of friendship.

In modern scholarship it is often taken for granted that *philia* at a royal court is at odds with the autocratic nature of Hellenistic kingship; 'royal' *philia*, it is commonly assumed, has to be fundamentally different from what the ideal of *philia* meant to the classical Greeks. Thus, David Konstan maintained that the *philia* between Hellenistic *philoi tou basileōs* and the ruler was 'less personal and affectionate, more formal and calculated than the classical ideal', and dismisses aulic *philia* as 'a striking instance of the application of the language of friendship to distinctly hierarchical relations between people of different social station' – itself a striking instance of the late twentieth-century apprehension of the Hellenistic era as a period of cultural and moral decline. Gabriel Herman also takes the absolutism of Hellenism more or less for granted, though in a very nuanced manner, assuming that, although *philia* may have lain at the root of the relationships at court, 'the basic obligations of friendship [ultimately] came to be superseded by obligations of service'.[10]

---

[7] Plut., *Cleom.* 32.3.

[8] See e.g. Polyb. 21.6.2–6.

[9] See Musti 1984: 179. Personal ties between king and friends: Mooren 1998: 124 with n. 12.

[10] Konstan 1997: 121; Herman 1987: 164. Cf. Walbank 1984a: 70. Cf. Smith Pangle 2002, discarding Aristotle's understanding of *philia* as potentially an aspect of monarchic relations because of the author's conviction that would be incompatible with the inherent equality of *philia*.

However, *philia* at royal courts, I would argue, was not more formal than genuine Greek *philia*, and mutual obligations and the *ideal* of equality determined *philia* relations at court too.

Philia may be defined as a personal, reciprocal bond of loyalty and solidarity between two or more individuals of approximately equal status who shared roughly the same interests; they were committed to each other by mutual obligations, and could rely on each other for help.[11] The objective of *philia* was normally to achieve a common goal, and united action towards that end was a means to strengthen and display the bond; by means of exchanging gifts and favours (*charites*) the friendship was kept alive.[12] Though *philia* may indeed not have been 'a subjective bond of affection and emotional warmth', as Heath defined it, neither was it an 'entirely objective bond of reciprocal obligations',[13] because loyalty between friends was regulated by morality and honour. Konstan defines *philia* as

> a mutually intimate, loyal and loving bond between two or a few persons that is understood not to derive primarily from membership in a group normally marked by native solidarity, such as family, tribe, or other such ties. Friendship is thus what anthropologists call an achieved rather than an ascribed relationship, the latter being based on status whereas the former is in principle independent of a prior formal connection such as kinship.[14]

However, achieved and ascribed relationships cannot be dissociated radically since *philia* can intensify solidarity between members of a pre-existing social group, as much as ethnic or social ties can strengthen *philia* ties, too. Violation of friendship was considered highly dishonourable, even impious.[15]

Kings, too, were subject to the obligations of *philia*. Diodoros relates how the Sicilian ruler Agathokles was punished by the divine powers that be because he had murdered a man who was his *philos* and *xenos*.[16] Traitors and rebels were severely punished when caught, their bodies dehumanised through mutilation, dismemberment and the refusal of proper burial; this happened notoriously with the rebel Achaios after he had been captured by Antiochos III: 'At the subsequent meeting of the *sunedrion*, there were many proposals as to the proper punishment to inflict on Achaios, and it was decided to lop off in the first place the unhappy prince's

[11] Goldhill 1986: 82.
[12] Herman 1996; Konstan 1997: 78. See also Scott 1982, characterising Homeric *philia* as 'based on self-interest but wholly co-operative in action'.
[13] Heath 1987: 73–4.
[14] Konstan 1997: 1.
[15] Belfiore 2000.
[16] Diod. 20.70–3–4; cf. Herman 1996: 612.

extremities, and then, after cutting off his head and sewing it up in an ass's skin, to impale his body.'[17]

Like *xenia*, *philia* had traits of fictive kinship.[18] Some royal *philoi* were honoured in inscriptions as the *sungeneis* or *adelphoi*, 'relatives' and 'brothers', of the king, even if they were not really related to him.[19] Equality is an aristocratic ideal, also known from Homeric and archaic Greece.[20] In the *Iliad* it is said that a good friend is 'in no way less than a brother'.[21] This reminds one of Aristotle's dictum that a *philos* is 'one's other self', which in turn is reminiscent of the famous anecdote, related by Curtius, in which Alexander exclaimed that Hephaistion 'is Alexander too'.[22] In other words, the parties involved in a *philia* relationship were ideally each other's equals, even when in actuality they were not.[23]

To sum up: *philia* at the royal courts had two functions. First, it was instrumental in creating unity by stressing that the *philoi* immediately surrounding the king belonged to the same status group and were ideally each other's peers. Second, it created a sense of accord which in turn facilitated collective action.

Patronage relations at the Hellenistic courts were characterised by obligations of loyalty and what may be called 'fictive equality'.[24] Like the companions in Alexander's council, the foremost *philoi* who had a seat in the *sunedrion* of a Hellenistic king discussed matters of state with him, often openly holding a view against the king's opinion.[25] Hierarchy within the *philoi* society at court was created

[17] Polyb. 8.21.2–3.
[18] Herman 1996: 611; the word φιλία can also signify actual blood relationship.
[19] Polyb. 4.48.5; Plut., *Mor.* 197a; 1 Macc. 3.32; 10.89; 11.31; 2 Macc. 11.12; *OGIS* 148; 259; cf. Liv. 30.42.6. In classical Athens συγγένεια connoted all blood relatives, within and without the *oikos*, and was distinguished from ἀγχιστεία (literally 'closest'), which was limited to blood relatives up to cousins.
[20] See Van Wees 1992: 45, who contrasts the hierarchy of the pre-Hellenistic courts in the Near East with the egalitarian ideology of the *Odyssey*.
[21] *Il.* 8.584–6. For *hetaireia* and *philia* as aristocratic ideals in Homeric epic see Scott 1982; Van Wees 1992: 44–8.
[22] Arist., *Eth.Nic.* 1169b 6; Curt. 3.12.17.
[23] Equality of friends in a *philia* relationship: Herman 1996: 611; Heath 1987: 74; Konstan 1997: 97.
[24] Patronage in itself can be defined as 'a political system based on personal relationships between unequals, between leaders (or patrons) and their followers (or clients). Each party has something to offer to the other. Clients offer patrons their political support and also their deference ... For their part, patrons offer clients hospitality, jobs and protection' (Burke 1992: 72). See, however, the objections to such a definition raised by Silverman 1977 and Gilsenan 1977.
[25] *Pace* Konstan 1997: 121. On the *sunedrion* see below. Note that the old Macedonian institution of companions of the king was named after a term, ἑταιρεία, designating a (political) confraternity too (Herman 1996: 611); the companions and the Macedonian king belonged to the same peer group in which the king was *primus inter pares* (though a strong king could of course in practice be more equal than his peers). Cf. Arist., *Pol.* 5.9.6, comparing

by various informal dynamics, to be discussed in the following sections.

HIERARCHY

As a social group, the *philoi* society at court was defined by the ideal of equality. At the same time, the *philoi* community was in reality hierarchical. Since the king was the focus for all aspects of the court society, a courtier's relative status was determined by the principle of proximity to the throne, or 'favour', that is, the degree to which he was able to gain access to the person of the king, or to persons near the king, or to persons near the persons near the king.[26] Gift-exchange, court titulature and etiquette were instrumental in determining a courtier's position within the subtle hierarchy of the court:

> Charges were brought against Menelaos about this incident. When the king [Antiochos Epiphanes] came to Tyros, three men sent by the council [of Jerusalem] presented the case before him … But Menelaos, already as good as beaten, promised a substantial gift to Ptolemaios son of Dorymenos to win over the king. Therefore Ptolemaios, taking the king aside into a colonnade as if for refreshment, induced the king to change his mind.[27]

In what follows, several aspects of the principle of proximity to the throne will be discussed. Specifically, we will look at gift-exchange as a mechanism for constructing social relations at court, the more or less formalised complex of aulic titles, membership of the royal council, and other status determinants. In *Die höfische Gesellschaft*, Norbert Elias listed what he believed to be the determinants of status at court.[28] Although many of Elias' views have in later research been adjusted, this particular inventory still holds good. Elias distinguishes the following status determinants: family prestige, wealth (possessed and received), rank, military achievements, the king's favour, and the ability to influence powerful persons (dignitaries, but also e.g. concubines of the king), membership of a certain clique, *esprit*, courtly behaviour and outward appearance. We will have to keep these mechanisms in mind when examining social behaviour at the Hellenistic courts.

---

the relationship between a king and his common subjects to the authority of a father over his children, i.e. an unequal relationship, while in *Eth. Eud.* 7.4.1–2 it is stated that a father–son relationship is *not* a form of *philia*.

[26] For the importance of 'access' and 'favour' see Starkey 1977 and Winterling 2004.

[27] 2 Macc. 4.43–7.

[28] Elias 1969: 153.

PROXIMITY TO THE THRONE AND THE ROLE OF BROKERS

In absolutist monarchies, kings attempted to regulate access to their own persons as an instrument to control the dynamics of court life. The Hellenistic monarchies were no exception to the rule. The king was distanced from other humans in terms of space and time: in space because people wishing to meet the king had to overcome various physical barriers before being able to address him, or were only allowed to see him from a distance; in time because people were forced to wait to see him.

The fact that most people could not approach the king, at least not directly, accentuated the privilege of those few individuals who did have routine access, such as the most prominent courtiers, the queen, the king's concubines, his personal physician or body-guards.[29] These individuals could act as mediators, or 'brokers', between the king and others.[30] Pyrrhos the Molossian, who as a young man stayed at the court of Ptolemy Soter as a hostage, 'culti-vated Berenike in particular, seeing that she was the most influential and the most virtuous and intelligent of the wives of Ptolemy'.[31] Diodoros, probably drawing from Hieronymos of Kardia, tells how in 316 Dokimos, a partisan of Eumenes, was captured by Antigonos Monophthalmos but made a dramatic escape by negotiating with Antigonos' wife Stratonike; he later rose to high office in Antigonos' army.[32] Josephus relates how a century later a certain Joseph, an aristocrat from Jerusalem, travelled to the Ptolemaic court to obtain certain privileges for his family: '[He] privately sent many presents to the king, and to [queen] Kleopatra, and to their friends, and to all that were powerful at court, and thereby purchased their goodwill to himself.'[33] Finally a meeting with the king was arranged by the queen. While Ptolemy was travelling from Memphis to Alexandria, Joseph waited along the road at a place agreed upon in advance, was invited into the royal carriage, and was given restricted time to convince the king: 'With his amusing and clever conversation he

[29] See for instance Diod. 30.10.2; Polyb. 5.26.8, 5.56.7; Jos., *AJ* 12.17–32. On physicians at the Hellenistic courts see Marasco 1996; Mastrocinque 1995.
[30] The key role of 'brokers' in patron–client relations was first recognised by Wolf 1956; cf. Kettering 1986; Burke 1992: 74; Duindam 1994: 86; Strootman 2005c: 192–3.
[31] Plut., *Pyrrh.* 4.
[32] Diod. 19.16; cf. Hornblower 1981: 125–8. Jones 1992: 94 comments that 'it is a likely suggestion that [Dokimos] betrayed his companions in return for a promise of advantage in the service of Antigonos'.
[33] Jos., *AJ* 12.185. Further examples of mediators arranging meetings with Hellenistic kings can be found in Jos., *AJ* 14.11.1 and Polyb. 8.18.10.

made a good impression on the king, who began to like him, and he was invited for dinner at the palace, as a guest at the royal table.'[34] Josephus also relates of the same queen how, when a man called Arion was thrown in jail although he was innocent, his wife 'informed Kleopatra of this … (for Arion was in great esteem with her), [and] Kleopatra informed the king of it'.[35]

GIFT-EXCHANGE

The principal instrumentality in creating and maintaining bonds between king and *philoi* was the exchange of gifts.[36] Gift-exchange was a pivotal element in the ideal of *philia*,[37] and furthermore was tantamount to the royal virtue of generosity, directly related to royal euergetism and the public display of wealth known as *tryphē*. Plutarch later sceptically remarked that 'kings hunt for men by attracting them with gifts and money, and then catch them'.[38] But the opposite also happened – that friends through gifts or services obliged rulers. But let us start with the generosity of the king.

In an encomiastic poem, the court poet Theokritos praises Ptolemy Philadelphos as a man who is 'generous with gifts, as a king befits, generous to cities and loyal friends'.[39] Magnanimity was a crucial component of the Hellenistic ideal of kingship. Kings were obliged to live up to that ideal. In a society where honour depended on appearances and behaviour, giving lavish gifts was a means to attain or confirm superior status. It was a means to demonstrate in a public setting the successful king's unlimited wealth. Royal gifts went out, first of all, to the gods, then to relatives and friends, and finally to cities and temples. Although royal euergetism in cities is at present the best-known and most studied form of royal gift giving, the munificence of Hellenistic kings towards their *philoi* was of equal significance, and more written about by ancient authors.[40]

In anthropological theory, the principal function of gift-exchange is the creation or affirmation of social relations.[41] The exchange of gifts is a reciprocal and normally highly ritualised process. It serves

[34] Jos., *AJ* 12.4.8.
[35] On Josephus' sympathy for Kleopatra III see Haider 1998.
[36] Strootman 2007: 143–8.
[37] Konstan 1997: 4.
[38] Plut., *Cleom.* 13.5.
[39] Theocr., *Id.* 17.124–5; cf. *Id.* 16.32–3.
[40] See for instance Ath. 48f; 49a; Sokrates of Rhodes, *FHG* III 96 *ap.* Ath. 148a; Jos., *AJ* 12.40–1; 12.59; 13.82.
[41] See generally Burke 1992: 69–71.

no economic aim, even though the circulation of goods brought about by it often has significant economic consequences.[42] Claessen in his work on the early state distinguishes four forms of royal gifts: 'gifts' (incidental donations), 'remunerations' (incidental gifts in return for a specific service), 'salary' (regular payment in return for services) and 'offerings' (various gifts to gods, priests or temples).[43] All forms are apparent in the Hellenistic kingdoms. The *philoi*, the people closest to the king, received 'remunerations' in exchange for gifts or as rewards for services, and not a regular salary. Unwritten rules regulated what kind of present was proper in a given context.[44]

The most rewarding gift, in economic as well as social terms, was land. The distribution of landed estates, often including buildings, labourers and slaves, provided the *philoi* with status, as well as a source of income.[45] Estates could be managed *in absento*. Thus Apollonios, the major-domo of Ptolemy Philadelphos' *oikos*, managed his possessions in the Fayum – some 2,500 ha of land, a gift of the king – through his steward, the Karian Zenon, as is well documented by the Zenon Papyri archive. In addition to landed estates, kings could give their friends trading privileges, or the revenues of villages and harbours, and even cities.[46] Thus the requirements of the court provide a partial explanation for the endemic warfare among the Hellenistic kings: territorial gains provided new sources of income and new estates to distribute among the *philoi*, not to mention plunder as a source of wealth for redistribution.[47] The centrality of land distribution in imperial states

[42] Kettering 1986 and 1988; cf. Burke 1992: 74. The influential 'archaic economy' model of the school of Polanyi emphasised the economic aspects of gift-exchange by strictly distinguishing between reciprocity (social) and redistribution (economic), though acknowledging that the latter was essentially a side effect of the first; cf. Dalton 1968: xxxv.

[43] Claessen 1978.

[44] Alexander gave fifty talents to the page who had warned him of a conspiracy (Curt. 8.10.26; cf. 8.6.19); Strato of Lampsakos received no less than eighty talents for tutoring the children of Ptolemy Philadelphos (Diog. Laert. 5.58). cf. Ath. 194a.

[45] Van der Spek 1986: 179–80. Although royal concern with agricultural economy was not unknown in the Seleukid and Ptolemaic empires, Van der Spek shows that land grants were primarily political measures. For gifts of land see e.g. Curt. 8.10.26; Plut., *Alex.* 15.2; 1 Macc. 10.39; Plut., *Pomp.* 36.4. See Hammond 1989: 55. On the difficult legal status and ambiguities of royal land grants consult Van der Spek 1986: 154–61. For some interesting case studies of aristocratic land-holding in Hellenistic Macedon and the northern Aegean see Hatzopoulos 1991 and 1999.

[46] Hammond 1989: 142. Van der Spek 1986: 159 lists several instances of cities given by the Seleukids and others to favourites, including Telmessos, Tarsos and Ptolemais in Palestine; it is difficult to say what this means exactly, but given the formal autonomy of most cities, their 'possession' probably meant a monopoly on levying tolls or taxes; the practice is known too from the Achaemenid kingdom; cf. Sancisi-Weerdenburg 1988.

[47] Plut., *Alex.* 15.3–6; 34.1; *Eum.* 3.14; Just. 11.5.5. Cf. Hatzopoulos 1988. Friends of Antiochos III shared in the war booty and received land grants in Asia Minor (Orth 1977:

explains why empires can grow so rapidly but often collapse spectacularly after one or two generations (though they sometimes re-emerge some generations later). Conquest provides rulers with an abundance of land to distribute among their followers, and thus secure their loyalty. After the initial conquest phase, however, these land-holdings easily become hereditary prerogatives, turning their owners into firmly established elites with provincial power bases, capable of opposing the king. A new king, therefore, must either acquire new lands to distribute in order to create a new group of loyal adherents, or accept the presence of a hereditary courtly elite sharing in the royal power.[48] The Seleukid empire contracted under the successors of Seleukos Nikator but re-emerged as a superpower in the late third century when Antiochos III succeeded in reshaping the social composition of his courts and reorganised the empire.[49] The Antigonid empire shows a similar dialectic, temporarily re-emerging as an imperial power under Philip V, a contemporary of Antiochos III.

In his seminal essay on the gift, Marcel Mauss theorised that all gift-exchange is subject to three rules: the obligations to give, to receive and to reciprocate.[50] Reciprocity, however, is not balanced – the person with the highest status is obliged to offer the most valuable gifts or favours. In an anecdote told by Plutarch, a courtier who requested of Alexander dowries for his daughters was offered fifty talents; when the courtier politely retorted that ten talents would be more than enough, the king retorted: 'Enough for you to receive, but not enough for me to give.'[51] Unbalanced reciprocity is first of all a matter of honour. However, in practice it is instrumental in ensuring that the lesser-ranking person remains indebted and dependent because he is neither able nor allowed to reciprocate fully. The anecdote furthermore shows that it was not considered dishonourable to *ask* for gifts.[52] In fact, any petitioner appearing before the king could expect his request to be complied with. Of course, he himself was to make an initial gift. This could be a material present, but also a

---

170). In the 'Military Regulation' from Amphipolis, the *philoi*'s sharing in the booty was formally regulated in the Antigonid empire in the reign of Philip V (Roussel 1934: 46).

[48] See Sinopoli 1994: 163: 'the engine of imperial expansion, once started, may be difficult to turn off especially as systems of economic and social rewards and privileges become associated with expansion and with military success. Overexpansion may ultimately contribute to political collapse or reorganization.'

[49] Strootman 2011c.

[50] Mauss 1925.

[51] Plut., *Mor.* 127b.

[52] For more instances see, among others, Ath. 211b; Aristodemos *ap.* Ath. 246e.

Fig. 7.1. Silver and gold *phalera* (horse trapping) showing a Seleukid or Graeco-Baktrian war elephant. The 'biography' of this object, found in a tomb in the Volga Region, may have started at a royal banquet (State Hermitage Museum, St Petersburg).

service.[53] Josephus informs us that if the initial gift was too small relative to one's status, the king might be displeased; if, however, the gift of the petitioner was accepted by the king, the request would be granted.[54] In Greek aristocratic morality, working for pay was considered tantamount to servitude, but to be rewarded for services with gifts, honours or privileges was fully honourable.[55] The value of a gift was determined not only by its exact worth, but also by the status of the giver. It was symbolic capital, too. To be rewarded by a king increased one's social status enormously. Moreover, it is customary in pre-industrial societies for objects that have been in contact with the body of the king to attain a certain 'sacred' quality (Fig. 7.1).[56] For this reason, Hellenistic kings, like the Achaemenids before them, after banquets not only allowed their guests to take with them the silverware from which the guests had eaten, but also

---

[53] Jansen 1984: 51.
[54] Jos., *AJ* 12.217 and 219.
[55] Konstan 1997: 81–2.
[56] Jansen 1984: 58.

gave away the cups and plates from their own table.[57] Thus, endur-
ing networks of personal links could be maintained even after the
moment of the feast, for which guests had temporarily come to the
court, had passed.[58]

The ostentatious distribution of gifts is inextricably intermixed
with its counterpart, the ostentatious, public *receiving* of gifts. The
value of the gifts that one received was an expression of personal
worth. In times of political change, notably conquest, gift-exchange
could be a means to alter existing social structures. Plutarch's
account of the elevation of a man to the status of an honoured *philos*
of Mithradates Eupator is worth quoting in full as an anecdotal
description of an instance of conspicuous receiving which cuts across
social boundaries:

> When the old man woke up that morning, he saw that tables were placed in
> his house upon which stood gold and silver vessels; and a band of servants,
> eunuchs and pages brought him rich garments; and a horse, caparisoned like
> those of the royal *philoi*, stood before his door … The pages informed him
> that the king had also bestowed on him the large estate of a man who had
> recently died, and that all this was a mere foretaste of what was yet to come
> … So he put on his purple robe, leaped upon his horse and rode through the
> city, crying: 'All this is mine!'[59]

Plutarch presents this story as a morality tale about a poor old
man's sudden turn of fate; but the story is rooted in actual history,
as the protagonist was in reality the father of Stratonike, one of the
king's favourite wives. The giving of a horse is reminiscent of
Achaemenid practice, too; protocol at the Irano-Hellenic court of the
Mithradatids will have been predicated on both Seleukid and Iranian
tradition.[60]

Next to land, the public distribution of clothing, dyed with purple
dye or adorned with purple-coloured borders, was arguably the most
significant gift in terms of honour and favour. It was a mark of
belonging to the circle of the king's friends, a tangible (and eye-
catching) representation of favour. When Eumenes of Kardia
distributed purple clothing among his followers, 'they were delighted
to receive from him the same honours as kings bestow upon their

---

[57] Hdt. 9.20; Xen., *Anab.* 1.2.27, 8.28–9. The Hellenistic custom of giving tableware
may have been a borrowing from the Achaemenid court. Among the Persians, robes and
swords given by the king were important tokens of royal favour; cf. Bigwood 1995; Sancisi-
Weerdenburg 1989.

[58] On ritual feasting as a context for the public distribution of gifts and favour see below,
Chapter 9.

[59] Plut., *Pomp.* 36.4–5.

[60] Xen., *Anab.* 1.2.27; for Mithradates' *philoi* consult Sullivan 1990: 42–4.

philoi; for Eumenes was empowered to distribute purple *kausiai* and *chlamudes*, and this was a special gift of royalty among the Macedonians.'[61] In the first book of the Maccabees it is related that the Makkabean leader Jonathan, an ally of Alexander Balas, was given the titles of *philos* and *adelphos* of the king, and received the accompanying gifts of a purple garment and a golden wreath (*stephanos*) as the tokens of his status.[62] Likewise Dorimachos, leader of the Aitolian League in the late third century, received a *kausia* and a *chlamus* when he became the ally of the Antigonid king in 221.[63] Such prestige symbols not only indicated social status and authority, but also emphasised that royal favour was the source of that status and authority.[64]

The public distribution of gifts thus could be a means of publicly allocating royal favour, and so establish the receiver's place within the court hierarchy. It could even be a means to control the exit from and entrance to the *philoi* group, as in the case of purple clothing. Jansen has shown with various examples from cultural anthropology that in the context of a court one's proximity to the throne not only determined what royal gifts one received, but also worked the other way round; as Jansen rightly points out, common soldiers who received their payment from the crown were closer to the king than common subjects. In the context of the Hellenistic kingdoms this means that Macedonian military settlers receiving farmland from the crown or regular payment when under arms were closer to the king than the average subject, and this may in part explain their proverbial loyalty to the dynasty.[65] Moreover, regular soldiers and mercenaries were paid in cash directly by the crown; the coins they received showed the portrait of the king and various symbols representing the Seleukid, Ptolemaic or Antigonid monarchies – the Seleukid anchor, elephant, horned horse, Apollo, Zeus, etc. Though there were notable temporal and regional variations in imperial coin iconography, the bottom line was that the soldiery were always reminded of who paid them.

The exchange of gifts created not only horizontal bonds of loyalty but also vertical bonds of dependence to hold the formal equality of the *philoi* in check. Norbert Elias, in *Die höfische Gesellschaft*, even

---

[61] Plut., *Eum.* 8.6–7.
[62] 1 Macc. 10.20; 6.15 and 10.62.
[63] Polyb. 4.4.5.
[64] As was argued with regard to Achaemenid gift distribution by Sancisi-Weerdenburg 1989: 139–40.
[65] Jansen 1984: 55–6.

maintained that the requirement for massive status expenditures
drained courtiers of their financial resources, to the benefit of the
absolutist monarch because it made them dependent on royal generosity. However, the obligation of generosity placed a much heavier
financial burden on the king, being the person of highest status. In
reaction to Elias' thesis, Duindam noted that the king, too, was the
prisoner of the spending pattern: 'He could not control the game
without participating in it. It is important to note that the pressure
to prove one's superior status was greater on the monarch than on
anyone else.'[66]

The obligation of kings to grant any request made in public is
amusingly illustrated by an anecdote in which King Lysimachos –
a practical joker with a dark sense of humour, but also a notorious
miser – once threw a scorpion into the mantle of one of his *philoi*;
the latter retaliated by requesting a gift of one talent from the king,
who was thus scared out of his wits, too.[67] This joke only works
because the audience knows that Lysimachos would not be able to
refuse. Conversely, Ptolemy IV met with conspiracies and *philoi*
going over to the Seleukids because he was not able to fulfil their
demands.[68] An impression of the vast expenses required of kings to
uphold the loyalty of followers is given by this description of one of
the 'gift hoards' stockpiled by Mithradates Eupator, which fell into
the hands of the Romans:

> In the city of Talauri, which Mithradates used as a storehouse of furniture,
> were found two thousand drinking-cups made of onyx welded with gold,
> and many cups, wine-coolers, and drinking-horns, also ornamental couches
> and chairs, bridles for horses, and trappings for their breasts and shoulders,
> all ornamented in like manner with precious stones and gold. The quantity
> of this store was so great that the transfer of it occupied thirty days.[69]

Note that this is not a hoard of silver for the payment of troops, but
a stockpile of typical status gifts – trappings for horses, and furniture
and tableware to be used and distributed at banquets. Plutarch
writes that before setting out to meet Antony for the first time at
Tarsos, Kleopatra 'provided herself with many gifts, much money,
and such ornaments as her high position and prosperous kingdom
made it natural for her to take'.[70]

Thus, kings ran the risk of over-consumption, which would erode

[66] Duindam 1994: 86 and 95.
[67] Ath. 246e.
[68] Polyb. 5.34.4, 10.
[69] App., *Mithr.* 12.17.15, trans. H. White.
[70] Plut., *Demetr.* 25.4.

the financial foundation of their military power, or even lead to dependence on wealthy *philoi*, a process that has been described for the early modern court by Duindam: 'Extravagant expenditures to confirm the pretence of power and status eroded the financial foundation. Status expenditures had to be reduced, resulting in the loss of face and thus loss of power. The king could avoid this by finding new sources of income. This in turn led to dependence – on the assemblies of estates or on private *financiers*.'[71]

When a courtier once asked Ptolemy V where the king would find sufficient money to finance a campaign against the Seleukids, the king pointed to his *philoi* and said: 'There, walking about, are my money-bags.'[72] Antiochos III was at the beginning of his reign financially dependent on a *philos* called Hermeias the Karian.[73] Governors in the Hellenistic kingdoms were responsible for levying troops, using the provincial revenues to arm and pay them. It is possible that *philoi* who received important commands in the king's army were likewise supposed to equip the soldiers under their command from their own resources, and that this was both compulsory and honourable, like liturgies in classical Athens; investing in war brought profits in the form of booty and slaves; Apollonios, the wealthy Ptolemaic courtier and land owner known from the Zenon Papyri, had become rich from trading slaves from Syria.

Kings could forestall the risk of running out of wealth to meet the demands of the *philoi* by distributing symbolic gifts. Privileges and titles were much desired gifts, too. Purple clothing and tableware used at royal symposia were in themsleves valuable, but had an added value as visible tokens of such intangible rewards as 'protection' or 'favour'.[74] Gold crowns (*stephanoi*), though costly, were essentially gifts of honour, bestowed upon *philoi* as rewards for bravery.[75]

ARTISTIC AND SCIENTIFIC PATRONAGE

Many Hellenistic kings were renowned patrons of the arts and sciences, particularly the first two Ptolemies. Indeed, in Ptolemaic

[71] Duindam 1994: 86.
[72] Diod. 29.29. On the wealth of *philoi*: Diod. 33.20; Polyb. 15.25.28; Agatharchides, *FHG* II 476 *ap*. Ath. 155d.
[73] Polyb. 5.50.1–3. His ethnic suggests that he was not a Greek.
[74] The purple garments given to *philoi* as status symbols may have been woven on the looms of the king's wives or daughters; it was customary at the Argead court for the royal women to weave the menfolk's clothing; cf. Hammond 1990: 270.
[75] 1 Macc. 10.20.

Alexandria such patronage was institutionalised through the Museum (*mouseion*) and the Library. But other dynasties too maintained museums and libraries, and in the fourth century several Argead kings, in particular Archelaos, Philip II and Alexander the Great, had been protectors of philosophers and poets. Art, poetry, philosophy and sciences were defining aspects of Hellenistic court culture.

Elsewhere I have dealt more extensively with court patronage, arguing that Hellenistic cultural and scientific patronage was integrated into court society.[76] The poets, scholars and scientists working for the king were for the most part not his employees but genuine courtiers, *philoi tou basileōs*. In Theokritos' sixteenth *Idyll*, royal patronage is presented by the poet as *xenia* for the benefit of both participants, and poems written for the ruler are conceptualised as gifts.[77] If they were accepted, the return gift would not necessarily be money; honours, privileges or a court title could be appropriate rewards, too. Indeed, some prominent men of letters belonged to the upper echelons of court society. Conversely, members of the *sunedrion* often distinguished themselves as philosophers or occasional poets.

Another argument central to my earlier work that perhaps needs repeating here is the thesis that competition for royal favour was the principal driving force encouraging poets and others to be original, inventive and pioneering. The production of literature and scholarship could be instrumental in obtaining access to the presence of the king, or more precisely, in being admitted to royal banquets and symposia. There, status, favours and privileges could be obtained, not only for oneself but also for one's family or friends. Being appreciated by kings and their *philoi* lent authority to works of literature or philosophy. *Philoi*, and notably the king himself, were certified arbiters of taste. Because of their rank and education they qualified as judges of quality and merit, and their approval contributed to the acceptance of new ideas and art forms. As everyone knew,

[76] Strootman 2007: 189–250 and 2010a (with an overview of the literature), developing some views expressed in Strootman 2001. I hope to return to this subject in a small monograph titled *The Birdcage of the Muses: Royal Patronage of the Arts and Sciences at the Early Ptolemaic Court, 305–222 BCE*.

[77] Apart from showing that the bond between patron and poet was defined in terms of *xenia* and that this relationship was *reciprocal*, *Idyll* 16 lists several more aims of literary patronage: first, that the hospitality and generosity offered to a poet are in themselves honourable and may boost a king's charism; second, that poetry is the means par excellence to make the deeds of kings public and spread their fame to the edges of the earth (lines 121–2); and third, that the patron's reputation may be boosted by the fame of the clients whom he patronises. Cf. Strootman 2010a.

Alexander had his portraits made by Lysippos, who therefore must be the greatest sculptor alive. Conversely, the fame of artists and scholars was added to the prestige of the patron. Writings and works of art were offered to kings and courtiers as gifts and subsequently became their personal possessions.

This interpretation runs counter to the notion that poets, scholars and artists working at a court were servants of kings and courtiers, giving up their integrity and producing second-rate works, including servile laudatory poems and insincere philosophical tracts in defence of monarchic rule.[78] In older scholarship one often encounters pains-taking efforts to disconnect Hellenistic poetry and science from its courtly context. Thus in a handbook on post-classical Greek science it is assured that 'there were many scientists who received no help whatsoever from rich patrons. Many of those who did scientific work were no doubt men of means.'[79] This statement is based on the presumption that the motive for seeking patronage was gaining material benefit. I believe this notion to be erroneous. Many poets and philosophers who did attend court were men of means. Further-more, there were opportunities for them to make a living outside the court; the increased number of *poleis* with their many festivals perhaps offered more opportunities for Greek poets than had existed in the classical Age. But in the Hellenistic age the impetus for *progress* and *innovation* in art and science came primarily from royal patronage.

The early Ptolemaic court in particular was a safe haven for intel-lectuals with unorthodox, even subversive views. At the court of Ptolemy II, Aristarchos of Samos developed his revolutionary helio-centric theory, even though this was widely criticised, not only on scientific but especially on moral grounds.[80] The Ptolemies enabled the physicians Herophilos and Erasistratos to perform systematic dissections of human cadavers – a practice that was as unique and progressive as Aristarchos' hypothesis, and provoked similar hostile reactions: it was rumoured that with the approval of the king, Herophilos performed vivisection on convicted criminals.[81]

---

[78] See, for instance, Africa 1968: 'In the Hellenistic age, many scientists exchanged independence for the patronage of kings' (p. 2), and they 'learned the arts of discretion and subservience' (p. 48). Green 1990: 241 sees 'blatant flattery' every time the Ptolemaic court poet Theokritos mentions the name of Ptolemy Philadelphos, and maintains that 'there is always a price to be paid for patronage'; Schwinge 1986: 40–82 even holds that kings actively *repressed* the freedom of poets and believes that the poets in revenge criticised their patrons in between the lines.

[79] Lloyd 1973: 6.

[80] Diog. Laert. 7.174.

[81] Celsus, *De Med.*, pr. 23–4.

The court, as a centre of social and economic distribution, was a place where the lines separating the hierarchical layers of society could be crossed. But to win favour one had to attract attention and have at one's disposal a network of personal contacts. Other *philoi* in all likelihood acted as brokers. This set-up challenged men to prove their worth and demonstrate their skills; in one word, to *distinguish* themselves. And as the focal point for the presentation of work was the banquet and the symposium, one also had to prove that one was able to *entertain*. Rivalry was perhaps behind much of the mannerism and erudition of Hellenistic literature, with its almost snobbish allusions and its partiality for obscure myths and rare words. Court poets needed to distinguish themselves before an audience of courtiers – an audience that was critical and perceptive, and wanted to be confirmed in its self-image as an educated upper class. Thus even 'propaganda' texts like Theokritos' encomium for Ptolemy Philadelphos or Kallimachos' *Hymn to Zeus* could become literary masterpieces.

The entire set-up was predicated on competition. Hence the envy that according to some sources spoiled the atmosphere at the *mouseion*, including the notorious enmity between Theokritos and Kallimachos. Competition for favour was a driving force behind technical innovation, and can also help explain the experimental nature of Hellenistic literature and art.[82] The court provided, on a regular basis, an educated audience that was both receptive and influential. At banquets and symposia poetry and treatises were read, inventions were demonstrated, new ideas proposed. Of course, not all court poetry aimed exclusively at court circles.[83] Some of it may have been written for a broader audience of Greek *politai*. We can be sure, however, that most of it was in the first instance written for an elite circle of educated royal friends, who were eager for new things and would return the most prestigious gifts. Honour was a major driving force in the life of a Greek poet, and to be associated with such an elite milieu increased one's status more than success among lower levels of society. The members of the upper level of court society all had their own networks of *xenoi* and maintained relations with their families' cities of origin. The court as a

---

[82] The competitive nature of Hellenistic science is emphasised by Netz 2004: 62; on poetic competition at the Ptolemaic court see Barbantani 2000 and Klooster 2009.

[83] Griffiths 1979 and Zanker 1987 identify only Ptolemaic royal *philoi* as the intended audience for Alexandrian poetry, for as Zanker says, Alexandrian poetry because of its complexity obviously was not written for 'the urban masses of Alexandria' (p. 18); Cameron 1995 agrees, stating that 'no one in pagan antiquity ever wrote (non-dramatic) poetry for such an audience' (p. 56).

result was the nucleus of an international elite infrastructure through which poems or ideas could circulate throughout the Hellenistic world.

A possibly striking feature of Hellenistic royal patronage is its overall Hellenic nature. The main difference between pre-Hellenistic and Hellenistic Greek literature is that the latter tended to iron out regional differences among the Greeks. Thus Greek culture was redefined in the light of a new, more cosmopolitan world view that was closely connected with the universalistic ideals of empire. Non-Greek artists, writers and scholars were virtually absent from the courts. And when they were present – Berossos, Manetho, perhaps the first Septuagint translators – they wrote in Greek. Egyptian pharaonic ideology may have informed Alexandrian panegyric,[84] but the influences (if any) were thoroughly transformed to become part of a new, 'Hellenistic' culture of empire that was, again, strikingly similar at the different Macedonian courts.

The Hellenism of the court was instrumental in creating an imperial elite culture, intensifying a process of Hellenisation also at work in the *poleis*. In world history, court culture often serves as a means to link dispersed local elites, creating coherence in culturally and ethnically heterogeneous empires, and binding these elites to the political centre by 'the power of memory, of imagination, and of language'.[85] In the Macedonian empires, it was Hellenism that helped define who did and who did not participate in the imperial order.[86] This is why in the Hellenistic period members of non-Greek civic elites strove after 'the Greek way of life', signified especially by membership of the gymnasion and the adoption of a second, Greek personal name. Conversely, those who did not benefit from the imperial order, or were excluded from it by their political opponents, reacted by accentuating (or inventing) indigenous culture; this was the case in Judaea in the 160s, when an orthodox version of Jewish culture was constructed in opposition to the Hellenised allies of the Seleukids, as is apparent from 1 and 2 Maccabees.[87]

By concerning themselves with Greek culture on a grand scale, and in the centres of their kingdoms, Macedonian rulers presented themselves as protectors and benefactors of the Greeks. In part, they did so because Hellenes formed the principal agents of empire in the

---

[84] See esp. Heerink 2010 on pharaonic influences in Theokritos' encomium for Ptolemy II (*Idyll* 17).
[85] Burke 1992: 57.
[86] Mehl 2003.
[87] Strootman 2006.

Macedonian Near East. Moreover, the culture of the court had a distinct 'cosmopolitan' character that cut across the multifarious cultural and linguistic zones within the Hellenistic empires. This may be what the historian Menekles of Barke meant when around 200 BCE he boasted that Alexandria had become the teacher to all Greeks and barbarians.[88] Thus, the Hellenism of the court could potentially create a sense of commonwealth and so contribute to the establishment of cohesion in states characterised by their political, ethnic and cultural heterogeneity.

Artistic and scientific patronage, furthermore, could be instrumental in two of the basic functions of the court: the court as a stage for the drama of kingship and the court as the focus for competition with other dynasties. In cultural and scientific patronage these two functions merged. The splendour of a court's system of patronage increased the glory of the king and his dynasty, and could be a means to outdo his rivals. Moreover, some forms of art were suitable for rather explicit propaganda. This was in particular the case with (panegyric) poetry, historiography and the visual arts.

[88] Fraser I: 517–18, with II: 165 n. 324.

8 *Hierarchy and Conflict*

In the Seleukid and Ptolemaic kingdoms, the ranking of *philoi* in the court hierarchy was regulated and explicated by means of court titles and offices.[1] In this chapter it will be argued that the distribution of titles was part of the complex of gift-exchange at court. Titles were presented by the king as gifts, comparable to, and presumably coming with, material gifts (clothing, crowns, horse trappings) so that the recipient would be able to show his rank to others and derive status from that. The institution of a more intricate system of court titulature after c. 200 BCE – first at the Seleukid and then at the Ptolemaic court – may have been an attempt to regain control of court society against the opposition of an established nobility of rich, land-holding *philoi* with hereditary prerogatives at court. Court titles potentially regulated access and relative status at court. Of the highest importance for kings was regulating access to the circle of royal advisors, the *sunedrion*. Another instrument to regulate access, discussed at the end of this chapter, was the promotion of a favourite: a loyal outsider who had direct access to the king and served as a protective shield between king and court society.

COURT TITLES

Hellenistic court titulature developed from the basal system of titles of the fourth-century Argead court, and developed through the adoption of Achaemenid influences at the courts of Alexander and the Seleukids into a more complex and refined system in the second century. The second-century system is best attested for the Ptolemaic kingdom. The system of court titles at the later Ptolemaic court

---

[1] For Hellenistic, especially Ptolemaic, court titulature see, among others, Willrich 1909; Peremans and Van 't Dack 1968; Mooren 1968, 1975, 1977; Herman 1980/1; Savalli-Lestrade 1998.

appears to have become somewhat formalised at the lower levels of
the dynastic household, perhaps in relation to the administration of
Egypt, but the higher echelons of the court surely did not change into
a bureaucracy.[2] The complex of aulic titulature in the second century
can be better described as a form of formalised informality. Therefore it is more likely that a *philos'* power position at court was
indicated by his title, not necessarily fixed by it.

Because of the disparate nature of the evidence, the meaning of
many known titles is unknown, and their relative status remains
elusive. In the context of the Ptolemaic court Léon Mooren distinguishes 'honorific titulature', i.e. titles awarded *honoris causa*,
and 'real aulic titulature', i.e. titles indicating concrete aulic functions, such as major-domo, chamberlain or master of the hunt.[3] Even
though Mooren does not include them, I would maintain that military titles (*stratēgos, elephantarchos, nauarchos*, etc.) belong to the
latter category too.[4] However, although these categories are helpful
for the modern historian, they do no justice to the complexity of
Hellenistic aulic titulature. Instead of enforcing such a distinction it
is perhaps better to speak of honorific offices – at *Ancien Régime*
courts, 'real' titles such as major-domo could be honorific *and* practical at the same time. Moreover, it appears that the Hellenistic
complex of court titles was not static but open to change.

Although most evidence for court titles stems from the Ptolemaic
empire of the second century, where indeed the most sophisticated
titles system seems to have developed, titulature at the Seleukid court
was in essence identical, though perhaps less elaborate. The similarities suggest that the Seleukid and Ptolemaic courts influenced each
other, presumably as the result of the mobility of *philoi* and dynastic
intermarriage, with the Seleukids initially having ascendancy over
the Ptolemies in this respect.[5] The Antigonids in Macedon were
content to stick to the old Macedonian titles predating Alexander,
retaining for instance the honorific office of *sōmatophulax* at the
heart of the inner court.[6] To be sure, the Seleukids retained the old
titles, too. For instance, an inscription from the royal city of Susa,
published by Cumont, honours the son of a Seleukid *sōmatophulax*.
The date formula is damaged; Cumont dates the text to the

  [2] *Pace* Walbank 1984a: 70; Herman 1987: 164.
  [3] Mooren 1975: 2.
  [4] Mooren 1975: 172–4 does distinguish a category of 'the king's military house', meaning the guards and household troops present at court.
  [5] Bickerman 1938: 31; Mooren 1975: 2 and 5.
  [6] Diod. 30.10.2; 30.11.1.

beginning of the first century BCE, but an earlier date is also possible (and perhaps more plausible): '(From) those of the middle service-group, to Lysimachos, son of Apollophanes, one of the Bodyguards (and) to him from amongst the others on account of his good service. In the year [2]14 (?). Diophantes inscribed the stele.'[7] In the Seleukid and Ptolemaic kingdoms, a process of subdivision of titulature took place, and new titles were created so that an elaborate court hierarchy and system of aulic offices developed after c. 200. At the Antigonid court a similar process began (and came to a halt) at the same time, in the reign of Philip V,[8] perhaps also under Seleukid influence as the Antigonid and Seleukid houses were closely connected through dynastic marriages.

But even when lesser positions of honour indeed declined into specific professions, at the uppermost levels there always remained an informal inner circle of powerful men surrounding the king whose positions were not determined by titles and whom Polybios describes correctly with an unofficial and rather vague term: 'the most prominent of the people of the court'.[9] Status and influence could have been indicated too by less tangible signs now lost to the historian, and perhaps we should not overestimate the value of court titles as indicators of real power. Although there is no Hellenistic Saint-Simon to inform us in any comprehensive manner about the subtleties of Seleukid and Ptolemaic court life, the ancient evidence sometimes does hint at the existence of subtle status indicators of a more temporal nature. For instance, when reconstructing meetings of the Seleukid *sunedrion*, Polybios always has the man who at that time was the most powerful speaking first – Epigenes at first, and later Hermeias – from which it may be deduced that the sequence of other speakers was determined by, and indicative of, status and/or favour. Invariably, the king is the last to speak – and, ideally, to decide. At the courts of Alexander, Antiochos the Great and Mithradates, etiquette required that a select band of courtiers had the right to greet the king when waking up in the morning – an indication of rank comparable to the well-known ceremony of the *petit lever* at the court of Louis XIV, a privilege that may have

---

[7] Cumont 1931: 234–8; cited by Potts 1999: 364; cf. p. 365 citing two more honorific inscriptions from Susa (of unknown date) in which 'one of [the First Friends and of the Bodyguards]' and 'one of 'the F[irst and Foremost Friends – –]' have been amended by Haussoullier 1903: 159 and 1909.

[8] Le Bohec 1985.

[9] Polyb. 5.41.3: τοῖς ἐν ὑπεροχαῖς οὖσι τῶν περὶ τὴν αὐλήν. For a different view see Herman 1997: 215.

entailed more actual influence at court than an impressive honorific title that one could show off with in non-aulic contexts.[10]

This said, let us have a closer look at the honorific titulature of the Ptolemaic and Seleukid kingdoms. The first striking feature is the fact that the word *philos* (in itself a title of honour) was at the basis of the system of honorific titulature. We hear of such titles as 'first friends' (πρῶτοι φίλοι), 'honoured friends' (τιμώμενοι φίλοι), 'first and highly honoured friends' (πρῶτοι καὶ πρωτιμώμενοι φίλοι) in both the Seleukid and Ptolemaic contexts after c. 200.[11] What exactly these titles implied is unknown, but we may assume that they indicated status differences at the very least.

Somewhat less elusive are two other notable titles attested for all Macedonian courts: kinsman of the king (συγγενὴς τοῦ βασιλέως) and foster-brother of the king (σύντροφος τοῦ βασιλέως).[12] The latter title, *suntrophos*, indicated that one had been a royal page with the ruling monarch. The Seleukids used to address their *suntrophoi* as 'brother' and their (former) *tropheus*, i.e. the man who had been in charge of the pages, as 'father'.[13] In this way, ties of personal loyalty were strengthened by means of fictive kinship. The second title, *sungenēs*, presumably had a similar connotation but apparently could also be awarded *honoris causa*.[14] The title may have had Achaemenid antecedents, because *sungeneis* is the word that Greek authors use to describe the Persian noblemen most closely attached to the Great King, forming a ceremonial bodyguard around his person.[15]

The category of 'real aulic titulature' comprises first of all titles connected with the domestic affairs of the royal household. At the Ptolemaic court the principal dignitary seems to have been the *dioiketes*, the major-domo; he was aided by a steward, who was responsible for the reception of guests and the progress of symposia

---

[10] Curt. 8.6.13 (Alexander); Polyb. 8.21.1 (Antiochos); Plut., *Pomp.* 32.4 (Mithradates).

[11] Walbank 1984a: 70; Mooren 1975: *passim*. With the addition, for the Seleukids, of Jos., *AJ* 12.53 (τιμιώτατοι φίλοι); Jos., *AJ* 13.13.85; 1 Macc. 11.27; 10.65 (Πρῶτοι φίλοι).

[12] Συγγενής: Arr., *Anab.* 7.11.1 (Argeads); 1 Macc. 11.31; 2 Macc. 11.12; *OGIS* 148, 259; cf. Liv. 30.42.6; Polyb. 4.48.5 (Seleukids); Plut., *Mor.* 197a (Antigonids); Jos., *AJ* 16.288; 17.93; 17.220 (Ptolemies). Συςντροφο : Polyb. 5.9.4 (Antigonids); Polyb. 5.82.8; 31.13.2; *OGIS* 247, 1–3; 2 Macc. 11.22 (Seleukids); Polyb. 15.33.11; 22.22.1–2 (Ptolemies); Polyb. 32.15.10 (Attalids).

[13] 1 Macc. 11.30; Jos., *AJ* 12.127, 12.148; 13.126; cf. Diod. 33.4.1.

[14] Ath. 48f; Jos., *AJ* 16.288; 17.93; 17.220; *OGIS* 148; Polyb. 4.48.5; 1 Macc. 10.20. Arr., *Anab.* 7.11.6, claims that only the *sungeneis* of Alexander had the right to greet the king with a kiss.

[15] Xen., *Cyr.* 1.4.27; Arr., *Anab.* 1.15.7; 3.11.5; 7.11.1; 7.11.6; Ath. 48e; Diod. 16.20.1–3; Curt. 3.3.14 (*cognati regis*).

and banquets.[16] *Dioiketes* is often translated as 'first minister' or 'chief financial minister', but such designations do not belong in the context of a court. A more useful comparison may be the 'grand-maître de l'hôtel' of the *Ancien Régime*, i.e. the dignitary responsible for the daily (economic) affairs of the householdand for access to the king. The office of *dioiketes* perhaps developed from the chiliarchate at the court of Alexander and Philip III Arrhidaios. The chiliarch, too, was presumably in charge of the affairs of the household, and perhaps of the bodyguard, regulating access to the king.[17] Other officials of high rank attested for the Ptolemaic court were chamberlain and captain of the guard.[18] There were several titles that can be translated as chancellor or (chief) secretary.[19] The financial affairs of the royal household were managed by a (chief) treasurer.[20] We also hear of more specialised offices like master of the pages and master of the hounds,[21] and in Alexandria the office of head of the

---

[16] *P.Tebt.* 8 = Austin 265 (reign of Ptolemy II); ἐδεατρος (Ath. 167b; Argead, c. 225); ἀρχεδεαοτρος (Jos., *AJ* 12.2.12; Ptolemaic, c. 250).

[17] Grainger 1990: 18–19 claims that the chiliarchate was created by Alexander as an ad hoc measure to meet the sudden increase of court affairs after the conquest of the Achaemenid empire; Sancisi-Weerdenburg 1980: 176 has drawn attention to the similarities between the Argead chiliarch and the Achaemenid office of *hazarpat*, the major-domo and commander of the bodyguard at the Persian court, who was second only to the king because he regulated access to the king. This explanation, however, is complicated by the fact that Alexander already had at his disposal bodyguard commanders regulating access, in the shape of the *sōmatophulakes*. At the Antigonid court the major-domo was called ἐπὶ τῆς θεραπεία (Polyb. 4.87.5, 8; cf. Diod. 18.27.1 and Walbank I: 536), and it seems that, like the *hazarpat*, this dignitary was at the same time captain of the bodyguard. See further Ehling 1998: 97–106, arguing that the designation ὁ ἐπὶ τῶν πραγμάτων attested for courtiers of Antiochos III and Antiochos IV in literary sources was a formal, initially non-military Seleukid office existing alongside an office of 'commander in chief' of the army.

[18] ἐπν τοῦ κοιτῶνος: Porphyr., *FGrH* 260 F 20; *RIG* no. 1158 (Seleukid, reign of Antiochos IX); ἡγεμον των ὑπασπιστων: Polyb. 7.16.2 (Seleukid, 216/15); Jos., *AJ* 12.17 (Ptolemaic, c. 300).

[19] ἐπὶ τοῦ γραμματευς: Polyb. 4.87.8 (Antigonid, c. 225); γραμματευς: Polyb 15.27.7 (Ptolemaic, 203); ἐπιστολογραφος: Polyb. 31.3.16 (Ptolemaic). Cf. Polyb. 5.54.12, who mentions an αρχιγραμματευς of the royal army (Seleukid, 220/1).

[20] ταμίας: Ath. 493f, 494a (Ptolemaic); ἐπὶ τοῦ νομίσματος: Plut., *Aem.* 23.3 (Antigonid, 168); cf. Plut., *Luc.* 29.8. Central treasury accountants in charge of the finances of the household should be distinguished from the regional treasure guardians and citadel commanders known as θησαυροφύλαξ or γαζοφύλαξ guarding hoards stored away in strongholds for the financing of campaigns; cf. e.g. Diod. 19.18.1 (Argead, 317 BCE) and 30.11.1 (Antigonid, 169 BCE). Allen 1983: 9 n. 4 may be mistaken when describing Philetairos' office of γαζοφύλαξ and commander of the Pergamon citadel for King Lysimachos as 'certainly not a military [position]'.

[21] Master of the pages (*tropheus*): Plut., *Alex.* 5 (Argeads); Polyb. 31.13.1; *OGIS* 148, 256; App., *Syr.* 68; 1 Macc. 11.1, 31–2 (Seleukid); Jos., *AJ* 12.127, 148; 13.126–7; Plut., *Ant.* 5.31 (Ptolemaic). On the *tropheus* see further below. Master of the hounds (ἀρχικυνηγος): Bevan 1902 II: 283 (Seleukid), perhaps indicating the position of master of the hunt in general; it may also mean just what it says: someone responsible for the royal hunting dogs.

royal museum and library, who was responsible for the intellectual education of the king's children and the royal pages.[22]

A special place of privilege and honour was held by the king's personal physician,[23] who was in charge of a staff of doctors and servants at the Seleukid court.[24] The physician's relative proximity to the person of the king or the queen made him well suited for the role of broker. Apollophanes, the personal physician of Antiochos III, was according to Polybios 'a great favourite' of his.[25] Ptolemy IV's physician Andreas was quartered in the king's own pavilion during the Raphia campaign.[26] Alexander's prodigious trust in his physician Philip the Akarnanian gave rise to a popular story recorded by Plutarch.[27] In the original version of a comparable Roman tale – a popular story recorded by no fewer than fourteen writers in various versions – the consul Fabricius rejects an offer from Pyrrhos' physician Nikias to poison his king; it is exactly his proximity to the king that makes Nikias' offer plausible.[28] Several Hellenistic court physicians were medical scientists of renown, in particular Herophilos, Erasistratos and Krataios. Herophilos and Erasistratos both worked at the court of Ptolemy II; the latter had earlier been the personal physician of Seleukos I. Krataios, the physician of Mithradates Eupator, was a famous pharmacist and botanist.[29]

Dignitaries such as the major-domo, chamberlain or chancellor were ultimately responsible for the duties indicated by their titles. But these, of course, were also honorific offices indicating status and proximity to the throne. Each of them presumably had the requisite staff and assistants to carry out their duties for them. In Josephus' account of the arrival of the seventy Judaean scholars who came to translate the Tora, the king ordered the steward to take care of the reception of the guests, but the steward forthwith delegated this to a lesser dignitary: 'Now the man who was appointed to take care of the reception of guests, Nikanor by name, called for Dorotheos,

[22] Strabo 17.1.8; *P.Oxy* 1241. Cf. Fraser II: 467 n. 34.
[23] ἀρχιατρος or simply ἰατρος: see, among others, Plut., *Alex.* 19; Diod. 17.31.6 (Argead); Plut., *Mor.* 195a–b (Molossian); *RIG* no. 1158; Polyb. 5.56.1, 81.6; Porphyr., *FGrH* 260 F 20 (Seleukid); Polyb. 5.81.6 (Ptolemaic).
[24] Polyb. 5.56.6–7.
[25] Polyb. 5.56–7. Compare the honours voted by Ilion for a doctor of Antiochos I in response to the king's publicising of this doctor's services (*Ilion* 34; *OGIS* 220).
[26] Polyb. 5.81.6; cf. Fraser I: 370.
[27] Plut., *Alex.* 19 and 77; cf. Just. 12.47.6.
[28] Plut., *Pyrrh.* 21.14–15; *Mor.* 195a–b; cf. Nederlof 1978: 170–4.
[29] Hdt. 3.129–37 ascribes a similar standing to Demokedes of Kos, the Greek physician of Darius the Great. On Hellenistic court physicians see, among others, Gorteman 1957; Mastrocinque 1995; Marasco 1996.

whose duty it was to make provisions for [guests], and ordered him to lodge and feed every one of them, as had been ordered by the king.'[30] The existence of more dignitaries such as this assistant steward at the middle levels of the Ptolemaic and Seleukid court hierarchy seems self-evident. At the lower levels there were, furthermore, various household servants who were not *philoi*: cashiers, grooms, cupbearers, stablehands, musicians, cooks, palace guards (all of whom have been attested), muleteers, clerks, bakers, barbers etc. (whose presence at court can be assumed), as well as slaves.[31]

Hammond claimed that there were no slaves at the Argead court, at least until Alexander's campaign in Asia: '[because] at the Macedonian court the royal women made their menfolk's clothes and the Pages waited on the king; it was a slaveless set-up'.[32] However, the royal women's responsibility for making clothes was, rather, the result of their status as daughters and (good) wives; at work, they may of course have been assisted by slaves. The pages certainly did not perform all of the duties Hammond suggests; on the contrary, they formed a screen between the king and his servants, as we are informed that grooms saddled the kings' horse but the pages subsequently brought the horses to the king and helped him to mount.[33] Likewise, the pages' duty of waiting on the king at table most probably meant that they took over food and drink from the kitchen personnel and placed it on the king's table.

As has already been suggested, military titles too were indicative of status within the court society, court and army being completely interwoven, notably at the Antigonid and Seleukid courts. High-ranking army officers were almost always at the same time *philoi*. Thus, the men included by Polybios as members of the royal councils of Antiochos III and Philip V also appear as the kings' supreme military commanders in the field.[34] For instance, Philippos, a counsellor and *suntrophos* of Antiochos III, was commander of the elephants in the battle of Raphia (217 BCE) and the battle of Magnesia, 27 years later.[35] The most common title was *stratēgos*, general, but more precise titles also existed, such as chief commander of the fleet in the

---

[30] Jos., *AJ* 12.2.12–13.
[31] Cooks: Ath. 405e. Cupbearers: Polyb. 14.11; Ath. 195e; Agesarchos, *FHG* 67 *ap*. Ath. 425e; 606b. Grooms: Arr., *Anab*. 4.13.1; cf. Curt. 5.1.42; 8.6.4. Musicians: Ath. 43bc (Argeads); Ath. 603d–e; Polyb. 14.11; Ath. 167a, 350a, 603b; mime actors and dancers: Diod. 34.34; Ath. 195e; 607c–d.
[32] Hammond 1990: 270.
[33] Arr., *Anab*. 4.13.1; Curt. 5.1.42; 8.6.4.
[34] For a different view: Herman 1997: 214; Ehling 1998: 104.
[35] Polyb. 5.82.8; Liv. 37.41.1; App., *Syr*. 33.

Ptolemaic kingdom or commander of the peltasts in the entourage of Philip V.[36]

THE ROYAL COUNCIL

At the heart of the court was the *sunedrion*, the royal council.[37] Membership of this council was a more substantial status marker than any court title or office. Such councils existed in most premodern monarchic states. In the Macedonian kingdoms, too, monarchs were obliged to hear the advice of the council before making important decisions, in particular matters of foreign affairs and war. They could not easily dissent from their council's advice when that advice was given unanimously. In the Ptolemaic kingdom, the council on various occasions managed the affairs of the monarchy in the name of a minor successor.[38] Members of the *sunedrion* were often present when kings received foreign ambassadors.[39] Yet the authority of the royal councils was unofficial and informal; in historiographical sources the *sunedrion* appears as the single most important body in the Hellenistic kingdoms, but the word is absent from inscriptions.

A *sunedrion* consisted of the king and the most powerful of his *philoi*, just as the council of Alexander had consisted of representatives of the high nobility of Macedon, the *hetairoi*. Ideally, these were men of the king's own choosing. In practice, however, the king did not necessarily have the last say in the composition of the *sunedrion*. In cases of disagreement, the most influential person or faction could enforce a decision against the king's will. Kings themselves needed to secure support for their plans in advance. To the outside world, however, king and council would always present an image of unity. Polybios understood this when he added the following concluding sentences to a lengthy reconstruction of a meeting of Philip V's council in 218/17:

[36] Polyb. 15.25.37: ἐπὶ τοῦ ναυτικοῦ; Polyb. 4.87.8: ἐπι; τοῦ πελταστων.

[37] Jos., *AJ* 12.25 (Ptolemy II). Polyb. 15.25.27 (Ptolemy V). App., *Syr.* 11.2.9; Polyb. 5.41.6; 5.49.1; 5.49.5–6; 5.50.3; 5.52.1; 5.58.2; 8.21.2; 11.3.13–14 (Antiochos III). Diod. 34.1.1; 34.16 (Antiochos VII). Polyb. 4.23.5; 4.24.8; 5.2.1; 5.4.13; 5.16.5; 5.102.1; Diod. 28.2 (Philip V). Other: App. 11.3.14; Jos., *AJ* 17.106; 17.132. Polyb. 7.5.2; 15.25.26; 16.22.10. Cf. Liv. 35.17.3, 42.50.1, 42.51.1 (*consilium*). A royal council existed in Argead Macedonia long before Philip II (Walbank I: 470). On Ptolemaic and Seleukid councils see Mooren 1998.

[38] Polyb. 4.76.1, 87.7; 7.5.2–3; 15.25.26; 18.53.5; Caes., *BCiv* 3.105. One of the council members was appointed guardian of the child-king (*epitropos*): Polyb. 15.25.21; 16.22.10; Diod. 30.15.1; 2 Macc. 3.7; 11.1; 13.2; Caes., *BCiv* 3.108 (*nutricius*).

[39] Diod. 28.12; Polyb. 2.50.1–2; 4.23.4–5.

Finally the king spoke, if indeed we are to suppose that he gave his own opinion; for it is hardly believable that a seventeen-year-old boy was able to decide about such grave matters of the kingdom. It is, however, the duty of writers to attribute to the supreme ruler the expression of opinion which prevailed at his council, while it is open to the reader to suspect that such decisions and the arguments on which they rest are due to his associates and especially to those closest to his person.[40]

A pivotal aspect of the ideal of equality among the *philoi* who were present at the council was forthrightness.[41] *Parrhēsia*, 'freedom of speech', is perhaps best known as a fundamental aspect of Athenian democratic ideology. But frankness of speech in itself is originally a typical aristocratic ideal, a central virtue in the concept of *philia*.[42]

Typically, many passages in Plutarch's *Moralia* dealing with the virtue of *parrhēsia* take the form of conversations between a king and a courtier. In a letter ascribed to Isokrates, the author praises the *parrhēsia* of the addressee, Diodotos, a former courtier of Philip II, noting that:

> Those rulers who have a praiseworthy earnestness of soul regard this [frankness] as useful, whereas those whose nature is weaker than the powers they possess despise it, believing that it would compel them to do what they do not want to do; they do not realise, however, that those who most dare to disagree concerning what is advantageous are the very ones who afford them the maximum capacity to do what they wish. For it stands to reason that monarchies ... cannot endure in power by relying on those who speak only to please ... But if they put their trust in those who speak frankly for the best then much is salvaged even in situations that seem headed for ruin.[43]

Compare Kleitos' sneer at Alexander, urging him to allow the Macedonian companions 'to speak out freely what [they] wished to say, or else not to invite to supper men who were free and spoke their minds, but to live with barbarians and slaves, who would do obeisance to his white tunic and Persian girdle'.[44]

The frankness expected from a good courtier, even when it meant disagreeing with the king, forms the basis of the historiographical

---

[40] Polyb. 4.24.1–2.
[41] See e.g. Curt. 3.12.16; Plut., *Alex.* 9; Polyb. 5.27.6.
[42] Konstan 1997: 93–4; Momigliano 1973. On *parrh sia* and classical democracy see Sluiter and Rosen 2004, esp. the contribution of Raaflaub, tracing the development of oligarchic freedom of speech among equals (*is goria*) to its broader, democratic meaning as the recognition that 'everyone had a right to say everything', for which the term *parrhēsia* was introduced. On *parrhēsia* and democracy see also Saxonhouse 2006. In the meantime, the aristocratic ideal of frankness among equals presumably never disappeared, least of all in Macedon. The significance of the freedom to approach the monarch in Macedonia has been analysed by Adams 1986.
[43] (Ps.)Isocr., *Ep.* 4.
[44] Plut., *Alex.* 51.3.

topos of the king who brings himself to ruin by not listening to his counsellors. To quote one example: 'When his *philoi* advised him to wait for reinforcements ... he (Ptolemy Keraunos) would not listen to their words. King Ptolemy was killed and the entire Macedonian army was destroyed by the Celts.'[45] Again, the reality may have been less ideal. This at least is suggested by another *topos*: that of the young king who after a promising start is corrupted by power and becomes a tyrant, surrounding himself with sycophants and parasites who typically do not (dare to) disagree with him:

> [Then] the king (Antiochos III) held a council regarding the Roman War. There each tried to outdo each other in fighting spirit, since each thought that he would win greater favour in proportion to the severity of his attitude towards the Romans, while others assailed the insolence of their demands, seeing that they (i.e. the Romans) were imposing terms upon Antiochos the Great King of Asia.[46]

In continuation of former Argead practice, the Hellenistic *sunedrion* acted as a tribunal in cases of treason against the king.[47] Like Alexander's council, the Hellenistic *sunedrion* was not a formal judicial court; its members tried their peers because treason was first of all violation of *philia*, and perhaps also because it was a noble prerogative to be tried by one's equals.[48]

FRIENDS OR FLATTERERS?

Behaviour, 'good manners', distinguished courtiers from non-courtiers. Rules of conduct form a central feature of court culture, the importance of which was recognised by Elias, although he wrongly attributed to the king a free rein in manipulating court etiquette to his own discretion.[49] Polybios provides a rare description of the ideal Hellenistic courtier, in his portrayal of the Egyptian *philos* Aristonikos:

> Aristonikos, a courtier of King Ptolemy, was a eunuch but in his youth had become a *suntrophos* of the king. As an adult he proved to be more masculine in courage and character than eunuchs usually are. For he was a born soldier and spent most of his time in the company of other such men, and studying military matters. He was also very good in the art of conversation. In addition to that he was by nature benevolent (which is rare) and generous.[50]

[45] Diod. 22.3.1.
[46] Liv. 35.17.3–4.
[47] Diod. 19.46.1–4.
[48] Arr., *Anab.* 1.25.1 (*hetairoi*); Diod. 19.46.1–4; Polyb. 5.29.6; 8.21.2–3.
[49] Elias 1969: 135; Duindam 1994: 97–101.
[50] *Suda* s.v. 'Aristonikos' (=Polyb. 22.22.1–5).

Erudition and *esprit* characterised the true courtier.[51] Good behaviour and sharp-wittedness were essential in the competition for favour and status. Hellenistic courtiers are often depicted as flatterers (*kolakes*) and parasites (*parasitoi*) who use words to please their royal hosts. The character of the flatterer, who would say anything to please a powerful host, is well known from Hellenistic comedy and moral writings from the imperial period.[52] 'At dinner I am a wit, and cause much laughter and praise my host', exclaims a parasite in a comedy of Epicharmos, and Philip II had already enjoyed being surrounded by men 'who could say funny things'.[53] The image of the courtier as a flatterer, although topical, does testify to the importance of the art of conversation at the Hellenistic courts, especially during banquets and symposia. Josephus tells how a jester at the Ptolemaic court, 'who was appointed for jokes and laughter at feasts', made jokes at the expense of one of the *philoi*; when this man retaliated with an even cleverer joke, 'the king admired his answer, which was so wisely made, and directed them all to make an acclamation, as a mark of their approval of his jest'.[54] And when Ptolemy Philadelphos entertained Jewish scholars at his court, 'he began to talk philosophically to them, and asked everyone of them a philosophical question ... and when they had explained all the problems that had been proposed by the king about every point, he was well pleased with their answers'.[55] The complexity and learnedness of court poetry, with its references to obscure versions of myths and ingenious literary allusions, give some idea of the level of sophistication that was required to take part in the table talk at court.[56]

FACTIONS AND FAVOURITES

Theoretically, the *philoi* depended on the king's grace for obtaining and preserving status at court. The king decided who would become his friend and who would receive titles and offices. Assignments in the army and the government were ideally given on a temporal and ad hoc basis. As Polybios says, kings 'measured friendship and

---

[51] Strootman 1993: 59. Various anecdotes about conversations between kings and philosophers attest to this; see, among others, Ath. 493e–494b; Diog. Laert. 50.7.177; cf. Polyb. 15.34.3–4.

[52] See notably the collection of anecdotes in Ath. 235.

[53] Epicharmos, *CGF* 96 *ap.* Ath. 235f; cf. Eupolis, *CAF* I 301 *ap.* Ath. 236f. Philip II: Ath. 435c.

[54] Jos., *AJ* 12.4.9.

[55] Jos., *AJ* 12.2.12.

[56] See Strootman 2007: 202–16.

enmity by the sole standard of expedience'.[57] Thus, kings tried to
forestall the emergence of a hereditary, independent court aristocracy. An anecdote about Antigonos Gonatas articulates the ideal:
'When a young man, the son of a brave father, but not himself
having any reputation for being a good soldier, suggested the pro-
priety of his receiving his father's emoluments, Antigonos said: "My
boy, I give money and presents for the excellence of a man, not for
the excellence of his father."'[58] In practice, however, royal power was
rarely in the hands of the king alone. The Hellenistic kingdoms were
governed by elites who were dependent on the monarchy as an institution, and perhaps loyal to the dynasty. Loyalty to an individual
monarch, however, was a different matter. Philip and Alexander had
been more or less successful in pacifying the hereditary nobility of
old Macedonia. In the course of the third century new land-owning
aristocracies with hereditary prerogatives came into existence, and
ancestry again became a condition for status at court. The longer the
kingdoms existed, the more the families of leading *philoi* – who were
rewarded for their services to the crown with riches, landed estates
and status – acquired sources of income and prestige of their own.
This could be particularly troublesome when the royal title passed
from a deceased king to his successor. If the succession had been
prearranged by the former king, the transition to a new *sunedrion*
might take place gradually and placidly, especially when the
companions of the new king included the sons of his father's *philoi*.
Frequently, however, a new king would find it troublesome to
replace the sitting members of the royal council with his own intimates.[59] Attalos III at his accession allegedly killed *all* the *philoi* of
his father.[60] Landed estates distributed among *philoi* may ideally
have been open to reconsideration by his successor – all land in
theory being royal land – but in practice this was not easily done.
Thus in a decree of Kassandros, the king confirms gifts of land made
by Philip II and Alexander III, even though Kassandros was an
enemy of the latter.[61] To be sure, even strong and able kings like
Antiochos the Great or Philip V took to secret negotiations,
scheming and even murder to get their predecessors' men out of the
way and replace them with their own friends.

[57] Polyb. 2.47.5.
[58] Plut., *Mor.* 183d.
[59] For an opposite view see e.g. Hammond 1989: 55; Herman 1997: 215; Roy 1998: 111.
[60] Diod. 35–35.3.
[61] Hammond 1989: 55, who, however, understands this decree as evidence of a new king's
freedom to appoint his own selection of leading companions; I, rather, believe this is evidence
of the exact opposite. For Kassandros' enmity towards Alexander see Bosworth 1986: 11–12.

Norbert Elias conceptualised the early modern court as an instrument for the creation of absolutist power. Later studies, however, have shown the limitations of royal power in the age of absolutism, even at court. Duindam, in his critique of Elias' model, has noted that:

> The monarch bestowed favours upon parts of the elite to bind them, and subsequently eliminated troublesome opponents in cooperation with those elites. The elite in turn interceded at court for its own clientele. The pyramids of clienteles kept the various parts of a territory together, ... [and] it was rare that the monarch was the sole source of income and prestige for nobles.[62]

At the Hellenistic courts, too, *philoi* had obligations towards their own friends and relatives. All powerful *philoi* maintained retinues of their own.[63] The size of a *philos'* personal following, and the status of his *xenoi*, were indicative of his own standing and power.[64] But being a patron also involved obligations to act in the interest of one's clients. *Philoi* furthermore often acted at court in the interest of their cities of origin.[65]

In other words, various, often opposite interests were represented at court. As a result, the Hellenistic courts were fundamentally discordant – not only because of the endemic disputes over precedence among the sons and wives of the king, but also because *philoi* competed with each other for the king's favour.[66] These two forms of power struggles were interwoven. *Philoi* joined forces in informal factions led by a powerful man or woman – a queen, a prince, a leading man from the *sunedrion* – to secure their position and overcome their rivals. Important men tried to gather around themselves a following as large as possible, both as a source of power and as a tangible sign of their importance at court.[67] For example, in 203, the

---

[62] Duindam 1994: 79.

[63] Plut., *Cleom.* 32.2; Diod. 34.3.1; Ath. 245a; Agatharchides, *FHG* II 476 *ap.* Ath. 155d. According to Ath. 251c the philosopher Persaios, a *philos* of Antigonos Gonatas, even boasted a parasite of his own, a certain Ariston of Chios.

[64] Herman 1997: 216; cf. Herman 1987: 151.

[65] Savalli-Lestrade 1996: 149–81 shows that the activities of five Attalid *philoi* were motivated not only by the king's interests but also by obligations to the *poleis* they represented.

[66] As Lane Fox 1979: 431 commented on the court Alexander: 'Men who love a powerful or popular man do not therefore love each other, and it is no surprise that Craterus, for example, hated Hephaestion, Hephaestion hated Eumenes and Eumenes hated the leader of the Shield Bearers [i.e. Hephaistion].' Note that in this listing the most powerful man, Hephaistion, is also the most hated; see the fundamental remarks of Burke 1992: 58 on social groups in general: 'It cannot be assumed that every group is permeated by solidarity; communities have to be constructed and reconstructed. It cannot be assumed that a community is homogeneous in attitudes or free from conflicts.' For conflict as characteristic of *Ancien Régime* courts consult Duindam 1994: 28–30; for the instability of the Greek *oikos* see Cox 1998: 130–67.

[67] Herman 1997: 216.

stratēgos Tlepolemos plotted against Agathokles, who at that time was the most powerful man among the Ptolemaic courtiers:

> Tlepolemos, who wished to win over generals, commanders and lesser officers, entertained such men most lavishly at banquets; and on these occasions ... he would make remarks about Agathokles and his family, cautiously at first, then putting him down more openly, and finally flagrantly insulting him ... As his guests always laughed with him and contributed something of their own witticism to his jokes, the matter soon reached the ears of Agathokles. Their enmity was now complete, and Agathokles lost no time in making insinuations against Tlepolemos himself, accusing him of disloyalty to the king and of planning to help [the Seleukid king] Antiochos take over control of the kingdom.[68]

Similarly, in what may be a fictional account, Aristaios, 'one of the most intimate friends', wished to obtain freedoms for the Jews in Alexandria, and therefore first secured the goodwill of two powerful *philoi*, Sosibios of Taras and Andreas, the captains of the guard; subsequently, when he made his request before the king and the *sunedrion*, Sosibios and Andreas supported him, and persuaded the king to make a decree in accordance with Aristaios' wish.[69]

Through their involvement in the rivalry between wives and half-brothers, *philoi* could win a lightning career if the prince they supported succeeded to the throne, but risked exile or death when this was not the case. The philosopher Demetrios of Phaleron was imprisoned by Ptolemy Philadelphos because he had backed Philadelphos' half-brother in the struggle over the succession won by Philadelphos' faction.[70] Kings tried, for better or for worse, to profit from the rivalries through the principle of divide and rule. Often, however, the king did not succeed in remaining a lofty arbiter but became himself a participant in factional conflicts. This is what happened when Philip V succeeded to the Antigonid throne in 218. The young king had inherited a council consisting of the former *philoi* of his predecessor, Antigonos Doson. The *sunedrion* instantly became divided into two factions, both trying to win the favour of the new king – even though Doson 'in his will ... had left orders how and by whom each matter was to be managed with the aim of leaving no pretext for rivalries and quarrels among the courtiers (περὶ τὴν αὐλήν)'.[71] One faction was led by a certain Apelles, the other by Alexandros, captain of the bodyguard, and Taurion,

---

[68] Polyb. 15.25.31–4; cf. 50.10–14; and Plut., *Cleom.* 32.3.
[69] Jos., *AJ* 12.17–32.
[70] Diog. Laert. 5.77–8.
[71] Polyb. 4.87.7.

'minister of Peloponnesian affairs'; Apelles was allied with Leontios, the captain of the peltasts, and Megaleas, the chief secretary.[72] Initially, Apelles was triumphant: 'the governors and dignitaries in Macedon and Thessaly referred all matters to him, while the Greek cities in voting gifts and honours made little mention of the king, but Apelles was all in all to them'.[73] The king, however, secured the collaboration of Apelles' enemies; when this was done, he publicly made it known that Apelles had fallen into disfavour by refusing to see him:

> After arriving with great pomp owing to the number of officers and soldiers who had flocked to meet him, [Apelles] proceeded immediately to the royal quarters. He was about to enter, as was his custom, when one of the guards, acting on orders, stopped him, saying that the king was engaged. Disconcerted by this unexpected affront, Apelles … withdrew much abashed, upon which his followers at once began to drop away quite openly, so that finally he reached his private quarters accompanied only by his own servants.[74]

Thereafter Apelles, because of his status, 'was still invited to state banquets and received other such honours, but took no part in councils and was no longer admitted to the daily service of the king. Apelles and several of their followers committed suicide; his remaining associates were put on trial before the *sunedrion* and the army assembly, on charges of cowardice and insult, and ultimately executed.[75] A similar conflict accompanied the accession of Antiochos III in 223/2. In Polybios' book 5 a detailed, and well-informed, account has been preserved of these events, which I have discussed in detail elsewhere.[76]

Attempting to curtail the autonomy of the *philoi*, kings sometimes promoted a 'favourite', an individual who was favoured by the king disproportionately in order to create a protective shield between himself and the nobility. A favourite was typically a relative outsider who had no previous independent power base or hereditary rights to warrant the high position to which he or she was elevated by means of 'favour', i.e. the measure of access to the king a courtier had.

Favourites are mainly associated with early modern Europe between c. 1550 and 1650, with Buckingham, Olivares and

[72] Polyb. 4.87.5–8: ἐπὶ τῆς θεραπείας; ἐπὶ των κατὰ Πελοπόννησην; ἐπὶ τῶν πελταστῶν; ἐπὶ τοῦ γραμματείου.

[73] Polyb. 5.25.5.

[74] Polyb. 5.26.9–14.

[75] Polyb. 5.26.15–29.6. Compare 2 Macc. 4.34–8, on Antiochos IV sacrificing his favourite Andronikos when rioting broke out in Antioch, blaming him for the murder of the high priest Onias: Andronikos' purple robe was taken from him, after which he was given over to the angry mob to meet his death.

[76] Strootman 2011a; these events are also discussed by Herman 1997.

Richelieu as the best-known examples. Favourites rise to power particularly when the political equilibrium in a monarchical state is being redefined, that is, at key moments in the evolution of absolutism and state centralisation (e.g. in France under Louis XIII). They appear at the Hellenistic courts in comparable contexts. We encounter them at the Argead court in the reigns of Philip and especially Alexander, who employed favourites in his struggle with the *hetairoi*. The Seleukids and Ptolemies from c. 220 BCE used favourites to offset the growing power of a land-owning class of Greek *philoi*.[77]

Various characteristics of favourites may be distinguished.[78] For instance, they often have no connections with the established court elite.[79] They often have no legal offspring.[80] They usually hold no formal position within the court hierarchy: their bond with the king is personal and they have exclusive routine access to his presence; if they do hold an aulic office, it is often connected with the king's personal sphere, for instance *sōmatophulax* at Alexander's court.[81] As the king distances himself more and more from established court society (Antiochos IX, Louis XIII and Mehmet IV notoriously left their courtiers behind to go hunting),[82] courtiers are forced to deal with the favourite instead. Because of his or her proximity to the monarch, the favourite functions as a screen between the king and court society, controlling access.[83] Because the favourite derives his or her elevated position not from pedigree, *Hausmacht* or aulic status but from the informal privilege of having direct access to the king, the king can potentially withdraw his favour by *denying* the favourite access.

Favourites are recognisable in history because throughout they are described in terms of the same stereotypes that reflect the opinion of the established court elite. First, there are often markers of 'otherness': they are Egyptians, eunuchs, priests, exiled men, women, and often of low birth. Second, they usually have a bad reputation. The favourite is the archetypal wicked counsellor, avaricious and hungry

[77] Strootman 2007: 94–101.
[78] See esp. Kaiser and Pe ar 2003: 11–14.
[79] Asch 2004: 528–9.
[80] Brockliss 1999: 281–2.
[81] Asch 2003: 24–5, 2004: 517–19; Brockliss 1999: 280; Kaiser and Pe ar 2003: 16.
[82] For Antiochos IX see Diod. 34.34: 'He would often slip away from his *philoi* at night and making his way to the country with two or three servants go in pursuit of lions, panthers, or wild boars.' The 'favourite' to whom he left political matters in his absence was a eunuch called Krateros (Diod. 33.28.1; *RIG* no. 1158; see also above), Antiochos' *tropheus*. whom we have already encountered in Chapter 6.
[83] Feros 1999: 219; Hirschbiegel 2004: 37–8; Paravicini 2004: 17.

for power. The other courtiers are said to hate him or her because of his or her unjustified influence on the king, whom he or she is said to have put under a spell, manipulating him in private with the purpose of taking control of the kingdom.[84] Herakleides, Philip V's notorious favourite, allegedly began his political career with an abortive attempt to betray his native city of Taras (Tarentum) to the Romans, only to betray the Romans in turn and go over to the court of Philip. This is how Polybios characterises him:

> He was ... of a low family of manual workers, and he had many qualities which fitted him for bold and unscrupulous undertakings. His boyhood had been stained by notorious immorality; ... in the presence of the vulgar no one could be more bullying and audacious; to those in high position no one more insinuating and servile.[85]

The favourite usually takes responsibility for unpopular measures but is sacrificed when things go wrong so that the king, while pleading his own innocence, may restore good relations with the court nobility. Here again is Herakleides, but now in the words of Diodoros:

> Philip, the king of the Macedonians, had by him a certain knavish fellow, Herakleides of Taras, who in private conversations made many false and malicious charges against the *philoi* whom Philip held in high esteem. Eventually Philip sank so low in impiety as to murder five leading members of the *sunedrion*. From that point on his situation deteriorated, and by embarking on unnecessary wars he came near to losing his kingdom at the hands of the Romans. For none of his friends any longer dared speak their minds or rebuke the king's folly for fear of his impetuous temper.[86]

When Philip's popularity dwindled because of his lack of success against the Romans, he blamed Herakleides for it and arranged the latter's downfall.[87]

A favourite rises to power through the arbitrary conferment of royal favour. The fear of falling from grace again theoretically secures a favourite's loyalty. But precisely because the king bestows favour on him or her disproportionally, the favourite in turn can

---

[84] Asch 2004: 526–7; cf. Feros 1999, a study of contemporary authors' reactions to the earlyseventeenth-century favourites: 'Even if the royal favourite did not attempt to usurp the king's crown, he surely transformed his monarch into a tyrant through his undeserved influence and evil advice' (p. 208). The promising young king who becomes a tyrant when corrupted by flattery and the advice of wicked counsellors is a recurring *topos* in Polybios; this is particularly the case in his account of the reign of Philip V, but see also e.g. the concise narrative in 8.22.1–3: 'Cavarus, king of the Thracian Gauls, being naturally kingly and high-minded, ... was corrupted by the flatterer Sostratos, a native of Chalcedon.'

[85] Polyb. 13.4.

[86] Diod. 28.2; cf. Polyb. 13.4.

[87] Diod. 28.9; Liv. 32.5.

bestow privileges on others and become himself or herself the hub of a web of patronage. As a result, the favourite's power becomes ingrained in the court system, giving him or her the opportunity actually to influence decision-making.[88] As Werner Paravicini noted, there is always the difficult question of whether we are dealing with rule *by means of* a favourite (to the advantage of the king) or rule *by* a favourite (for the favourite's own benefit).[89] A Hellenistic example of the latter situation is the case of Apelles, a mighty man in the entourage of Antigonos Doson who, as we saw above, retained his position in the early years of Philip V: 'The governors and dignitaries in Macedonia and Thessaly referred all matters to him, while the Greek cities in voting gifts and honours made little mention of the king, but Apelles was all in all to them' (Polyb. 5.25.5). This is why kings often contrive the downfall of their favourites before they become too powerful. Indeed, the fact that sooner or later they always fall from grace may be considered another defining characteristic of a true favourite.[90] As we also saw above, Philip V arranged the downfall of the aforementioned Apelles by first securing the collaboration of Apelles' enemies and then *publicly* denying him 'access'.

At the Ptolemaic court of the second and first centuries BCE, Egyptians, as well as eunuchs, turn up in very powerful positions. Their relative prominence contrasts with the fact that Egyptians in general were conspicuously absent from the Alexandrian *philoi* society. Above, we have already encountered the Egyptian courtier Aristonikos, a prominent *philos* of an unknown Ptolemy of the second century, whose uniqueness was emphasised by Polybios.[91] Between 169 and 164, Ptolemy VI ruled through an Egyptian favourite called Petosarapis, known also by the Greek name of Dionysios. Diodoros says that Petosarapis wielded greater influence at court than anyone else; he also stereotypes Petosarapis as a typical favourite by saying that he tried to stir rebellion and wished to win control of the kingdom himself.[92]

Palace women could become favourites, too. Apart from the official royal wives, concubines of the king often acquired power and influence at court on account of their closeness to the king. In the

[88] Kaiser and Pečar 2003: 12–13.
[89] Paravicini 2004: 18; cf. Polyb. 5.50.4–5, emphasising that Hermeias' power rested on his prerogative of being in the presence of King Antiochos at all times.
[90] Asch 2004: 516.
[91] Polyb. 22.22.1–5 *ap. Suda* s.v. 'Aristonikos'.
[92] Diod. 31.15.1–4.

literary sources one often finds the *topos* of the royal concubine as a vulgar, unscrupulous, power-hungry courtesan who turns the king into a 'slave':

> In the temples of Alexandria there were many statues of Kleino, the cup-bearer of Ptolemy Philadelphos, representing her in a *chiton* and holding a rhyton. And are not some of the richest houses [in Alexandria] owned by Myrtion, Mnesis and Potheine? But what are Mnesis and Potheine but flute-players, and was Myrtion not one of those vulgar professional mime actors? And was Ptolemy Philopator not the slave of the courtesan Agathokleia, who brought the kingdom to the brink of collapse?[93]

This passage unwittingly underlines the power that 'official' royal mistresses might have. In the often antipathetic historiography they are stereotyped as depraved common girls or even prostitutes who seduce and enthral the king. For instance, the principal concubine of Ptolemy Philopator, the 'courtesan' Agathokleia, is described by Plutarch as a 'Samian dancing girl'[94] – in reality she was the full sister of Agathokles, Ptolemy's minister-favourite. Polybios' claim that Ptolemy Soter set up statues of his concubines in sanctuaries indicates that being a royal concubine was also a formal *public* role – an aulic office *avant la lettre*, reminiscent of the official *maîtresse en titre* at the court of Louis XIV.[95] Because concubines were in a position to communicate with the king in private, without other people being present, they could potentially help regulate access to the king by acting as brokers, as well as perhaps being intermediaries between a 'minister-favourite' and the king, as in the example of Agathokles and Agathokleia.[96]

The increasing presence of favourites at the courts of the Ptolemies and Seleukids provides indirect evidence for the development of the society of *philoi* into a landed aristocracy with a firm hold on the

---

[93] Polyb. 14.11.2–5. Similar characterisations of Agathokleia in Plut., *Kleom.* 33; Just. 30.1.7; Strabo 17.795; Ionn. Antioch., *FHG* IV 558. Both Justin and Polybios accuse Agathokleia of having murdered Queen Arsinoë, the latter (15.25.12) even holding her responsible for the death of Philopator himself. Diod. 33.13 relates how Ptolemy VIII's concubine Eirene persuaded the king to become a murderer. Nikolaos of Damascus, *FHG* III 414 *ap.* Ath. 593a, says about Myrrhine, a concubine of Demetrios Poliorketes: 'although he did not give her the diadem, he gave her a share in the royal power'.

[94] Plut., *Amat.* 9.

[95] For the official concubine at the French court see Horowski 2004: 98–107 and Hanken 1996. An additional reason for Hellenistic kings to maintain relationships with concubines may have been to produce offspring: either loyal 'bastard' sons to whom responsibilities could be delegated, or girls to be given away in marriage to cement alliances inside or outside the court. Thus a more complex set of connections may have interlinked the members of the court than is visible to us at first sight.

[96] A similar intermediary role could be performed by the king's personal physician, as in the case of Antiochos III and his doctor Apollophanes (Polyb. 5.56.2–3 and 6–7), who later acquired a seat in the royal council (Polyb. 5.58.3).

army and the court. The rise of favourites at the Hellenistic courts after c. 220 BCE was in all probability a reaction to that, directly connected to the increasing power of local vassal dynasties that we see in the Seleukid empire from the reign of Antiochos III onward.

PART III

Ceremonial and Ritual

9 *Ceremonial and Protocol*

Polybios reports that Antiochos III was awakened each morning at the same time by a select group of *philoi*.[1] This custom has also been attested for the court of Alexander and Mithradates Eupator, and is reminiscent of the ceremonial of *lever* known from the French court of the seventeenth and eighteenth centuries.[2] To be present when the king got dressed was a form of 'favour', a privilege that gave a courtier direct influence through access to the king. Like being a companion of the king in the hunt or a guest at his dinners and drinking bouts, this was a privilege indicative of a courtier's relative status within the informal hierarchy of the court. Polybios makes it clear that controlling court hierarchy was not at all a simple task for the king. In this specific instance it proved impossible for Antiochos to change the persons whose prerogative it was to be present. The king had to feign an illness to be alone in the early morning and be able to talk in private with one of his confidants, his personal physician Apollophanes, who subsequently secretly acted as messenger between the young king and his supporters.[3] Thus, although the selection of men attending the royal dressing room *could* be turned into an instrument of the king to manipulate access to his person, as Elias would have suggested, it could as well be a reflection of established positions and prerogatives beyond the grasp of the ruler.

Details of daily life at the Macedonian courts are in short supply. We know, however, enough to be sure that there existed a high degree of protocol regulating access to the king. Protocol no doubt varied from court to court, but the evidence does not allow us to see these differences clearly. A topical passage in Plutarch's biography of Kleomenes contrasts the modesty of the Spartan king with his Antigonid, Ptolemaic and Seleukid contemporaries:

[1] Polyb. 8.21.1.
[2] Curt. 8.6.13; Plut., *Pomp.* 32.4; for the French ceremony see Mieck 1982: 163.
[3] Polyb. 5.56.6–7.

When men came to Kleomenes, who was a real as well as a titled king, they saw no profusion of purple robes or mantles about him, and no array of couches and litters; [and] they saw, too, that he did not make the work of his petitioners grievous and slow by employing a throng of messengers and door-keepers or by requiring written memorials.[4]

Polybios says that Antiochos III in his early years as king 'was beset and preoccupied by court etiquette and by a host of guards (*phulakai*) and courtiers (*therapeia*), [so that] he was not his own master'.[5]

Besides daily ceremonial, opportunities for incidental celebrations were provided by the religious calendar, weddings and births, and private cults of the royal household.[6] In the Ptolemaic kingdom, the birth of a prince or princess was celebrated with a festival called *paidogonia*.[7] Several of the many festivals celebrated in Alexandria were organised by the court, such as the Ptolemaia and the Adonis festival described in Theokritos' fifteenth *Idyll*.[8] Anniversaries – birthdays of kings and queens,[9] as well as anniversaries of the coronation – were also occasions for religious celebration, involving the distribution of gifts and privileges, the reception of ambassadors and petitioners, and the demonstration of royal pomp and circumstance.

BANQUETS AND SYMPOSIA

Symposia and banquets were central to Hellenistic court life. In the time of the Argeads the symposium was already 'the key meeting place of king and court'.[10] It was said that Alexander dined among sixty or seventy companions almost every day.[11] In Greek domestic architecture, the *andron* was the central part of the house. In this room the male members of the family dined and gave banquets and

[4] Plut., *Cleom.* 13.2.
[5] Polyb. 5.50.2–3.
[6] See Plut., *Cleom.* 33.2, for cults for Dionysos and Kybele at the Ptolemaic court under Ptolemy IV.
[7] Diod. 33.13; cf. Jos., *AJ* 12.4.7: when Ptolemy VIII 'had a son just born, ... all the principal men of Syria and the other countries subject to him were to keep a festival, on account of the child's birthday'.
[8] For a complete overview of the evidence for Alexandrian festivals see Visser 1938; on the Adonis festival see Hölbl 2001: 98–9.
[9] See e.g. Diod. 34.15 on the celebration of the birthday of Kleopatra II in the *basileion* at Alexandria, in 126 BCE. Annual birthday celebrations of Seleukid kings: *OGIS* no. 212 and 222, 1.2; see Bickerman 1938: 246.
[10] Cameron 1995: 73. On the symposium at the Macedonian court under the Argeads: Borza 1983, 1990: 241–2; Lane Fox 1979: 63. The drinking habits of Hellenistic kings are discussed in Ath. 10.438d–440b; for Alexander's excessive drinking see Plut., *Mor.* 623d–624a; cf. O'Brien 1992. It was said that Mithradates Eupator 'put up prizes for the greatest eater and the greatest drinker ... He himself won the prizes for both' (Plut., *Mor.* 624a; cf. Nikolaos of Damascus, *FHG* II fr. 73 *ap.* Ath. 415e; Ath. 212d).
[11] Ephippos. *FGrH* 126 F 2.

symposia for their guests. As we saw in Chapter 3, the *andron* formed a basic element of Macedonian palatial architecture. Hellenistic palaces normally comprised many such rooms. The first floor (and perhaps there was no more than one) of the palace of Aigai consisted almost entirely of *andrones*. The palace at Pella consisted for a major part of *andrones*.

The many attestations of semi-private banquets and symposia taking place at royal courts, together with the archaeological evidence for the centrality of *andrones* in palaces, confirm their importance as loci for communication at court. Feasts, moreover, were pivotal occasions for the public distribution of status gifts, and offered a possibility of hierarchising and awarding favour through the positioning of guests relative to each other and to the king's place. The symposium in particular was a formalised, even sacralised, occasion for contact between courtiers and guests, and between courtiers and courtiers. Symposia thus were at the heart of court life on a regular basis – the context in which king and courtiers met, where political matters were discussed, where poets, scientists and technicians presented their work, and courtiers entered into erudite competition in the field of literature and philosophy.

State banquets, on the other hand, taking place more irregularly on specific festive occasions, were meant to entertain the court as well as guests from outside, although smaller regular sacrifices provided meals for only the courtiers and military commanders: 'Having pitched his camp early in the day, [Philip V] sacrificed a thank-offering to the gods for the success of his late enterprise and invited all his commanding officers to a banquet.'[12] By the eating of communal food, cohesion was probably created: members of separate households through the sharing of food were transformed into members of one household.[13] Lavish banquets for a multitude of guests furthermore served the purpose of advertising the wealth of the king and demonstrating the typical royal virtues of hospitality and generosity. By feeding many guests, a king acted as a nourisher of the people, which added to his superhuman status.[14] These banquets, too, could be sacrificial. The procession of Antiochos Epiphanes in Daphne was concluded with the sacrifice of no fewer

---

[12] Polyb. 5.14.8 (218 BCE).

[13] Paraphrased from Just and Monaghan 2000: 108.

[14] In various Near Eastern religions, the principal god had the task of feeding gods and humans; in a document from ancient Ugarit, Ba'al says: 'I alone am the one who can be king over the gods, who can fatten gods and men, who can satisfy the multitudes of the earth' (*CAT* 1.4, vii, lines 49–52; cited after Paul Sanders in *RBL* 06–2006); cf. Korpel 1990: 407–8, 411–13; and Claassens 2004 on the role of Yahweh as a giver of food to the people.

than 1,000 oxen and 300 cows, the greater part of the meat being eaten by the human participants in the ritual: apparently a huge crowd. During banquets the guests were entertained in various ways.[15] Some of the 'entertainment' was apparently of a ritual, religious nature: Demetrios of Skepsis says that at the court of Antiochos III 'it was the habit not merely of the royal *philoi* but also of the king himself to dance in arms at dinner'.[16] Antiochos IV danced naked before his guests during the sacrificial meal of the Daphne festival.[17] At the party's end, gifts were distributed, first of all tableware.[18] After having feasted his guests at a great banquet, Ptolemy Philadelphos 'gave to every one of them three garments of the best sort, and two talents of gold, and a cup worth one talent, and the furniture of the room in which they were feasted'.[19] A special honour at the Ptolemaic court was to be allowed to eat from the food provided for the king's own table.[20] This practice was presumably a continuation of an Achaemenid custom,[21] and may therefore have existed at the Seleukid court, too.

In Roman and western Greek sources, Hellenistic royal table manners are not always properly valued. Livy, who as a champion of Roman moral values was supposed to speak pejoratively about eastern royalty, writes that Antiochos Epiphanes made a fool of himself with his weird behaviour at banquets: 'He used to ignore his friends but smiled most amiably to unimportant people, and he was so inconsistent in his benefactions that he made a laughing stock of himself as well as his beneficiaries.'[22] Polybios, perhaps Livy's source, accuses Epiphanes of distributing gifts in a crazy manner.[23] The king's

---

[15] See for instance Jos., *AJ* 12.4.6 (187); Ath. 13.607c–d.

[16] Ath. 4.155b; cf. 12.550b on the heavyweight Ptolemy X Alexandros: '[but] when it came to the rounds of dancing at a *symposion* he would jump from a high couch barefoot as he was, and perform figures in a livelier fashion than those who had practised them'.

[17] Ath. 5.195e–f.

[18] Sokrates of Rhodes, *FHG* III 96 and 326 *ap.* Ath. 148a and 147f; Poseidonios, *FHG* III 263 *ap.* Ath. 540c; 1 Macc. 11.58; Jos., *AJ* 12.2.13–14; Plut., *Ant.* 25.4; *Mor.* 179f; Esther 2.18. See also Plut., *Ant.* 25.4, on the distributions of gifts during Kleopatra's banquet for Antony at Tarsos. For the significance of gift-exchange at the Hellenistic courts see also above, Chapter 4. For Hellenistic royal tableware consult Zimmer 1996: 130–5.

[19] Jos., *AJ* 12.2.14 (116). According to Poseidonios, *FHG* III 257 *ap.* Ath. 210d–e, Antiochos Grypos gave his guests after a banquet live geese, hares and antelopes, as well as horses, camels and slaves. Normally it was tableware that was distributed among the guests.

[20] Jos., *AJ* 12.2.13 (105).

[21] In the Achaemenid empire symbolic gift-exchange developed from a system of semi-economic redistribution of goods (Sancisi-Weerdenburg 1980: 145–73). On banqueting and the distribution of tableware and food at the Persian court see Briant 1989; see further Sancisi-Weerdenburg 1980: 154–5; Sancisi-Weerdenburg and Henkelman 1998; Briant 2002: 286–96. See further Lewis 1987: 79–87; Parpola 2004.

[22] Liv. 41.20.3.

[23] Polyb. 16.1.

inconsistency in giving presents is mentioned by other authors as well. Diodoros says that during banquets Epiphanes supposedly gave to one person a large number of gold coins but to another worthless things such as figs.[24] It is not difficult to see what really lay behind Epiphanes' strange manners – the king symbolically bestowed favour *and* disfavour. In the context of Achaemenid ceremonial banquets Sancisi-Weerdenburg has noted the distribution of 'negative gifts' by the king, especially giving plain pottery instead of gold and silver tableware.[25] Seen in this light, Livy's remark that the king ignored his *philoi* may be understood as an attempt by the king to favour men from outside the existing *clique* of courtiers. At least Livy did acknowledge that smiling at people in public was a means of signalling royal favour, implying that *not* being smiled at meant the opposite.

HOLDING COURT

Under the Roman emperors, Greek writers and their readers indulged in the opulence of Hellenistic court spectacle. In the writings of authors such as Plutarch and, particularly, Athenaios, the decadence and *hubris* of Hellenistic rulers is a recurrent *topos* that supplanted the classical theme of Persian luxury.[26] Fortunately, Athenaios often cites writers who were less far removed from the Hellenistic courts than he himself was; for instance, this colourful description by Phylarchos of a public audience at the court of Alexander:

> His tent was furnished with one hundred couches and was supported by fifty gilded pillars. The roof was covered with carpets embroidered with gold thread and sumptuously ornamented. Inside first five hundred Persian *mēlophoroi* stood, dressed in colourful robes of purple and yellow; behind them no fewer than one thousand archers were standing, some in flame-coloured clothing and many in dark blue clothes. In front of these were five hundred Macedonian *arguraspides*. In the centre of the pavilion stood a golden throne on which Alexander was seated, giving audience; at either side [of the throne] were his *sōmatophulakes*, standing close by him. Outside the pavilion the elephant contingent was arrayed in a circle, fully equipped, and also a thousand Macedonians in Macedonian costume, besides ten thousand Persians and a large company of five hundred who were all clad in purple, as Alexander had granted them permission to wear such clothes. And the

---

[24] Diod. 29.32.1; Ath. 194a. Some *philoi* received dice from Antiochos – one can only guess at what *that* may have meant.
[25] Sancisi-Weerdenburg 1980: 156 on Ath. 464a.
[26] See Gambato 2001.

number of friends (*philoi*) and guards[27] was so large that nobody dared to approach Alexander; such was the majesty of his presence.[28]

Phylarchos' source is Douris, who in turn drew upon the *Histories of Alexander* by Chares of Mytilene, Alexander's chamberlain.[29] Douris describes the setting as if it were theatre décor. The men put on stage here are a mixture of Persians and Macedonians (and apparently no Greeks), as well as a mixture of guardsmen and courtiers. The pavilion in which Alexander sits enthroned is reminiscent of the canopy under which the Achaemenid king was seated when giving audience.[30] Phylarchos' use of the words *arguraspides* and *philoi*, instead of *hypaspistai* and *hetairoi* respectively, is congruent with conventions at the courts of his own time, the late third century. Note that Alexander's closest confidants were gathered around his throne. Outside the tent were five hundred 'friends' dressed in purple clothing as a sign of their close proximity to the king. The Persian *mēlophoroi*, 'apple-bearers', so called by Greek sources because of the apple-shaped counterweight at the bottom of their spears, come straight out of the Achaemenid world. They formed a part of the company of *doruphoroi*, 'lance-bearers', appearing on the reliefs of the Great Apadana in Persepolis; they also figure in Persian royal texts, in particular the so-called Persepolis Fortification archive, besides being mentioned in various Greek sources such as Xenophon. In the Achaemenid empire, lance-bearers acted as the king's body-guards. They are sometimes called 'guards' or 'protectors' in Persian sources but were in fact high-ranking courtiers whose presence beside the throne was ceremonial and indicative of their status. They may be compared to the Macedonian *sōmatophulakes*.[31] The 'archers' (τοξόται) standing behind the *mēlophoroi* are either members of the Persian nobility, equipped with bows and quivers as befits their character as warrior-horsemen, or a detachment of the elite regiment

---

[27] Or 'attendants', 'courtiers': (θεραπευόντοι).

[28] Phylarchos, *FGrH* 81 F 41 *ap*. Ath. 539e–f. This evidence is discussed more extensively, in the light of Alexander's adoption of Persian court ceremonial, by Spawforth 2007b.

[29] Douris, *FGrH* 125 F 4; Lissone 1969: 141.

[30] On the canopy as signifier of majesty in the Achaemenid kingdom, see Paspalas 2005: 73–4.

[31] Lance-bearers and apple-bearers probably did not form part of the elite unit of 10,000 'Immortals', as Ath. 514b claims. On μηλοφόροι and δορυφόροι at the Achaemenid court see Henkelman 2002: besides establishing that both designations were in effect honorific titles, Henkelman mentions two interesting tablets (*PF* 11A and C) in which the king issues lances for his 'bodyguards'; the Achaemenid evidence mentions lance-bearers as members of royal travel parties and as such as the inspectors of the king's workmen, the royal sheepfold and the Royal Road. In the Greek Esther (2.21 and 6.2), δορυφόροι are high-ranking courtiers rather than guardsmen (but this may reflect Seleukid practice). Ath. 514c claims that the Persian *mēlophoroi* were noblemen.

of 10,000 'Immortals'. The presence of so many Iranians near the throne of Alexander is neither surprising nor unhistorical. This fragment of Phylarchos has been taken to reveal Alexander's attempt to replace Macedonian custom with Persian court ceremonial, or even his desire to mix Macedonians and Persians. It would be mistaken, however, to ascribe the presence of Persian nobles at this ceremonial occasion simply to the reportedly unique personality of Alexander. The ceremony in all likelihood took place in Persia before a largely Persian audience. By presenting himself as a Persian king – the golden throne and the forest of pillars are also reminiscent of the Achaemenid court – Alexander aimed at gaining acceptance among the Iranian nobility as the new Great King. On the other hand, he also had to reckon with his Macedonian following – hence the apparent 'mixture' of Macedonians and Persians (note, however, that the two groups are strictly separated from each other). Comparable pageantry may have taken place at the court of the Seleukids when on the road in Iranian lands. Notably, Seleukos Nikator in creating his empire depended on cooperation with Iranian aristocrats for his control of the east at least as much as Alexander did.

In this context the issue of the *proskynēsis* may also be mentioned. *Proskynēsis* is an inappropriate Greek umbrella term for a disparate variety of ritualised greetings performed before the king at the former Achaemenid court. Depending on his status, a man seeking audience would prostrate himself, kneel, bow or blow a kiss towards the monarch.[32] Alexander naturally took over this ceremonial in his dealings with Persians after his assumption of the status of Great King in 330. In 327 he went too far, perhaps deliberately, by demanding such obeisance from Macedonian aristocrats as well (although probably not in the form of prostration), thus violating the fiction of the equality of king and *hetairoi* – a far more plausible reason for their resistance than the alleged Greek and Macedonian association of this ceremonial with an act of worship.[33] Alexander's successors in the east perhaps continued the ceremony when playing the role of Great King before Iranians, but exempted the closest of their *philoi* and noble *Makedones* from the obligation to humiliate themselves publicly, since we no longer hear about it in Greek sources.

One interesting aspect of the Phylarchos fragment remains to be mentioned. This is the image of the king as a lonely figure distanced from the rest of the world, as apparent especially in the last sentence:

[32] Hdt. 1.134.
[33] Arr., *Anab.* 4.10.5–12.5; Plut., *Alex.* 54.

'the number of friends and guards was so large that nobody dared to approach Alexander'. But Alexander was giving audience! Even a more reliable historian like Polybios chastises Ptolemy Philopator because

> he began to conduct himself as if his chief concern were the idle pomp of royalty, showing himself as regards the members of his court (περὶ τὴν αὐλὴν) and those who administered Egypt inattentive to business, and difficult to approach, and treating with entire negligence and indifference those charged with the empire outside Egypt, to which the former king had paid much more attention than to the government of Egypt itself.[34]

This amounts to a paradox: kings were distanced from everybody and at the same time were expected to be accessible and amenable – a paradox that is akin to the one encountered when discussing the society of courtiers, namely that the king was elevated above all others and at the same time a *primus inter pares* among his peers, namely the members of the *sunedrion*. Furthermore, kings were still supposed to give audience to common people, hearing their requests and grievances. Anyone who presented a gift or petition to the king would as a matter of course receive whatever he wished from the benevolent lord. But access to the king was not easily obtained.

The evidence attesting to a ritualised, 'oriental' distancing of Hellenistic kings shows only one of two distinct faces of monarchic representation. For, on the other hand, we also hear of a strong moral obligation on the part of kings to be *easily* accessible for the rank and file of the army and even common people. This is best illustrated by two Hellenistic morality tales about kingship attributed to Demetrios Poliorketes and surviving in Plutarch's biography of the king as anecdotal mirror for the Roman emperor:

> One day when Demetrios was riding abroad and appeared to be in a more obliging mood than usual, and more willing to converse with his subjects, a large crowd gathered to present him with written petitions, all of which he accepted and placed in the fold of his cloak. The people were delighted and followed him on his way, but when he came to the bridge over the River Axios, he shook out the fold and emptied all the petitions into the water. This infuriated the Macedonians, who felt that Demetrios was insulting them, not governing them, and they recalled or listened to those who were old enough to remember the accessibility (κοινός) of Philip and how considerate he had been in such matters. On another occasion an old woman accosted Demetrios and kept asking him to give her an audience. Demetrios replied that he could not spare the time, whereupon the old woman screamed at him, 'Then don't be king!' This rebuke stung Demetrios to the quick. He went back to his

---

[34] Polyb. 5.34.2–5.

house, put off all other business and for several days gave audience to everybody who asked for it, beginning with the old woman.[35]

Several more anecdotes attest to a public image of the king who should lend an ear to even his humblest subjects at any time, publicly accepting petitions en route from people standing at the side of the road. Seleukos Nikator 'constantly repeated that if people would know what a task it was merely to read and write so many letters, they would not even pick up a diadem that had been thrown away'.[36] And Antiochos Sidetes 'held daily receptions to great crowds', distributing food to all.[37]

THE RECEPTION OF AMBASSADORS

As the male head of the household, the king was expected to maintain relations with the outside world, negotiating with other royal houses, vassals, civic elites and the odd republic. Like the individual petitioner in the Demetrios anecdote cited above, ambassadors of cities often found it hard to gain an audience with the king. For cities, too, the acceptance by the king of a gift (a golden crown, a statue to be set up in the agora, cultic honours) implied the granting of (part of) the accompanying request (the withdrawal of a garrison, exemption of taxes, the favourable settlement of a border dispute).

Foreign embassies, until being led before the king and the *sunedrion*, were entertained and feasted according to their rank.[38] Formal receptions were an opportunity to demonstrate wealth and military strength. When a Roman embassy led by Scipio Africanus arrived at Alexandria, 'Ptolemy [VIII] welcomed the men with a great reception and much pomp, held costly banquets for them, and conducted them about, showing them the *basileia* and all of the royal treasures.'[39] In the palace in second-century Alexandria, public receptions took place in a large propylon gatehouse, located in between the semi-public royal district (the *basileia*) and the palace proper on the Lochias peninsula (cf. Chapter 3).[40]

---

[35] Plut., *Demetr.* 42, trans. I. Scott-Kilvert. Cf. Plut., *Mor.* 173f; *Artax.* 5.
[36] Plut., *Mor.* 790a.
[37] Poseidonios, *FHG* III 257 *ap.* Ath. 210d.
[38] E.g. Diod. 28.12 (Roman commissioners before Antiochos III in 196); Polyb. 2.50.1–2; cf. 2.47.5 (Aratos before Antigonos III in 225); Polyb. 4.23.4–5 (Lakedaimonian envoys before Philip V in 221).
[39] Diod. 33.28b.1; cf. Polyb. 5.67.2: during the Fourth Syrian War, 'the chief object of Antiochos [III] was to prove himself in his interviews with the embassies coming from Alexandria decidedly superior both in military strength and in the justice of his cause'.
[40] Polyb. 15.31.2–3.

Envoys had to wait before being granted an audience, and sometimes also had to wait afterwards for an answer. Waiting is an instrument of power. Waiting ritually accentuated the king's distance from other people.[41] It could be used to hierarchise petitioners and apportion favour or disfavour. Most of all it could be used to prevent petitioners from offering the king a gift and irreversibly setting in motion the process of mandatory reciprocity, a process in which the king, as we saw in Chapter 7, was obliged to offer a counter-gift of higher value than the initial offering. Not accepting a gift was perhaps difficult for reasons of honour and morality, but the restricting of access to the person of the king was feasible because that would be in accordance with the king's higher status.[42]

During the Social War (or War of the Allies, 220–217), an Achaian embassy appeared before Philip V to ask for military support: 'The king, after listening to them, kept the envoys with him [at his court], saying that he would give their request consideration.'[43] The necessity for official consultation of the *sunedrion* before an answer was given was a matter of protocol, in accordance with the status of the *sunedrion*'s members as the king's peers. It was protocol facilitating games of power. Hellenistic court etiquette is mocked in an anecdote, recorded by Plutarch, about Sparta dispatching a single envoy to negotiate with Demetrios Poliorketes. '"What is this supposed to mean?" the king cried out. "Did the Spartans send one man only?" To which the ambassador replied, "Yes, o king, to one man."'[44] The anecdote emphasises what was *not* customary – in reality, even the Spartans would show the respect due to a king, sending an embassy of no fewer than ten envoys to Philip V, according to a more sober historical authority.[45] Violation of protocol is the crux in a notorious incident known as the Day of Eleusis in 168 BCE:

[41] This is a universal characteristic of despotic power. In 1995, UN secretary-general Boutros Boutros-Ghali travelled to the former republic of Zaire because President Mobutu had urgently requested a tête-à-tête with him. Michael Ignatieff, who accompanied the secretary-general on this trip, later recalled how surprised he was to see that Mobutu was nowhere to be seen when the head of the UN and his staff had arrived: 'President Mobutu, we are told, is still at mass. So we cool our heels in his guest palace, a suburban bungalow in a heavily guarded compound in the middle of the forest. Boutros-Ghali walks about, looks at his watch, runs his hands over Mobutu's collection of gold African figurines on their cool white marble plinths ... Why are we kept waiting? I ask one of the secretary-general's aides. Because, he whispers, Mobutu is king' (Ignatieff 1998: 82–3).

[42] Plut., *Cleom.* 13.1–2.

[43] Polyb. 4.64.2–3; cf. 10.41.8: '[Philip V] dismissed all the embassies after promising each to do what was in his power and devoted his whole attention to the war [against the Romans and their allies].'

[44] Plut., *Demetr.* 42.2.

[45] Polyb. 4.23.5.

When Antiochos [IV] had advanced against Ptolemy in order to take control of Pelousion, he was met by the Roman commander Popilius (Laenas). The king greeted him vocally from a distance and offered him his right hand, but Popilius presented to him the tablet he had in his hand which contained the Senate's decree, and asked Antiochos to read it first … When the king had read it, he said he wanted to consult with his friends on these new developments, but Popilius in reply did something which seemed insolent and arrogant to the highest degree. With a vine stick which he had in his hand he drew a circle around Antiochos and told him to give his reply to the message before he stepped out of that circle.[46]

Polybios contrasts the success of Popilius Laenas' straightforward approach with the failure of some Achaian ambassadors who had come the Seleukid court some time earlier with a peace proposal; when the Achaians were admitted to the *sunedrion* some time after their arrival (in which interval the king discussed matters with the *sunedrion*) they were first politely heard, then received from the king a prearranged refusal.[47]

An impression of reception protocol at the Ptolemaic court of the second century BCE is provided by the *Letter of Aristeas*, a second-century document paraphrased by Josephus. When emphasising the exceptional honours given to the seventy translators who were invited to Ptolemy Philadelphos' court to translate the Jewish scriptures, this document contrasts the reception they receive with standard procedures. First, the Jewish translators were given the extraordinary honour of being granted an audience without other guests and the royal entourage being present. Nor did they have to wait:

> [The king] ordered that all people who were normally present should be sent away, which was a surprising thing, something that was unusual for him to do. For those who were received there for such occasions used to come to him on the fifth day, but ambassadors always on the last day of the month.[48]

A more direct source, a late second-century papyrus containing a royal order concerning a Roman ambassador visiting the Egyptian countryside, contains first-hand, contemporary information:

> Let him be received with special magnificence and take care that at the proper spots the guest-chambers be prepared and the landing-places to them be got ready with great care, and that the gifts of hospitality mentioned below be

---

[46] Polyb. 29.27, trans. Austin; cf. Liv. 45.12.3–8; App., *Syr.* 66; Just. 34.3.1–4; Vell. Pat. 1.10.1. For the historical context and consequences of the Day of Eleusis see Mørkholm 1966: 64–101; Gruen 1984: 647; Mittag 2006: 214–24.

[47] Polyb. 28.20.1–9; cf. Plut., *Pyrrh.* 20, for a similar reception of Fabricius at the court of Pyrrhos.

[48] Jos., *AJ* 12.2.11 (87–8).

presented to him at the landing-places ... In general take the utmost pains in everything that the visitor may be satisfied.[49]

ROYAL WEDDINGS

Weddings belong to the category of those 'great events' when the household expanded to include an outer court consisting of many guests, among them representatives of subject states and foreign powers. Royal weddings were widely advertised. The coincidental survival of a variety of official communications connected with the politically important marriage in 177 BCE of the Antigonid king Perseus and Laodike, a daughter of Seleukos IV, shows that this was so both before and after the actual wedding.[50] Encomiastic poetry, too, could be used to celebrate a wedding.[51] The marriage of Mithradates I Kallinikos of Kommagene with the Seleukid princess Laodike Thea Philadelphos, a crucial marriage that linked the vassal dynasty of Kommagene with the imperial family, 'was endlessly celebrated in the dynasty's inscriptions', and after the wedding Mithradates adopted his epithet *kallinikos* to stress his ties with his father-in-law, Antiochos VIII Kallinikos.[52] It was this union that later gave Laodike's and Mithradates' offspring a legal claim to the title of Great King after the disappearance of the Seleukids.[53]

When Antiochos III married Laodike, the daughter of Mithradates III of Pontos, she was brought from her father's house by an embassy of Antiochos led by the admiral Diognetos of Seleukeia: 'Antiochos received the maiden with all due pomp and at once celebrated his nuptials with right royal magnificence. After the wedding festival was over he went down to Antioch, where he proclaimed Laodike *basilissa*.'[54] Weddings were celebrated with all due pomp, in the presence of many guests.[55] Even the relatively insignificant political

---

[49] *Sel. Pap.* II.416 (112 BCE).

[50] Habicht 1989: 339; the attestations of the Antigonid–Seleukid marriage alliance include a dedicatory inscription to Laodike from Delos (*IG* XL.1074); a dedication on Delos for King Perseus by a courtier, dated to 178 (*I.Del.* 140 A 43 and 443 B 71); and a hoard of 100 magnificent silver coins bearing the portrait of Perseus, found at Mersin in Kilikia; the coins were perhaps a reward given to the Seleukid *philos* who had accompanied the princess to Macedon (Seyrig 1973: 47–8).

[51] Kallimachos wrote a poem for the marriage of Ptolemy Philadelphos and Arsinoë, of which a fragment has remained (*fr.* 392); Theocr., *Id.* 17, 128ff., compared this brother–sister marriage to the *hieros gamos* of Zeus and Hera, whose love-making creates the fertility of the earth.

[52] Sullivan 1990: 60–1.

[53] Strootman 2010b.

[54] Polyb. 5.43.3–4.

[55] Diod. 16.92.1; 29.29.1; 31.16.1; Polyb. 5.43.3, 20.8; 30.25.1; Liv. 36.11.

marriage of Antiochos III with the daughter of a notable of the city of Chalkis in 192/1 BCE was a time-consuming event with 'brilliant assemblies and festivals' – although all this seems also to have been staged to keep the troops busy during the winter season.[56] Royal marriage ceremonial in the Hellenistic kingdoms could attain the character of a coronation when the bride upon her marriage was elevated to the status of principal royal consort, receiving the title of *basilissa* and a royal diadem.[57] At the Ptolemaic court, a brother–sister marriage could coincide with the royal couple's inauguration *and* the rites of royal deification of the deceased predecessor(s).[58]

HUNTING

Hunting was a central activity of royal households.[59] It had ceremonial and symbolic meaning related to the ideal of kingship, as an emblem of conquest and victory that reflected battle and vice versa. The great battle scene on one long side of the Alexander sarcophagus in Istanbul is mirrored by a hunting scene on the other. Just as the king ought to be a good warrior, so also he should be a good hunter.[60] The hunt provided opportunities to learn or practise skills needed for war: horsemanship, the use of weapons, courage and persistence, and the ability to take life.[61] Hunting helped creating group identity and cohesion among the *philoi*, and was potentially a means to hierarchise court society. To be the companion of the king in the hunt was a privilege like the honour of being invited to his table. Most of all, the hunt was a paradigm of the aristocratic notion of courage and manliness.[62]

It was normally a king's prerogative to kill the hunted animal.

---

[56] Diod. 29.2; cf. Polyb. 20.8; Liv. 36.11.

[57] Plut., *Luc.* 18.3; Polyb. 5.43.4; Nikolaos of Damascus, *FHG* III 414 *ap.* Ath. 593a.

[58] Diod. 16.92.1; Lanciers 1988.

[59] Significance of hunting for Hellenistic monarchy: Diod. 31.27.8; 34.34; Plut., *Mor.* 184c; *Demetr.* 50; Plin., *NH* 7.158; 35.138; Polyb. 31.29; Arr., *Anab.* 4.13.2; cf. Rostovtzeff 1967 I: 296; Bevan 1902 II: 278. For representations of the royal hunt in Hellenistic art see Pollitt 1986: 38–41; for Greek and Macedonian hunting in general consult Anderson 1985 and Barringer 2002. Specifically on the royal hunt in (early) Hellenistic Macedonian context: Briant 1993; Carney 2002; Tripodi 1992 and 1998.

[60] In Polyb. 22.3.8–9 a Ptolemaic envoy in Greece praises Ptolemy V for his 'skill and daring in the chase, ... expertness and training in horsemanship and the use of weapons'. Cf. Phylarchos, *FHG* 81 fr. 49; Plut., *Pyrrh.* 4.4; *Demetr.* 50; Diod. 34.34; Polyb. 5.37.10. While staying at the court of Ptolemy I as a hostage, Pyrrhos distinguished himself while hunting with the king (Plut., *Pyrrh.* 4.4). Prousias II of Bithynia was surnamed 'the Hunter' (ὁ κυνηγὸς: App., *Mithr.* 12.1.2).

[61] In Greek classical literature the educational value of hunting is emphasised, e.g. Pl., *Leg.* 822d; Xen., *Cyn.* 1.

[62] Roy 1998: 113.

Antiochos IX, who was 'addicted to hunting', hunted lions, panthers and wild boars and was '[so] reckless, [that] he frequently put his own life in extreme peril'.[63] To kill a ferocious animal was like defeating a mighty enemy, ideally in single combat. Symbolically this was tantamount to saving the land from danger and creating peace and order. The image of the royal hunt as a battle between (natural) chaos and (human) order is also well known from the pre-Hellenistic Middle East, in particular Assyrian palace reliefs and Achaemenid royal propaganda.[64] In Greek mythic tradition, saviour heroes like Herakles and Theseus rid the land of dangerous beasts and thereby lay the foundation for civilised human society. At Versailles under Louis XV an entire gallery of paintings, the Petite Galerie, was devoted to the 'exotic hunt', with hunting pieces associating the French king with heroes from Greek mythology and ancient history, based on Greek and Roman authors such as Pliny and Diodoros; the hunting of exotic animals on these paintings symbolised the victory of civilisation over barbarity.[65]

Hunting had been the leading pastime of the Argead aristocracy long before Alexander.[66] In Greece and the Balkans, in both reality and myth, the wild boar and the lion were considered the hunter's most formidable antagonists. Apart from Alexander himself, Lysimachos, Krateros and Perdikkas were famous lion-slayers too.[67] On two mosaics from Pella youthful hunters (sometimes identified as Alexander and Krateros) adopt a heroic pose, expressing heroic *andreia*. Barringer argued that in aristocratic cultures of the Hellenistic age the image of hunting became more mythological, and developed into a means of turning (contemporaneous) mortal men into heroes.[68]

In the case of the boar hunt – a more common activity among the Macedonians than the lion hunt prior to the conquests of Alexander, although mountain lions and leopards did exist in the Balkans – the meat of the victim was eaten by the hunters in a festive banquet following sacrifice, thus making the hunt a double opportunity for ritualised male bonding. This is similar to the practice in epic

---

[63] Diod. 34.34.
[64] Weissert 1997.
[65] Salmon 1995: 33; two notorious royal hunting addicts of early modern Europe, Louis XIII and Mehmet IV, more probably used the hunt as a means to make themselves inaccessible: while the ruler was out hunting in the Bois de Boulogne or Belgrade Forest, the courtiers and others were forced to deal instead with a favorite (Richelieu and Kara Mustafa respectively).
[66] Hammond 1989: 142; Carney 2002. Cf. Polyb. 22.3.8; Arr., *Anab.* 4.13.2.
[67] Lund 1992: 6–8.
[68] Barringer 2002.

tradition (e.g. *Odyssey* 10.153) but perhaps in contrast to classical Athens, where, it has been argued, aristocrats hunted for status but not for meat, since it seems that on Attic vases and funeral reliefs noble banqueters are provided with game meat by professional hunters of lower status.[69]

Ancient sources claim that traditionally a young Macedonian aristocrat came of age upon ritually killing his first wild boar in the wilderness, after which he took his place among the adults and was allowed to recline at banquets (instead of sitting, as *paides* did); it was even said that killing a boar had replaced a more ancient *rite de passage* in which a man was killed.[70] After the conquests of Alexander, Macedonian kings had the opportunity to stage (lion) hunting parties on a grand scale, using former Achaemenid *paradeisoi* as hunting grounds, besides creating new ones themselves. The Near Eastern notion of the relation between hunting and royalty blended with Macedonian ideology.

The fact that the royal hunt is a more common motif in Mesopotamia than in Greece and the Balkans before Alexander does not in itself warrant the conclusion that the Macedonian royal hunt was originally 'eastern'.[71] The 'heroic' hunting of dangerous animals, of course, may be characteristic of any aristocratic society in a country where such animals lived. Indeed, Asiatic mountain lions did exist in northern Greece and the Balkans. Their presence is mentioned by Aristotle and has been archaeologically confirmed; in Greece, lions became extinct only in c. 80–100 CE, and they probably lasted longer in the Balkans to the north of the Macedonian plain; in Anatolia, the last lion was shot as late as 1870.[72] The fact that (visual) evidence for Macedonian royal hunts is more abundant for the period after Alexander may be due to the general lack of archaeological evidence for early Argead court culture. All this, of course, does not preclude cultural interaction, especially regarding the *imagery* of hunting at Pella and Vergina, as Olga Palagia has shown.[73] In like manner Hellenistic royal art consequently influenced the development of

---

[69] Chorus 1994; Schmitt Pantel and Schnapp 1982; Ghedini 1992.

[70] Hegesander F 33 *ap.* Ath. 18a; cf. Curt. 8.6.5. See Hammond 1989: 56; Cameron 1995: 83 n. 82.

[71] *Pace* Briant 1991a and 1991b. Palagia 2000 is more nuanced, arguing that the hunting scenes from Pella and Vergina, which she dates to the late fourth century, were inspired by the hunts staged by Alexander in Persian *paradeisoi*; see Palagia 1998. Carney 2002 argues for the continuity of Argead hunting traditions in the Hellenistic period; on the mosaics and their significance see now also Cohen 2010.

[72] Guggisberg 1961; cited from the website of the Asiatic Lion Information Centre, www.asiatic-lion.org; visited January 2006.

[73] Palagia 2000; cf. Paspalas 2005: 72 with n. 4.

hunting imagery in Roman imperial representation, especially as an expression of the emperor's *virtus*.[74]

DRESS CODES FOR (EARLY) HELLENISTIC (MACEDONIAN) COURTIERS?

Social roles are expressed and in part determined through the display of material status symbols, clothing and personal adornment, notably on ceremonial occasions. Clothing is communicative of an individual's social, economic or official identity, and is thereby instrumental in the construction of group identity. The Russian anthropologist Bogatyrev understood that 'in order to grasp the social functions of costumes we must learn to read them as signs in the same way we learn to read and understand languages'.[75] This basic idea was elaborated by Schwarz, who added the observation that clothing not only expresses social roles but may actually influence social behaviour: 'The ability of clothing to move [other] men to act in the culturally appropriate manner may be called its symbolic or rhetorical power; through their capacity to symbolize a social order, clothes are related to social action and communication in a dynamic way.'[76] Status markers can be monopolised – by their expensiveness and rarity, by morality, and even by legislation or by rulers.[77]

Evidence for dress codes for Hellenistic *philoi* is somewhat scarce. It is impossible to say what subtle signs indicated differences in rank and status among the *philoi*, what distinguished the important from the very important, or how courtly clothing developed through time and what differences there were between the kingdoms. Some general principles of court dress may be reconstructed, although most of the evidence dates to the early Hellenistic period, in the decades after the Macedonian conquest, when the courts of the respective monarchies were more similar to one another than in later ages.

Clothing helped construct cohesion among the *philoi* group at court. By dressing in a similar manner the *philoi* expressed their loyalty to each other. And to the king: the dress of the *philoi* was basically derived from the dress of the king. Moreover, they could receive their clothing from the king as a status gift, especially mantles

---

[74] Tuck 2005.

[75] Bogatyrev 1971: 83.

[76] Schwarz 1979: 23; cf. Eicher and Roach 1979: 7: '[Costume] suggests the behaviors (roles) of people on the basis of their ... multiple connections with each other and can, therefore, distinguish the powerful from the weak, the rich from the poor, ... the leader from the follower.'

[77] Reinhold 1969: 300; Bonfante 1994: 5.

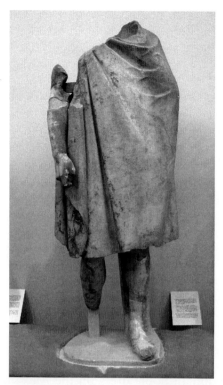

Fig. 9.1. Daochos I, tetrarch of Thessaly, wearing a *chlamus* on the Daochos monument in Delphi, c. 335 BCE (author's photograph).

with purple ornamentation that were the material tokens of aulic offices (see below; cf. Chapter 7).

The most distinctive elements of the costume in which *philoi* appeared in public, as it is known from written sources, mosaics and frescoes, were riding boots (*krepides*), hat (*kausia*) and short mantle (*chlamus*),[78] the traditional costume of the Macedonian nobility, and also worn by kings.[79] *Chlamus* and *krepides* were used in the whole of Greece, but the combination was typical of aristocracies in Thessaly and Macedon. The Macedonian *chlamus* differed in shape and size from the Greek version. It was a short mantle in the shape of a semicircle, attached with a clip on one of the shoulders. The mantle originated in Thessaly or Macedon as a rider's cloak and could be worn over a cuirass (Fig. 9.1). It is this variant of the *chlamus* that is

[78] *Krepides*: Plut., *Ant.* 54.5; *Mor.* 760b; Hdn. 4.8; *krepides* were perhaps originally sandals with straps bound as high as the knees, worn with cloth underneath (Neuffer 1929: 24). *Kausia* and *chlamus*: Polyb. 15.33.4; Plut., *Cleom.* 13.2.

[79] Plut., *Mor.* 178d; *Ant.* 54.5; *Demetr.* 41.4–5; cf. Ath. 253d–254b; 535f; Val. Max. 5.1 ext. 4. Plut., *Ant.* 54.5; Eusthatios *ad Od.* 1399; Hdn. 4.8.1–2.

Fig. 9.2. Alexander's battledress. Detail of the Alexander mosaic from Pompeii
(Museo Nazionale in Naples).

depicted as Macedonian noble dress on the Alexander sarcophagus
and the mosaics of Pella.[80] On the Alexander mosaic, Alexander
wears a long-sleeved tunic under his armour, and this piece of
clothing too seems typical of northern Greece and Macedon
(Fig. 9.2). The companion cavalrymen on the Alexander sarcophagus
wear long-sleeved tunics over Greek-style *chitons* (Fig. 9.3). The
kausia was a piece of traditional Macedonian costume; it was a cap
made of wool, leather or felt. It looked a little like a beret, but according to some the word could also refer to the mushroom-shaped
soldier's cap known best from Hellenistic genre terracotta figurines
(see below).[81] In pre-Hellenistic Macedon, *kausiai* were worn by the
ruling classes and had military connotations (Fig. 9.4).

   The origin of the *kausia* is obscure since the word is not mentioned
in Greek literature before 326 BCE. It has been related to the better-
known Thessalian *petasos* and has therefore often been translated
as 'broad-brimmed hat'. In his overview of Hellenistic terracotta
figurines, Thompson identified the *kausia* as the mushroom-shaped

   [80] Neuffer 1929: 22; Saatsoglou-Paliadeli 1993: 143. Evidence for the *chlamus* in Greek
culture is collected by Heuzey 1922: 116–41. Plut., *Alex.* 26.5 and Plin., *NH* 5.62 compare the
ground plan of Alexandria with the shape of a *chlamus*.
   [81] Saatsoglou-Paliadeli 1993: 122–47; the material evidence is catalogued by Dintsis 1986.

Fig. 9.3. Companion cavalrymen on the Alexander sarcophagus in the
Archaeological Museum, Istanbul (author's photograph).

common soldier's cap.[82] Since that cap was then not known from
pre-Hellenistic times, he suggested an oriental origin. Taking this
to heart, Kingsley argued in three articles that the *kausia* originated
in Baktria and can be identified with the modern *chitrali*, the well-
known mushroom-shaped woollen cap worn by men in eastern
Afghanistan and northwest Pakistan.[83] It seems more probable,
however, that the word *kausia* – mentioned in the sources mainly in
relation to kings and aristocrats – refers to the berets depicted e.g. on
Baktrian coins and the hunting mosaics of Pella.[84] Prestianni-
Galliombardo maintained that the *kausia* was a piece of exclusive
royal headgear introduced by Alexander.[85] It is, however, more likely
that the cap originated in the Balkans earlier, as Neuffer had already
argued,[86] but made its debut in the Greek sources only after the

[82] Thompson 1963: 53–5.
[83] Kingsley 1981a, 1981b, 1984.
[84] Fredricksmeyer 1986.
[85] Prestianni-Galliombardo 1989: 9.
[86] Neuffer 1929: 23–4.

Fig. 9.4. Tetradrachm of Philip II showing the laureate head of Zeus (obverse) and the king on horseback wearing the Macedonian *kausia* and a *chlamus* (courtesy of the Classical Numismatic Group Inc.).

Macedonian expansion under Philip and Alexander. Later archaeological findings support this conclusion: 'The new archaeological evidence reaffirms the reliability of the ancient sources, attributing [*kausia, chlamus* and *krepides*] to the Macedonians long before their campaign to the east. Therefore *argumenta e silentio* seem to be on the retreat in the face of ... new archaeological material being discovered in Northern Greece'.[87]

At the Argead court under Philip II and Alexander this attire was the distinctive dress of the companion aristocracy. It remained in use in the successor kingdoms as the standard (ceremonial) costume of the court nobility, at least in the generation of the Diadochs.[88] Other Hellenistic courts (Pergamon, Pontos, Bithynia) presumably followed suit. Antigonid courtiers dressed in the Macedonian manner because Macedon was the power base of the Antigonid dynasty. Ptolemaic and Seleukid nobles dressed in the Macedonian manner because Macedon was *not* the power base of these dynasties – Macedonians in Egypt and Asia formed a privileged imperial elite, having all the more reason to make their ethnicity visible. The further away from Macedon, it seems, the stronger the need to cling to Macedonian 'traditions'. This is demonstrated by the fact that Baktrian kings often appear on their coins wearing conspicuous *kausiai*, whilst Antigonid kings apparently did not find it important to be portrayed with it (Fig. 9.5). It is impossible to say whether this attire was the prerogative of ethnic Macedonians. If not, Greek *philoi* may have worn the Macedonian costume, too; Egyptians or Iranians who

---

[87] Saatsoglou-Paliadeli 1993: 145.
[88] Plut., *Mor.* 760b; *Pyrrh.* 11.6; cf. *Demetr.* 44; *Eum.* 6.1–2, 8.6–7; *Ant.* 54.4–6; *Mor.* 760b; Polyaen. 5.44.5; Diod. 17.7.3; Onesikritos, *FGrH* 134 F 17a *ap.* Strabo 15.1.63–5; cf. Plut., *Alex.* 65. For the reliability of Plutarch as a source for Hellenistic royal dress see Tatum 1996: 135–51.

Fig. 9.5. Silver tetradrachm of Antimachos I of Baktria, c. 180–165 BCE. The king on the obverse wears a diadem, *chlamus* and *kausia*. The reverse shows Poseidon holding a trident and palm branch (courtesy of the Numismatic Association, Inc.).

managed to gain access to the courts of the Ptolemies and Seleukids may have donned the prescribed clothing, just as they would assume Greek names to express their allegiance with the monarchy.

By wearing Macedonian costume, courtiers also expressed their commitment to the non-noble *Makedones* who constituted the royal phalanxes. Plutarch relates how feelings of ethnic identity among the *Makedones* could be stirred by ethnic costume: 'For the Macedonians longed for him [i.e. Krateros] exceedingly, and if they should only see his *kausia* and hear his voice, they would go over to him with a rush, with all their arms.'[89] The fact that the Macedonian troops were to recognise Krateros by his *kausia* implies that the cap was not worn by the common rank and file but only by their commanders. The same conclusion may be drawn from the well-known lion hunt mosaic from Pella (Fig. 9.6). The mosaic dates to the Antigonid period and perhaps represents the famous tale of how Krateros saved the life of Alexander during a lion hunt near Susa, the same incident that was commemorated on the votive monument erected by Krateros at Delphi.[90] The two young men depicted on the mosaic are nude, but despite their heroic nakedness and idealised, almost god-like features, both wear a *chlamus* and one of them a *kausia*, being the only attributes to make them recognisable as noblemen of the Macedonian court.

Yet the wearing of *kausiai* and *chlamudes* as such was not itself the principal prerogative of kings and courtiers. What qualified such clothing as aristocratic was the use of purple dye. Purple was the

[89] Plut., *Eum.* 6.1–2. Polyaen. 5.44.5 relates how the Achaemenid commander Memnon together with his officers put on *kausiai* to make some Macedonian soldiers believe that they really were their general Kalas and his staff.
[90] Petsas 1978: 55; cf. pp. 95–7 with figures 8 and 9, and pp. 99–102 with figures 12–15.

Fig. 9.6. Lion hunt mosaic from Pella (author's photograph).

attribute of royalty par excellence.[91] There were various forms of purple colour, a dye made from sea snails in an extraordinary, labour-intensive process, the most valuable, reddish variant being the famous 'royal purple' or 'Tyrian purple'. The sheer cost as well as tradition prohibited non-elite groups from using it. In the ancient Near East, the wearing of costumes dyed with royal purple was monopolised by kings and royal dignitaries; in classical Greece, 'royal' purple was associated with the gods. The clearest indication that purple was the crucial badge of rank of Hellenistic courtiers is the fact that the standard Latin translation of *philos tou basileōs* is *purpuratus*.[92] There is some evidence that apart from the king only *philoi* had the right to wear clothing that was in part dyed with the royal purple of Tyre.[93] The two young men on the lion hunt mosaic from Pella wear white *chlamudes* with purple borders.[94] The remains of paint on the Alexander sarcophagus show that companion caval-rymen also had red-purple borders on their *chlamudes*. According to written evidence, the dress of later Greek *philoi* was coloured with this dye as well.[95]

Philoi received their purple clothing from the king. Purple garments were perhaps the most prestigious gifts dealt out by kings to their courtiers. Plutarch says that purple *kausiai* and *chlamudes*

---

[91] See Reinhold 1970 (arguing that there was no royal or divine monopoly on wearing purple clothing).

[92] Liv. 30.42.6; 32.39.8; 37.23.7; 37.59.5; 42.51.2. Cic., *Cat.* 4.12; *Tusc.* 1.102; Curt. 3.2.10; 3.13.13; 5.1.37; Vitr. 2 *pr.* 1. Quint. 8.5.24. Cf. Ath. 211b.

[93] Ath. 211b; Phylarchos, *FGrH* 81 F 41 *ap.* Ath. 539e; ibid. *ap.* Ath. 540a; Ath. 211b.

[94] Petsas 1978: 95–7.

[95] Ath. 211b; 539f; Diod. 17.77.4–5; Plut., *Eum.* 8.6–7; Justin. 12.3.8 (adding gold embroidery to the purple dress).

'were a special gift of royalty among the Macedonians'.[96] When in 326 BCE Onesikritos of Astypalaia was sent as an ambassador to the Indian gymnosophists near Taxila, Alexander gave him a *chlamus* and a *kausia* as the tokens of his assignment.[97] At the time that 1 Maccabees was written, purple *kausiai* and *chlamudes* were still symbols of royalty in the Seleukid kingdom, for when Antiochos Epiphanes lay dying in c. 164 and appointed his *philos* Philippos – presumably an ethnic Macedonian – as regent for his son Antiochos (V Eupator), a minor, Philippos received the king's mantle and hat as badges of his office.[98] We know from the same source that purple clothes were also given to allies and friends outside the court.[99] Receiving such gifts was a mark of being accepted into the circle of the king's friends.

[96] Plut., *Eum.* 8.6–7.
[97] Strabo 15.1.63–5.
[98] 1 Macc. 6.15.
[99] 1 Macc. 10.20; cf. 10.62; Polyb. 4.4.5.

10 *Death and Resurrection: Inauguration Ritual*

Ancient sources suggest that the installation of a new king and the burial of his predecessor were interrelated ritual events: the transmission of *basileia*, preferably from father to son. The successor was transformed into the new master of the household. This obliged him to pay the last honours to his predecessor and, if necessary and possible, to revenge his death. Thus, in 336, Alexander, 'succeeding to the kingship, first inflicted due punishment on his father's murderers, and then devoted himself to the funeral of his father'.[1]

Before succession could take place, a period of mourning had to be observed. This allowed time for the burial and inauguration to be prepared and announced. It took time for people to travel to the court to attend the inauguration of the new ruler. Also, the army had to be assembled and its allegiance secured.[2] The presence of the army at the coronation was imperative.[3] The period of mourning was a period of ritually enacted anomy. When Antiochos, the favourite son and intended successor of Antiochos the Great, died, relations between the Seleukid court and the outside world were formally brought to a standstill, as if time itself had temporarily stopped: 'There was a great sorrow at the court [and] grave mourning filled the palace for several days; and the Roman ambassador, who did not want to be an untimely guest at such an inconvenient moment, retired to Pergamon ... [for] the court was closed during the mourning.'[4] Concerning a remarkably similar, but better documented, ritual of mourning in another time and place – the 'closed palace' during the

---

[1] Diod. 17.2.1.
[2] See Polyb. 18.55.3–4 – 'The courtiers began to occupy themselves with the celebration of the inauguration (*anaklētria*) of the king' – and 15.25.3–19, cited below.
[3] Walbank 1984b: 226.
[4] Liv. 35.15.3–7, presumably following Polybios; cf. Bickerman 1938: 32.

mourning for the Venetian doge – Boholm concluded that the palace temporarily became a tomb of sorts, its inhabitants being symbolically dead during the interregnum.[5] This enabled the successor to emerge after mourning as if reborn.

An important piece of evidence for the subsequent ritual of the transmission of kingship is Polybios' account of the inauguration of the infant king Ptolemy V. His parents, Ptolemy IV and Arsinoë III, had both been murdered in c. 204. Polybios describes how first the death of the ruling couple was announced by the leading men of the *sunedrion* by means of a formal proclamation to the members of the court, the palace guards, and representatives of the army:

> After four or five days, erecting a tribune in the largest colonnade of the palace (*aulē*), they summoned a meeting of the hypaspists, the courtiers (*therapeia*), as well as of the commanders of the infantry and cavalry. When all these had assembled, Agathokles and Sosibios mounted the tribune, and in the first place acknowledged the death of the king and queen and ordered the audience to go into mourning in accordance with custom. After this they gave the diadem to the boy and proclaimed him king ... They beseeched the army officers to remain loyal and maintain the boy in his rule (*archē*).[6]

Then the silver urns containing the ashes of the king and the queen were brought out, and after the funeral rites had been celebrated, the mourning began:

> The people fell into such a state of distraction and affliction that the city was full of groans, tears, and ceaseless lamentation, a testimony. [Agathokles,] after depositing the urns in the vault of the Royal House, ordered the public mourning to cease, and as a first step granted two months' pay to the troops, ... and in the next place imposed on them the oath they were accustomed to take on the proclamation of a new king.[7]

In Polybios' account, the rites of inauguration and burial are presented as fully integrated. Both seem to have been divided into two distinct phases. First, the former monarch is cremated and his death announced, and at the same time the new king is adorned with the diadem. Then the period of mourning begins 'according to custom'. Polybios' subsequent description of the mourning among the citizens of Alexandria hints at ritualised anomy: 'The people fell into such a state of distraction and affliction that the city was full of groans, tears, and ceaseless lamentation.' Similar behaviour of the citizens of a royal city is described by Diodoros in relation to the death of Antiochos Sidetes in 129 BCE: 'When Antioch received the

---

[5] Boholm 1990: 266–71.
[6] Polyb. 15.25.3–19.
[7] Polyb. 15.25.3–19 (continued).

news of Antiochos' death, not only did the city go into public mourning, but every public house as well was dejected and filled with lamentation.'[8] During the period of mourning, courtiers and relatives wore dark clothing.[9] Finally, in Polybios' account of the death ritual for Ptolemy IV, the mourning was after some days ended at the command of Agathokles, who acted on behalf of the new king, Ptolemy V, whose *epitropos* he was. Then the twofold second part of the burial-cum-inauguration ritual took place: the silver urns containing the ashes of the deceased royal couple were placed in their tombs near the Sema, and the new king was proclaimed king (ἀναδείξις τῶν βασιλέων) in a rite of acclamation performed by the army and the household. With this last ritual the situation returned to normality. The successor emerged from mourning to be invested with kingship, signified by his putting off the mourning clothes and assuming the diadem and royal robe.[10]

The actual burial – the placing of the urn or the body in its tomb – was a pivotal royal pageant. The transportation of the urn, or the coffin containing the king's embalmed body, to its final resting place was attended by the army and the court. Accounts of such processions show that the last progress of the king could be spectacularly staged, the divinised king's body being now more sacral than during life. An example is the funeral procession of Demetrios Poliorketes, whose urn was brought from Syria to Greece by the Antigonid fleet commanded by Demetrios' successor Antigonos Gonatas (283 BCE):

> There was something dramatic and theatrical even in the funeral ceremonies of Demetrios. For his son Antigonos, when he learned that his remains had been sent home, put to sea with his entire fleet and met them off the islands. They were given to him in a golden urn, and he placed them in the largest of his admiral's ships. Of the cities where the fleet touched in its passage, some brought garlands to adorn the urn, others sent men in funeral attire to assist in escorting it home and burying it. When the fleet put in at Corinth, the vase was conspicuous on the vessel's poop, adorned with royal purple and a diadem, and young men (νεανίσκοι) stood around it in arms as a bodyguard … After garlands and other honours had been bestowed upon the remains at Corinth, they were brought by Antigonos to Demetrias for burial, a city

---

[8] Diod. 34.17.1; cf. Polyb. 8.21.6–7: when a messenger from Antiochos III brought news of the death of Achaios, who had proclaimed himself king in Asia Minor, to his soldiers in Sardis (also demanding their immediate surrender), 'there was at first no answer from those in the citadel but loud wailing and extravagant lamentation'.

[9] Plut., *Mor.* 184a; Jos., *AJ* 16.266; Liv. 14.7.4; 45.7.4; Diod. 34.14.

[10] See Plut., *Demetr.* 18.3, on the fundamental change of character of the Diadochs when they became kings. The *topos* of character change is also recurrent in Polybios. Comparable is Dio 37.10.4, on the abdication of Ariobarzanes I of Kappadokia, a variant of the Damokles motif: 'Happy was he who lay down the kingship, sad he to whom it was given.'

named after his father, who had settled it from the small villages around Iolkos.[11]

In other words, the new king and the ashes and regalia of his father toured along the coastal cities of Greece to win acclaim for the succession in a magnificent show of royal splendour and military power. The disembarking at Corinth is of special significance. Demetrios had restored the Corinthian League in 302, and Corinth could still be considered the symbolic heart of a politically united world of *poleis*, whose *dēmokratia*, *autonomia* and *eleutheria* had been defended by the Antigonids. Thus, the veneration for Demetrios in Corinth signified his being honoured by the entire Greek world, and consequently pan-Hellenic acceptance of Gonatas' leadership.

Written and material information attesting to the burial of Hellenistic kings is, however, in short supply,[12] but Josephus' description of the burial of Herod the Great in 4 BCE may give some idea of a regular Hellenistic royal burial. Apart from a single reference to Yahweh, and of course the fact that Herod was buried instead of cremated, the ritual has a very Hellenistic flavour, including the fact that the burial was a component of the accession of Herod's principal successor, Archelaos.

> Vociferous congratulations were at once heaped upon Archelaos, and the soldiers came forward in companies with the citizens, pledged their loyalty, and joined in prayer for the blessing of God. Then they turned to the task of the king's burial. Everything possible was done by Archelaos to add to the magnificence: he brought out all the royal ornaments to be carried in procession in honour of the dead monarch. There was a solid gold bier, adorned with precious stones and draped with the richest purple. On it lay the body wrapped in royal purple, with a diadem resting on the head and above that a golden victory wreath, and the sceptre by the right hand. The bier was escorted by Herod's sons and the whole body of his kinsmen, followed by his bodyguards and the Thracian Guard, and the Germans and Celts, all in full battle array. The rest of the army led the way, fully armed and in perfect order, headed by their commanders and all the officers, and followed by five hundred household servants and freedmen carrying spices. The body was borne twenty-four miles to Herodion, where by the late king's command it was buried.[13]

Hellenistic royal tombs have only rarely been discovered, and seldom intact. The Argead kings were buried in the cultic centre of Aigai

---

[11] Plut., *Demetr.* 53.1–3, trans. B. Perrin. Cf. Plutarch's account of Kleopatra's advent to Tarsos, discussed below.

[12] An exception is Diodoros' description of Alexander's funerary catafalque (Diod. 18.26; cf. Curt. 10.6.4; 10.7.13; 10.8.20; Just. 7.2.2–4).

[13] Jos., *BJ* 1.671, trans. G.A. Williamson, with minor adjustments. Cf. Diod. 31.21; 17.115.4 (burial of Hephaistion); App., *Syr.* 63 (Seleukos I); Just. 100.42N (Antiochos VII).

(Vergina) in Macedonia, but the findings in Vergina cannot be used as evidence for burial practices in Egypt and the Near East. Several kings were buried in cities they themselves had (re)founded, receiving cult as *hērōs ktistēs* at their *heroon*: Alexander at Alexandria, Demetrios Poliorketes at Demetrias, Lysimachos at Lysimacheia, Seleukos Nikator at Seleukeia in Pieria, Antiochos Epiphanes at Antioch. Royal burial ground was sacred space. Not all kings were deified after death, but when this was the case, the placing of the remains inside the *heroon* probably involved some ritual marking the apotheosis. The sources only hint at such rites. In a fragment of a poem of Kallimachos, written for the occasion of the apotheosis of Arsinoë Philadelphos and perhaps performed during a public ritual of deification, the deified queen is taken to heaven by the Dioskouroi, where she is given a place in 'the circle of the god'; in Alexandria she received a *temenos* and altar near the Emporion Harbour.[14] At least since the reign of Ptolemy IV the Ptolemies were buried in the same *temenos* where the Sema, the *heroon* of the city's deified founder Alexander, was also located, suggesting both a relationship with Alexander and dynastic continuity; Kleopatra VII broke with this tradition and built a separate mausoleum for herself and Antony, signalling the advent of a new era.[15] In addition to the early Hellenistic tumulus graves excavated at Vergina (Aigai) in Macedonia, whose occupants are still to be decisively identified, only two late Hellenistic royal tombs have remained more or less intact, both of them tumuli but neither of them belonging to the great Macedonian dynasties: the elevated shrine of Antiochos of Kommagene at Nemrut Dağı (Fig. 10.1) and the Herodion of Herod the Great near Bethlehem.

Before we can continue with an evaluation of the sources for the actual ritual of inauguration, it is necessary first to discuss the principal Hellenistic regalia, in particular the diadem.

HELLENISTIC REGALIA: PURPLE, SCEPTRE AND THE DIADEM

The principal royal insignia in the Hellenistic world from the late fourth century BCE until the first century CE were purple dye and the diadem. Besides the diadem, Hellenistic kings were equipped with sceptres and signet rings. The sceptre (*skeptron*), though in itself a rather generic symbol of authority in both Greek and non-Greek

[14] Call., fr. 228.
[15] Strabo 794; Plut., *Ant.* 86; cf. Fraser II: 33–4 n. 81. For the new era of Kleopatra see Volkmann 1953: 116–22; Grant 1972: 171–5; Schrapel 1996: 209–23; Strootman 2010b.

Fig. 10.1. Nemrut Dağı: view of the eastern terrace and the tumulus of Antiochos I of Kommagene (author's photograph).

traditions, in the Hellenistic age may have taken the form of a lance with the spearhead pointing down towards the ground; as such it can be associated with the concept of *doriktētos chōra*, 'spear-won land', and Hellenistic kings' image as heroic spear-fighters (Fig. 10.2).[16] To my knowledge there are no contemporary images of sceptres apart from the spears carried by Hellenistic kings in art and on coins (Fig. 10.3).

Purple already had a long tradition as a status symbol in both the Near East and the Aegean world. Purple was not a single colour but a dye, obtained from boiling vast numbers of marine snails of the *gastropeda* species. Purple dye was produced principally along the Levantine coastline. It existed in several colour variants, only one of which was an exclusive emblem of royalty: the colour better known as 'royal purple' or 'Tyrian purple'.[17] This dye, probably of a deep reddish hue and extremely hard to obtain, had long been a symbol of royalty in the Near East. In Aegean religious cult, 'royal purple' was

[16] Strootman 2007: 372–4.
[17] Strootman 2007: 374–84; for a different view see Reinhold 1970, arguing that in the Near East purple was not an emblem of royalty.

Fig. 10.2. Detail of a fresco from Boscoreale, showing a Hellenistic nobleman or king wearing *kausia* and *chlamus* (left); the figure has been variously identified as, among others, Achilles, king Antigonos I Gonatas and (perhaps most likely) a personification of the Macedonian people casting a spear across the Hellespont to claim a female Asia as his *doriktētos chōra*.

connected with the divine.[18] In their use of royal purple, Hellenistic kings presumably benefited from both associations.

The diadem, by contrast, was a rather simple and unassuming object.[19] It was essentially a band of cloth tied about the head with a knot at the back, from which two long, loose-hanging ribbons hung down (Fig. 10.4). It attained the quality of a royal diadem only after it had been tied round one's head. The diadem appears to have been a personal emblem, and was not transmitted from father to son.[20] It was an exclusive monarchic emblem, worn only by the king and

[18] Stulz 1990.
[19] Modern literature on the Hellenistic royal diadem is not very extensive; it includes Grenz 1914, Ritter 1965 and 1987 – arguing for an Achaemenid background – and Smith 1988; the present paragraphs summarise Strootman 2007: 366–72.
[20] Plut., *Demetr.* 53.2.

Fig. 10.3. First-century BCE relief from Arsameia-on-the-Nymphaios showing Antiochos I of Kommagene, a descendant of the Seleukid house, shaking hands with Herakles. The king is clad in 'Persianistic' Armenian attire and is holding a spear with its head pointing down (after Wagner 2000).

perhaps his co-*basileus* and first queen, the *basilissa*. People associated with the court could wear purple clothing but not diadems. Apparently it was a new symbol, introduced by Alexander as a personal ornament and institutionalised as a generic royal emblem only after his death.[21] With the assumption of the diadem by the Diadochs in 306/5, its use became widespread, not only among the great Macedonian dynasties of the Hellenistic age but among all monarchic states of the Near East for many centuries to come. From Constantine the Great onward, Roman emperors, too, wore the diadem,[22] and through them the band became the ancestor of

[21] This had already been maintained by Grenz 1914: 36–8; there is no evidence that the diadem existed in Macedon before the reign of Alexander; cf. Ritter 1984: 106–8 and Smith 1988: 35 with n. 35. Evidence for Alexander wearing the diadem: e.g. Arr., *Anab.* 7.9.9; Diod. 17.116.4; 18.60.6–61.1; Curt. 10.6.4.

[22] Alföldi 1970; Smith 1988: 38 with n. 59.

Fig. 10.4. Obverse of a silver tetradrachm of the Seleukid king Antiochos VIII
showing a portrait of the king wearing the diadem (photo and collection of
the Geldmuseum, Utrecht).

medieval European crowns.[23] In the course of the Hellenistic
centuries the physical shape of the diadem remained more or less the
same, although tending to become broader and more conspicuous.[24]

What did the diadem signify? Apart from the suggestion that
the Hellenistic diadem was of pre-Hellenistic Macedonian origin, the
diadem has been interpreted as a reference to Persian kingship, as a
symbol of Dionysos, and as a Greek victory wreath.[25]

The Persian connotation of the diadem has been defended notably
by Ritter.[26] Diodoros and Curtius both claim that Alexander took
over his diadem from the Persian king, but Arrian apparently thinks
differently.[27] There are, however, two compelling arguments against
a purely Persian origin: the Achaemenid variant of the diadem was
not the primary sign of royalty, and wearing it was not the exclusive
prerogative of the king. The association of the diadem with Dionysos
stems from Diodoros and Pliny, who, drawing on the same uniden-
tified Hellenistic author, stated that the Diadochs took over the
diadem from Dionysos, who wore it as a symbol of his eastern
conquests.[28] The problem is that diadem and Dionysian fillet are only

<hr/>

[23] Schramm 1955: 381.
[24] Smith 1988: 55.
[25] For an overview see Smith 1988: 35–6, who is strongly opposed to a 'fictitious'
Achaemenid background, and Strootman 2007: 369–71.
[26] Ritter 1965: 31–41, and 1984.
[27] Diod. 17.77.6; Curt. 6.6.4; Arr., *Anab.* 6.29.5.
[28] Diod. 4.4.4; Plin., *NH* 7.191. Cf. Smith 1988: 37–8.

Fig. 10.5. Head of the Delphi charioteer, a bronze votive statue connected with the Pythian Games of 474 BCE; the charioteer is adorned with a fillet that looks much like a diadem (collection of the Delphi Museum; author's photograph).

superficially similar in shape.[29] Alföldi argued that the diadem was derived from the Greek victory fillet: originally a reward for athletes and poets participating in games, it developed into a more general symbol of exceptional victory and merit.[30] Again, the objection can be made that the this was a different sort of band, but the similarities are more obvious (Fig. 10.5).

None of the proposed origins of the diadem is fully persuasive. However, to find the historical origin of the diadem is only relevant as far as it can help us to understand the meaning of the Hellenistic diadem. The objections raised against the respective theories of origin do not preclude the possibility that contemporaries *could* understand the diadem as referring to – and not necessarily originating from – the Greek agonistic fillet, the Dionysian headband or oriental royal insignia. Perhaps the Hellenistic diadem may even have referred

[29] Smith 1988: 37 with n. 55.
[30] Alföldi 1970, and again in the posthumously published 1985: 105–32, to which Ritter 1987 expressly responds.

to several meanings simultaneously. All we know for certain is that ancient sources claim that Alexander bound a piece of cloth around his head and made this the principal symbol of his power. Alexander was presumably aware of the varied associations it invoked. But what must have counted most was the need to introduce a novel symbol for a new form of kingship, without arousing any of his subjects' aversion to change or foreign culture.

Smith argued that the diadem '[i]n "origin" ... probably meant precisely nothing. In this lay its real value and success as a symbol. Originally empty of meaning, it could take on whatever significance Alexander gave it.'[31] However, the diadem need not necessarily have been empty of meaning to become a new symbol, as meanings assigned to symbols can always be renegotiated by using them differently, in a dialectic with actual behaviour.[32]

Thus, Alexander's diadem was at the same time familiar and new – a token of kingship that was linked to his personal, charismatic rulership. It marked a break with the Macedonian tradition of a limited, hereditary kingship that probably knew no exclusive, distinguishing regalia.[33] When in 306/5 the Diadochs proclaimed themselves kings and used the diadem as the central symbol of their new monarchies,[34] a shift in the diadem's meaning occurred. To Alexander, the diadem had been personal; with the Diadochs, the diadem became a generic symbol of royal power.

Whatever its exact origin and meaning, the diadem became the royal insignium that was most closely connected with inauguration ritual. In Greek historiography after Alexander, putting on a diadem or binding a diadem around one's head (sometimes in combination with the assumption of purple garments) is the standard metaphor for the assumption of kingship itself.[35] Conversely, to put *off* a diadem is the standard metaphor for the downfall of kings, often used by Plutarch and other ancient authors in the contexts of decisive battles.[36]

---

[31] Smith 1988: 36.
[32] Boon 1982: 52–3.
[33] Smith 1988: 37 n. 49, and 58–62, draws attention to the problem that Alexander's diadem is only attested in literary sources; on his portraits he never wears one, with only two, rather doubtful, exceptions: the Kyme and Getty Alexanders (cat. nos. 15 and 16). It may be, therefore, that the Diadochs instead of Alexander were the first to use the diadem.
[34] The literary sources are collected and extensively discussed by Ritter 1965: 78–127.
[35] See e.g. Plut., *Mor.* 184a–b; Diod. 31.15.2; 36.2.4; Jos., *AJ* 196–7; *BJ* 1.671.5.
[36] E.g. Plut., *Aem.* 23.1 (Perseus at Pydna); Plut., *Luc.* 28.5–6 (Tigranes after the battle of Tigranokerta); more examples in Ritter 1965: 172–3.

INAUGURATION RITUAL

It has often been assumed that Hellenistic coronations were unpresumptuous: 'the diadem ... was not like a crown and there was no coronation'.[37] This notion is presumably due to the lack of sources describing the details of such a ritual and the absence of iconographic evidence. Even Polybios in his relatively detailed account of the inauguration of Ptolemy V mentions the diadem only in passing. This is quite remarkable. The diadem was the key signifier of royal status in iconography and writing. Hellenistic and later Greek historiography is packed with men 'assuming the diadem', the standard phrase for the transition of man to king.[38] When ancient authors mention the act of binding on the diadem, this happens most often in the context of a military victory.[39] Success in battle was prodigious; it proved that one was worthy of kingship. Military prestige enabled would-be kings to rally the support of citizens and soldiers. Achaios, who rebelled in Asia Minor against Antiochos III in 220 and 'was eagerly urged by the army to assume the diadem', at first was reluctant to do so; 'but when he met with a success that surpassed his expectations, having confined Attalos to Pergamon and made himself master of all the rest of the country, he was so elated by his good fortune [that he] assumed the diadem and styled himself king, [since] he was at this moment the most imposing and formidable king on this side of the Taurus'.[40] Achaios' enemy, Attalos of Pergamon, first assumed the diadem and styled himself king after having defeated the Galatian Celts in battle; his claim that with this victory he had saved the Greeks of Asia Minor from the barbarians instantly turned him into a *sōtēr*, and hence a king.[41]

When ancient authors write about dynastic succession, however, assumption of the diadem is *not* the preferred expression. Rather they speak of 'succession', or 'accession to the [ancestral] kingship (*basileia*)', normally translated as 'succession to the throne'.[42] Perhaps 'assumption of the diadem' is not the principal *terminus technicus* for the inauguration of a king. Perhaps we must look elsewhere for the pivotal act of inauguration. Polybios' account of the

---

[37] Smith 1988: 36–7. Evidence for the diadem is collected in Ritter 1965 (arguing for an eastern origin of the diadem; cf. also Ritter 1987).

[38] E.g. Polyb. 4.48.12; 5.42.7, 57.2, 57.5; 1 Macc. 1; 11.13; Diod. 31.15.3; 40.1a; Plut., *Demetr.* 17–18; *Pyrrh.* 11; Diod. 20.53; 33.28; App., *Syr.* 54; Polyb. 1.8–9.

[39] E.g. Plut., *Demetr.* 17–18; *Pyrrh.* 11; Diod. 20.53; App., *Syr.* 54; Polyb. 1.8–9.

[40] Polyb. 4.48.10–12.

[41] Strabo 13.4.2; cf. Strootman 2005a.

[42] E.g. Polyb. 7.11.4: τῶν πρόρερον βασιλέων (Philip V).

inauguration of Ptolemy V may provide a clue: 'The courtiers began to occupy themselves with the celebration of the proclamation (*anaklētēria*) of the king ... After preparations had been made on a grand scale they carried out the ceremonies in a manner worthy of the kingship.'[43] Other sources mention the proclamation of the new king, usually by the army, too.[44] Given the conspicuous lack in the sources of descriptions of public acts of binding on the diadem – except in the context of battle – new kings may have presented themselves before the army and the populace with the diadem already fastened. It remains possible that some ritual took place in seclusion, in the presence of a select group of spectators or with only the gods as witnesses, but this we will never know.[45] What does seem sure, however, is that kings could perform the act themselves.[46] When ancient authors write that someone else ties a diadem around a king's head, this indicates that (illegal) king-makers or rivals are putting a pretender on the throne. For instance, when the Arab dynast Aziz made Philip (II) Seleukid king in opposition to Antiochos XIII in 67/6 BCE, we read that '[Aziz] gave him a ready welcome, bound a diadem around his head, and restored him to the kingship'.[47] This rare passage, emphasising the powerlessness of the later Seleukids, is purposely at odds with normal practice. The same is true for the central source in the present discussion, the inauguration of Ptolemy V: Agathokles and Sosibios put the infant Ptolemy V on the throne to serve their own purposes, and that is why Polybios writes 'they crowned the boy with a diadem and proclaimed him king'.[48] This, then, may be the fundamental difference between the *basileus* as 'emperor' or Great King – who binds the diadem round his head himself because there is no higher authority – and the *basileus* as 'vassal', who receives the diadem from his (Seleukid, later Parthian or Roman) overlord.

Polybios has more to say about the inauguration ritual of Ptolemy V. After the fastening of the diadem, the Alexandrian people, who were assembled in the stadion, shouted 'the cry of the king' (or: 'shouted "bring the king"'), after which the new *basileus* was

[43] Polyb. 18.55.3–4.
[44] Plut., *Demetr.* 18.1 (Antigonids); App., *Syr.* 54 (Seleukids).
[45] 'Hidden' coronations are known from e.g. the Ashante monarchies of Ghana: thus, in the small kingdom of Akuapem the ritual of enthronement on the sacred Black Stool is secret and takes place behind closed doors; the king appears for the first time in public when he is carried outside seated on his throne, where a ritual of acclamation by the people takes place (Gilbert 1987, 1994). Cf. Plut., *Luc.* 18.3; *Demetr.* 17.2–18.1.
[46] Polyb. 4.48.10; Diod. 31.15.3; 1 Macc. 11.13.
[47] Diod. 40.1a.
[48] Polyb. 15.25.5.

brought out of the palace and presented to the populace.[49] Diodoros describes a similar sequence of events when relating the affirmation of Ptolemy Euergetes and Ptolemy Philometor as joint kings between 169 and 164: 'Both of them, donning on their royal attire, went out [from the palace and into the stadion] and appeared before the populace, making it manifest to everybody that they were in harmony.'[50] It may therefore be maintained that it was not the binding of the diadem itself but the acclamation of the already diademed king by the army that was the central *public* rite of inauguration in the Hellenistic kingdoms. To describe the Hellenistic inauguration ritual, it may be better to speak of the *consecration* of the new king rather than the *coronation*.[51]

The ritual of acclamation was a Macedonian tradition, but it could have developed independently in any state with a military monarchy. The question of whether the Macedonian army assembly in the Argead kingdom had the right to elect the new king has been exhaustively but indeterminately discussed by modern historians.[52] This controversy should not concern us here. Acclamation is not the same as election and all this has nothing to do with constitutional rule: no legitimate successor to the throne would have become king without the allegiance of the army, let alone against the army's wishes. The importance of the Macedonian element in the armed forces of the Ptolemies and Seleukids should not be underestimated. Macedonian infantry and 'Macedonian' military settlers constituted the phalanx, the core of any Hellenistic imperial army. The question of whether or not these men were 'real' Macedonians is immaterial; group identity can be a situational and changeable social construct and what matters most is that these military settlers are identified in our sources as 'Macedonians' – they probably thought of themselves as Macedonians too. And since they received their land or regular payment directly from the king's treasury, the common soldiers and their families were the recipients of benefactions coming directly from the king. This means that they stood closer to the king than the average subject, closer even than members of rural and civic elites without direct access to the court.[53] It is not surprising, therefore, that the

[49] Polyb. 15.31.2; cf. 3–4.
[50] Diod. 31.15.2–3.
[51] This distinction was suggested in the context of medieval English coronation by Everett 1997: 7, 'because ["consecration"] is without question what the rite is about, whereas "coronation" refers specifically to a small part of the rite, and by no means the most important'.
[52] For the continuation of the army assembly in the Hellenistic kingdoms see Plut., *Eum.* 8.3; Diod. 18.37.2; 19.51.1; Polyb. 5.27.5.
[53] See Jansen 1984.

Macedonian troops played a central role in the consecration of the king, and that their role was reminiscent of that of the Macedonian army assembly under Philip and Alexander. When in 203 Agathokles sought acceptance for his status as regent in the name of the child Ptolemy V, the first thing he did was to summon a meeting of the Macedonian household troops (*Makedones*) and appear before them with his sister Agathokleia, formerly the *maîtresse en titre* of Ptolemy IV, who held the young king in her arms. Agathokles thereupon addressed the troops, saying: 'Take the child whom his father on his death-bed placed in the arms of this woman, ... and confided to your faith, o you Macedonian men.'[54]

Two more elements of the accession rite described in Polybios' account of the inauguration of Ptolemy V are of interest here: the army swearing allegiance to the new king by taking oaths, and the distribution of lavish gifts, first of all among the army. The oaths taken by the army were apparently part of the inauguration, as they had already been in Macedonia under Philip and Alexander, a practice that was also continued in the Antigonid kingdom.[55] Oaths were taken by units of the standing army and by military settlers, all of whom would have been drawn together for the occasion. Josephus claims that at the beginning of the Hellenistic age, Jewish soldiers in the service of Ptolemy Soter took the same oath as the Macedonians, suggesting that the tradition was modified to include the entire army.[56] The soldiers received extra payment and gifts.

The acclamation was followed by the presentation of the new king before the people in a stadion, hippodrome or theatre,[57] where a temporary tribune (*bēma*) was erected for this purpose:

> The Macedonians took the king and at once setting him on a horse conducted him to the stadion. His appearance was greeted with loud cheers and clapping of hands, and they now stopped the horse, took him off, and leading him forward placed him on the royal seat.[58]

In the Ptolemaic context incidental gratuities were promised to Egyptian temples and amnesties were granted, as we read on e.g. the Rosetta Stone, but this was presumably not exclusive to Egypt. The granting of amnesties was a necessary measure to pacify the kingdom after a discordant succession, which often happened.[59] At

---

[54] Polyb. 15.26.1–3.
[55] Walbank 1984b: 226; for army oaths in general see Pritchett 1979: 230–9.
[56] Jos., *AJ* 12.1.
[57] Polyb. 15.31.2; Diod. 31.15a.1–3.
[58] Polyb. 15.32.1–5.
[59] Bevan 1927: 291.

his accession in 179, Perseus' first act was to proclaim the redemption of all debts to the crown and a general pardon for the *philoi* who had fled the Antigonid court during the succession struggle between him and his brother Demetrios; Polybios comments that Perseus' conduct was 'truly royal'.[60] In his account of the accession of Ariarathes V of Kappadokia in c. 163, Diodoros puts the actions to be taken by the king in an interesting, hierarchical, sequence:

> Ariarathes, surnamed Philopator, on succeeding to his ancestral kingship, first of all gave his father a magnificent burial. Then, when he had duly attended to the interests of his philoi, of the military commanders and lesser officials, he succeeded in winning great favour with the populace.[61]

In the Memphite Decree in honour of Ptolemy V, gifts to the army and the temples, as well as amnesties and the cancellation of debts, are summed up; the proclamation, made by the synod of priests, is dated to the eighteenth day after the inauguration of the new king in 196:

> Whereas King Ptolemy ... has given much money and much grain to the temples of Egypt, [and having undertaken great expenses] in order to create peace in Egypt and to establish the temples, and has rewarded all the forces that are subject to his rulership; and of the revenues and taxes that were in force in Egypt he had reduced some or had renounced them completely, in order to cause the army and all the other people to be prosperous in his time as [king; the arrear]s which were due to the king from the people who are in Egypt and all those who are subject to his kingship, and (which) amounted to a large total, he renounced; the people who were in prison and those against whom there had been charges for a long time, he released; ... moreover, he ordered concerning those who will return from the fighting men and the rest of the people who had gone astray (*lit.* been on other ways) in the disturbance that had occurred in Egypt that [they] should [be returned] to their homes, and their possessions should be restored to them.[62]

After the initial inauguration a new king often embarked on a ceremonial journey, showing himself to his subjects and taking possession of the land.[63] The inauguration ceremonies could be repeated during such journeys, or when new territories had been conquered. We have already encountered Antigonos Gonatas on his tour of the cities of Greece in 283. Best known is the 'repetition' of the Ptolemaic inauguration at Memphis, where new kings were enthroned as pharaohs in the central hall of the great temple of

---

[60] Polyb. 25.3.3–5; cf. 7.11.4.
[61] Diod. 31.21; cf. Polyb. 31.3 and 7.
[62] Trans. Simpson 1996: 258–71. See also Thompson 1988: 106–25 and Hölbl 2001: 77–90.
[63] See Clarysse 2000: 35.

Fig. 10.6. Crowning of Ptolemy VIII as pharaoh by the goddesses Nechbet (right) and Wadjet. Relief from the temple of Horus at Edfu (Wikimedia Commons).

Ptah; for instance, Ptolemy VIII, who 'was enthroned as king in Memphis in accordance with Egyptian custom (κατὰ τοὺς Ἀιγυπτίων νόμους)' in 144 (Fig. 10.6).[64] Compelling evidence exists only from the reign of Ptolemy IV, but Koenen has argued that the Ptolemies were enthroned as pharaohs at least from the time of Ptolemy II and perhaps even earlier.[65] Various sources claim that Alexander had already made a ceremonial advent into Memphis, where at least he sacrificed to the Apis bull.[66] Stanley Burstein, however, argued that it is not very likely that Alexander was enthroned as pharaoh,[67] although that does not exclude his being accepted as pharaoh by the Egyptian priesthood and populace.

---

[64] Diod. 33.13. The pharaonic consecration was a ritual of enthronement. On the instal-lation of the Ptolemies as pharaohs in Memphis see Thompson 1988: 146–54, and for a general overview of the 'survival' in Ptolemaic times of Egyptian rituals connected with kingship see Fairman 1958.

[65] Koenen 1977: 58–62; Clarysse 2000: 35. The Ptolemies also took responsibility for the cults of Memphis when they were absent (Thompson 1980).

[66] Arr., *Anab.* 3.1.4, 5.2; Iul. Val. 1.33; Diod. 17.49.2; Curt. 4.7.1.

[67] Burstein 1991; cf. 1994. For Alexander's activities in Egypt see Hölbl 2001: 9–14.

The Seleukids likewise performed the supposedly ancient rites in non-Greek contexts. They were involved in the Babylonian new year festival of Akitū, sometimes even taking part in the ritual personally. The latter is evidenced by a fragmentary astronomical diary that was first published in 1989; it is dated to 6 April 205 BCE:

> That [month,] on the 8th, King Antiochos (III) and the [...] went out [from] the palace to the gate ... of Esagila ... [...] of Esagila he made before them. Offerings to (?) [...] Marduk-etir ... [...] of their descendants (?) were set, entered the Akitū temple [...] made [sacrifices for] Ishtar of Babylon and the life of King Antiochos [...].[68]

Akitū, the yearly ritual of purification in honour of (notably) Marduk, was a (returning) coronation ritual of sorts, in which the king temporarily abdicated in order to be ritually reborn and reinstalled.[69] The festival survived during the Achaemenid period, and was still performed under Seleukid rule.[70] The Seleukids' concern with this Babylonian cult is also apparent from their taking responsibility for the maintenance and restoration of the Ezida and Esagila, the temples that marked the beginning and the end of the Akitū procession, as is apparent from the cuneiform building inscription of Antiochos I (268 BCE).[71] Of course, Seleukid kings could not be present each year; Amélie Kuhrt has shown, however, that the absence of the king did not affect his legitimacy as king of Babylon since his son and co-ruler could represent him, as Kambyses probably had done for Cyrus and as Antiochos I did for Seleukos I. If neither the king nor his son was present, a curtailed ritual could be enacted, in which perhaps a royal robe served as substitute for the king's physical presence.[72]

THE CORONATION OF THE DIADOCHS

Perhaps the best-known Hellenistic inauguration is the coronation of Antigonos Monophthalmos. In 306, Antigonos and his son Demetrios openly took the diadem and presented themselves as kings for the first time to Greeks and Macedonians. Within a year,

---

[68] Sachs-Hunger II: no. 204, C. rev. 14–18; cf. Kuhrt and Sherwin-White 1993: 130–1.
[69] Akit took place in various Mesopotamian cities from the early period to the Parthian period, but most evidence comes from Babylon and Uruk; see generally Cohen 1993: esp. 300–53; on the Akitū as a ritual of reversal see Versnel 1993: 32–7; cf. 1970: 220–8.
[70] Continuity of the Akitū festival in the Achaemenid and Hellenistic periods: Van der Spek 1999; Linssen 2004: 71–9. Cf. Downey 1988: 7–15 (Babylon) and 15–47 (Uruk) for the archaeological backdrop to the continuity – 'or perhaps more accurately the revival' – of Mesopotamian religion under the Seleukids.
[71] *ANET* 317; Austin 189; cf. Kuhrt and Sherwin-White 1991 and 1993: 36–7; on Babylonian building rituals in general see Linssen 2004: 103–11 and Ambos 2004.
[72] Kuhrt 1987: 49–50.

Seleukos, Lysimachos and Ptolemy had followed their example. This ended a chaotic period of interregnum that had lasted four years. It is usually assumed that the Diadochs waited so long out of respect for the extinct Argead dynasty. But the assumption of kingship by the Diadochs was not an attempt at becoming successors of the Argeads – by assuming the diadem without being related to the house of Philip and Alexander, each of the Diadochs created his own *basileia* and thereby proclaimed the establishment of new empires to replace the Argead state.[73] Before 306 several Diadochs had already accepted royal honours as king vis-à-vis indigenous people: Antigonos in Iran, Seleukos in Babylonia, and perhaps Ptolemy in Egypt.[74] Still, 306/5 BCE, the 'Year of the Kings', was a milestone in the evolution of Hellenistic kingship.[75]

The universal declaration of Antigonos' overlordship was legit-imised by military success, namely his son Demetrios' naval victory over the Ptolemaic fleet off Salamis (Cyprus), and the subsequent surrender of Cyprus to the Antigonids.[76] It was a resounding victory: about a hundred Ptolemaic fighting ships had been captured un-damaged; Ptolemy's brother and son, Menelaos and Leontiskos, had been taken prisoner; and over 16,000 Ptolemaic soldiers had surren-dered and could be enlisted in the Antigonid army.[77] The victory off Salamis seemed to testify that Antigonos and Demetrios were the strongest of the Macedonian warlords. To boost Antigonid prestige even more, Demetrios himself arranged the burial of the enemy dead, released prisoners of war without ransom, and made rich dedications to the gods, including a magnificent gift of 1,200 suits of armour to Athena in Athens.[78] Since the Diadochs may already have been kings in the eyes of eastern peoples more accustomed to autocratic kingship, the victory and subsequent assumption of kingship were advertised mainly among the Greeks of the Mediterranean. By presenting their *basileia* as a pan-Hellenic phenomenon, Antigonos and Demetrios changed the meaning of *basileus* from 'king' to 'Great King' – a role that Antigonos had already assumed when he made his declaration of Greek freedom in 315/14. The principal symbol of this new form of monarchy, which eventually came to incorporate aspects

---

[73] Strootman 2013b.
[74] Plut., *Demetr.* 18.2 (Seleukos). Diod. 19.48.1; 55.2; Plut., *Demetr.* 10.3 (Antigonos).
[75] Müller 1973; Gruen 1985; Billows 1997: 155–60.
[76] Plut., *Demetr.* 16.1–4.
[77] Diod. 20.53,1; Plut., *Demetr.* 16.4; cf. Billows 1990: 155 n. 40. For the campaign see Wheatly 2001.
[78] Plut., *Demetr.* 17.1.

of Near Eastern universal kingship, traditional Macedonian monarchy, and Greek notions of cosmopolitism,[79] was the diadem – the victory emblem Alexander had introduced as a consciously created, hybrid token of kingship that could be taken to refer to either Greek or Achaemenid traditions, but was in effect a wholly new sign of victorious rulership.[80]

The public proclamation of Antigonos as king had appeared as a spontaneous bottom-up occurrence, a dramatic play in with Antigonos acted as if surprised by the honour that been bestowed upon him by, ultimately, the gods, since it was they who had granted him victory. Plutarch accounts how immediately after the battle of Salamis, Demetrios dispatched a courier, a *philos* called Aristodemos of Miletos, in his own flagship to bring the news to Antigonos, who was overseeing the construction of his new capital Antigoneia in Syria:

> After [Aristodemos] had crossed over from Cyprus, he ... landed alone, and proceeded towards Antigonos, who was anxiously awaiting news of the battle ... Indeed, when he heard that Aristodemos was coming, he was more disturbed than before, and, with difficulty keeping himself indoors, sent servants and friends, one after the other, to learn from Aristodemos what had happened. Aristodemos, however, would make no answer to anybody, but step by step and with a solemn face approached in perfect silence. Antigonos, therefore, thoroughly frightened, and no longer able to restrain himself, came to the door to meet Aristodemos, who was now escorted by a large throng which was hurrying to the palace. Accordingly, when he had come near, he stretched out his hand and cried with a loud voice: 'Hail, King Antigonos, we have conquered Ptolemy in a sea-battle, and we have Cyprus, with twelve thousand eight hundred soldiers as prisoners of war.' ... Upon this the multitude for the first time saluted Antigonos and Demetrios as kings. Antigonos was immediately proclaimed king by his *philoi*, and Demetrios received a diadem from his father, with a letter in which he was addressed as *basileus*.[81]

This 'spontaneous' ritual was certainly prearranged. Antigonos had no doubt received the news of the victory by a real courier, well in advance of the arrival of the official messenger Aristodemos.[82] The proclamation was a theatrical performance: only after an anxious multitude of men had assembled on the square before the palace did Antigonos come out to show himself. The moment that he stepped

[80] Strootman 2007: 366–72, with further literature, i.e. references to scholars arguing in favour of (esp. Ritter) or against (e.g. Alföldi, R. R. R. Smith) an Achaemenid origin for the diadem.
[81] Plut., *Demetr.* 17.2–18.1. Cf. Diod. 20.53.1; Justin 15.2.7. For the historicity of this passage see Gruen 1985: 255–7 and Billows 1990 157–8.
[82] See Billows 1990: 155, demonstrating that Demetrios waited to secure full control of Cyprus before sending Aristodemos on his mission to Antigoneia.

outside, Aristodemos hailed him as *basileus*, followed by a general acclamation by the army and the *philoi*. Again, the account does not mention the binding on of a diadem, which means that Antigonos was probably already wearing a diadem when he came out of the palace to confront the crowd.

KLEOPATRA VII AND THE DONATIONS OF ALEXANDRIA

A special case is the extravagant coronation ritual known as the Donations of Alexandria, a Ptolemaic royal ceremony in 34 BCE of which relatively detailed accounts survive in Plutarch's biography of Mark Antony and Dio Cassius' *Roman History*. It took place in the gymnasion of Alexandria as part of a series of celebrations that had started with Antony's entry into Alexandria as 'Neos Dionysos' (see Chapter 11). Before a large audience, Kleopatra VII Philopator and her infant children were proclaimed rulers of the entire east, from Cyrenaica and the Hellespont to India. Kleopatra and her eldest son Ptolemy XV Caesar ('Caesarion'), with whom she shared the kingship, received the titles of Queen of Kings and King of Kings. This is Dio's account of the ceremonial:

> Next Antony organised sumptuous celebrations for the population of Alexandria. He appeared before the assembled people with Kleopatra and her children seated at his side. In his speech to the people he ordered them to call Kleopatra Queen of Kings, and the Ptolemy whom they named Caesarion King of Kings. He then made a new distribution of countries and gave them Egypt and Cyprus ... Besides these donations he gave to his own children by Kleopatra the following lands: to Ptolemy [Philadelphos] Syria and the whole region to the west of the Euphrates as far as the Hellespont; to Kleopatra [Selene] the country of Cyrenaica in Libya; to her brother Alexandros [Helios] Armenia and all of the other lands east of the Euphrates as far India; and he bestowed these regions as if they were already in his possession.[83]

In the account of Plutarch, who used a different or additional source, more details are preserved:

> [Antony] assembled a great crowd in the gymnasion, where he had erected a stage covered with silver, whereupon he had placed two golden thrones, one for himself and one for Kleopatra, as well as two lower thrones for the children ... Alexandros [was] dressed in Median garb with a *tiara* and a *kitaris*, and Ptolemy in *krepides*, *chlamus*, and a *kausia* encircled with a diadem. For the latter was the attire of the kings who had come after Alexander and the

---

[83] Dio Cass. 49.40.2–41.3.

former that of the kings of Media and Armenia. And after the children had embraced their parents, one was given a guard of Armenians, the other of Macedonians. Kleopatra was on this occasion, as indeed she always was when she appeared in public, dressed in a robe sacred to Isis and she was hailed as the New Isis.[84]

The Donations claimed for Kleopatra and her children the combined diadems of the Ptolemaic and Seleukid houses.[85] The new world empire was in turn amalgamated with Roman rule by means of Caesar's paternity of Caesarion and Antony's paternity of Kleopatra's other children.[86] Antony also possessed the authority of a father over Caesar's son, whose *kyrios* he was, as was made visible by the fact that the throne of Caesarion, the King of Kings, was placed lower than Antony's chair.

The Donations ceremony should be seen in relation to an earlier royal ritual that had taken place in the winter of 37/6 when Kleopatra visited Antony in Antioch.[87] In a ritual performance, presumably of comparable magnitude to the Donations of Alexandria (no details of the ritual itself have been preserved), Kleopatra received the city of Kyrene in Libya, estates on Crete, and various strongholds in the Levant.[88] Also, Antony acknowledged paternity of Kleopatra's twins Alexandros and Kleopatra. A new era in history was announced, with 37/6 BCE as year 1.[89] To emphasise the coming of an everlasting golden age, Antony and Kleopatra made abundant use of solar symbolism. In the Hellenistic east the sun was the principal symbol of the expectation of a golden age, and this it would remain. The twins Alexandros and Kleopatra received the epithets Helios and Selene as a reference to the eternal power exercised in the universe by the sun and the moon.[90] Unfortunately, neither Dio nor Plutarch describes the attire and regalia worn by Caesarion.

The titles Queen of Kings and King of Kings signified that Kleopatra and Caesarion were the rulers of the kingdoms in the Near East, most of which were former vassals of the Seleukids. By then, the

---

[84] Plut., *Ant.* 54.3–6; cf. Fraser II: 219 n. 223.

[85] Strootman 2010b.

[86] Dio Cass. 49.41.4 significantly adds that afterwards '[Antony] sent a despatch to Rome in order that it might also secure ratification from the people there.' At 49.41.2, Dio also explicitly states that Antony made Caesarion 'King of Kings' because of his descent from Caesar, 'and that he had arranged all this for the sake of Caesar'; cf. Schrapel 1996.

[87] Plut., *Ant.* 36.3–4; Dio Cass. 49.32–1–5.

[88] Jos., *AJ* 15.4.88 and 92, at 15.4.96; cf. Hölbl 2001: 242 with n. 102.

[89] Volkmann 1953: 116–22; Schrapel 1996: 209–23.

[90] The Ptolemaic-Roman New Era as a golden age: Grant 1972: 171–5; cf. Strootman 2010b. On Kleopatra's solar propaganda in general see Grant 1972: 142–4 and Śnieżewski 1998: 135–8.

east had come under Roman hegemony, but republican Rome lacked the monarchic prestige and legitimacy needed to unite the east. The titles both replaced and capitalised upon the Seleukids' prestige as Great Kings and kings of Asia, and challenged Parthian rule in Mesopotamia and the Upper Satrapies.[91] Kleopatra's status as 'Empress of the World'[92] was not only apparent from her new title but also inherent in her presentation as the New Isis. Identification with Isis had already been crucial for Kleopatra's rule in Egypt. She had already appeared as an imperial 'universal' goddess at Tarsos in 41, and perhaps she had done so more often, as Plutarch also seems to imply.[93] After the Donations of Alexandria, and perhaps already after the ceremonial in Antioch in 37/6, Kleopatra appeared as 'Thea Neōtera', the 'Younger Goddess' – presumably a reference to both Isis and Levantine universal goddesses – on coins minted in Cyrenaïca and the Levant.[94]

CONCLUSION

In this chapter, several arguments have been made in relation to Hellenistic rituals of inauguration. First, it was argued that the rituals connected with the installation of a new ruler were, as far as we can tell, interwoven with the death rituals of his predecessor. This reinforced the image of dynastic continuity, presenting kingship as something eternal and immortal. Second, it was argued that the new king who emerged from the ritual mourning for his predecessor, ending this period of anomy by leaving the 'closed palace', was already adorned with the diadem when he first showed himself in public. The central *public* inauguration rite was therefore not the binding on of the diadem, which was done behind closed doors, but the acclamation of the newly diademed king by the court and the army. Third, it was argued that inauguration or acclamation could be 'repeated' in various local places, especially when a king went on a tour of his realm. It is here that we see the greatest cultural particularities, for instance at Memphis, where the Ptolemaic *basileus* was enthroned as king of Egypt.

---

[91] Strootman 2010b; Volkmann 1953: 117 has suggested that the names Helios and Selene had been consciously chosen to rival the Parthian king's title 'Brother of the Sun and the Moon'.

[92] Bevan 1927: 377.

[93] On Kleopatra's appearance as the goddess at Tarsos, see below. Probably related is the placing of a gold statue of Kleopatra in the temple of Venus Genetrix in the Forum Iulium during her stay in Rome, and her being proclaimed 'Isis Regina' by Caesar: Cic., *Att.* 14.8.1; 15.17.2; cf. Hölbl 2001: 290.

[94] Nock 1953; Moretti 1958.

11 *The Royal Entry*

This is the first of two chapters discussing the pomp and pageantry of courtly ritual. We will first take a closer look at the ceremonial entries of kings into cities. The context will be kings visiting subjects. Chapter 12 will deal with centralised royal ritual; here the focus will be on subjects visiting the king. The main premise underlying the present discussion is that in entering particular cities Hellenistic kings played a variety of cultural roles – Egyptian, Greek, Judaean, Phoenician – but these roles were not necessarily 'traditional': tradition was constantly renegotiated, and manipulation *by both parties* of the formal aspects of the rituals ordering the royal entry was part of the bargaining process that determined the relationship of city and empire.[1] The two forms of rituals, both involving a procession, overlapped: the Grand Procession of Ptolemy Philadelphos in Alexandria Chapter 12) was both a central event emanating from the palace *and* a ritual of entry, in which the king was equated with Dionysos victoriously returning from the east.

RITUALS OF ENTRY

Macedonian supremacy in the eastern Mediterranean was largely founded on the support of cities. A city was the key to routine access to the military resources of its hinterland. The ritual of entry into a city was therefore of prime importance, since it strengthened the bond between monarchy and town.

Royal entries into cities could take place on various occasions: the arrival of a travelling king, the presentation of a new king making a tour of his realm, the arrival of a royal bride, the return of a victorious king from war, or the arrival of the king for the celebration of a local festival. Ceremonies of entry varied depending on local

---

[1] See Strootman 2013b.

religious and cultural traditions. But this public pageant seems to have had a more or less universal basic structure consisting of three stages. (1) The first part of the ceremony was a joyful welcome of the king outside the main gate. This seems to have been a standard procedure in Greek and Hellenised cities, as well as in cities with a distinct non-Greek identity. A procession of citizens, headed by the magistrates and priests, all clothed in festive garments, left the city to welcome the king. Often the entire population was present for this joyful event, but the only interaction was between the royal entourage and members of the city's elite.[2] (2) After the king had been welcomed, he was taken into the city by the people. There followed a solemn ceremonial passage along the city's main artery, i.e the processional road, culminating in (3) offerings by the king in the town's principal sanctuary.

The significance of the welcoming ceremony outside the city was, I would argue, twofold. On the one hand, the fact that the king was *invited* to enter by the citizens emphasised the city's autonomy. On the other hand, the citizens' vulnerable position outside the protection of the city walls paradoxically amounted to a formal capitulation as well, a ceremonial opening of the gates.[3] Both aspects are part of Josephus' account of Alexander the Great's entry into Jerusalem in 332.[4] Alexander's visit to Jerusalem is usually considered a fable, although a visit by his representatives in that same year is highly likely.[5] Still, the passage provides valuable information, as it is quite clear that the ceremony of welcome that Josephus describes is based on Ptolemaic or Seleukid practices, and may even go back to actual visits of Hellenistic kings or governors to Jerusalem.[6] In Josephus' narrative the ruler of Jerusalem, the high priest Iaddous (Yaddua), fears the coming of the conqueror and makes offerings to Yahweh in the Temple. That same night the god appears before him in a dream,

---

[2] Compare the elaborate reception of Ptolemy III at Antioch during the Third Syrian War (246–241) as reported in the Gourob Papyrus (Holleaux 1900; see also below); cf. Bevan 1927: 198–200.

[3] In Renaissance Italy, princely entries had a prelude *extra moenia* – outside the city walls – where the city fathers symbolically surrendered the town by proffering the keys (Garbero Zorzi 1986: 160).

[4] Jos., *AJ* 11.326–39.

[5] Belenkiy 2005 does not exclude the possibility that Alexander could have entered Jerusalem. Gruen 1998: 189 dismisses the story as entirely fictitious and advocates the older view that '[the] Jews wrote themselves into the campaign of Alexander the Great'.

[6] See Belenkiy 2005, arguing that the account is based on the surrender of Jerusalem by the high priest Shimon II to Antiochos the Great in 199 BCE.

telling him to take courage and adorn the city with wreaths, open the gates and go out to meet him, and that the people should dress in white garments, and only himself and the priests in the robes prescribed by the law; and that they should not look to suffer any harm, for God was watching over them ... When he learned that Alexander was not far from the city, he went out with the priests and the citizens, and, making the reception sacred in character and different from other nations, met him at a certain place called Saphěïn.[7]

When Alexander approached Babylon a few years later, he was met outside the city by the Babylonian governor and a procession of citizens, and was led into the city along a road strewn with aromatic branches and flowers, and accompanied by musicians.[8] Amélie Kuhrt, drawing attention to similarities with the entry of Cyrus into Babylon in 539, comments that Alexander modelled his entry on typical Mesopotamian, particularly Assyrian tradition.[9]

Typically Greek was the reception of the king as if he were a god. An early, pre-Hellenistic example of this is Dion's entry into Syracuse in 357, shortly after the Syracuseans had awarded him 'absolute power' in return for his restoration of *dēmokratia* and *eleutheria*:

Meanwhile Dion drew near the city and was presently seen, leading the way in brilliant armour, with his brother Megakles on one side of him, and on the other, Kallippos the Athenian, both crowned with wreaths. A hundred of his mercenaries followed Dion as a body-guard, and his officers led the rest in good order, the Syracuseans looking on and welcoming as if it were a sacred religious procession for the return of liberty and democracy into the city ... After Dion had entered the city by the Temenid Gate, he stopped the noise of the people by a blast of the trumpet, and made proclamation that Dion and Megakles, who were come to overthrow the tyranny, declared the Syracuseans and the rest of the Sicilians free from the tyrant [Dionysios II]. Then ... the Syracuseans set out tables and sacrificial meats and mixing-bowls, and all, as he came to them, pelted him with flowers, and addressed him with vows and prayers as if he were a god.[10]

After having defeated Philip V in a naval battle off Chios (201 BCE), Attalos I Soter was offered a grand reception in Athens. When the Athenians heard that the king was approaching their city, they sent out ambassadors who congratulated him on his victory and invited him to enter Athens:

[7] Jos., *AJ* 11.326–8; cf. 11.342. There are also several Talmudic versions in which the high priest is named Shimon the Just; cf. Gruen 1998: 190 with n. 2.

[8] Curt. 5.1.19–23; cf. Arr., *Anab.* 3.16. One can still witness the use of scented twigs during civic religious festivals in present-day Andalusia, where aromatic branches are strewn upon the streets before processions; when trodden upon by the carriers of the cult image, the branches become intensely sweet-smelling and thereby suggestive of a divine epiphany.

[9] Kuhrt 1987: 48-9; cf. Kuhrt 1990; entry of Cyrus into Babylon: *ANET* 13.

[10] Plut., *Dion* 18.3-19.1, trans. B. Perrin; cf. Diod. 16.20.6, 16.11. For the historicity of this passage see Sanders 1991; cf. Habicht 1970: 8. Robert 1984 gives many examples of the Greek ritual of welcome (*apantesis*).

The Athenians, hearing that he would soon arrive, made a most generous grant for the reception and the entertainment of the king, [who] went up to Athens in great state accompanied by ... the Athenian archonts. For not only all the archonts and the knights, but all the citizens with their wives and children went out to meet him. As he entered the Dipylon, they drew up the priests and priestesses on either side of the road. After this they threw all the temples open, brought offerings to all the altars, and begged him to perform sacrifice. Lastly they voted him such honours as they had never readily paid to any former benefactors. For in addition to other distinctions they named one of the tribes Attalis after him and they added his name to the list of the eponymous heroes of the tribes. [Then] they summoned the council and invited the king to attend.[11]

The king's presence at the city council – giving a speech to, and perhaps presiding over, the meeting – seems to have been a standard element in the reception of a king by a Greek *polis* or *koinon*. In 220 Philip V presided over the annual meeting of the council of the Aitolian League, and addressed the council at length, after which the council voted to renew, through Philip, 'their friendly relations with the kings, his ancestors'.[12] A public ceremony of acclamation of the visiting monarch by the populace in the theatre may also have been standard procedure. According to Plutarch's account of the acclamation of Mithradates the Great in Pergamon, the king, at that time at the height of his power, sat enthroned on the stage of the theatre, watched by the entire populace. By means of a theatrical mechanism a huge statue of a winged Nike was lowered towards the king, holding a *stephanos* in her outstretched hand, as if descending from the heavens to crown Mithradates victor, and thus king.[13]

An important piece of evidence for the royal advent is the Gourob Papyrus, a contemporaneous propaganda text documenting Ptolemy III Euergetes' military exploits in Syria in 246 during the Laodikean War. The best-preserved part describes the triumphal arrival of the king at Seleukeia in Pieria and Antioch:

Embarking on as many ships as the harbour of Seleukeia was likely to hold, we sailed to the fortress called Poseideion and anchored about the eighth hour of the day. Then we weighed anchor at dawn and entered Seleukeia. The priests, magistrates and the general citizenry, the commanders and the soldiers, wearing crowns met us on the [road] to the harbour. [No excess of]

[11] Polyb. 16.25.3–26.1. The summoning of the council presumably means that the king will give a speech; cf. Polyb. 4.14.6–7 and 4.25.8.

[12] Polyb. 4.14.6–7 and 25.8; cf. App., *Syr.* 11.3.13 (Antiochos III giving a speech at Thebes in Greece); when Philip visited the Achaean League at Sikyon in 218, he and his *philoi* were invited to stay in the houses of the archonts (Polyb. 5.27.3).

[13] Plut., *Sulla* 11.1. Plutarch's 'moral' intention in relating this story is the fact (?) that the statue 'broke to pieces just as she was about to touch his head, and the crown went tumbling from her hand to the ground in the midst of the theatre, and was shattered'.

goodwill and [friendliness towards us was missing. When we entered] the city, [the ordinary people invited us to sacrifice] the animals provided [at the altars which they had built before their houses].[14]

The king then proceeded to Antioch, where he was met outside the gates by a procession of priests, magistrates and commanders, accompanied by the populace and the 'youths from the gymnasion', all wearing festive garments and wreaths: 'They brought all the animals for sacrifice to the road outside the gate; some shook our hands, and some greeted us with clapping and shouts of acclamation' (μετὰ κρότου καὶ κραυγῆς). The involvement of (gymnasion-related) age groups is reminiscent of on an honorific inscription from Pergamon describing the festive entry of Attalos III, who is welcomed by the civic magistrates (*stratēgoi* and archonts), *hieronikai* (victors), ephebes and *neoi* led by the gymnasiarch, *paides* led by a *paidonomos*, and *politai*.[15]

Using the Gourob Papyrus, among other sources, as evidence, Jones was able to show that a passage in Chariton's romance *Chaereas and Callirhoe*, probably written in the second half of the first century CE, and describing the arrival of Callirhoe as a bride in Miletos, is in fact a genuine Hellenistic ritual of welcome (παράστασις ἱερῶν) and may have been modelled on the historical marriage of Demetrios Poliorketes and Ptolemais, daughter of Ptolemy Soter, in Miletos in 286.[16] This is Chariton's description of the ritual:

At daybreak the whole town was already decorated with garlands of flowers. Every man offered sacrifice in front of his own house, and not just in the temples ... They spread purple cloth and scattered roses and violets in her path; they sprinkled her with perfume as she passed; not a child nor an old man remained in the houses, [but] the crowd packed tight, and people even climbed on the roofs of houses.[17]

In Josephus' story about Alexander's visit to Jerusalem, 'the priests led the king into the city; and he entered the Temple and made a sacrifice to God, at the instruction of the priests'. The king in his turn paid homage to the principal local deity, Yahweh, granted the city autonomy and reinstalled the high priest.[18] Although Josephus

---

[14] *FGrH* II b no. 160, trans. Jones 1992. Cf. Holleaux 1942; Lehmann 1988; Downey 1963: 51; on the campaign see Hauben 1990.

[15] *OGIS* 332 = *I.Pergamon* 246.

[16] Jones 1992; for the date of Chariton's novel see Tilg 2010. Marriage of Demetrios and Ptolemais: Plut., *Demetr.* 46.5.

[17] *Chaereas and Callirhoe* 3.2.14–17, trans. Jones 1992: 101.

[18] Jos., *AJ* 11.329.

presents the favours Alexanders bestowed on Jerusalem as the result of his special reverence for the Judaean god – which is ultimately caused by that powerful god's control of even Alexander the Great – the king's behaviour is in fact not very dissimilar from standard approaches of kings to cities. Josephus' account is probably based on Ptolemaic or Seleukid rituals of entry, some more historically sound accounts of which have survived.

For instance, in a report by Agartharchides of Knidos, preserved in Josephus,[19] the people of Jerusalem opened the gates for Ptolemy Soter when the king requested permission to perform sacrifice in the Temple. This turned out to be a cunning plan to capture the city (which is strange, since by opening the gates for Ptolemy and allowing him into the Temple, the Jerusalemites had already acknowledged his overlordship). Such a request was considered so normal that the plan could become a cliché – the same stratagem has been attributed to Philip V and to Antiochos III or IV.[20] Antiochos IV Epiphanes' infamous entering of the Temple was, even in the hostile Maccabees, a regular sacrifice to Yahweh performed by Antiochos in accordance with his role as king and in cooperation with the Judaean high priest Menelaos.[21] According to the same source, Antiochos Epiphanes had also in 172 made his entry into Jerusalem, likewise on the invitation of the high priest, and he had been 'splendidly received and had held his advent under torchlight and amid shouts of acclamation'.[22]

Sacrificing to local deities, it seems, was a king's duty upon entering cities. It may be surmised that by sacrificing to a city's patron deity the king not only acted as one who respected local traditions, but could be viewed as 'one of us'. A person's place and role in civic cult usually defined civic hierarchy, with participation in the central sacrificial ritual being a marker of high social status.[23] By being allowed to perform this ritual act, surpassing the local (high) priest(s), the king became the city's most highly honoured 'citizen'.

The typically Hellenistic integration of local religion into the representation of kingship is already apparent in the reign of Alexander. Curtius tells how Alexander ascended a mountain during the night prior to the battle of Issos (333), and performed sacrificial rites to local gods 'in accordance with local traditions'.[24] Alexander also

[19] Jos., *AJ* 12.4.
[20] Polyb. 7.12.1; 2 Macc. 1.14.
[21] Strootman 2006; cf. 2 Macc. 5.11–16 and 1 Macc. 1.20–5.
[22] 2 Macc. 4.21–22. In 2 Macc. 3.2–3 and 5.16, it is furthermore acknowledged that the Seleukid dynasty paid for offerings and the upkeep of the Temple.
[23] Blok 2003.
[24] Curt. 3.8.22: *Ipse in iugum editi montis escendit multisque collucentibus facibus patrio*

offered sacrifice to Ister, the god of the Danube, to Apis at Memphis, and to 'Minerva' at Magarsos in Kilikia, perhaps Anat or a similar goddess.[25]

It seem there was no real distinction between Hellenistic kings offering sacrifice to Greek and non-Greek local deities. Compare, for instance, Antiochos IV's sacrifice to Yahweh with Philip V's sacrifice to Zeus in Messene:

> He told the magistrates of that city that he wished to visit the citadel and sacrifice to Zeus. He went up with his following (*therapeia*) and sacrificed, and [then], *as is the custom*, the entrails of the slaughtered victim were offered to him [and] he received them in his hands.[26]

In addition to the relatively well-documented participation of the Seleukids in the Jerusalemite cult, and the various sources recording Hellenistic royal offerings to local deities in Greek cities, several documents from Babylonia give a similar picture. A cuneiform chronicle from the early third century, for instance, records a visit of Antiochos I (apparently still co-*basileus* with his father Seleukos Nikator), who makes an offering to the moon god Sin:

> That month, the 20th day, Antiochos, the [crown] prince [entered Babylon. … [Month … , the …] the [day], the crown prince at the instruction of a certain Bab[ylonian] [performed] regular [offerings] for Sin of Egišnugal and Sin of Enit[enna]. [Antiocho]s, the son of the king, [entered] the temple of Sin of Egišnugal and in the tem[ple of Sin of Enitenna] [and the s]on of the king aforementioned prostrated himself. The son of the king [provided] one sheep for the offering [of Sin and he bo]wed down in the temple of Sin, Egišnugal, and in the temple of Sin, En[itenna].[27]

The interesting thing here is that Antiochos I performs the ritual under guidance of 'a certain Babylonian', presumably a (high) priest, exactly as Antiochos IV later did in Jerusalem. Another cuneiform document from Babylon records how an unnamed Seleukid co-ruler (Akkadian: *mar šarri*, 'crown prince') makes offerings at the Esagila, the temple of Marduk, and personally oversees the restoration of the building. Several bad omens take place: the king falls while sacrificing and a stroke of lightning hits the top of a ziggurat:

---

more sacrificium dis praesidibus loci fecit. After the battle, Alexander erected altars dedicated to Zeus, Athena and Herakles: Curt. 3.12.27; see also Bing 1991, who associates these altars with the preceding sacrifice to a local deity, and identifies Curtius' *Iovis*, *Minerva* and *Hercules* as Latin representations of the Syrian deities Ba'al, Nergal and Anat.

[25] Diod. 17.49.1; Curt. 3.7.3; 4.7.5; Arr., *Anab.* 1.4.5; 3.1.4; 2.5.8, 6.4, 24.6; 3.5.2; Plut., *Alex.* 29. Cf. Atkinson 1980: 467; Bing 1991: 161 n. 2.

[26] Polyb. 7.12.1.

[27] Glassner 32; Grayson 1975: 11; *ANET* 317; Austin 189; trans. R.J. van der Spek (*BCHP* 5).

Fig. *11.1*. View of the Isis temple on the sacred isle of Philai, an important Ptolemaic sanctuary in Upper Egypt. Watercolour by David Roberts, c. 1830.

[A]n offering on the ruin of Esagila they [arran]ged. On the ruin of Esagila he fell. Oxen [and] an offering in the Greek fashion he made. The son of the king, his [troop]s, his wagons, [and his] elephants removed the debris of Esagila. [...] on the empty lot of Esagila they ate. That [month], the 17th (?) day, a stroke of lightning within Eridu against the [building] in the middle of its roof took place.[28]

In Egypt, the Ptolemies first of all visited Memphis – for the occasion of their enthronement as pharaoh (see Chapter 10) but apparently also en route to Alexandria when returning victoriously from a campaign.[29] In the later Ptolemaic period, when the importance of Egypt for the Ptolemies increased, they visited cities and shrines in more southerly parts of the country, making a ceremonial boat journey up and down the Nile (Fig. 11.1).[30]

In sum, because kings participated in local, civic cults upon entering cities, the king was turned into a citizen.[31] And because the king within that local cult almost always personally performed the crucial act of offering the sacrificial animal on the altar, he became the most highly honoured citizen. Since cultic ritual has a hierarchising

[28] *BCHP* 6, lines 2–10.
[29] See Clarysse 1980, discussing a victorious entry into Memphis in July 253.
[30] See Clarysse 2000, listing all evidence for royal visits to Egyptian towns and temples in an appendix at pp. 44–53.
[31] For the functionality of religious cult in accommodating outsiders in civic society see now Sara Wijma's study of the integration of metics in classical Athens (Wijma 2010).

Fig. 11.2. Bases for statues of the eponymous heroes Antigonos and Demetrios in the Athenian agora, one of several divine honours awarded to the Antigonids by the Athenian *politai* (author's photograph).

function, especially in cities, it may be presumed that the place of individual citizens relative to the sacrificing king was instrumental in the creation of hierarchy by association (with the empire).

DEMETRIOS POLIORKETES IN ATHENS

Particularly in Greek cities, the ritual entry of a king was sometimes shaped as a divine epiphany, a *parousia*. Besides various other divine honours for his father and himself, Demetrios Poliorketes was on several occasions hailed as a god manifest in Athens (Fig. 11.2). When he visited the city for the first time in 306, the spot where he descended from his chariot and first touched Athenian soil was made into sacred ground on which an altar was erected dedicated to 'Demetrios Kataibatos', 'Demetrios the Descended [God]' – an epithet of Zeus.[32] In June 304, Demetrios entered Athens for the

[32] Plut., *Demetr.* 10.4: καθιερώσαντες καὶ βωμὸς ἐπιθέντες Δημητρίου Καταιβάτου προσηγόρευσαν. The altar's location is unknown. Demetrios visited Athens at least four times. The remarkable honours he received on these occasions are described in detail by Plutarch (*Demetr.* 10.1–4; cf. 12.1–4 and 13.1–2) and confirmed by other sources. On Demetrios and

second time. Because he had relieved the city from a siege by Kassandros and had declared Athens to be henceforth autonomous and free, the Athenians bestowed upon him an even more grandiose and unique honour than the first time: they offered him the *opisthodomos*, the back room of the Parthenon, to use as his quarters,[33] as if, being himself a god, he could only be the *xenos* of another divinity.[34] Indeed, Plutarch says that Demetrios called Athena his 'elder sister' because of their identical roles as *sōtēres* of Athens. It is possible that the same honour was later offered to Pyrrhos, who declined.[35]

The staging of the royal entry as a divine *parousia* is especially apparent from the so-called Ithyphallic Hymn of the poet Hermokles, which the Athenians sang when they welcomed Demetrios Poliorketes at his third ceremonial entry in 291/0:

> See how the greatest and the most beloved gods in our city are present. For here Demeter and Demetrios one lucky moment brought us. She has come to celebrate the holy mysteries of Kore. Joyous, as the god befits, beautiful and laughing, he is present. An august picture is revealed. All friends around him and he is in the centre. Just as the friends are like the stars, He resembles the sun. O son of mighty god Poseidon and Aphrodite, hail you! Now, know that other gods are far away, or have no ears or don't exist or do not care about us. But thee, we see here present,– not wood, nor stone but real to the bone, to thee we send our prayer. So first of all make peace, o most beloved, For thou hast the power.[36]

The hymn continues with an explication of the *sōtēria* expected from Demetrios to save the city and 'make peace': the king is asked to make war against the Aitolian enemies of the Athenians and destroy them. But despite its overtly political intentions, the hymn is thoroughly religious. The association with Demeter follows from the fact that Demetrios arrived at Athens in concurrence with the celebration of the mysteries of Kore, for which occasion Demeter was supposed to be present in the city, too. Of interest also is the

Athens in general see Dimitrakos 1937; Habicht 1997: 87–97; Kralli 2000; Woodhead 1981. For the divine honours Antigonos Monophthalmos and Demetrios Poliorketes received at Athens see Habicht 1970: 44–8; Billows 1997: 149–50; Dreyer 1998 (discussing Antigonid influences on Athenian offices); Kertész 1983; Landucci Gattinoni 1981.

[33] The whole episode of Demetrios' stay in the Parthenon is recorded in Plut., *Demetr.* 23 and 24; cf. 26.3 and Diod. 20.100.5–6.

[34] When Alexander offered to pay for the completion of the temple of Artemis at Ephesos on condition that his name be inscribed on the building, a citizen suggested to him 'that it was not fitting for one god to make gifts to another'; cf. Trell 1989: 83.

[35] Plut., *Pyrrh.* 12.4.

[36] Douris, *FGrH* 76 F 13 *ap.* Ath. 6.253b–f; cf. Demochares, *FGrH* 75 F 2; after a (literal) translation by H.S. Versnel. Recent discussions of the hymn include Mikalson 1998; Bergmann 1997; Marcovich 1988. I was not able to consult Thonemann 2005.

comparison of Demetrios and his *philoi* with the sun and the stars. Solar symbolism was a central feature of Hellenistic royal propaganda. Demetrios himself is said to have owned a magnificent mantle (*chlamus*) into which representations of the *kosmos* and the heavenly bodies were woven.[37] The elaborate mantle was still unfinished when Demetrios died; it may have been intended to be worn by the king during processions, not unlike the sacred robes used to adorn cult statues during festivals.[38] The message seems clear: the kingship of Demetrios was universal and mirrored the rule of the sun in the heavens.

The image of the king as a manifested god whose presence struck the people with awe and joy at the same time is also present in other descriptions of royal entries, discussed below. As we will see, kings associated themselves quite openly with saviour gods, most of all Dionysos.[39]

KLEOPATRA AND ANTONY

Plutarch reports how Kleopatra in 41 sailed to Tarsos in a magnificent barge, dressed as Aphrodite, for her first meeting with Mark Antony:

> She sailed up the river Kydnos in a barge with gilded poop and purple sails, its rowers urging it on with silver oars to the sound of the flute blended with pipes and lutes. She herself reclined beneath a canopy spangled with gold, adorned like Aphrodite in a painting, while boys like Cupids in paintings stood on either side and fanned her. Likewise also the fairest of her ladies in waiting, attired like Nereids and Graces, were stationed at the rudder-sweeps, and others at the reefing-ropes. Wondrous odours from countless incense-offerings diffused themselves along the river-banks. Of the inhabitants, some accompanied her on either bank of the river from its very mouth, while others went down from the city to behold the sight ... And a rumour spread on every hand that Aphrodite had come to revel with Dionysos for the benefit of Asia.[40]

The marriage of Aphrodite and Dionysos, otherwise unknown in extant Greek mythology, may have been based on the Greeks'

[37] Plut., *Demetr.* 41.6; Ath. 12.535f.
[38] Conversely, images of Antigonos and Demetrios were woven into the sacred peplos of Athena Polias for the Panathenaic festival of 306 BCE, depicting the two kings fighting giants together with Zeus and Athena (Plut., *Demetr.* 10.4; 11.2).
[39] On the image of the entering king as the bearer of good fortune in various ancient cultures, but especially the (Hellenistic) Near East and Rome, see Versnel 1970: 371–96. Association with Dionysos is particularly evident in the Ptolemaic dynasty, as has been elucidated particularly by Tondriau (1946, 1948, 1950, 1953); cf. Cerfaux and Tondriau 1957: 189–227.
[40] Plut., *Ant.* 26.1–3, trans. B. Perrin (Loeb), with modifications. On the *hieros gamos* see Śnieżewski 1998: 134; cf. Hölbl 2001: 244 with n. 110.

equation of Aphrodite with Isis and of Dionysos with her divine consort Osiris.[41] And when Antony went on board to attend a banquet in his honour, Plutarch writes that:

> What he found there was beautiful beyond compare, but he was most amazed at the multitude of lights. For, as we are told, so many of these were let down and displayed on all sides at once, and they were arranged and ordered with so many inclinations and adjustments to each other in the form of rectangles and circles, that few sights were so beautiful or so worthy to be seen as this.[42]

Kleopatra did not dress up as Aphrodite in order to seduce an unprepared Antony. The coming together of queen and *triumvir* was carefully prearranged as a celebration of the marriage of Dionysos and Aphrodite, the beginning of a golden age of peace and prosperity in Asia. Antony had earlier that same year appeared as the New Dionysos in Athens and Ephesos. The representation of Kleopatra as Aphrodite, attended by nereids, graces and cupids, was a Ptolemaic tradition which had equated the queen with Aphrodite since the days of Arsinoë II Philadelphos. Kleopatra also associated herself with Isis in Egypt, and later associated Isis with Aphrodite.[43] But Kleopatra's 'Aphrodite' was a deity designed for a wide audience – a universal goddess who could be equated with the Hellenistic Isis as well as with Asian supreme goddesses such as Atargatis, Astarte and Ishtar. The image of a divine *parousia* was enhanced by the incense spreading from her barge towards the onlookers on the river-banks, the flute music, and the abundant use of lights at nightfall. In Greek religious cult, notably of Artemis, Dionysos and the Eleusinian deities, torches were associated with the cleansing of pollution, and the victory of light over darkness.[44]

How at that same period a male Ptolemaic ruler would enter a city as a god is shown in the surviving accounts of the entry of the *triumvir* Mark Antony into Alexandria in 34.[45] Hoping to pacify the Hellenistic world, Antony – who as the representative of Rome in the east between 40 and 30 faced the task of imposing republican rule on a monarchic world – styled himself *basileus* in all but title. Crucial for his 'monarchic' representation were his association with Kleopatra

---

[41] Dio Cass. 50.5.3.

[42] Plut., *Ant.* 26.4, trans. Perrin.

[43] For the association of Aphrodite with Isis in this context see Grant 1972: 117–20.

[44] Parisinou 2000.

[45] Precisely because it was a *Roman* who entered Alexandria as if he were a king and a god, the event was described, pejoratively, by Dio Cass. 49.40.2–3 and Vell. Pat. 2.82 in relative detail, and mentioned by Plut., *Ant.* 50.4. Here, too, it may be assumed that by the award of a (central) place in local civic religion to the Roman Antony, he became a citizen of sorts and was no longer a foreigner and an outsider.

VII, 'Thea Neotera', the Younger Goddess Isis-Aphrodite, as well as his self-presentation as her hierogamous consort, the 'Neos Dionysos'. Already in 41, Antony had entered Ephesos in a bacchanal procession, dressed as the victorious Dionysos,[46] and had received cultic honours as Neos Dionysos in Athens.[47] When Antony and Kleopatra prepared for the war against Octavian on Samos, they held many celebrations in honour of Dionysos.[48] It has become customary to interpret Antony's association with Dionysos as a claim to be a new Alexander. But the epithet 'Neos Dionysos' indicated first of all that he wished to be looked upon as a new Dionysos. In this he followed the example of various Ptolemaic and Seleukid kings. The identification with Dionysos, the conqueror of the east, fore-shadowed his invasion of the Parthian empire.[49]

After subjugating Armenia in 34, Antony left his legions behind and went to Alexandria to celebrate the victory and to propagate – in the public ceremony later known as the Donations of Alexandria (see Chapter 10) – his far-reaching designs for a united Ptolemaic Near East under Roman hegemony. He entered Alexandria in a spectacu-lar *pompē*, adorned as Dionysos incarnate, riding a carriage and carrying a thyrsos and other Dionysian paraphernalia,[50] and paraded the spoils of Asia, including the captured Armenian king Artavasdes and his family:

> [Antony] made them walk at the head of a kind of triumphal entry into Alexandria, together with the other captives, while he himself entered the city upon a chariot. And he not only presented to Kleopatra all the spoils that he had won, but even led the Armenian together with his wife and children before her, bound in chains of gold. She herself was seated upon a golden throne on a stage plated with silver, amidst a great multitude.[51]

The procession ended with offerings in the great temple of Sarapis, the Ptolemaic god of kingship.[52] Antony probably also received divine honours on this occasion.[53] Later, Antony's enemies accused him of having celebrated a *triumphus* outside Rome, an allegation that is often accepted as true in modern scholarship.[54] But from the

---

[46] Plut., *Ant.* 24.4.
[47] Sokrates of Rhodes, *FGrH* 192 F 2; Sen., *Suas.* 1.6.7.
[48] Plut., *Ant.* 56.6–10.
[49] Versnel 1970; Tondriau 1953.
[50] Vell. Pat. 2.82.
[51] Dio Cass. 49.40.2–3.
[52] Vell. Pat. 2.82; Plut., *De Is. et Os.* 28.
[53] Hölbl 2001: 291; cf. Śnieżewski 1998.
[54] So e.g. Volkmann 1953: 141–2; Bradford 2000: 196–8; Southern 2000: 113–15; Weill Goudchaux 2001: 139. Cf. Strootman 2005a.

details (Dionysian imagery, Sarapis) it is clear that the entry was a Hellenistic affair, akin to the earlier Grand Procession of Ptolemy Philadelphos, discussed in the following chapter, and designed to impress the Hellenistic east.

12 Royal Processions: Enacting the Myth of Empire

In the previous chapter we looked at the ritual arrangement of royals visiting cities. We will now focus on centralised public ritual – the religious festivals and processions that drew people from the periphery to the centre. Whereas in entering particular cities Hellenistic kings played a variety of cultural roles, as we saw in Chapter 11, in centralised public rituals kings assumed a *supracultural* imperial persona. In the context of the imperial centre, Graeco-Macedonian religious festivals provided a template for the development of new monarchical ritual – a process going back to at least Philip II's imperial festival at Aigai in 336. Of particular importance, especially in the Ptolemaic empire, for the creation of Hellenistic royal pomp were the developing mythology and iconography of Dionysos, the semi-human epiphanic god, whose prestige as conqueror and bringer of peace and joy to the world was manipulated to become a model of kingship closely connected with the Ptolemaic 'royal gods' Sarapis and Osiris.

In this chapter the ideological dimensions of monarchical ritual and symbolism will also be evaluated. The main argument will be that the two principal, interconnected, 'messages' that were symbolically conveyed in royal rituals were (1) an articulation of the militaristic, heroic nature of the monarchy, and (2) an image of peaceful universal rulership. Here, too, the Ptolemies were able to advance successfully their version of Dionysos. Since the image of Dionysos the conqueror of the east was intrinsically anti-Seleukid, just as he had been an anti-Persian role-model for Alexander, Dionysos was very much a Ptolemaic deity. The Seleukids were apparently wary of utilising his image in political religion. Instead, they promoted Apollo almost exclusively from the reign of Antiochos I to the reign Antiochos IV. As an imperial icon, Apollo clearly had universalistic

Fig. 12.1. Silver tetradrachm of Antiochos I from Seleukeia on the Tigris.
The reverse shows Apollo Delphios seated on the *omphalos* (courtesy
of the Numismatic Association, Inc.).

pretensions because of his equation with the sun and his association
with Delphi and the Omphalos, the geographical centre of the world
(Fig. 12.1). Apollo, like Artemis, moreover, could be associated with
various deities in the Near East, for instance with Nabû in Babylonia.

Finally, it will hopefully be shown how the simultaneous participation in royal rituals of court society and the citizens of capital
cities – e.g. the citizenry of Antioch in the Daphne parade of
Antiochos Epiphanes and the citizenry of Alexandria in the Grand
Procession of Ptolemy Philadelphos – created emotional bonds
between city and empire, while simultaneously enhancing group
solidarity among the *philoi*.

ROYAL PROCESSIONS

On the central, imperial level, it appears that the religious procession
was the basic form for the development of the Hellenistic royal
progress: a festive pageant in which cult images and cultic attributes,
and many participants, followed a prescribed route through the city,
culminating in a sacrificial ritual in a major sanctuary, and followed
by athletic and artistic competition. Thus, Hellenistic royal festivals
revealed the relation between the earthly, royal order and the divine
order of the gods. The shared characteristic of the two best-known
Hellenistic royal processions – the Grand Procession of Ptolemy
Philadelphos and the procession of Antiochos Epiphanes at Daphne
a century later – show once again that the two major dynasties
influenced one another rather than going their separate ways.

In the first instance, statues of the reigning king and queen were
added to the images of the gods and the ruling couple's deified

parents; in the latter case, the living king was centre stage in person. In monarchical-led cities in the Near East, and in Egypt, processions with the king as focal point of course pre-existed this. But the divine honours awarded to the living king were a significant innovation of the Hellenistic era. Ptolemaic and Seleukid rulers apparently drew upon earlier Aegean examples, for instance the divine honours awarded to Pausanias and Lysander.

Combining royal and religious festival ensured that 'great numbers of people flocked together from all directions'.[1] Monarchies attempted to create in their capitals new festivals with pan-Hellenic status. Successful examples are the Ptolemaia at Alexandria and the Nikephoria at Pergamon.[2] The festival for Apollo (and perhaps Artemis) at Daphne in northern Syria was presumably based on a pre-existing religious celebration, but was thoroughly transformed to become a Seleukid imperial festival with international appeal in the second century. Eratosthenes, in a treatise dedicated to Arsinoë II Philadelphos, says that her husband Ptolemy Philadelphos 'founded all kinds of festivals and sacrifices, *particularly those connected with Dionysos*' (my emphasis).[3] The lavishness of royal festivals and their rich processions was meant not only to impress those who were present but to stun the entire world for generations to come; the more sumptuous a procession was, the more and longer it would be talked about, and persist in memory or be commemorated in writing.[4]

The earliest recorded royal procession that may be called typically Hellenistic took place in the reign of Philip II at Aigai, and was part of the Macedonian games of 336. The festival combined a religious feast with a court event, namely the marriage of Philip's daughter Kleopatra to the Molossian king. An impressive spectacle was staged in the theatre of Aigai, which was situated – and not by coincidence, as we have seen in Chapter 3 – below the royal palace. The procession took place before an audience of notables from Philip's Balkan empire, representatives of the Greek *poleis*, and leading Macedonians.[5] For maximum effect, the spectators had been brought to their seats early in the morning while it was still dark, so that the appearance of King Philip – the last and most important element of a *pompē* that was led through the theatre – would coincide with the rise of the sun:

[1] Diod. 16.91.1, on the royal festival celebrated in Aigai in 336 (see below).
[2] For an exhaustive list of Hellenistic royal *pompai* see Bömer 1952: esp. 1954–74.
[3] Ath. 27b.
[4] Moevs 1993: 123; cf. Hesberg 1989.
[5] Diod. 16.92.5–93.1–2; Just. 9.6.3–4.

Along with various other riches, Philip included in the procession statues of the Twelve Gods, made with great skill and richly adorned, so that this show of dazzling wealth would strike the beholder with awe; and together with these came a thirteenth statue, fit for a god, that of Philip himself, so that the king presented himself as enthroned among the Twelve Gods.[6]

Then the king entered the stage of the theatre in person, wearing a white cloak. He was accompanied by his son, Alexander, and his new son-in-law (and vassal), Alexander the Molossian, while the *sōmatophulakes* fanned out behind them at the back of the stage. Since at that very moment Philip was killed by Pausanias, no further description of the festivities survives.

In 333, Alexander staged a procession of his army in honour of Asklepios at Soli in Kilikia, in which the entire Macedonian army participated.[7] Ellen Rice suggested that the participation of the army was an innovation from necessity, since no Macedonians other than the troops were present.[8] But among the *Makedones*, army and people coincided. Before Alexander's reign, the companion cavalry had already paraded in full armour at the Xanthika, the Macedonian spring festival, demonstrating their horsemanship and war-like skills.[9] The inclusion of armed men and other symbols of monarchical power in this and later Hellenistic royal processions did not make them any less solemn.

Two comprehensive accounts of royal processions have been preserved. The so-called Grand Procession of Ptolemy Philadelphos dates to the early third century; the Seleukid festival at Daphne in Syria dates to the reign of Antiochos IV Epiphanes. There are several similarities between the two processions. Both linked royal symbols to divine symbols, and in both entire armies participated. Both processions will now be discussed in more detail.

---

[6] Diod. 16.92.5; cf. Ath. 6.25.1b; Neoptol. *ap.* Stob. 4.34.70. The meaning of the (cult?) image of Philip is controversial; see, among others, Versnel 1974: 140–1; Cerfaux and Tondriau 1957: 123–5; Habicht 1970: 14 n. 3. At the very least, however, Philip was *in some way* presenting himself as a thirteenth Olympian, though this put him on a par with his ancestor Herakles rather than directly with Zeus or Apollo (cf. Strootman 2005a: 133–4 with n. 120). Diod. 16.95.1 comments that Philip made himself the companion of the gods 'because of the extent of his kingdom'.

[7] Arr., *Anab.* 2.5.8; cf.2.24.6; 3.5.2; Plut., *Alex.* 29.

[8] Rice 1983: 26–7.

[9] Hammond 1989: 55 with n. 19; cf. Lane Fox 1979: 62–3, evoking the martial atmosphere at the Argead court, 'where single combat was the recurrent business [of the aristocracy]'. For a comprehensive overview of the evidence for religious festivities at Alexander's court consult Berve I: 89–90.

THE PROCESSION OF ANTIOCHOS
EPIPHANES AT DAPHNE

The grand procession mounted by Antiochos IV Epiphanes at Daphne in 166 or 165, near Antioch, was part of a festival in honour of Apollo.[10] It was a Hellenistic festival, and clearly not an imitation of Roman triumphal spectacle, as has sometimes been presumed.[11] The festival had also been celebrated before the reign of Antiochos Epiphanes and it continued after his death.[12] Epiphanes did, however, increase the festival's importance and size. He thereby transformed the originally local cult of Apollo (and Artemis) at Daphne in Syria into a central imperial cult for the dynasty's tutelary deities – perhaps to compensate for the loss of direct access to Didyma after the Roman–Seleukid War of 191–188, and indeed an oracle of Apollo is later attested for the sacred grove of Daphne.[13] However, the Apollo festival at Daphne may originally have been an indigenous religious festival.[14] Elsewhere I have argued that the Daphne festival was a new year festival: Livy states that it took place in *medio aetate*, and Polybios' negative report on the peculiar behaviour of the king during the procession and later the ritual meal suggests that Polybios' account was based on an (intentional?) misinterpretation of a ritual of reversal in which the king partook.[15] The fact that all the gods came to Daphne to celebrate the festival is also indicative of a new year festival. Finally, there is an indication that Antiochos was impersonating Dionysos, a deity associated with the new year, behaving as if he were directing a bacchic procession in Dionysos' chaotic

[10] The date remains an open question. Scholars have tried to connect the festival with known historical events. Thus Mørkholm 1966: 97–8 believed it was really a victory parade celebrating the end of the Sixth Syrian War; this view was defended at greater length by Bunge 1976, who dated the festival to September/October 166. Bar-Kochva 1989 rejected this, arguing instead that the *pompē* was a prologue to Epiphanes' expedition to the east and dating it to August 165.

[11] See e.g. Edmondson 1999: 84–8, maintaining that Epiphanes had imported the traditional Roman *triumphus* to the east; however, the Roman triumph had eastern origins rather than the other way round (Versnel 1970). Cf. Raup Johnson 1993, who compares the parade with the Grand Procession of Ptolemy Philadelphos to show that it is fully intelligible as purely Hellenistic ceremonial.

[12] Liv. 33.48.4–6 and 33.49.6, on the festival being celebrated in 195 BCE; cf. Ath. 12.540a; *OGIS* 248 l. 52–3.

[13] It may be no coincidence that the earliest irrefutable evidence for Seleukid veneration of the Daphne shrine is a letter in which Antiochos III appoints priests for the joint cult of Apollo and Artemis, dated to 189, immediately after the battle of Magnesia (Welles 1934: no. 44).

[14] Strootman 2007: 309–10. Lib., *Or.* 11.94–99 and Sozomen 5.19 claim that Seleukos Nikator had founded the sanctuary at Daphne, but according to Malalas 204.9–16, the temple predated Seleukos.

[15] Strootman 2007: 309–10.

manner:[16] 'He rode on an inferior horse by the side of the procession, ordering one part to advance, and another to halt, as occasion required; so that, if his diadem had been removed, no one would have believed that he was the king and the master of all.'[17]

Antiochos, writes Polybios, 'in putting on these lavish and stupendous games outdid all his rivals'.[18] The confident presentation of Seleukid strength – a military parade of more than 50,000 soldiers was part of the parade – was intended to advertise his power, and to challenge especially the Romans.[19] Antiochos sent out sacred ambassadors to the Greek cities to request pan-Hellenic status for the festival.[20]

The procession is described in detail by Polybios.[21] A splendidly outfitted army of more than 40,000 infantry plus about 10,000 cavalry marched at the head.[22] More than half of the infantry consisted of Macedonian shock troops: the elite regiments of the Bronze Shields and Silver Shields, each numbering 5,000 men, another 10,000 regular phalangites, and 5,000 soldiers wearing breast-plates and chain armour 'after the Roman fashion'; although the introduction of 'legionaries' into the Seleukid army is usually taken as evidence for Epiphanes' admiration for the Romans, one rather gets the impression that the objective of this innovation was to be able to fight them better. The remainder were light infantry from Kilikia and Mysia, and Celtic mercenaries from Galatia. There also marched 600 *basilikoi paides* and 250 pairs of *monomachoi*. The latter are usually understood to be 'Roman' gladiators, but that seems most unlikely.[23] The cavalry included such guard regiments as the Royal Companions, the Royal Ag_ma and the kataphrakts – all of them wearing parade dress adorned with purple to emphasise their close connection to the monarchy – and mounted citizens of the cities

---

[16] Ibid. 310; *pace* Köhler 1996: 156, who explains Antiochos' wild riding around as stemming from the king's sense of responsibility, inducing him to direct the progress of the parade personally.

[17] Polyb. 30.25; cf. Liv. 36.1: 'it was not really clear either to himself or to others what kind of person he was'.

[18] Polyb. 31.16.1.

[19] Polyb. 30.25.1 links the festival with the games celebrated by Aemilius Paullus in Macedonia and claims that Antiochos '[was] ambitious of surpassing Paullus in magnificence'; cf. Diod. 31.16 and Polyb. 31.16.1. In defiance of the treaty of Apameia, Antiochos paraded elephants and Anatolian troops.

[20] Polyb. 30.25.1.

[21] Polyb. 30.25–26 *ap.* Ath. 5.194 and 10.439.

[22] Polyb. 30.25.1–11.

[23] They may have been elite troops or swordsmen. Carter 2001 suggests that the 500 μονομάχωι were athletes from Antioch.

of the Seleukis wearing gold crowns.[24] Next came 1,000 Iranian horsemen.[25] A thousand mounted *philoi*, wearing purple mantles with gold embroidery, followed. Behind the *philoi* were a thousand 'picked horsemen'.[26] At the end of the military parade came 140 horse-drawn chariots, two chariots drawn by elephants, and finally sixty-four fully armoured war elephants.

Behind the soldiers came an impressive number of sacrificial victims: about 1,000 fat oxen and nearly 300 cows, provided by the various sacred embassies of the Greek cities, as well as 800 ivory tusks and other rich gifts to the god(s) of Daphne. The offerings were carried by 800 ephebes wearing gold crowns.[27] The third and last part of the procession was a parade of deities attending the festival, and this too may be indicative of a new year festival:

> The vast quantity of images of the gods is impossible to enumerate. For representations of every god or demigod or hero known or worshipped by mankind were carried along, some gilded and others adorned with gold-embroidered robes; and there were representations of all the myths, belonging to each according to accepted tradition, made with precious materials.[28]

The universalistic pretensions of Seleukid kingship were made even clearer by the appearance of an image of earth and heaven, which was carried at the end of the procession together with representations of night and day and of dawn and noon.[29] This imagery, embodying the course of the day, can be easily associated with the sun god Apollo and the moon goddess Artemis – both of whom were worshipped at Daphne – but also with Antiochos IV Theos Epiphanes, the god manifest, himself, who equated his kingship with the sun, the all-powerful centre of the universe.[30] Here, too, the symbolism may have been connected with Dionysian myth, as was the case in the Grand Procession of Ptolemy Philadelphos, to which we will now turn.

---

[24] Polyb. 30.25.6: χίλιοι πολιτικοὶ δὲ τρισχίλιοι.
[25] Ibid. Polybios does not specify their ethnicity but describes them as ἱππεῖς Νισαῖοι.
[26] Polyb. 30.25.8: ἐπίλεκτοι χίλιοι.
[27] Polyb. 30.25.12. These young men may have been royal pages; but as they went on foot and were not included in the military parade, it is more likely that they were ephebes from Antioch.
[28] Polyb. 30.25.13–16.
[29] Polyb. 30.25.16.
[30] *Pace* Bunge 1975: 174, explaining Antiochos' solar propaganda as intended to legitimise his usurpation of the throne and reducing its meaning to the mere claim that Antiochos was the unchallenged sole ruler of the Seleukid kingdom; cf. Bunge 1974. Comparison of kingship with the *hēgemonia* of the Divine Sun occurred more often (e.g. in Call., *Hymn* 4.168–70) and presumably had imperial connotations.

THE GRAND PROCESSION OF PTOLEMY
PHILADELPHOS

The most detailed account of a Hellenistic royal progress is the description of the so-called Grand Procession of Ptolemy II Philadelphos in Alexandria. This *pompē* – in actuality a whole series of lesser processions in honour of various gods – is described in rich detail by Kallixeinos of Rhodes in the fourth book of his *Alexandria* (late third century BCE). Lengthy excerpts from this now lost report have been preserved in the fifth book of Athenaios' *Deipnosophistai*, of the late second century BCE.[31] Kallixeinos in turn cites from official records: γραφὰ τῶν πεντετηρίδων, illustrated accounts of the four-year festivals, commissioned by the king to keep the memory of these events alive.[32] These were the forerunners of the *descrizioni* of Renaissance Italy: official descriptions of ceremonies and *fêtes* at princely courts, made public, and even divulged to rival courts.[33] Another text based on Ptolemaic *descrizioni*, in the introduction of Appian's *Syrian Wars*, reveals how Hellenistic processions were meant to impress the world with images of unlimited wealth and military might:

> The empire of Alexander was splendid in its magnitude, in its armies, in the success and rapidity of his conquests, and it wanted little of being boundless and unexampled, yet in its shortness of duration it was like a brilliant flash of lightning. Although broken into several satrapies even the parts were splendid. The kings of my own country alone had an army consisting of 200,000 foot, 40,000 horse, 300 war elephants, and 2,000 armed chariots, and arms in reserve for 300,000 soldiers more ... They had money in their treasuries to the amount of 740,000 Egyptian talents. Such was the state of preparedness for war shown by the royal accounts as recorded and left by the king.[34]

Extensive as it is, the account of Ptolemy Philadelphos' Grand Procession as preserved in Athenaios is far from complete. Athenaios only cites Kallixeinos' description of a single procession (in honour of Dionysos) verbatim and paraphrases some other parts. No context is given, only abundant detail. Kallixeinos' account is genuine

---

[31] Kallixeinos, *FHG* III 58 = *FGrH* 627 F 2 *ap.* Ath. 5.196–203. The most valuable study of this text remains Rice 1983, focusing on the relation of the procession's imagery and political reality. Other significant discussions of Philadelphos' *pompē* are (in chronological order) Versnel 1970: 250–4; Heinen 1978; Dunand 1981: 21–6, 1986; Wikander 1992; Moevs 1993; Köhler 1996; Walbank 1996; Thompson 2000; Hazzard 2000: 59–79; Hölbl 2001: 39–40; Bell 2004.
[32] Ath. 197d.; cf. Moevs 1993: 125; Hesberg 1989. On the (un)reliability of Athenaios' view of Ptolemaic Egypt see Thompson 2001a.
[33] Garbero Zorzi 1986: 155.
[34] App., *Syr.* x.

ekphrasis, concentrating on the vast quantities of precious materials, valuable incense, purple dye, the enormous sizes of the statues, the vast numbers of people participating. Athenaios, too, made selections: 'I have selected for mention only those things which contained gold and silver.'[35] It may be tempting to dismiss the presentation of riches as meaningless 'ultramontane extravagance',[36] but the exhibition of royal *tryphē*, that is, the ostentatious display of luxury and wealth, was an expression of power that itself was instrumental in creating power.[37]

The religious calendar of Alexandria contained various festivals pertinent to the monarchy.[38] It is usually believed that the occasion for the Grand Procession of Ptolemy Philadelphos was the Ptolemaia, the principal four-year festival celebrated in honour of the dynasty.[39] Kallixeinos repeatedly shows that the *pompē* was held in commemoration of the first two Ptolemies, the deified 'saviour gods' Ptolemy I Soter and Berenike I, the parents of the 'brother–sister gods' Ptolemy II Philadelphos and Arsinoë II Philadelphos. Simultaneously with the festival, Ptolemy Soter and Berenike were honoured with sanctuaries at Dodona.[40] Hazzard, who dates the procession relatively late (262 BCE), argues that the procession was exceptionally spectacular because it was meant to announce a new imperial era, which he names the 'Soter Era'.[41] Both date and occasion, however, remain elusive.[42]

A festival such as the Ptolemaia was an international event. In Greece, friends of the Ptolemaic family endeavoured to have the Ptolemaia accepted as a festival of pan-Hellenic status.[43] People flocked to Alexandria from far and near, and many guests, including foreign ambassadors, were entertained by the king and the queen; they were feasted in the palace gardens in the grand banqueting

---

[35] Ath. 201f.

[36] Green 1990: 158–60.

[37] The importance of this aspect is stressed by Dunand 1981: 25–6. For the display of τρυφή by the Ptolemies in general see Heinen 1983.

[38] Fraser I: 230–3; Weber 1993: 165–82.

[39] The conventional date for the first celebration of the Ptolemaia is winter 279/8 (Hölbl 2001: 94); the date, however, is debated (below).

[40] Ath. 203a.

[41] Hazzard 2000: 18–46. The start of this new era coincided with the posthumous styling of Ptolemy I as 'Ptolemy Soter' by his son, which Hazzard also redates to 263/2. Huss 2001 rejects Hazzard's suggestion of a 'Soter Era'; cf. Peter Nadig in *BMCR* 2002–09, 2.

[42] The earliest possible date is the first celebration of the Ptolemaia in 282 *or* 279. Fraser I: 513 and II: 738 date the procession to the winter of 271/0, suggesting that the Grand Procession was a victory celebration after the First Syrian War; so also Ager 2003: 38. Using astronomical data, Foertmeyer 1988 set the date at winter 275/4.

[43] Hölbl 2001: 94; cf. Austin 218, with n. 4.

pavilion. Thus, the festival linked the various parts of the Mediterranean empire of the Ptolemies with the imperial centre, Alexandria.

The route of the procession is unknown. All that is sure is that the processions passed through the royal district – the procession in honour of Dionysos that Kallixeinos/Athenaios describe started in the stadion (near the palace) and passed by (or ended at?) the tombs of Ptolemy Soter and Berenike,[44] which in their turn were located near the Sema, the *heroon* of Alexander. In the stadion, the processions were shown to a large audience. Whether the king and the queen took part in the procession personally or were among the audience has not been recorded

The *pompē* was divided into several separate processions. The first of these was called the Procession of the Morning Star, and the last the Procession of the Evening Star. This implies that the *pompē* lasted from sunrise to sunset – though not necessarily of the same day.[45] Although the exact organisation and duration of the entire procession are not wholly clear, it may be reconstructed thus:

1. Procession of the Morning Star
2. Procession in honour of Ptolemy and Berenike
3. Procession of Zeus
4. Processions of Dionysos
5. Procession of the [other] gods
6. Procession of the Evening Star

Each of these divisions may have lasted a full day; the Dionysiac procession began with satyrs bearing torches, symbolising the transition from night to day, from darkness to light. Rich offerings were made to the gods (and thus lavish banquets given): the Procession of Zeus was preceded by *hekatombai* of 2,000 bulls, 'all of the same colour and with gilded horns, having gold stars on their foreheads, wreaths between the horns, and necklaces with aegises on their breasts'.[46] The procession in honour of 'other gods in great number' also honoured the city's deified founder, Alexander. An *agōn* was held after the procession; the first of twenty persons to be crowned victor with golden wreaths were statues of Ptolemy Soter and Berenike. The last *pompē* was a military parade of c. 80,000 men, elephants and more than 23,000 horses.

In the Dionysiac procession alone there marched more than 10,000

[44] Kallixeinos *ap.* Ath. 5.202d.
[45] Clarysse 1985: 204.
[46] Ath. 5.202a.

people,[47] all of them wearing wreaths and dressed in festive attire. Some of them impersonated mythical creatures associated with the worship of Dionysos. Between the carts walked satyrs, sileni and maenads, clad in purple and crowned with gold and silver garlands in the shape of ivy, pine or vine leaves. There were men carrying precious things, simply displaying these to the spectators, and several male and female age groups, including a group of 120 *basilikoi paides*. On three of the large, four-wheeled carts – drawn by respectively 300, 600 and 600 men – the process of wine-making was demonstrated by satyrs, supervised by sileni: 'and the new wine streamed through the whole line of march'. These were followed by carts with *tableaux vivants* showing various scenes from the life of Dionysos. One showed the god as a new-born before the grotto on Mount Nysa, where he was raised by the nymphs Makris, Erato, Bromie, Bakche and Nysa:

> A four-wheeled cart, ten metres long and six metres wide, drawn by six hundred men; on it stood a deep cavern that was profusely overgrown with ivy and yew. Out of it pigeons, ring-doves and turtle-doves flew forth along the whole route, with ribbons tied to their feet so that the spectators could more easily catch them. And from it also gushed forth two springs: one of milk, the other of wine. And all the nymphs standing round him were crowned with wreaths of gold, and Hermes held a gold staff, and they were dressed in rich garments.[48]

Although the *pompē* was supervised and paid for by the court, it was a meaningful event for the entire Alexandrian population. The number of participants indicates that not only the members of the court society were involved, but also huge parts of the citizenry of Alexandria. The Grand Procession was not just meant to be looked at; it was first of all meant to be participated in, creating group solidarities as well as strong emotional bonds between the dynasty and the Alexandrian people: participants in *pompai*, Burkert summarised, 'separate themselves from the crowd … and move towards a common goal [i.e. sacrifice at a sanctuary], though the demonstration, the interaction with the onlookers, is scarcely less important than the goal itself'.[49] The Grand Procession was a celebration of monarchy and empire, and established Alexandria as the heart of empire. By their participation in the processions and festivities, the

---

[47] Athenaios gives a total number of participants of 8,170, including 2,240 men pulling six carts; for the five other carts no number is given (Clarysse 1985: 205).

[48] Ath. 5.200c.

[49] Burkert 1994: 99. For the importance of the goodwill of the Alexandrian citizens to the royal family see Mittag 2000.

citizens of Alexandria expressed their central place in the imperial system – which at that time was still a Mediterranean thalassocracy and not yet an Egyptian kingdom – and celebrated their own sharing in the wealth, power and prestige of the monarchy.

The Procession of Dionysos was loaded with images illustrating various aspects of the monarchical charisma. The Dionysiac imagery in the procession emphasised in particular the god's prestige as civiliser and conqueror; he was the triumphant hero who had defeated the forces of chaos and bestowed peace upon the *oikoumenē*.[50] The procession therefore began at dawn with a *thiasos* of satyrs, their naked skins smeared with purple dye, who chased away the chaos and darkness of the night with torches and ivy branches. The epiphany of Dionysos was heralded by 120 *paides* burning incense on gold trenchers.[51] The god was preceded by an unspecified number of live 'victories' (*Nikai*) with golden wings, women dressed as personifications of the new year and the four-year period between the festivals – carrying a gold horn of plenty and a palm branch respectively – and as personifications of the seasons, carrying the produce appropriate to each of them, promising the spectators a prosperous future.[52] Finally the god himself appeared in the shape of a 4.5-metre-high statue, clad in a purple *chiton*, holding a mixing bowl, and pouring an offering of wine from a libation goblet.

The apex of the procession of 'King Dionysos' was the last part of the procession, dedicated to the god's victorious return from the east. An image of Dionysos led the march from the back of a huge statue of an elephant. Again the god was clad in royal purple. He was accompanied by an army of satyrs, equipped as heavy infantrymen, or riding on asses outfitted as war horses. Thereafter came a cart drawn by mules carrying 'barbaric tents, under which sat Indian and other women dressed as captives', followed by African tribute-bearers carrying 600 ivory tusks, 200 ebony logs, and 60 mixing bowls filled with gold dust and silver.[53] A train of camels brought frankincense, myrrh, saffron, cassia and cinnamon from Arabia and Yemen. Three flocks of 300 sheep of three different breeds represented the three continents of Europe, Asia and Libya. There

---

[50] López Monteagudo 1999: 40.

[51] For the significance of a delightful scent as indicator of divine epiphany see Versnel 1987.

[52] Ath. 198a–b: Ἐνιαυτος, Πεντερίς, Ὧραι. Moevs 1993: 143 has pointed out the resemblance to Dionysos' triumphal entrance into Athens during the Anthesteria festival as a celebration of the coming of the new year.

[53] Ath. 200f. The exhibition of captives after victory or the depiction of tribute-bearers in itself is not per se typically Egyptian (*pace* e.g. Hölbl 2001: 39).

followed a spectacular display of exotic animals – symbols of the Ptolemies' vast imperial power. There were parrots, zebus and antelopes from India; bears, deer and antelopes from the Levant; goats and cows from the lands along the southern Nile; and wild asses and antelopes from the Libyan desert. From equatorial Africa and the Near East came leopards, lions, ostriches, various exotic birds, and even a rhinoceros and a giraffe.

The triumphal march was concluded with a tableau depicting the purification of Dionysos in Phrygia. Directly after this came a tableau in which Ptolemy Philadelphos was the central figure. The statue of the king was crowned with an ivy wreath made of gold, which affiliated him with Dionysos. Next to him stood Alexander, also wearing an ivy wreath. Also on this cart were statues representing Aret and the city of Corinth. Next walked women personifying cities, 'some from Ionia, while all the rest were the Greek cities which occupied Asia and the islands and had been under the rule of the Persians'.[54] Ellen Rice suggested that the personification of Corinth, wearing a gold royal diadem and standing near Alexander and Ptolemy, referred to the Corinthian League, and presented the Ptolemies – in defiance of Antigonos Gonatas – as the successor of Alexander as *hegemon* of the Greeks.[55] The personifications of cities 'that were once under the rule of the Persians' likewise presented the Ptolemies – in defiance of Antiochos Soter – as Alexander's successor as liberator of the *poleis* of Asia Minor. *Aret* was a typical royal virtue and figures prominently in panegyric for Ptolemy Philadelphos.[56]

And the Procession of Dionysos was still not finished. The visual climax was a group of golden statues in golden chariots set atop golden columns. The statues represented Ptolemy Philadelphos and his sister–consort Arsinoë Philadelphos, as well as their deified parents, Ptolemy Soter and Berenike, together with the deified Alexander (to whose cult that of the ruling couple was linked, Philadelphos and Arsinoë being its high priests).

Imagery referring to Alexander was also present in the rear part of the procession in honour of 'various gods': a statue of Alexander, seconded by Athena and crowned victor by Nike, stood in a chariot drawn by elephants. The triumphant Alexander was followed by carts carrying thrones made of ivory and gold:

[54] Ath. 5.201e.
[55] Rice 1983: 106–9. Ptolemy Soter had attempted to formally restore the Corinthian League in 309/8.
[56] Call., *Hymn* 1.94–96; Theocr., *Id.* 17.135. Cf. Rice 1983: 110.

On one of these lay a gold diadem [στεφάνη], on another a gilded horn [κέρας], on still another a gold wreath [στεφάνος] and on another a horn of solid gold. Upon the throne of Ptolemy the Saviour lay a crown made of ten thousand gold coins.[57]

All kinds of enormously enlarged royal paraphernalia were displayed, including diadems and suits of armour, as well as enormous gold eagles, a gilded thunderbolt, and horns of plenty. Kallixeinos also mentions a 'mystic' (μυστικὸς) *stephanos*. It was 3.5 metres in circumference, made entirely of gold, and adorned with precious stones. This super-diadem was later hung above the portal of the Berenikeion, the shrine of the deified Berenike.[58]

The last procession was a military parade, which lasted perhaps a whole day.[59] There marched 57,600 infantry and 23,200 cavalry. These are the numbers of a campaigning army at full strength, larger even than the Ptolemaic army at the battle of Raphia in 217, and far too large to have been troops permanently stationed at Alexandria (or at any place).[60] It was probably about the complete military force available to the Ptolemies for campaigns at that time, temporarily brought together in Alexandria. The presence of an army of more than 80,000 men underlined the military foundations of empire and the heroic nature of the monarchy. These soldiers were the living assurance that the Ptolemies, too, were capable of what in the Athenian hymn for Demetrios Poliorketes was presented as the ultimate proof of god-like status: to *really* 'have the power to bring peace'.

The army included cleruchs, the Macedonian military settlers who made up the royal phalanxes, as well as the royal household troops and guard regiments that constituted the standing core of the Ptolemaic army. Their presence at the Ptolemaia was not only intended to impress the spectators (including foreign ambassadors),[61] but also to strengthen the soldiers' bond with the king – the rank and file of the common soldiers probably had stronger emotional ties

---

[57] Ath. 5.202a–b. The other three thrones probably belonged to Berenike, Arsinoë and Ptolemy Philadelphos.

[58] Ath. 202d.

[59] Rice 1983: 125.

[60] *Pace* Rice 1983: 125, who identifies these troops as the 'Army of Alexandria', following Fraser I: 69 and II: 152–3. Tarn 1948 II: 229 assumed it was a campaigning army returning from war, and rendered the whole of the Grand Procession in essence a triumphal parade; Hölbl 2001: 39 presumed the same, but believed that that army was paraded directly *before* the beginning of the First Syrian War, and thus dated the festival to 275/4. Note that the number of cavalrymen, 23,200, is unusually large for a Ptolemaic army; at the battle of Raphia the Ptolemies had at their disposal 68,000 infantry and only 4,700 cavalry.

[61] Rice 1983: 126.

with the king than did other subjects.[62] For these Macedonians living in Egypt – albeit by then including young men with Egyptian mothers – the main focus for identity was the empire and the king, who had granted them farmland and relatively high social status in Egypt, and who incidentally distributed gratuities among them – at least on the occasion of the coronation but perhaps also on coronation anniversaries. Nothing is said about the origins of the soldiers apart from the cleruchs and household troops. At Raphia, they consisted of allied units, mercenaries, light troops levied notably in Libya and Egyptian phalanx infantry, but the last had been levied for that occasion for the first time.

Besides all these troops (and many horses and elephants), the procession displayed the Ptolemies' financial resources to wage war and reward their supporters with gifts:

> There were 400 cartloads of silver vessels, 20 of gold vessels, and 800 of spices … Beside the arms and equipment worn by all the troops, there were many others stored in chests, of which it is not easy to set down even the number.[63]

The pan-Hellenic Ptolemaia with their international appeal established Alexandria as the heart of the Ptolemaic empire, and the centre of Greek civilisation. The imagery of the Grand Procession attests how far-reaching the imperial claims of the Ptolemies were at that time. Personifications of *poleis* presented the Ptolemies as the protectors and liberators of all the Greeks. Exotic animals and objects, notably those from peripheral areas such as Ethiopia and India, amounted to a symbolic claim to almost the whole world.[64] Even as the display of Nubian captives bringing a tribute of ivory and gold mirrored New Kingdom pharaonic victory display,[65] it was definitely not an Egyptian kingdom that was put on stage here, but an *empire*.

---

[62] The direct (and often emotional) bond between king and common soldier in pre-industrial monarchies, and the importance of gift distribution for maintaining this bond, is emphasised by Jansen 1984: 56.

[63] Ath. 5.202f and 203a.

[64] Rice 1983: 109 needlessly tries to explain the discrepancy between ideology and political reality by stating that the imperial imagery represented '*past* Ptolemaic interest in the mainland' (my emphasis) and *perhaps* referred to future political aims; however, nominal claims to universal dominance are typical of imperial ideology, and the Hellenistic empires were no different in this respect from e.g. the Assyrian or Sasanian kingdoms; cf. Strootman 2013c and, specifically on Ptolemaic claims to world power, 2010b.

[65] Ath. 5.200f–201c; the same products appear as Nubian booty on the temple of Ramesses the Great at Beit el-Uali; cf. Kitchen 1982; I owe this reference to Stefano Caneva (*BMCR* 2011–05, No. 59).

CONCLUSION: THE SYMBOLISM OF POWER

In this chapter, evidence for Hellenistic royal processions has been collected and discussed. Of course, there was no single, unchanging Hellenistic ritual of *adventus*. The sparseness of the sources makes it difficult to find details of regional variation or development through time. However, it does appear that there were notable similarities between the respective kingdoms. The necessity of presenting rituals as tradition precluded blatant innovation of what was supposed to be ancient and eternal – for instance, the amalgamation of monarchical and religious festival to suggest sacredness, the manifold claims to world power, or the presentation of empire as peace.

Throughout this chapter, attention has been given to the symbolism of royal ritual. The most important elements were the display of wealth (*tryphē*) and military power, and what may be called *the theatrical enactment of the myth of kingship*. I have tried to show how the imagery of Hellenistic royal entries amounted to the presentation of the ruler as bringer of peace, prosperity and justice. Since Greek ruler cult and various indigenous forms of reverence for the ruling monarch created an image of the king's eternal presence in the cities, even if he were physically absent, the actual entry of the ruler was like a divine *parousia*. The emphasis on victory and military prowess connected the ceremony of entry with the ideology of the ruler as a manifested *sōtēr* who had overcome chaos and darkness.

Among the divinities with whom kings affiliated themselves when entering a city, Dionysos was most prominent, especially in the Ptolemaic context. Dionysos was a royal god par excellence.[66] He was *der kommende Gott*, the epiphanic deity above all others.[67] Versnel has argued that Dionysos became such a suitable model for Hellenistic kingship because in defeating human adversaries instead of supernatural opponents, and in conquering *real* territory, Dionysos' conquest of Asia was mythical and historical at the same time. He was the victorious god who triumphed over man and world; he was not the god *of* victory, but himself a victorious god, whose return from the east signalled the dawn of an age of good fortune.[68]

The public adulation of visiting Hellenistic kings in a city theatre or hippodrome was a form of repeated inauguration. As we saw in

---

[66] Tondriau 1953.
[67] Burkert 1994: 162, with n. 6 on p. 412.
[68] Versnel 1970: 250–3. The theme of the bacchic triumphal march is best known from (late) Roman mosaics and sarcophagi; cf. Dunbabin 1971; representations of bacchic triumphs on Roman mosaics may be directly influenced by the Grand Procession of Ptolemy Philadelphos (López Monteagudo 1999: 45).

Chapter 10, the central element of Hellenistic inauguration rites was the presentation of the new king before audiences – before the army, court society, and the population of the city where the inauguration took place. Such public presentations could be repeated during an entire reign in many cities, where the king could be acclaimed as the city's own particular saviour and liberator. For the practice of empire, visibility of the king was key,[69] and the *Reisekönigtum* of the Seleukids especially must at times have been a never-ending road show of monarchical performance.

The Hellenistic kingdoms were empires, loosely uniting multifarious peoples and societies. This was notably the case in the Seleukid empire, but the Ptolemies and even the Antigonids also had to reckon with diverse ethnic, cultural and political entities within their spheres of influence. In none of these kingdoms could kings very easily appeal to a common set of social values endorsed by all the subjects. Instead, the symbols of power were adjusted to circumstances. Put into a simple model, two main forms of royal symbolism can be discerned: the local and the central. Locally, kingdoms adopted and reformed culturally specific forms of monarchic representation for specific audiences. This category includes, for example, the coronation of the later Ptolemies at Memphis, the Seleukids' taking part in the Babylonian Akitū ritual, and the utilisation of the Greek religious procession upon entering Greek cities. Centrally, the respective courts, in interaction, gradually developed an all-embracing, imperial symbolism to appeal to subjects (and especially elites) of various nationalities. These generic symbols of empire were rooted mainly in Greek and Macedonian traditions; but they were consciously chosen to be comprehensible to both Greeks and non-Greeks. The principal emblem of Hellenistic kingship, the diadem, was basically Greek in origin, but modified in such a way as to turn it into a generic symbol of kingship, acceptable to all willing to affiliate themselves with the empire.[70]

---

[69] For the theoretical aspects of 'visibility' as an instrument of monarchical rule see Hekster and Fowler 2005; cf. Hekster 2005.

[70] Strootman 2007: 367–86.

Conclusion

By approaching the Hellenistic kingdoms from the angle of the court I have attempted to shed a different light on the ideology and nature of Hellenistic monarchy and imperialism. Crucial to the approach has been the understanding of the monarchies of the Antigonids, Seleukids and Ptolemies as empires. Empire was defined as essentially both a supranational (military) organisation, characterised by a universalistic ideology and an expansionist policy, and a negotiated enterprise – although the enterprise was, of course, ultimately founded on the use of force. But like the European monarchs of the age of absolutism, the Hellenistic (and, for that matter, Achaemenid) emperors were in reality not as powerful as official propaganda claimed they were, and imperial control was constantly (re)negotiated or fought over.

As an analytical category, the paradigm of empire allows us to accommodate within the hegemonic spheres of the Macedonian monarchies not only multifarious cultures, languages and religions, but also a variety of sub-imperial polities, many of which were quite autonomous. It also allows us to distinguish between on the one hand the monarchies' diversified adaptation to, and manipulation of, varying local cultures (e.g. Egyptian, Babylonian, Greek), and on the other hand an overarching imperial culture emanating from the imperial centre and connecting the various local elites affiliated with that centre. Because the imperial elites were initially recruited from the ruling families of Aegean cities, the culture of the court at first had a rather 'Greek' countenance. Cooperation with civic elites (who controlled the infrastructure and the accumulation of economic surpluses) and local aristocracies (who controlled access to manpower and military resources) was vital for the practice of empire.

Two basic models explaining political power in premodern societies have been used for the investigation of Hellenistic imperialism and monarchy. The first is the understanding of the court as a political system, and potentially an instrument of power, in Norbert Elias' seminal study *Die höfische Gesellschaft*, but with the addition of Jürgen von Kruedener's important comprehension of the court's theatrical function as an instrument of legitimisation and a means of competition with rival courts. The second main influence is Charles Tilly's model explaining monarchical power as the interplay of coercion, cities and capital. The (integrated) models of Elias and Kruedener and of Tilly have informed the argument throughout the book, even though they are not always explicitly referred to.

Following Elias, I have defined the court in socio-political terms. The court was the social environment of the king, consisting of the royal household and various hangers-on who not only served the king but also maintained lines of communication and patronage with civic elites and rural aristocracies. As we saw in Chapter 1, writers in the ancient world also thought of the Hellenistic courts mainly in social terms. Working from Jürgen von Kruedener's model, four dimensions or functions of the court were discerned: the court as a political arena where status, power and offices were distributed through the intangible instrument of 'favour'; the court as administrative centre where the (mostly military) affairs of the king were administered; the court as symbolic centre – a microcosmic model of the world at the centre of the world where knowledge of the world was collected; and the court as a stage for monarchic representation through royal ritual, court poetry and the exposition of luxury, good taste, strength and wisdom.

Although king and courtiers usually presented an outward image of unity and concord, the court was riddled with conflicts. Contrary to Elias' thesis that the court was essentially an instrument developed by the monarchy to pacify the nobility and thereby consolidate absolutism, it has been argued throughout this book that one should be wary of imagining the king as being always in full control of the distribution of titles and offices, wealth and favour. Attempts by kings to rearrange the social composition of their households was an important source of conflict. Another major source of discord was conflict over the succession. Royal courts were not the only source of political power in the Hellenistic world. As long as the monarchy was strong and wealthy, kings were able to attract powerful men to their courts and control cities and territory with their aid. But when a monarchy became impoverished or lost charisma – usually the result of military failure – regional leaders turned away from the court or became political rivals. As we have seen, sometimes the court was an instrument of the king to control the nobility, to use Elias' terms, but sometimes the court could be an instrument of the nobility to control the king.

THE COURT AND IMPERIAL INTEGRATION

The court was key in keeping the empires together. In this book three integrative qualities of the court have been emphasised. The first was ideological. Architecture, iconography and theatrical perform-ances worked together to create an image of the empire as limitless, peaceful and all-powerful, and of the ruler as the greatest source of protection and munificence in the world.

The second quality was cultural: the development and trans-mission of an aulic 'high culture' that spread among local elites deriving power and status from their relations with the central power, and who internalised and displayed this affiliation by (partially) adopting the culture of the court. Thus, some form of 'Hellenism' may have spread through the Middle East after all, only not because of any 'nationalistic' promotion of Greek culture: the Hellenism of eastern (civic) elites was *imperial* – 'Seleukid' or 'Ptolemaic' – culture. It was unconnected with the land of Greece.

The (partial) adoption of a supranational, imperial identity, depending on context, by members of local elites contributed to the creation and maintenance of lines of communication between centre and periphery; it also allowed elite members to distance themselves from their local rivals and to connect with their peers elsewhere in the empire (e.g. in other cities). Hellenism, in other words, helped in crossing cultural boundaries, facilitating negotiations between the imperial centre and the locally powerful. It was only from the second century BCE onward, when the Seleukid imperial centre increasingly linked up with Iranian provincial elites and vassal rulers, bypassing the by now established landed *philoi* aristocracy, that Hellenism was supplemented by Persianism in, inter alia, Parthia, Fars (Persis) and post-Seleukid Kommagene. In the Ptolemaic context a process of Egyptianisation began in the second century, though here the main motivation was not the wish to remain in control of a huge, diver-sified empire, but rather the fact that the Ptolemaic empire had been destroyed by the Seleukids in the Sixth Syrian War, and Ptolemaic rule had become restricted to Cyprus and the land of Egypt.

The third integrative quality of the court was of a socio-political nature. The court was the point of contact between the monarchy and the various ruling classes at the regional and local levels of the kingdoms, the hub of a complex network of kinship, friendship, gift-exchange, redistribution and patronage.

The *philoi* functioned as intermediaries between the court and the cities. They were linked to the king and his family through kinship, ritualised friendship (*philia, xenia, philoxenia*), and other personal bonds. The *philoi* maintained ties with their cities and families of origin, and acted as private benefactors of other cities. They became local magnates because they were royal *philoi*, or vice versa. This permitted cities and elite families to exert influence at court through royal *philoi*.

Periodic special events such as birth ceremonies, royal marriage, inauguration rites or religious festivals attracted representatives of cities and provincial elites to the imperial centre, so that the household, the *inner court* of royal family and royal friends, temporarily expanded to include an extensive *outer court*. Collective participation in monarchic rituals and feasts, together with the allure of the refined and prestigious culture of the court, strengthened the attachment of elites to the monarchy and the imperial system. The significance of (religious) festivals, both at the imperial centre and locally, for elite integration into the Hellenistic empires could be, I would suggest, a fruitful subject of future research (see the final section of this Conclusion).

PERFORMATIVE SPACE: THE PALACE AS STAGE FOR THE THEATRE OF ROYALTY

The third chapter addressed the question of how royal palaces were incorporated into cities and what this tells us about the relationship between the royal and the civic in Hellenistic cities. It was argued that through the use of elements from religious architecture, a royal precinct was demarcated from civic space as if it were a sacred *temenos*. As in sanctuaries, there could be varying degrees of accessibility. For instance, the huge royal quarter between the *polis* and the palace of Alexandria was a more or less public 'contact zone' accessible to all or most citizens, while the sacred *temen* containing the tombs of Alexander and the Ptolemies inside this quarter, as well as the palace gardens, were semi-public, accessible to some at certain religious occasions. The private palace on the Lochias peninsula, again, was *mutatis mutandis* a closed inner sanctum, accessible only to a happy few. The same organisation of space can be seen in Pergamon and Demetrias, and earlier at Halikarnassos. Thus the sacredness of kingship was accentuated, and a means was created to separate *and* connect royal and civic space. In such quintessentially royal cities as Pergamon and Alexandria, the principal sanctuaries were in one way or another connected with the monarchy.

In order to facilitate communication between king and subject, theatres, stadia and other structures that could contain large crowds were constructed in the intermediate spaces between palace and *polis*. But the entire area with monarchic-religious or purely royal monuments – e.g. the Alexandrian *basileia* district, or the Pergamene processional road that led from the extramural Nikephoria sanctuary to the *temenos* of Athena Nikephoros, opposite the royal quarters on the top of the akropolis – was performative space, a stage for the theatre of royalty that linked up city and monarchy. The use of akropoleis for palace construction and the incorporation of fortifications into palatial architecture furthermore accentuated the king's heroic ethos and his ability to protect.

THE DYNASTIC HOUSEHOLD

Hellenistic monarchy was essentially a family affair. At the centre of the Hellenistic royal courts was the royal family. Chapter 4 therefore discussed the place of the king, his wife or wives and his sons in the dynastic household.

In reaction to Ogden's thesis that endemic 'amphimetric disputes' structurally broke up the Hellenistic courts and ultimately caused the decline and fall of the Macedonian empires, it was argued that Hellenistic kings potentially had at their disposal various means to appoint a 'crown prince'. For instance, the co-rulership of father and son was a successful strategy for arranging the succession in advance. The inter-dynastic conflicts that broke up the Seleukid and Ptolemaic empires in the second century BCE must therefore have had other roots, the failure to contain 'amphimetric disputes' being the result rather than the cause of decline.

The extraordinarily powerful position of women at the Hellenistic courts had two principal causes. The first was the pivotal role that Macedonian noblewomen traditionally had in transferring inheritance. The ancestral title of *basileus*, once acquired by a family through right of victory, could be passed on through the female line as well as the male line. The main rationale behind Ptolemaic full-sibling marriage may have been the consequence of this: the wish to make the two lines of inheritance converge and prohibit rival claims to the throne. The second explanation was that royal women were the ideal 'favourites' to whom kings could delegate power. Because

Macedonian monarchs were polygamous, and favour could be transferred from one queen to another (and her offspring), favoured queens were loyal and thus reliable associates.

Indeed, the principal purport of the title of *basilissa* may have been to distinguish a 'first queen' among the royal wives – a means to hierarchise royal women, prearrange the succession, and transform a queen's sub-court into a most loyal segment of the dynastic household. Dynastic marriage was instrumental in the creation of imperial elite networks. Especially in the Seleukid empire, royal women had an important role to play in maintaining lines of communication between the imperial family and vassal dynasties, and vice versa.

HELLENISTIC COURT SOCIETY AS A SOCIAL AND POLITICAL SYSTEM

The *philoi tou basileōs*, 'the friends of the king', were the most conspicuous group of courtiers in the Hellenistic kingdoms (though presence at court was not strictly speaking a prerequisite for being a royal *philos*). They mostly came from Aegean *poleis* and cultivated a Greek social identity. They helped maintain relations between the imperial centre and (Greek) cities. The *philoi* represented the interests of the cities at court, and the interests of the court in the cities. Thus, kings could directly influence civic politics through their *philoi*, whose families or adherents at the local level benefited from royal favour: it gave them an advantage over other families or factions in the internal political rivalries of the cities, and this in turn secured their loyalty to the dynasty.

Patronage relations at the Hellenistic courts were characterised by obligations of loyalty and what may be called 'fictive equality'. The aristocratic ideal of *parrhēsia*, i.e. speaking frankly and without fear, was an aspect of the ideal of equality. However, hierarchy within the *philoi* society was created by various means. Since the king was the nucleus of court society as a social system, status at court was determined by the principle of proximity to the throne, or 'favour': the degree to which one was able to gain access to the person of the king, or to persons near the king, or to persons near the persons near the king. Gift-exchange, court titulature, etiquette and, we may assume, various subtle indicators like one's distance from the king during banquets or processions, or the time one had to wait before being admitted into the king's presence, all worked together to determine a courtier's relative position within the subtle hierarchy of the court. It is doubtful whether the king was always able to manipulate 'favour' in order to control the nobility, as Elias suggested he could at the French court in the age of absolutism. It may have differed from case to case, but the Hellenistic examples suggest that status at court was sometimes the result of prerogative instead of the will of the monarch. Moreover, as Elias rightly saw, there were various other status determinants besides the favour of the king: inherited family prestige and wealth, military achievements, and the ability to influence powerful persons, courtly behaviour and outward appearance, etc. A similar ambiguity can be seen in relation to the royal pages, the *basilikoi paides* discussed in Chapter 6: it is never fully clear whether the presence of the young sons of aristocrats at court is a sign of the king's power or their fathers' power.

Gift-exchange was the principal mechanism underlying social relations at court. The complex of gift-exchange included the bestowment of honorific titles, aulic offices and the accompanying tokens of status and honour. The distribution of clothing, dyed with purple dye or adorned with purple-coloured borders, was in this respect arguably the most significant gift. It accompanied the distribution of aulic titles and was a mark of belonging to the circle of the king's friends. For kings, the public distribution of gifts thus had the additional advantage of allowing them to allocate favour publicly, and thus establish the receiver's place within the court hierarchy.

The exchange of gifts created not only horizontal bonds of loyalty but also vertical bonds of dependence. In *Die höfische Gesellschaft*, Elias even maintained that the requirement of massive status expenditures drained courtiers of their financial resources, making them dependent on royal generosity. However, being the person of highest status, the ruler was expected to deal out the most valuable gifts. This could even lead to the king's financial dependence on wealthy *philoi*, as in the case of the young Antiochos III and the powerful courtier Hermeias (Chapter 7). Kings could forestall the risk of running out of wealth to meet the demands of the *philoi* by distributing symbolic gifts. Privileges, titles and the king's favour were much-desired gifts, too, and only the king could give them. Purple clothing and tableware used at royal symposia were in themselves valuable, but had an added value as visible tokens of proximity to the throne, which in turn boosted one's status and prestige in other social contexts.

FESTIVALS, BANQUETS AND GIFT-EXCHANGE: THE COURT AND ELITE INTEGRATION

At the courts, multifarious festive events took place. Besides the daily ceremonial of the inner court, incidental occasions for celebration were provided by royal weddings and births, the inauguration of new rulers, and anniversaries. The influx of guests for occasions like these brought about the formation of a temporary 'outer court'. This, in turn, facilitated diplomatic interaction between centre and periphery, and – during 'great events' such as royal weddings or inaugurations – bilateral diplomacy between the dynasty and foreign states. Court festivities involved the distribution of gifts and privileges, the reception of ambassadors and petitioners, and a lot of pomp and circumstance. The dynasty's participation in religious cults, too, created opportunities to expand the court temporarily. In Ptolemaic Alexandria various religious festivals seem to have been created, or at least organised by the court, for precisely that reason. Seleukid kings, on the other hand, preferred to move around their empire and attend pre-existing local festivals.

The locus for the distribution of gifts was the royal banquet, notably the sacrificial meal that followed on rituals of offering. The gifts often included the tableware that one had used during the banquet. Such a gift was a *symbolon*: physical evidence of having enjoyed the king's hospitality, and thus of a certain degree of proximity to the throne. In local contexts, royal favour and the ability to stand up for the interests of one's home town at court could boost one's status, elevating a person above his rivals. At the same time, participation in royal banquets, hunting parties, and other ceremonials and rituals of the court potentially created bonds between representatives of geographically dispersed elites. Collective ritual action emphasised the unity of the court by conveying images of harmony and solidarity among the *philoi*, and a strong bond between the *philoi* and the king.

Clothing, too, had an integrative quality, creating cohesion among the *philoi* at court and outside it. Clothing (partly) dyed purple and other badges of rank given by the king were tangible tokens of favour. In local contexts, gifts received from the hands of the ruler expressed allegiance to the imperial centre, creating bonds between elite families in one city and their peers in other cities, *and* expanding the social gap between them and their rivals in the home town.

ROYAL RITUAL: ENACTING THE MYTH
OF EMPIRE

As we saw in Chapter 2, the similarity of royal ceremonial to theatrical performance was explicitly recognised in the Hellenistic age. In Part III (Chapters 9–12), the rituals and pageantry of the court were discussed. Chapter 10 focused on inauguration ritual, Chapter 11 on the ceremonial entry of kings into cities, and Chapter 12 on centralised royal festivals.

The installation of a new king and the burial of his predecessor were interrelated ritual events making possible the transmission of *basileia*. For the successor, it was a ritual of transformation. As we have seen, when the new Ptolemaic king emerged from the ritual mourning for his predecessor in the 'closed palace', he presumably came out already adorned with the diadem and presented himself in public already transformed. The central *public* inauguration rite was the acclamation of the new king by the court and the army. The ritual of inauguration and/or acclamation could be repeated in other places. The (later) Ptolemies went at least to Memphis to be enthroned as Egyptian pharaohs. New Seleukid emperors could go on a tour to find the support of civic elites.

For the practice of empire, the visibility of the king was key, and the itinerant Seleukid court's journeys especially must at times have amounted to a walkabout demarcating territory through a series of monarchical performances, just as the later Ptolemies demarcated their territory by means of ritual trips up and down the Nile. As we saw in Chapter 11, in entering particular cities Hellenistic kings played a variety of cultural roles – Egyptian, Greek, Judaean, Phoenician – but the local conventions they seemed to comply with could also be manipulated to connect them to a wider standard of imperial representation and so bridge the gap between the local and the imperial. The Macedonian kings' participation in the Babylonian Akitū festival or the Memphite enthronement ritual, in Greek and Jewish rituals of sacrifice – it all seems very traditional. But the ritual practices and the ideas connected with them were constantly in flux.

Generally speaking, the imagery of Hellenistic royal entries amounted to the presentation of the ruler as a bringer of peace, prosperity and justice. The emphasis on victory and military prowess connected the ceremony of entry with the ideology of the ruler as a manifested *sōtēr* who had overcome chaos and darkness. Among the divinities with whom kings affiliated themselves when entering a

(Greek or 'Hellenised') city, the 'epiphanic god' Dionysos was most prominent, particularly in the Ptolemaic context.

The key act in ceremonies of entry was the king's sacrifice in the city's principal sanctuary. The king's participation in local cult made him a citizen of sorts. He became 'one of us'. But by being assigned the honour of performing the central ritual act of offering, surpassing the local (high) priest(s), the king was also singled out as the city's most important citizen. The subsequent public adulation of visiting kings in a theatre or stadion was a form of inauguration; only now the king was acclaimed as the city's own private saviour and liberator.

Chapter 12 focused on centralised public ritual: religious festivals and processions that drew people from the periphery to the centre. In understanding the symbolic meaning of monarchical imagery, Geertzian cultural interpretation was merged with Tilly's model explaining the relationship between power, coercion and capital. The basic assumption was that monarchical ideology and representation do not cover up but, on the contrary, emphasise the essentially violent foundation of imperial rule – though of course this was presented in the positive light of heroism and *sōtēria*. Through the theatrical display of wealth (*tryphē*) and multifarious symbols representing the monarchy's universal pretensions and the king's charisma as a heroic spear-fighter and saviour, the myth of kingship was enacted.

Graeco-Macedonian religious festivals provided a template for the development of Hellenistic monarchical ritual – a process going back to at least Philip II's imperial festival at Aigai in 336. Of particular importance, especially in the Ptolemaic empire, was the developing mythology and iconography of Dionysos, the semi-human epiphanic deity, who was transformed into a model for kingship: the victorious god whose return from the east signalled the dawn of an age of peace and good fortune. Thus, monarchical ritual symbolically conveyed two interconnected images: (1) an articulation of the militaristic, heroic nature of the monarchy, and (2) an image of peaceful, universal rulership.

THE ROAD AHEAD

A potentially fruitful focus for future research, I would suggest, is to investigate what the role of the court was in integrating territories and peoples, especially in the Seleukid Near East. In other words, how could the court be a means of accessing military resources and the surpluses accumulated in cities? In antiquity, a supranational imperial state was, to paraphrase Patricia Crone and Martin Hinds, something which sat on top of societies, not something which was rooted in them. It would go too far, however, to maintain that 'given that there was minimal interaction between the two, there was also minimal political development: dynasties came and went, but it was only the dynasties that changed'.[1] The influence of empires on societies, even in the fields of culture and religion, was considerable.

This problem has been central to the present book, but more detailed research may be needed. By what unofficial, often highly ritualised means did empires interact with societies? How were rural and civic elites integrated into the imperial commonwealth through the instrumentality of the court? As we have seen, imperial rulers tried to gain a foothold in cities and regions by means of participation in local cults and through patronage of local sanctuaries. Cities in turn needed imperial protection to maintain their autonomous status and gain privileges. Religious institutions structured negotiations between empire and local elites for their mutual benefit. Conversely, members of local elites were drawn to the court and participated in the 'great events' and festivals of the dynastic household, and some-times the two – the civic and the aulic festival – merged, as was most clearly the case with the Grand Procession of Ptolemy Philadelphos in Alexandria.

If civic and courtly ritual indeed created 'contact zones' between the empire and localised communities, how then did this function? What strategies were employed to attract members of local elites to the great feasts at the (outer) court? What can we say about logistics? How was interaction between the imperial elite and local elites, who net temporarily in the 'outer court', structured by court ritual and the court feast? How did negotiations take place and who were the brokers? Who was excluded and by what means? What strategies exactly did kings have at their disposal for manipulating access and hierarchy at court – more precisely, what actions could they take to be able to use 'favour', and its opposite, *disgrace*, as instruments of control? Here, a comparative perspective might be helpful: the history of the ancient and Islamic east is characterised by a suc-cession of empires and a strong continuity of the ideal of political unity, which developed into an ideal of political-religious unity (Christianity, Islam). Achaemenids, Seleukids, Arsakids, Sassanians, Ummayads and Abbasids were faced with comparable problems

---

[1] Crone and Hinds 1986: 109.

and chances within largely the same geographical and climatic parameters.

A thorough investigation of the royal entry and court rituals, particularly the court feast, in other words, would take us further in understanding the significance of the court as an instrument of imperial rule. A specific subject, briefly discussed in this book, that merits further research in this context is the agency of royal women and concubines, especially their role as brokers between king and courtiers, and as representatives of their dynasties after marriage. A focused look at the benefactions and building activities of dynastic women in cities, moreover, could shed light on their agency vis-à-vis cities and the demarcation between specific male and female political roles.

Connected with the subject of female agency is the question of how imperial households interacted with vassal dynasties. During the Hellenistic age, a transformation of the political landscape of the Near East took place through the emergence of such minor kingdoms as Atropatene, Charakene, Fratarakā Persis, Kommagene, Kappadokia, Armenia, Pontos, Tarkondimotid Kilikia, the Nabataean Kingdom, the Hasmonean and Herodean kingdoms in Judaea-Palestine, and various smaller political units focused on cities and sanctuaries. The majority were governed by indigenous rulers, or so these rulers claimed. Many were created by the Seleukids, others emerged in the wake of Seleukid retreat, but they had one thing in common: they all flourished notably in the political void that followed the collapse of the Seleukid dynasty in 129 BCE, when Parthian claims to be the Seleukids' successors as imperial overlords of the east were challenged by the rising power of Rome. In their monarchical representation, some of the new kingdoms developed a cultural style that combined Hellenism with what may be called 'Persianism'. Rather than a real revival of any actual Achaemenid legacy, this was mostly invented tradition. It was closely connected with the transformation of the east under the later Seleukids (and to a lesser extent, the later Ptolemies) and, to complicate matters, can best be termed a Seleukid phenomenon. The role of the court, and dynastic marriage, in the genesis of these states may provide a fruitful focus of future research, too. To understand the fragmented Near Eastern and Anatolian state system, especially as it existed in the first century BCE and the first century CE, as essentially Hellenistic rather than as something Roman with only superficial Hellenistic antecedents, and to trace back its roots to the earlier period of Seleukid imperial policy, might be a refreshing way of looking at things. A

Hellenistic viewpoint might, moreover, award a more solid place to the Parthians in the *longue durée* of Middle Eastern history. To what extent and in what ways did Parthian kings and Roman emperors take over the role of Great King from their Macedonian predecessors, and continue to act as 'king-makers'? This may sound self-evident, but the ways in which Roman emperors legitimised and ritualised their role in the east are not yet understood. What, for instance, was the connection between Nero's self-presentation as a Macedonian-style sun king and his crowning (with a diadem) of Tiridates as king of Armenia in 62 BCE?[2]

In sum, four fields of study help us to understand better the history and culture of the Near East after the Achaemenids: (1) the relation between religion and politics, more precisely the use of the religious sphere (other than ruler cult) as a means to ritualise and structure negotiations between the imperial and the local; (2) the significance of the court feast for the realisation of imperial control; (3) the agency of royal women as mediators and representatives; and (4) the relation between empire and culture, particularly 'Hellenism' and 'Persianism'.

---

[2] Dio Cass. 61.4.

Bibliography

Adams, W. L. (1986), 'Macedonian kingship and the right of petition', *Ancient Macedonia* 4, 43–52.

Adamson, J. (ed.) (1999a), *The Princely Courts of Europe, 1500–1750*, London.

— (1999b), 'The making of the ancien-régime court, 1500–1700', in J. Adamson (ed.), *The Princely Courts of Europe, 1500–1750*, London, 7–42.

Africa, T. W. (1968), *Science and the State in Greece and Rome*, New York.

Ager, S. L. (2003), 'An uneasy balance: From the death of Seleukos to the battle of Raphia', in A. Erskine (ed.), *A Companion to the Hellenistic World*, Oxford, 35–50.

Akkermans, P. M. M. G., and Schwartz, G. M. (2003), *The Archaeology of Syria: From Complex Hunter-Gatherers to Early Urban Societies (ca. 16000–300 BC)*, Cambridge.

Al-Azmeh, A. [1997] (2001), *Muslim Kingship: Power and the Sacred in Muslim, Christian and Pagan Polities*, 2nd edn, London and New York.

Alföldi, A. (1970), *Die monarchische Repräsentation im römischen Kaiserreiche*, Darmstadt.

— (1985), *Caesar in 44 v.Chr. I*, Bonn.

Allen, R. E. (1983), *The Attalid Kingdom: A Constitutional History*, Oxford.

D'Altroy, T. N. (2001), 'Empires in a wider world', in S. E. Alcock, C. M. Sinopoli, T. N. D'Altroy and K. D. Morrison (eds), *Empires: Perspectives from Archaeology and History*, Cambridge, 125–7.

Ambos, C. (2004), *Mesopotamische Baurituale aus dem 1. Jahrtausend v. Chr.*, Dresden.

Anderson, J. K. (1985), *Hunting in the Ancient World*, Berkeley.

Andreae, B. (1996), 'Dating and significance of the Telephos frieze in relation to the other dedications of the Attalids of Pergamon', in R. Dreyfus and E. Schraudolph (eds), *Pergamon. Volume I*, San Francisco and New York, 121–6.

Andronikos, M. B. (1984), *Vergina: The Royal Tombs and the Ancient City*, Thessaloniki.

— (1987), 'Some reflections on the Macedonian tombs', *British School at Athens* 82, 1–16.

— (1994), 'The "Macedonian Tombs"', in M. B. Hatzopoulos (ed.), *Macedonia From Philip II to the Roman Conquest*, Princeton, 144–91.

Andronikos, M. B., and Mpakalakis, G. (1960), *Excavation Reports about the Palace in Vergina*, Athens.

— (1964), *Excavation Reports about the Palace in Vergina*, Athens.

— (1969), *Excavation Reports about the Palace in Vergina*, Athens.

Anson, E. M. (2004), *Eumenes of Cardia: A Greek among Macedonians*, Ancient Mediterranean and Medieval Texts and Contexts 3, Leiden.

Aperghis, M. (2001), 'Population, production, taxation, coinage: A model for the Seleukid economy', in Z. H. Archibald, J. Davies, V. Gabrielsen and G. J. Oliver (eds), *Hellenistic Economies*, London and New York, 69–102.

— (2004), *The Seleukid Royal Economy: The Finances and Financial Administration of the Seleukid Empire*, Cambridge.

Asch, R. G. (1991), 'Court and household from the fifteenth to the seventeenth centuries', in R. G. Asch and A. M. Birke (eds), *Princes, Patronage, and the Nobility: The Court at the Beginning of the Modern Age, c. 1450–1650*, London and Oxford, 1–38.

— (2003), '"Lumine solis": Der Favorit und die politische Kultur des Hofes in West-Europa', in M. Kaiser and A. Pečar (eds), *Der zweite Mann im Staat: Oberste Amtsträger und Favoriten im Umkreis der Reichsfürsten in der Frühen Neuzeit*, Berlin, 21–37.

— (2004), 'Schlußbetrachtung: Höfische Gunst und höfische Günstlinge zwischen Mittelalter und Neuzeit – 18 Thesen', in J. Hirschbiegel and W. Paravicini (eds), *Der Fall des Günstlings: Hofparteien in Europa vom 13. bis zum 17. Jahrhundert*, Ostfildern, 515–31.

Asch, R. G., and Birke, A. M. (eds) (1991), *Princes, Patronage, and the Nobility: The Court at the Beginning of the Modern Age, c. 1450–1650*, London and Oxford.

Atkinson, J. E. (1980), *A Commentary on Q. Curtius Rufus' Historiae Alexandri Magni: Books 3 and 4*, Amsterdam.

Aust, M., Miller, A., and Vulpius, R. (eds) (2010), *Imperium inter Pares: The Role of Transfers in the History of the Russian Empire: 1700–1917. Collected Articles*, Moscow.

Austin, M. M. (2003), 'The Seleukids and Asia', in A. Erskine (ed.), *A Companion to the Hellenistic World*, Oxford, 121–33.

Aymard, A. (1967), '*Basileôs Makedonôn*', in A. Aymard, *Études d'histoire ancienne*, Paris, 100–22.

Badian, E. (1965), 'Orientals in Alexander's army', *JHS* 85, 160–1.

— (1982), 'Greeks and Macedonians', in B. Barr-Sharrar and E. N. Borza (eds), *Macedonia and Greece in Late Classical and Early Hellenistic Times*, Studies in the History of Art 10, Washington, DC, 33–51.

— (2000), 'Conspiracies', in A. B. Bosworth and E. J. Baynham (eds),

Alexander the Great in Fact and Fiction, Oxford and New York, 50–95.

Bagnall, R. S. (1988), 'Greeks and Egyptians: Ethnicity, status, and culture', in R. S. Bianchi (ed.), *Cleopatra's Egypt: Age of the Ptolemies*, New York.

— (2001), 'Archaeological work on Hellenistic and Roman Egypt, 1995–2000', *AJA* 105, 227–43.

Baldry, H. C. (1959), 'Zeno's ideal state', *JHS* 73, 3–15.

Ball, W. (2000), *Rome in the East: The Transformation of an Empire*, London.

Balty, J.-C. (ed.) (1969), *Apamée de Syrie: Bilan de recherches archéologiques 1965–68*, Brussels.

— (ed.) (1972), *Apamée de Syrie: Bilan de recherches archéologiques 1969–1971*, Brussels.

— (2004), 'Antioche, centre d'art sous Séleucos I Nicator', in B. Cabouret, P.-L. Gatier and C. Saliou (eds), *Antioche de Syrie: Histoire, images et traces de la ville antique*, Topoi Supplément 5, Lyon, 11–19.

Barbantani, S. (2000), 'Competizioni poetiche tespiesi e mecenatismo tolemaico: Un gemellaggio tra l'antica e la nuova sede delle muse nella seconda metà del III secolo a.C. ipotesi su SH 959', *Lexis* 18, 127–72.

— (2001), Φάτις Νικηφόρος: *Frammenti di elegia encomiastica nell'età delle Guerre Galatiche*, Supplementum Hellenisticum, Milan, 958–69.

Barkey, K. (2008), *Empire of Difference: The Ottomans in Comparative Perspective*, Cambridge.

Bar-Kochva, B. (1989), 'The chronology of Antiochus Epiphanes' expedition to the eastern satrapies', in B. Bar-Kochva, *Judas Maccabaeus: The Jewish Struggle Against the Seleucids*, Cambridge, 466–73.

Barringer, J. M. (2002), *The Hunt in Ancient Greece*, Baltimore.

Baynham, E. J. (1988), *Alexander the Great: The Unique History of Quintus Curtius*, Ann Arbor.

Belenkiy, A. (2005), 'Der Aufgang des Canopus, die Septuaginta und die Begegnung zwischen Simon dem Gerechten und Antiochus dem Grossen', *Judaica* 61.1, 42–54.

Belfiore, F. S. (2000), *Murder among Friends: Violation of Philia in Greek Tragedy*, Oxford.

Bell, A. (2004), *Spectacular Power in the Greek and Roman City*, Oxford and New York.

Bell, C. (1992), *Ritual Theory, Ritual Practice*, New York and Oxford.

Bellinger, A. R. (1949), 'The end of the Seleucids', *Transactions of the Connecticut Academy of Arts and Sciences* 38, 51–102.

Bergmann, B., and Kondoleon, C. (eds) (1999), *The Art of Ancient Spectacle*, Washington, DC.

Bergmann, M. (1977), 'Hymnos der Athener auf Demetrios Poliorketes', in W. Barner (ed.), *Querlektüren: Weltliteratur zwischen den Disziplinen*, Göttingen, 25–47.

Bernard, A. [1956] (1966), *Alexandrie la grande*, 2nd edn, Paris.

Bernard, P. (1967), 'Ai Khanoum on the Oxus: A Hellenistic city in Central

Asia', *Proceedings of the British Academy* 53, 71–95.

— (1982), 'An ancient Greek city in Central Asia', *Scientific American* 246, 126–35.

— (2001), 'Aï Khanoum en Afghanistan hier (1964–1979) et aujourd'hui (2001): Un site en péril, perspectives d'avenir', *Comptes Rendus de l'Académie des Inscriptions et Belles-Lettres*, 971–7.

Bernsdorff, H. (2001), *Hirten in der nicht-bukolischen Dichtung des Hellenismus*, Palingenesia 72, Stuttgart.

Bertelli, S. (1986), 'The courtly universe', in S. Bertelli, F. Cardini and E. Garbero Zorzi (eds), *The Courts of the Italian Renaissance*, trans. M. Fitton and G. Culverwell, Milan, 7–38.

Bertelli, S., Cardini, F., and Garbero Zorzi, E. (eds) (1986), *The Courts of the Italian Renaissance*, trans. M. Fitton and G. Culverwell, Milan.

Bevan, E. R. (1902), *The House of Seleucus*, 2 vols, London.

— (1927), *A History of Egypt under the Ptolemaic Dynasty*, London.

Beyer-Rotthoff, B. (1993), *Untersuchungen zur Außenpolitik Ptolemaios' III*, Bonn.

Bickerman, E. J. (1938), *Institutions des Séleucides*, Paris.

— (1983), 'The Seleucid period', in E. Yarshater (ed.), *The Cambridge History of Iran. Volume 3: The Seleucid, Parthian, and Sassasian Periods*, Cambridge, 3–20.

Bielman Sanchez, A. (2003), 'Régner au féminin : Réflexions sur les reines attalides et séleucides', in F. Prost (ed.), *L'Orient méditerranéen de la mort d'Alexandre aux campagnes de Pompée: Cités et royaumes à l'époque hellénistique*, Rennes and Toulouse, 41–61.

Bigwood, J. M. (1995), 'Ctesias, his royal patrons and Indian swords', *JHS* 115, 135–40.

Bilde, P., Engberg-Pedersen, T., Hannestad, H. and Zahle, J. (eds) (1990), *Religion and Religious Practice in the Seleucid Kingdom*, Aarhus.

— (1992), *Ethnicity in Hellenistic Egypt*, Aarhus.

— (1996), *Aspects of Hellenistic Kingship*, Aarhus.

Billows, R. A. [1990] (1997), *Antigonos the One-Eyed and the Creation of the Hellenistic State*, 2nd edn, Berkeley, London and Los Angeles.

— (1995), 'The succession of the Epigonoi', *Syllecta Classica* 6, 1–11.

Bing, J. D. (1991), 'Alexander's sacrifice *dis praesidibus loci* before the battle of Issus', *JHS* 111, 161–5.

Blok, J. H. (2002), 'Women in Herodotus' *Histories*', in E. J. Bakker, I. J. F. de Jong and H. van Wees (eds), *Brill's Companion to Herodotus*, Leiden, Boston and Cologne, 225–42.

— (2003), 'Oude en nieuwe burgers', *Lampas* 36, 5–26.

Bogatyrev, P. G. (1971), *The Function of Folk Costume in Moravian Slovakia*, Approaches to Semiotics 5, trans. R. G. Crun, The Hague.

Bohec, S. le (1985), 'Les philoi des rois antigonides', *REG* 98, 93–124.

— (1987), 'L'entourage royal a la cour des Antigonides', in E. Levy (ed.), *Le système palatial en Orient, en Grèce et à Rome, Actes du colloque de*

Strasbourg 19–22 juin 1985, Leiden, 315–26.

Boholm, Å. (1990), *The Doge of Venice: The Symbolism of State Power in the Renaissance*, Göteborg.

Bömer, F. (1952), 'Pompa', in *RE* 21: 1878–994.

Bonfante, L. (1994), 'Introduction', in L. Bonfante and J. L. Sebesta (eds), *The World of Roman Costume*, Madison, 3–10.

Boon, J. A. (1982), *Other Tribes, Other Scribes: Symbolic Anthropology in the Comparative Study of Cultures, Histories, Religions, and Texts*, Cambridge.

Borza, E. N. (1982), 'The Macedonian royal tombs at Vergina: Some cautionary notes', *Archaeological News* 10, 8–10.

— (1983), 'The symposium at Alexander's court', *Ancient Macedonia* 3, 45–55.

— (1987), 'The royal Macedonian tombs and the paraphernalia of Alexander the Great', *Phoenix* 41, 105–21.

— (1988), 'The divinity of Alexander', in E. N. Borza, *Conquest and Empire*, Cambridge, 278–90.

— [1990] (1992), *In the Shadow of Olympus: The Emergence of Macedon*, 2nd rev. edn, Princeton.

— (1992), 'Ethnicity and cultural policy at Alexander's court', *Ancient World* 23, 1–25.

Bosworth, A. B. (1986), 'Alexander the Great and the decline of Macedon', *JHS* 106, 1–12.

— [1988] (1993), *Conquest and Empire: The Reign of Alexander the Great*, 2nd edn, Cambridge.

— (1998), *Alexander and the East: The Tragedy of Triumph*, Oxford.

— (2002a), *The Legacy of Alexander: Politics, Warfare, and Propaganda under the Successors*, Oxford.

— (2002b), 'The politics of the Babylon settlement', in A. B. Bosworth, *The Legacy of Alexander: Politics, Warfare, and Propaganda under the Successors*, Oxford, 29–63.

— (2002c), 'Hieronymus' ethnography: Indian widows and Nabataean nomads', in A. B. Bosworth, *The Legacy of Alexander: Politics, Warfare, and Propaganda under the Successors*, Oxford, 169–209.

— (2002d), 'The rise of Seleucus', in A. B. Bosworth, *The Legacy of Alexander: Politics, Warfare, and Propaganda under the Successors*, Oxford, 210–45.

— (2002e), 'Hellenistic monarchy: Success and legitimation', in A. B. Bosworth, *The Legacy of Alexander: Politics, Warfare, and Propaganda under the Successors*, Oxford, 246–78.

Bosworth, A. B., and Wheatley, P. V. (1998), 'The origins of the Pontic house', *JHS* 118, 155–64.

Boucharlat, R. (1990), 'Suse et la Susiana à l'époque achéménide: Données archéologiques', *AchHist* 4, 149–75.

— (2006), 'Le destin des résidences et sites perses d'Iran dans la seconde moitié du IVe siécle avant J.-C.', in P. Briant and F. Joannès (eds), *La transition entre l'empire achéménide et les royaumes hellénistiques*, Persika 9, Paris, 443–70.

Bourdieu, P. (1979), *La distinction: Critique sociale du jugement*, Paris.

Bradford, E. (2000), *Cleopatra*, 2nd edn, London.

Brands, G., and Hoepfner, W. (eds) (1996), *Basileia: Die Paläste der hellenistischen Könige, Internationales Symposion in Berlin vom 16.12.1992 bis 20.12.1992*, Mainz am Rhein.

Breebaart, A. B. (1967), 'King Seleucus I, Antiochus, and Stratonice', *Mnemosyne* 20, 154–64.

Briant, P. (1974), *Alexandre le Grand*, Paris.

— (1978), 'Colonisation hellénistique et populations indigènes: La phase d'installation', *Klio* 60, 57–92.

— (1985), 'Les Iraniens d'Asie Mineure après la chute de l'empire achéménide (à propos de l'inscription d'Amyzon)', *DHA* 11, 167–85.

— (1988a), 'Ethno-classe dominante et populations soumises dans l'empire achéménide: Le cas de l'Égypte', *AchHist* 3, 137–73.

— (1988b), 'Le nomadisme du Grand Roi', *Iranica Antiqua* 23, 253–73.

— (1989), 'Table du roi, tribut et redistribution chez les Achéménides', in P. Briant and C. Herrenschmidt (eds), *Le tribut dans l'empire perse*, Paris, 35–44.

— (1990), 'The Seleucid kingdom, the Achaemenid empire and the history of the Near East in the first millennium BC', in P. Bilde, T. Engberg-Pedersen, H. Hannestad and J. Zahle (eds), *Religion and Religious Practice in the Seleucid Kingdom*, Aarhus, 40–65.

— (1991a), 'Chasse royale macédonienne et chasse royale achéménide: La chasse au lion sur la fresque de Vergina', *DHA* 17.2, 211–55.

— (1991b), 'Chasses royales macédoniennes et chasses royales perses: Le thème de la chasse au lion sur la Chasse de Vergina', *DHA* 17.1, 211–55.

— (1993), 'Les chasses d'Alexandre', *Colloque d'Etudes Macédoniennes*, 267–77.

— (1994), 'Sources gréco-hellénistiques, institutions perses et institutions macédoniennes: Continuités, changements et bricolages', *AchHist* 7, 283–310.

— (1999), 'The Achaemenid empire', in K. Raaflaub and N. Rosenstein (eds), *War and Society in the Ancient and Medieval Worlds*, Cambridge, 105–28.

— (2002), *From Cyrus to Alexander: A History of the Persian Empire*, trans. P. T. Daniels, originally pub. 1996, Winona Lake.

— (2010), *Alexander the Great and his Empire: A Short Introduction*, trans. A. Kuhrt, originally pub. 1974, Princeton and Oxford.

Bringmann, K. (1993), 'The king as benefactor: Some remarks on ideal kingship in the age of Hellenism', in A. W. Bulloch, E. S. Gruen, A. A. Long and A. Stewart (eds), *Images and Ideologies: Self-Definition in the Hellenistic World*, Berkeley, Los Angeles and London, 7–24.

— (2005), 'Königliche Ökonomie im Spiegel des Euergetismus der Seleukiden', *Klio* 87, 102–15.

Brockliss, L. W. B. (1999), 'The anatomy of the minister-favourite', in J. H. Elliott and L. W. B. Brockliss (eds), *The World of the Favourite*, New Haven and New York, 279–309.

Broderson, K. (1985), 'Der Liebeskranke Königssohn und die Seleukidische Herrschaftsauffassung', *Athenaeum* n.s. 63, 459–69.

Brosius, M. (1996), *Women in Ancient Persia (559–331 BC)*, Oxford.

— (2007), 'New out of old? Court and court ceremonies in Achaemenid Persia', in A. J. S. Spawforth (ed.), *The Court and Court Society in Ancient Monarchies*, Cambridge, 17–57.

Brown, R. (2000), *Group Processes*, 2nd rev. edn, Malden and Oxford.

Buck, A., Kauffmann, G., Spahr, B. L., and Wiedemann, C. (eds) (1981), *Europäische Hofkultur im 16. und 17. Jahrhundert*, 3 vols, Hamburg.

Bulloch, A. W., Gruen, E. S., Long, A. A., and Stewart, A. (eds) (1993), *Images and Ideologies: Self-Definition in the Hellenistic World*, Berkeley, Los Angeles and London.

Bunge, J. G. (1974), '"Theos Epiphanes" in den ersten fünf Regierungsjahren des Antiochos IV. Epiphanes', *Historia* 23, 57–85.

— (1975), '"Antiochos-Helios": Methoden und Ergebnisse der Reichspolitik Antiochos' IV. Epiphanes von Syrien im Spiegel seiner Münzen', *Historia* 24, 164–88.

— (1976), 'Die Feiern Antiochus' IV: Epiphanes in Daphne 166 v.Chr.', *Chiron* 6, 53–71.

Buraselis, K. (1994), 'Des Königs Philoi und des Kaisers Amici: Überlegungen zu Ähnlichkeiten und Unter-schieden zwischen dem hellenistischen und dem römischen Modell monarchischer Regierung', in K. Buraselis (ed.), *Unity and Units of Antiquity*, Athens, 19–31.

Burke, P. (1992), *History and Social Theory*, Cambridge.

— (2009), *Cultural Hybridity*, Cambridge.

Burkert, W. (1994), *Greek Religion*, trans. J. Raffan, Cambridge.

Burstein, S. M. (1977), '*I.G.* II² 561 and the court of Alexander IV', *ZPE* 24, 223–5.

— (1991), 'Pharaoh Alexander: A scholarly myth', *AncSoc* 22, 139–45.

— (1994), 'Alexander in Egypt', *AchHist* 8, 381–7.

Calandra, E. (2011), *The Ephemeral and the Eternal: The Pavilion of Ptolemy Philadelphos in the Court of Alexandria*, Athens.

Calder, W. M. (1981), 'Diadem and barrel-vault: A note', *AJA* 85, 334–5.

Callaghan, P. J. (1981), 'On the date of the Great Altar of Zeus at Pergamon', *BICS* 28, 115–21.

Callataÿ, F. de (1996), 'La richesse des rois séleucides et le problème de la taxation en nature', in V. Chankowski and F. Duyrat (eds), *Le roi et l'économie*, Paris, 23–47.

Cameron, A. (1995), *Callimachus and his Critics*, Cambridge.

Campbell, W. A. (1934), 'The circus', in G. W. Elderkin (ed.), *Antioch-on-*

the-Orontes. Volume I: The Excavations of 1932, Princeton, 34–41.

Canepa, M. P. (2009), *The Two Eyes of the Earth: Art and Ritual of Kingship between Rome and Sasanian Iran*, Transformation of the Classical Heritage 45, Berkeley, Los Angeles and London.

— (2010), 'Technologies of memory in early Sasanian Iran: Achaemenid sites and Sasanian identity', *AJA* 114, 563–96.

Cannadine, D. (1987), 'Divine rites of kings', in D. Cannadine and S. R. F. Price (eds), *Rituals of Royalty: Power and Ceremonial in Traditional Societies*, Cambridge, 1–19.

Cannadine, D., and Price, S. R. F. (eds) (1987), *Rituals of Royalty: Power and Ceremonial in Traditional Societies*, Cambridge.

Cardascia, G. (1991), 'La ceinture de Parysatis', in D. Charpin and F. Joannès (eds), *Marchands, diplomates et empereurs*, Paris, 363–9.

Carney, E. D. (1991), '"What's in a name?" The emergence of a title for royal women in the Hellenistic period', in S. B. Pomeroy (ed.), *Women's History and Ancient History*, Chapel Hill and London, 154–72.

— (1994), 'Women and *basileia*: Legitimacy and female political action in Macedonia', *CJ* 90, 367–91.

— (2000a), *Women and Monarchy in Macedonia*, Norman.

— (2000b), 'Artifice and Alexander history', in A. B. Bosworth and E. J. Baynham (eds), *Alexander the Great in Fact and Fiction*, Oxford and New York, 263–85.

— (2002), 'Hunting and the Macedonian elite: Sharing the rivalry of the chase', in D. Ogden (ed.), *The Hellenistic World: New Perspectives*, London, 59–80.

— (2003a), 'Elite education and high culture in Macedonia', in W. Heckel and L. A. Tritle (eds), *Crossroads of History: The Age of Alexander*, Claremont, 47–63.

— (2003b), 'Women in Alexander's court', in J. Roisman (ed.), *Brills' Companion to Alexander the Great*, Leiden, 227–52.

— (2005), 'Women and *dunasteia* in Caria', *AJPh* 126.1, 65–91.

— (2006), *Olympias: Mother of Alexander the Great*, New York and London.

— (2008), 'The role of the *basilikoi paides* at the Argead court', in T. Howe and J. Reames (eds), *Macedonian Legacies: Studies in Ancient Macedonian History and Culture in Honor of Eugene N. Borza*, Claremont, 145–64.

Carsana, C. (1996), *Le dirigenze cittadine nello stato seleucidico*, Como.

Carter, M. (2001), 'The Roman spectacles of Antiochus IV Epiphanes', *Nikephoros* 14, 45–62.

Cartledge, P., Garnsey, P., and Gruen, E. S. (eds) (1997), *Hellenistic Constructs: Essays in Culture, History and Historiography*, Berkeley, Los Angeles and London.

Castritius, H. (1971), 'Zum höfischen Protokoll in der Tetrarchie: Introitus (adventus) Augusti et Caesaris', *Chiron* 1, 365–76.

Caubet, A. (1998), 'The international style: A point of view from the Levant and Syria', in E. H. Cline and D. Harris-Cline (eds), *The Aegean and the Orient in the Second Millennium, Proceedings of the 50th Anniversary Symposion, Cincinnati, 18–20 April 1997*, Aegaeum 18, Liège and Austin, 105–11.

Cavenaille, R. (1972), 'Pour une histoire politique et sociale d'Alexandrie: Les origines', *AC* 41, 94–112.

Cerfaux, L., and Tondriau, J. (eds) (1957), *Un concurrent du christianisme: le culte des souverains dans la civilisation gréco-romain*, Paris and Tournai.

Chamoux, F. (1988), 'Pergame et les Galates', *REG* 101, 492–500.

Chaniotis, A. (1997), 'Theatricality beyond the theatre: Staging public life in the Hellenistic world', in B. le Guen (ed.), *De la scène aux gradins: Théâtre et représentations dramatiques après Alexandre le Grand dans les cités hellénistiques*, Toulouse, 219–59.

— (2003), 'The divinity of Hellenistic rulers', in A. Erskine (ed.), *A Companion to the Hellenistic World*, Oxford, 431–45.

Chankowski, A. S. (2004), 'L'entraînement militaire des éphèbes dans les cités grecques d'Asie mineure à l'époque hellénistique: Nécessité pratique ou tradition atrophiée?', in J.-C. Couvenhes and H.-L. Fernoux (eds), *Les cités grecques et la guerre en Asie Mineure à l'époque hellénistique*, Paris, 55–76.

Chorus, J. (1994), 'Jacht en maaltijd', *Hermeneus* 66.5, 298–301.

Claassens, L. J. M. (2004), *The God Who Provides: Biblical Images of Divine Nourishment*, Nashville.

Claessen, H. J. M. (1978), 'The early state: A structural approach', in H. J. M. Claessen and P. Skalník (eds), *The Early State*, The Hague, 533–96.

— (1991), *Verdwenen koninkrijken en verloren beschavingen: Opkomst en ondergang van de vroege staat*, Assen and Maastricht.

Claessen, H. J. M., and Skalník, P. (eds) (1978), *The Early State*, The Hague.

Clarke, M. L. (1971), *Higher Education in the Ancient World*, London.

Clarysse, W. (1980), 'A royal visit to Memphis and the end of the Second Syrian War', in W. Clarysse, D. J. Thompson and W. Quaegebeur (eds), *Studies on Ptolemaic Memphis*, Studia Hellenistica 24, Leuven, 83–9.

— (1985), 'De grote processie van Ptolemy Philadelphos', *Hermeneus* 57, 204–6.

— (1995), 'Greeks in Ptolemaic Egypt', in S. Vleeming (ed.), *Hundred-Gated Thebes: Acts of a Colloquium on Thebes and the Theban Area in the Graeco-Roman Period*, Leiden, 1–19.

— (2000), 'The Ptolemies visiting the Egyptian Chora', in L. Mooren (ed.), *Politics, Administration and Society in the Hellenistic and Roman World*, Leuven, 29–43.

Cohen, A. (2010), *Art in the Era of Alexander the Great: Paradigms of manhood and their Cultural Traditions*, Cambridge.

Cohen, D. (1991), *Law, Sexuality and Society*, Cambridge.

Cohen, G. M. (2006), *The Hellenistic Settlements in Syria, the Red Sea Basin, and North Africa*, Hellenistic Culture and Society 46, Berkeley.

Cohen, M. E. (1993), *The Cultic Calendars of the Ancient Near East*, Bethesda.

Colledge, M. (1987), 'Greek and non-Greek interaction in the art and architecture of the Hellenistic east', in A. Kuhrt and S. M. Sherwin-White (eds), *Hellenism in the East*, Berkeley and Los Angeles, 134–62.

Collins, N. L. (1997), 'The various fathers of Ptolemy I', *Mnemosyne* 50, 436–76.

Cook, J. (1985), 'The rise of the Achaemenids and the establishment of their empire', in I. Gershevitch (ed.), *The Cambridge History of Iran. Volume 2: The Median and Achaemenian Periods*, Cambridge, 200–91.

Cordwell, J. M., and Schwarz, A. (eds) (1979), *The Fabrics of Culture: The Anthropology of Clothing and Personal Adornment*, The Hague, Paris and New York.

Corradi, G. (1929), 'Studi sulla corte ellenistica', in G. Corradi, *Studi Ellenistici*, Turin, 229–343.

Cox, C. A. (1998), *Household Interests: Property, Marriage Strategies, and Family Dynamics in Ancient Athens*, Princeton.

Cribiore, R. (2001), *Gymnastics of the Mind: Greek Education in Hellenistic and Roman Egypt*, Princeton.

Crone, P., and Hinds, M. (1986), *God's Caliph: Religious Authority in the First Centuries of Islam*, Cambridge.

Cumont, F. (1931), 'Nouvelles inscriptions grecques de Suse', *Comptes Rendus de l'Academie des Inscriptions et Belles-Lettres*, 233–50; 278–92.

Dalton, G. (ed.) (1968), *Primitive, Archaic, and Modern Economies: Essays of Karl Polanyi*, New York.

Davies, M. (2001), 'Greek personal names and linguistic continuity', in S. Hornblower and E. Matthews (eds), *Greek Personal Names: Their Value as Evidence*, Oxford, 15–39.

Delia, D. (1996), 'All army boots and uniforms? Ethnicity in Ptolemaic Egypt', in M. True and K. Hamma (eds), *Alexandria and Alexandrianism, Papers Delivered at a Symposium Organized by the J. P. Getty Museum, April 1993*, Malibu, 41–52.

Demir, A. (2004), 'The urban pattern of Antakya streets and houses', in B. Cabouret, P.-L. Gatier and C. Saliou (eds), *Antioche de Syrie: Histoire, images et traces de la ville antique*, Topoi Supplément 5, Lyon, 221–38.

Dickens, E. G. (ed.) (1977), *The Courts of the Italian Renaissance: Politics, Patronage, and Royalty, 1400–1800*, London.

Dimitrakos, G. (1937), *Demetrios Poliorketes und Athen*, Hamburg.

Dintsis, P. (1986), *Hellenistische Helme*, Rome.

Downey, G. (1941), 'Strabo on Antioch: Notes on his methods', *TAPhA* 72, 85–95.

— (1961), *A History of Antioch in Syria: From Seleucus to the Arab Conquest*, Princeton.

— (1963), *Ancient Antioch*, Princeton.

Downey, S. B. (1988), *Mesopotamian Religious Architecture: Alexander through the Parthians*, Princeton.

Dreyer, B. (1998), 'The *hiereus* of the *soteres*: Plut., *Dem.* 10.4, 46.2', *GRBS* 39, 23–38.

Dreyfus, R., and Schraudolph, E. (eds) (1996), *Pergamon: The Telephos Frieze from the Great Altar*, 2 vols, San Francisco and New York.

Ducat, J. (1995), 'Grecs et Égyptiens dans l'Égypte lagide : Hellénisation et résistance à l'hellénisme', in J. Leclant (ed.), *Entre Égypte et Grèce, Cahiers de la Villa Kérylos* 5, Paris, 68–81.

Duindam, J. (1994), *Myths of Power: Norbert Elias and the Early Modern European Court*, Amsterdam.

— (2003), *Vienna and Versailles: The Courts of Europe's Dynastic Rivals, 1559–1780*, Cambridge.

Dunand, F. (1981), 'Fête et propagande à Alexandrie sous les Lagides,' in F. Dunand, *La fête: Partique et discours*, Paris, 13–41.

— (1986), 'Les associations dionysiaques au service du pouvoir lagide (IIIe s. av. J.-C.)', in *l'Association dionysiaque dans les sociétés anciennes, Actes de la Table Ronde 1984*, Rome, 85–104.

Dunbabin, K. M. D. (1971), 'The triumph of Dionysos on the mosaics in North Africa', *Papers of the British School of Rome* 39, 52–65.

Durkheim, E. (1915), *The Elementary Forms of the Religious Life*, trans. J. W. Swain, London.

Eddy, S. K. (1961), *The King is Dead: Studies in Near Eastern Resistance to Hellenism 334–31 BC*, Lincoln.

Edmondson, J. C. (1999), 'The cultural politics of public spectacle in Rome and the Greek east, 167–166 BC', in B. Bergmann and C. Kondoleon (eds), *The Art of Ancient Spectacle*, Washington, DC, 77–95.

Edson, C. (1958), 'Macedonicum *imperium*: The Seleucid empire and the literary evidence', *C Phil.* 53, 153–70.

Ehling, K. (1998), 'Der "Reichskanzler" im Seleukidenreich', *Epigraphica Anatolica* 30, 97–106.

Eicher, J. B., and Roach, M. A. (1979), 'The language of personal adornment', in J. M. Cordwell and A. Schwarz (eds), *The Fabrics of Culture: The Anthropology of Clothing and Personal Adornment*, The Hague, Paris and New York, 7–21.

Elderkin, G. W., et al. (eds) (1934–72), *Antioch-on-the-Orontes*, Princeton.

Elias, N. (1936), *Über den Prozess der Zivilisation: Soziogenetische und psychogenetische Untersuchungen*, 2 vols, Bern and Munich.

— [1969] (1994), *Die höfische Gesellschaft: Untersuchungen zur Soziologie des Königtums und der höfischen Aristokratie*, 7th edn, Frankfurt am Main.

Elliott, J. H., and Brockliss, L. W. B. (eds) (1999), *The World of the*

Favourite, New Haven and New York.

Elton, G. (1983), 'Tudor government. The points of contact III: The court', in G. Elton, *Studies in Tudor and Stuart Politics and Government*, Cambridge, 38–57.

El-Zein, M. (1972), *Geschichte der Stadt Apameia am Orontes von den Anfängen bis Augustus*, dissertation, Heidelberg.

Empereur, J.-Y. (1998), *Alexandria Rediscovered*, London.

— (1999), 'Travaux récents dans la capitale des Ptolémées', in J. Leclant (ed.), *Alexandrie: Une mégapole cosmopolite*, Paris, 25–9.

Engels, D. (2011), 'Middle Eastern "feudalism" and Seleukid dissolution', in K. Erickson and G. Ramsey (eds), *Seleucid Dissolution: The Sinking of the Anchor*, Philippika 50, Wiesbaden, 19–36.

Erickson, K. (2011), 'Apollo-Nabû: The Babylonian policy of Antiochus I', in K. Erickson and G. Ramsey (eds), *Seleucid Dissolution: The Sinking of the Anchor*, Philippika 50, Wiesbaden, 51–66.

Errington, R. M. (1969), 'Bias in Ptolemy's history of Alexander', *CQ* 19, 233–42.

— (1978), 'The nature of the Macedonian state under the monarchy', *Chiron* 8, 77–133.

— (1983), 'The historiographical origins of Macedonian *Staatsrecht*', *Ancient Macedonia* 3, 89–101.

— (1990), *A History of Macedonia*, Berkeley, Los Angeles and London.

Erskine, A. (ed.) (2003), *A Companion to the Hellenistic World*, Oxford.

Erskine, A., and Llewellyn-Jones, L. (eds) (forthcoming), *The Hellenistic Royal Court*.

Etienne, R. (1998), '*Basileia*', *Topoi* 8, 347–55.

Everett, H. (1997), 'The English coronation rite: From the Middle Ages to the Stuarts', in P. Bradshaw (ed.), *Coronations: Past, Present and Future*, Cambridge, 5–21.

Fabricius, J. (1999), *Die hellenistischen Totenmahlreliefs: Grabrepräsentation und Wertvorstellungen in ostgriechischen Städten*, Studien zur antiken Stadt 3, Munich.

Fairman, H. W. (1958), 'The kingship rituals of Egypt', in S. H. Hooke (ed.), *Myth, Ritual and Kingship: Essays on the Theory and Practice of Kingship in the Ancient Near East and in Israel*, Oxford, 74–104.

Feldman, M. H. (2006), *Diplomacy by Design: Luxury Arts and an 'International Style' in the Ancient Near East, 1400–1200 BCE*, Chicago and London.

Feros, A. (1999), 'Images of evil, images of kings: The contrasting faces of the royal favourite and the prime minister in early modern European political literature, c. 1580–c. 1650', in J. H. Elliott and L. W. B. Brockliss (eds), *The World of the Favourite*, New Haven and New York, 205–22.

Fleischer, R. (1990), 'Physiognomie, Ideologie, dynastische Politik: Porträts seleukidischer Könige', in *Akten des XIII. Internationalen Kongress für klassische Archäologie, Berlin 1988*, Mainz am Rhein, 33–6.

Foertmeyer, V. (1988), 'The dating of the *pompe* of Ptolemy II Philadelphus', *Historia* 37, 90–104.

Foreman, L. (1999), *Cleopatra's Palace: In Search of a Legend*, n.p.

Foss, C., and Hanfmann, G. M. A. (1975), 'Regional setting and urban development', in G. M. A. Hanfmann and J. C. Waldbaum (eds), *A Survey of Sardis and the Major Monuments Outside the City Walls*, Cambridge and London, 17–34.

Fraenkel, H. (1890), *Altertümer von Pergamon*, Berlin.

Fredricksmeyer, E. A. (1986), 'Alexander the Great and the Macedonian *kausia*', *TAPhA* 116, 215–27.

Funck, B. (1996), 'Beobachtungen zum Begriff des herrscherpalastes und seiner machtpolitischen Funktion im hellenistischen Raum: Prolegomena zur Typologie der hellenistischen Herrschaftssprache', in G. Brands and W. Hoepfner (eds), *Basileia: Die Paläste der hellenistischen Könige, Internationales Symposion in Berlin vom 16.12.1992 bis 20.12.1992*, Mainz am Rhein, 44–55.

Gambato, M. (2001), 'The female kings: Some aspects of the representation of the eastern kings in the Deipnosophistae', in D. Braund and J. Wilkins (eds), *Athenaeus and his World: Reading Greek Culture in the Roman Empire*, Exeter, 227–30.

Garbero Zorzi, E. (1986), 'Court spectacle', in S. Bertelli, F. Cardini and E. Garbero Zorzi (eds), *The Courts of the Italian Renaissance*, Milan, 127–87.

Garnsey, P., and Saller, R. (1987), *The Roman Empire: Economy, Society and Culture*, London.

Geertz, C. (1964), 'Ideology as a cultural system', in D. E. Apter (ed.), *Ideology and Discontent*, New York, 47–76.

— (1973), *The Interpretation of Cultures*, New York.

— (1977), 'Centers, kings, and charisma: Reflections on the symbolics of power', in J. Ben-David and T. N. Clark (eds), *Culture and its Creators: Essays in Honour of Edward Shils*, Chicago, 150–71.

— (1980), *Negara: The Theatre State in Nineteenth Century Bali*, Princeton.

Gehrke, H.-J. (2005), 'Heroen und Grenzgänger zwischen Griechen und Barbaren', in E. S. Gruen (ed.), *Cultural Borrowings and Ethnic Appropriations in Antiquity*, Stuttgart, 50–67.

Gershevitch, I. (ed.) (1985), *The Cambridge History of Iran. Volume 2: The Median and Achaemenian Periods*, Cambridge.

Ghedini, F. (1992), 'Caccia e banchetto: Un rapporto difficile', *Rivista di Archeologia* 16, 72–88.

Gilbert, M. (1987), 'The person of the king: Ritual and power in a Ghanaian state', in D. Cannadine and S. R. F. Price (eds), *Rituals of Royalty: Power and Ceremonial in Traditional Societies*, Cambridge, 298–330.

— (1994), 'Aesthetic strategies: The politics of a royal ritual', *Africa* 64.1, 99–125.

Gilsenan, M. (1977), 'Against patron–client relations', in E. Gellner and

J. Waterbury (eds), *Patrons and Clients in Mediterranean Societies*, London, 167–83.

Goddio, F., Bernand, A., Bernand, E., Darwish, I., Kiss, Z., and Yoyotte, J. (1998), *Alexandria: The Submerged Royal Quarters*, London.

Goldhill, S. (1986), *Reading Greek Tragedy*, Cambridge.

Goodin, R. E. (1978), 'Rites of rulers', *British Journal of Sociology* 29.3, 281–99.

Gorteman, A. (1957), 'Médecins de cour dans l'Égypte du IIIe siècle avant J.-C.', *CE* 32, 313–36.

Goudriaan, K. (1988), *Ethnicity in Ptolemaic Egypt*, Amsterdam.

Grainger, J. D. (1990), *The Cities of Seleukid Syria*, Oxford.

— (1992), *Seleukos Nikator: Constructing a Hellenistic Kingdom*, London.

— (1997), *A Seleukid Prosopography and Gazetteer*, Leiden.

Grant, M. (1972), *Cleopatra*, London.

Grayson, A. K. (1975), *Assyrian and Babylonian Chronicles*, Locust Valley.

Green, P. (1982), 'The royal tombs at Vergina: A historical analysis', in W. L. Adams and E. N. Borza (eds), *Philip II, Alexander the Great, and the Macedonian Heritage*, Washington, DC, 129–51.

— (1990), *Alexander to Actium: The Historical Evolution of the Hellenistic Age*, Berkeley and Los Angeles.

— (ed.) (1993), *Hellenistic History and Culture*, Berkeley and Los Angeles.

— (2007), *The Hellenistic Age: A Short History*, New York.

Greenwalt, W. (1989), 'Polygamy and succession in Argead Macedonia', *Arethusa* 22, 19–45.

Grenz, S. (1914), *Beiträge zur Geschichte des Diadems in den Hellenistischen Reichen*, PhD thesis, University of Greifswald.

Griffiths, F. T. (1979), *Theocritus at Court*, Mnemosyne Supplement 55, Leiden.

Griffiths, R. A. (1991), 'The king's court during the Wars of the Roses: Continuities in an age of discontinuities', in R. G. Asch and A. M. Birke (eds), *Princes, Patronage, and the Nobility: The Court at the Beginning of the Modern Age, c. 1450–1650*, London and Oxford, 42–67.

Grimal, N., Briant, P., Chauveau, M., et al. (eds) (1998), *La gloire d'Alexandrie*, Paris.

Grimm, G. (1998), *Alexandria: Die erste Königsstadt der hellenistischen Welt*, Mainz am Rhein.

Gruen, E. S. (1984), *The Hellenistic World and the Coming of Rome*, 2 vols, Berkeley, Los Angeles and London.

— (1985), 'The coronation of the Diadochoi', in J. Eadie and J. Ober (eds), *The Craft of the Ancient Historian: Essays in Honour of Chester G. Starr*, Lanham, 253–71.

— (1996), 'Hellenistic kingship: Puzzles, problems, and possibilities', in P. Bilde, T. Engberg-Pedersen, H. Hannestad and J. Zahle (eds), *Aspects of Hellenistic Kingship*, Aarhus, 116–25.

— (1998), 'Kings and Jews', in E. S. Gruen, *Heritage and Hellenism*,

Berkeley, Los Angeles and London, 189–245.

Guggisberg, C. A. W. (1961), *Simba: The Life of the Lion*, Cape Town.

Gygax, M. D. (2002), 'Zum Mitregenten des Ptolemaios II. Philadelphos', *Historia* 51, 49–56.

Habicht, C. (1956), 'Über die Kriege zwischen Pergamon und Bithynien', *Hermes* 84, 90–110.

— (1958), 'Die herrschende Gesellschaft in den hellenistischen Monarchien', *Vierteljahrschrift für Sozial- und Wirtschaftsgeschichte* 45, 1–16.

— (1970), *Gottmenschentum und griechische Städte*, Zetemata 14, Munich.

— (1997), *Athens from Alexander to Antony*, trans. D. L. Schneider, Cambridge and London.

— (1989), 'The Seleucids and their rivals', *CAH* 8, 324–87.

— (2005), 'Kronprinzen in der Monarchie der Attaliden', in V. A. Troncoso (ed.), ΔΙΑΔΟΧΟΣ ΤΗΣ ΒΑΣΙΛΕΙΑΣ: *La figura del sucesor en la realeza helenística*, Gerión Anejos 9, Madrid, 119–26.

Hadley, R. A. (1978), 'The foundation of Seleucia-on-the-Tigris', *Historia* 27, 228–30.

Haider, P. W. (1998), 'Judith: Eine zeitgenössische Antwort auf Kleopatra III. als Beschützerin der Juden?', *Grazer Beiträge* 22, 117–28.

Hall, J. (1997), *Ethnic Identity in Greek Antiquity*, Cambridge.

Hämäläinen, P. (2008), *The Comanche Empire*, New Haven and London.

Hammond, N. G. L. (1970), 'The archaeological background to the Macedonian kingdom', *Ancient Macedonia* 1, 53–67.

— (1980), *Alexander the Great: King, Commander and Statesman*, London.

— (1989), *The Macedonian State: Origins, Institutions, and History*, Oxford.

— (1990), 'Royal pages, personal pages, and boys trained in the Macedonian manner during the period of the Temenid monarchy', *Historia* 39.3, 261–90.

— (1994), *Philip of Macedon*, London.

Hammond, N. G. L., and Griffith, G. T. (1979), *A History of Macedonia. Part II: 550–336 BC*, Oxford.

Hammond, N. G. L., and Walbank, F. W. (1988), *A History of Macedonia. Part III: 336–167 BC*, Oxford.

Hanfmann, G. M. A. (1977), 'On the palace of Croesus', in U. Höckmann and A. Krug (eds), *Festschrift für F. Brommer*, Mainz am Rhein, 145–54.

Hanfmann, G. M. A., Robert, L., and Mierse, W.E. (1983), 'The Hellenistic period', in G. M. A. Hanfmann (ed.), *Sardis: From Prehistoric to Roman Times. Results of the Archaeological Exploration of Sardis 1958–1975*, Cambridge and London, 109–39.

Hanken, C. (1996), *Gekust door de koning: Over het leven van koninklijke maîtresses*, Amsterdam.

Hansen, E. V. [1946] (1972), *The Attalids of Pergamon*, 2nd rev. and enlarged edn, Ithaca and London.

Hansen, M. H. (1996), 'City-ethnics as evidence for *polis*-identity', in M. H. Hansen and K. Raaflaub (eds), *More Studies in the Ancient Greek Polis*, Stuttgart, 169–96.

Hardie, P. (1986), *Virgil's Aeneid: Cosmos and Imperium*, Oxford.

Harris, W. V., and Ruffini, G. (eds) (2004), *Ancient Alexandria between Egypt and Greece*, Leiden.

Harrison, T. (2011), *Writing Ancient Persia*, Classical Essays 5, Bristol.

Hatzopoulos, M. B. (1988), *Une donation du roi Lysimaque*, Meletemata 5, Athens.

— (1991), *Actes de vente d'Amphipolis*, Meletemata 14, Athens and Paris.

— (1996a), *Macedonian Institutions under the Kings*, 2 vols, Athens.

— (1996b), 'Aigéai: La localisation de la premier capitale macédonienne', *REG* 109, 264–9.

— (1999), 'La Macédoine de Philippe II à la conquête romaine: L'apport des récents documents épigraphiques', in *XI Congresso Internazionale de Epigrafia Greca e Latina: Roma 18–24 Settembre 1997*, Rome, 257–73.

— (2001), 'Macedonian palaces: Where king and city meet', in I. Nielsen (ed.), *The Royal Palace Institution in the First Millennium BC*, Monographs of the Danish Institute at Athens 4, Athens, 189–99.

Hauben, H. (1990), 'L'expédition de Ptolemée III en orient et la sédition domestique de 245 av. J.-C.', *ArchPF* 36, 29–37.

Hauben, H., and Meeus, A. (eds) (forthcoming), *The Age of the Successors and the Creation of the Hellenistic Kingdoms*, Leuven.

Haussoulier, B. (1903), 'Inscriptions grecques de l'extrême-orient grec', in *Mélanges Perrot: Receuil de mémoires concernant l'archéologie classique, la littérature et l'histoire anciennes dédié à Georges Perrot*, Paris, 155–9.

— (1909), 'Inscriptions grecques de Babylone', *Klio* 9, 352–63.

Hazzard, R. A. (2000), *Imagination of a Monarchy: Studies in Ptolemaic Propaganda*, Phoenix Supplementary Vol. 37, Toronto, Buffalo and London.

Heath, M. (1987), *The Poetics of Greek Tragedy*, Stanford.

Heckel, W. (1992), *The Marshals of Alexander's Empire*, London and New York.

— (1997), 'Resistance to Alexander the Great', in L. A. Tritle (ed.), *The Greek World in the Fourth Century: From the Fall of the Athenian Empire to the Successors of Alexander the Great*, London and New York, 189–227.

— (2003), 'King and "companions": Observations on the nature of power in the reign of Alexander', in J. Roisman (ed.), *Brill's Companion to Alexander the Great*, Leiden, 197–226.

Heerink, M. (2010), 'Merging paradigms: Translating pharaonic ideology in Theocritus' Idyll 17', in R. Rollinger, B. Gufler, M. Lang and I. Madreiter (eds), *Interkulturalität in der Alten Welt: Vorderasien, Hellas Ägypten und die vielfältigen Ebenen des Kontakts*, Wiesbaden, 383–406.

Heerman, V. (1986), *Studien zur makedonischen Palastarchitektur*, Nürnberg.

Heilmeyer, W.-D. (ed.) (1997), *Der Pergamonaltar: Die neue Präsentation nach Restaurierung des Telephosfrieses*, Tübingen.

Heinen, H. (1978), 'Aspects et problèmes de la monarchie ptolémaïque', *Ktema* 3, 177–99.

— (1983), 'Die Tryphè des Ptolemy VIII. Euergetes II: Beobachtungen zum ptolemaïschen Herrscherideals und zu einer römischen Gesandtschaft in Ägypten, 140/39 v.Chr.', in H. Heinen, K. Stroheker and G. Walser (eds), *Althistorische Studien: Hermann Bengtson zum 70. Geburtstag dargebracht von Kollegen und Schülern*, Wiesbaden, 116–27.

Hekster, O. (2005), 'Captured in the gaze of power: Visibility, games and Roman imperial representation', in O. Hekster and R. Fowler (eds), *Imaginary Kings: Royal Images in the Ancient Near East, Greece and Rome*, Oriens et Occidens 11, Stuttgart, 157–76.

Hekster, O., and Fowler, R. (2005), 'Imagining kings: From Persia to Rome', in O. Hekster and R. Fowler (eds), *Imaginary Kings: Royal Images in the Ancient Near East, Greece and Rome*, Oriens et Occidens 11, Stuttgart, 9–38.

Held, W. (2002), 'Die Residenzstädte der Seleukiden: Babylon, Seleukeia am Tigris, Ai Khanum, Seleukeia in Pieria, Antiocheia am Orontes', *JDAI* 117, 217–49.

Henkelman, W. (2002), 'Exit der Posaunenbläser: On lance-guards and lance-bearers in the Persepolis fortification archive', *Arta* 7, 1–35.

Henshall, N. (1992), *The Myth of Absolutism: Change and Continuity in Early Modern European Monarchy*, London and New York.

Herman, G. (1980/1), 'The "friends" of the early Hellenistic rulers: Servants or officials?', *Talanta* 12–13, 103–49.

— (1987), *Ritualised Friendship and the Greek City*, Cambridge.

— (1996), 'Friendship', in S. Hornblower and A. Spawforth (eds), *The Oxford Classical Dictionary*, 3rd edn, Oxford and New York, 611–13.

— (1997), 'The court society of the Hellenistic age', in P. Cartledge, P. Garnsey and E. S. Gruen (eds), *Hellenistic Constructs: Essays in Culture, History, and Historiography*, Berkeley, Los Angeles and London, 199–224.

Hermann, P. (1965), 'Antiochos der Große und Teos', *Anadolu* 9, 29–159.

Herz, P. (1992), 'Die frühen Ptolemaier bis 180 v.Chr', in R. Gundlach and H. Weber (eds), *Legitimation und Funktion des Herrschers: Vom Pharao zum neuzeitlichen Diktator*, Stuttgart, 52–97.

Hesberg, H. von (1989), 'Temporäre Bilder oder die Grenzen der Kunst', *JDAI* 104, 61–82.

— (1999), 'The king on stage', in B. Bergmann and C. Kondoleon (eds), *The Art of Ancient Spectacle*, Washington, DC, 65–75.

Heuzey, L. (1922), *Histoire du costume antique*, Paris.

Hinske, N. (ed.) (1981), *Alexandrien: Kulturbegegnungen dreier Jahrt-*

ausende im Schmelztiegel einer mediterranen Großstadt, Mainz am Rhein.

Hintzen-Bohlen, B. (1990), 'Die Familiengruppe: Ein Mittel zur Selbstdarstellung hellenistischer Herrscher', *JDAI* 105, 129–54.

Hirschbiegel, J. (2004), 'Zur theoretischen Konstruktion der Figur des Günstlings', in J. Hirschbiegel and W. Paravicini (eds), *Der Fall des Günstlings: Hofparteien in Europa vom 13. bis zum 17. Jahrhundert*, Ostfildern, 23–40.

— (2010), 'Hof. Zur Überzeitlichkeit eines zeitgebundenen Phänomens', in B. Jacobs and R. Rollinger (eds), *Der Achämenidenhof*, Wiesbaden, 13–38.

Hoepfner, W. (1996a), 'Das vollendete Pergamonaltar', *AA*, 115–34.

— (1996b), 'Zum Typus der *Basileia* und der königlichen Andrones', in G. Brands and W. Hoepfner (eds), *Basileia: Die Paläste der hellenistischen Könige, Internationales Symposion in Berlin vom 16.12.1992 bis 20.12.1992*, Mainz am Rhein, 1–43.

— (2004), '"Antiochia die große": Geschichte einer antiken Stadt', *AW* 35, 3–9.

Hoepfner, W., and Schwandner, E.-L. (1994), *Haus und Stadt im klassischen Griechenland*, Munich.

Hof, P. van 't (1955), *Bijdrage tot de kennis van Antiochus IV Epiphanes, koning van Syrië*, Amsterdam.

Hölbl, G. (2001), *A History of the Ptolemaic Empire*, trans. T. Saavedra, London and New York.

Holland, T. (2011), 'The greatest of them all: Revisionist professors, Hollywood turkeys, even the pacifist spirit of our age cannot wither the incomparable mystique and terrifying glamour of Alexander of Macedon', *Wall Street Journal*, 15 January.

Holleaux, M. (1900), 'Un prétendu décret d'Antioche sur l'Oronte', *REG* 13, 258–80; reprinted in M. Holleaux (1942), *Études d'épigraphie et d'histoire grecques III: Lagides et Séleucides*, Paris, 281–316.

— (1942), *Études d'épigraphie et d'histoire grecque III: Lagides et Séleucides*, Paris, 281–31.

Hölscher, T. (1987), *Römische Bildsprache als semantisches System*, Heidelberg.

Holt, F. L. (1989), *Alexander the Great and Bactria: The Formation of a Greek Frontier in Central Asia*, Mnemosyne Supplement 104, Leiden.

Hoover, O. D. (1996), *Kingmaker: A Study in Seleukid Political Imagery*, Hamilton.

Hornblower, J. (1981), *Hieronymus of Cardia*, Oxford.

Hornblower, S. [1983] (2002), *The Greek World 479–323 BC*, Routledge History of the Ancient World 3, 2nd edn, London.

Horowski, L. (2004), 'Das Erbe des Favoriten: Minister, Mätressen und Günstlinge am Hof Ludwigs XIV', in J. Hirschbiegel and W. Paravicini (eds), *Der Fall des Günstlings: Hofparteien in Europa vom 13. bis zum 17. Jahrhundert*, Ostfildern, 77–126.

Huebner, S. R. (2007), '"Brother–sister" marriage in Roman Egypt: A curiosity of humankind or a widespread family strategy?', *JRS* 97, 21–49.

Huss, W. (1994), *Der makedonische König und die ägyptischen Priester: Studien zur Geschichte des ptolemäischen Ägypten*, Historia Einzelschriften 85, Stuttgart.

— (2001), *Aegypten in hellenistischer Zeit (332–30 v. Chr.)*, Munich.

Huttner, U. (1997), *Die politische Rolle der Heraklesgestalt im griechischen Herrschertum*, Historia Einzelschriften 112, Stuttgart.

Ignatieff, M. (1998), *The Warrior's Honour: Ethnic War and the Modern Conscience*, London.

Invernizzi, A. (1993), 'Seleucia on the Tigris: Centre and periphery in Seleucid Asia', in P. Bilde, T. Engberg-Pedersen, H. Hannestad and J. Zahle (eds), *Centre and Periphery in the Hellenistic World*, Aarhus, 230–50.

Jacobs, B., and Rollinger, R. (eds) (2010), *Der Achämenidenhof, Akten des 2. Internationalen Kolloquiums zum Thema 'Vorderasien im Spannungsfeld klassischer und altorientalischer Überlieferung', Landgut Castelen bei Basel, 23–25 Mai 2007*, Classica et Orientalia 2, Wiesbaden.

Jähne, A. (1974), 'Die "Syrische Frage": Seleukeia in Pierien und die Ptolemäer', *Klio* 56, 501–19.

— (1981), 'Die "Ἀλεξανδρέων χώρα"', *Klio* 63, 63–103.

Jameson, M. (1990), 'Private space and the Greek city', in O. Murray and S. Price (eds), *The Greek City: From Homer to Alexander*, Oxford, 172–92.

Jansen, J. J. (1984), 'Het geschenk des konings', in H. J. M. Claessen (ed.), *Macht en majesteit: Idee en werkelijkheid van het vroege koningschap*, Utrecht, 51–9.

Jones, C. P. (1974), 'Diodorus Pasparos and the Nikephoria of Pergamon', *Chiron* 4, 183–205.

— (1992), 'Hellenistic history in Chariton of Aphrodisias', *Chiron* 22, 91–102.

Jones, S. (1997), *The Archaeology of Ethnicity: Constructing Identities in the Past and Present*, London and New York.

Just, P., and Monaghan, J. (2000), *Social and Cultural Anthropology: A Very Short Introduction*, Oxford and New York.

Just, R. (1989), *Women in Athenian Law and Life*, London.

Kaiser, M., and Pečar, A. (2003), 'Reichsfürsten und ihre Favoriten: Die Ausprägung eines Strukturphänomens unter den politischen Bedingungen des Alten Reiches', in M. Kaiser and A. Pečar (eds), *Der zweite Mann im Staat: Oberste Amtsträger und Favoriten im Umkreis der Reichsfürsten in der Frühen Neuzeit*, Berlin, 9–19.

Karttunen, K. (1997), *India and the Hellenistic World*, Helsinki.

Kawerau, G., and Wieland, T. (1930), *Die Paläste der Hochburg,*

Altertümer von Pergamon 5.1, Berlin.

Kemp, B. (1977), 'The palace of Apries at Memphis', *Mitteilungen des Deutschen Archäologischen Instituts in Kairo* 33, 101–8.

Kern, O. (1900), *Die Inschriften von Magnesia am Meander*, Berlin.

Kertész, I. (1982), 'Der Telephosmythos und der Telephosfries', *Oikumene* 3, 203–15.

— (1983), 'Religionsgeschichtliche Voraussetzungen zur Herausbildung des Herrscherkultes in Athen', *Oikoumene* 4, 61–9.

Kertzer, D. I. (1988), *Ritual, Politics and Power*, New Haven and London.

— (1974), 'Politics and ritual', *Anthropological Quarterly* 47, 374–89.

Kettering, S. (1986), *Patrons, Brokers, and Clients in Seventeenth-Century France*, New York.

— (1988), 'Gift-giving and patronage in early modern France', *French History* 2, 133–51.

Kienast, D. (1971), *Philipp II. von Makedonien und das Reich der Achaimeniden*, Abhandlungen der Marburger Gelehrten Gesellschaft 6, Munich.

Kingsley, B. M. (1981a), 'The "chitrali": A Macedonian import to the west', *Afghanistan Journal* 8.3, 90–3.

— (1981b), 'The cap that survived Alexander', *AJA* 85, 39–46.

— (1984), 'The *kausia diadematophoros*', *AJA* 88, 66–8.

Kitchen, K. A. (1982), *Pharaoh Triumphant: The Life and Times of Ramesses II, King of Egypt*, Warminster.

Kleiner, D. E. E. (2005), *Cleopatra and Rome*, Cambridge.

Kloft, H. (ed.) (1979), *Ideologie und Herrschaft in der Antike*, Darmstadt.

Klooster, J. (2009), *Poetry as Window and Mirror: Hellenistic Poets on Predecessors, Contemporaries and Themselves*, dissertation, University of Amsterdam.

Koehn, C. (2007), *Krieg – Diplomatie – Ideologie: Zur Außenpolitik hellenistischer Mittelstaaten*, Stuttgart.

Koenen, L. (1977), *Eine agonistische Inschrift aus Ägypten und frühptolemäische Königsfeste*, Meisenheim am Glan.

Koester H. (ed.) (1998), *Pergamon, Citadel of the Gods: Archaelogical Record, Literary Description, and Religious Development*, Harrisburg.

Kohl, M. (2004), 'Sièges et défense de Pergame : Nouvelles réflexions sur sa topographie et son architecture militaires', in J.-C. Couvenhes and H.-L. Fernoux (eds), *Les cités grecques et la guerre en Asie Mineure à l'époque hellénistique*, Paris, 177–98.

Köhler, J. (1996), *Pompai: Untersuchungen zur hellenistischen Festkultur*, Frankfurt am Main.

Konstan, D. (1997), *Friendship in the Classical World*, Cambridge.

Korpel, M. (1990), *A Rift in the Clouds*, Münster.

Kosmetatou, E. (2003), 'The Attalids of Pergamon', in A. Erskine (ed.), *A Companion to the Hellenistic World*, Oxford, 159–74.

Kralli, I. (2000), 'Athens and the Hellenistic kings (338–261 B.C.):

The language of the decrees', *CQ* 50, 113–32.

Kramolisch, H. (1989), 'Demetrias', in S. Lauffer (ed.), *Griechenland: Lexikon der historischen Stätten. Von den Anfängen bis zur Gegenwart*, Munich, 190–1.

Kreissig, H. (1978), *Wirtschaft und Gesellschaft im Seleukidenreich: Die Eigentums- und die Abhängigkeitsverhältnisse*, Berlin.

Kruedener, J. von (1973), *Die Rolle des Hofes im Absolutismus*, Stuttgart.

Kuhrt, A. (1987), 'Usurpation, conquest and ceremonial: From Babylon to Persia', in D. Cannadine and S. R. F. Price (eds), *Rituals of Royalty: Power and Ceremonial in Traditional Societies*, Cambridge, 20–55.

— (1990), 'Alexander in Babylon', *AchHist* 5, 121–30.

— (1995), *The Ancient Near East, c. 3000–330 BC*, 2 vols, London and New York.

Kuhrt, A., and Sherwin-White, S. M. (eds) (1987), *Hellenism in the East*, London.

— (1991), 'Aspects of Seleucid royal ideology: The cylinder of Antiochus I from Borsippa', *JHS* 111, 71–86.

— (1993), *From Samarkhand to Sardis: A New Approach to the Seleucid Empire*, London.

Künzl, E. (1971), *Die Kelten des Epigonos von Pergamon*, Beiträge zur Archäologie 4, Würzburg.

Kutbay, B. L. (1998), *Palaces and Large Residences of the Hellenistic Age*, Lewiston, Queenston and Lampeter.

Lanciers, E. (1988), 'Die Vergöttlichung und die Ehe des Ptolemy IV. und der Arsinoë III', *ArchPF* 34, 27–32.

Landucci Gattinoni, F. (1981), 'La divinizzazione di Demetrio e la coscienza ateniese', *Contributi dell'Istituto di Storia antica dell'Università del Sacro Cuore, Milan* 7, 115–23.

Lane, C. (1981), *The Rites of Rulers. Ritual in Industrial Society: The Soviet Case*, Cambridge.

Lane Fox, R. (1979), *Alexander the Great*, 2nd edn, Harmondsworth.

Lauter, H. (1986), *Die Architektur des Hellenismus*, Darmstadt.

Lawrence, A. W. (1979), *Greek Aims in Fortification*, Oxford.

Leach, E. R. (1968), 'Ritual', in D. L. Sills (ed.), *The International Encyclopedia of the Social Sciences* 13, New York, 521–3.

Lehmann, G. A. (1988), 'Das neue Kölner Historiker-Fragment (P. Köln. Nr. 247) und die chroniké sýntaxis des Zenon von Rhodos (FGrHist 523)', *ZPE* 72, 1–17.

Le Rider, G. (1965), *Suse sous les Séleucides et les Parthes*, Mémoires de la mission archéologique en Iran 38, Paris.

Lewis, D. M. (1987), 'The king's dinner (Polyaenus IV 3,32)', *AchHist* 2, 79–87.

Linssen, M. J. H. (2004), *The Cults of Uruk and Babylon: The Temple Ritual Texts as Evidence for Hellenistic Cult Practice*, Leiden.

Lissone, F. L. V. M. (1969), *De fragmenten van de geschiedschrijver*

Phylarchus: Vertaling en Commentaar, Indagationes Noviomagenses VI, Nijmegen.

Liverani, M. (1979), 'The ideology of the Assyrian Empire', in M. T. Larsen (ed.), *Power and Propaganda: A Symposium on Ancient Empires*, Copenhagen, 297–317.

— (1990), *Prestige and Interest: International Relations in the Near East ca. 1600–1100*, Padua.

Llewellyn-Jones, L. (2012), *King and Court in Ancient Persia*, Edinburgh.

Lloyd, A. B. (2002), 'The Egyptian elite in the early Ptolemaic period: Some hieroglyphic evidence', in D. Ogden (ed.), *The Hellenistic World: New Perspectives*, London, 117–36.

Lloyd, G. E. R. (1973), *Greek Science after Aristotle*, London.

López Monteagudo, G. (1999), 'The triumph of Dionysus in two mosaics in Spain', *Assaph: Studies in Art History* 4, 35–60.

Lukes, S. (1975), 'Political ritual and social integration', *Sociology* 9, 289–308.

Lund, H. S. (1992), *Lysimachus: A Study in Hellenistic Kingship*, London.

Ma, J. (2003), 'Kings', in A. Erskine (ed.), *A Companion to the Hellenistic World*, Oxford, 177–95.

MacCormack, S. G. (1981), *Art and Ceremonial in Late Antiquity*, Berkeley, Los Angeles and London.

MacDowell, D. (1989), 'The *oikos* in Athenian law', *CQ* 39, 10–21.

Macurdy, G. H. (1927), 'Queen Eurydice and the evidence for woman-power in early Macedonia', *AJPh* 48, 201–7.

— (1932a), *Hellenistic Queens: A Study of Woman-Power in Macedonia, Seleucid Syria, and Ptolemaic Egypt*, Baltimore.

— (1932b), 'Roxane and Alexander IV in Epirus', *JHS* 52.2, 256–61.

Maguire, H. (ed.) (1998), *Byzantine Court Culture from 829 to 1204*, Cambridge.

Mairs, R. (2006a), *Ethnic Identity in the Hellenistic Far East*, PhD thesis, University of Cambridge.

— (2006b), 'Hellenistic India', *New Voices in Classical Reception Studies* 1, 19–30.

— (2008), 'Greek identity and the settler community in Hellenistic Bactria and Arachosia', *Migrations and Identities* 1.1, 19–43.

Malkin, I. (ed.) (2001), *Ancient Perceptions of Greek Ethnicity*, Cambridge and London.

Mann, M. (1986), *The Sources of Social Power. Volume 1: A History of Power from the Beginnings to A.D. 1760*, Cambridge.

Manning, J. (2003), *Land and Power in Ptolemaic Egypt: The Structure of Land Tenure, 332–30 BCE*, Cambridge.

Marasco, G. (1996), 'Les médecins de cour à l'époque hellénistique', *REG* 109, 435–66.

Marcovich, M. (1988), 'Hermocles' Ithyphallus for Demetrius', in M. Marcovich, *Studies in Graeco-Roman Religions and Gnosticism*,

Studies in Greek and Roman Religion 4, Leiden, 8–19.

Marinoni, E. (1972), 'Le capitale del regno di Seleuco I', *Rendiconti dell'Istituto Lombardo* 106, 579–631.

Martinez-Sève, L. (2002), 'La ville de Suse à l'époque hellénistique', *RA* n.s., 31–54.

Marzolff, P. (1994), 'Développement urbanistique de Démétrias', in Θεσσαλια: Δεκαπεντε χρονια αρξαιολογικησ ερευνασ 1975–1990. Αποτελεσματα και προοπτικες, *Proceedings of an International Conference, Lyon 17–22 April 1990*, Athens, 57–69.

— (1996), 'Der Palast von Demetrias', in G. Brands and W. Hoepfner (eds), *Basileia: Die Paläste der hellenistischen Könige, Internationales Symposion in Berlin vom 16.12.1992 bis 20.12.1992*, Mainz am Rhein, 148–63.

Mastrocinque, A. (1995), 'Les médecins des Séleucides', in P. van Eijk, H. F. J. Horstmanshoff and P. Schrijvers (eds), *Ancient Medicine in its Socio-Cultural Context*, Amsterdam, 143–51.

Mauss, M. (1925), *Essai sur le don*, Paris.

McCormick, M. (1986), *Eternal Victory: Triumphal Leadership in Late Antiquity, Byzantium, and the Early Medieval West*, Cambridge.

McKenzie, L. (1994), 'Patterns in Seleucid administration: Macedonian or Near Eastern?', *Mediterranean Archaeology* 7, 61–8.

Mehl, A. (2003), 'Die antiken Griechen: Integration durch Kultur', in K. Buraselis and K. Zoumboulakis (eds), *The Idea of European Community in History, Conference Proceedings. Volume II*, Athens, 191–204.

Meillier, C. (1979), *Callimaque et son temps: Recherches sur la carrière et la condition d'un écrivain à l'époque des premiers Lagides*, Lille.

Meißner, B. (2000), 'Hofmann und Herrscher: Was es für Griechen hieß, Freund eines Königs zu sein', *Archiv für Kulturgeschichte* 82, 1–36.

Merker, I. L. (1979), 'Lysimachus, Thessalian or Macedonian?', *Chiron* 9, 31–6.

Meyer, M. (1992/3), 'Mutter, Ehefrau und Herrscherin: Darstellungen der Königin auf Seleukidischen Münzen', *Hephaistos* 11/12, 107–32.

Mieck, I. (1982), *Die Entstehung des modernen Frankreichs 1450–1610: Strukturen, Institutionen, Entwicklungen*, Stuttgart, Berlin, Cologne and Mainz.

Mikalson, J. D. (1998), *Religion in Hellenistic Athens*, Hellenistic Culture and Society 29, Berkeley and Los Angeles, 94–7.

Millar, F. (1987), 'The problem of Hellenistic Syria', in A. Kuhrt and S. M. Sherwin-White (eds), *Hellenism in the East*, London, 110–33.

Miller, S. G. (1982), 'Macedonian tombs: Their architecture and architectural decoration', in B. Barr-Sharrar and E. N. Borza (eds), *Macedonia and Greece in Late Classical and Early Hellenistic Times*, Washington, DC, 153–71.

Miron, D. (2000), 'Transmitters and representatives of power: Royal women in ancient Macedonia', *AncSoc* 30, 35–52.

Mitchell, L. (2007), 'Born to rule? Succession in the Argead royal house', in W. Heckel, L. Tritle and P. Wheatley (eds), *Alexander's Empire: Formulation to Decay. A Companion to Crossroads of History*, Claremont, 61–74.

Mittag, P. F. (2000), 'Die Rolle der hauptstädtischen Bevölkerung bei den Ptolemäern und Seleukiden im 3. Jahrhundert', *Klio* 82, 409–25.

— (2006), *Antiochos IV. Epiphanes: Eine politische Biographie*, Klio Beihefte 11, Berlin.

Moevs, M. T. M. (1993), 'Ephemeral Alexandria: The pageantry of the Ptolemaic court and its documentations', in R. T. Scott and A. R. Scott (eds), *Eius Virtutis Studiosi: Classical and Postclassical Studies in Memory of Frank Edward Brown (1908–1988)*, Washington, DC, 123–48.

Momigliano, A. (1973), 'Freedom of speech in antiquity', in P. P. Wiener (ed.), *Dictionary of the History of Ideas 2: Studies of Selected Pivotal Ideas*, New York, 252–63.

Mooren, L. (1968), 'Über die ptolemäischen Hofrangtitel', in L. Cerfaux et al. (eds), *Antidoron W. Peremans Sexagenario ab Alumnis Oblatum*, Studia Hellenistica 16, Leuven, 161–81.

— (1975), *The Aulic Titulature in Ptolemaic Egypt: Introduction and Prosopography*, Brussels.

— (1977), *La hierarchie de cour ptolémaïque: Contribution à l'étude des institutions et des classes dirigeantes à l'époque héllenistique*, Studia Hellenistica 21, Leuven.

— (1979), 'Die diplomatische Funktion der hellenistischen Königsfreunde', in E. Olshausen (ed.), *Antike Diplomatie: Wege der Forschung 462*, Darmstadt, 256–90.

— (1985), 'The Ptolemaic court system', *CE* 60, 214–22.

— (1998), 'Kings and courtiers: Political decision-making in the Hellenistic states', in W. Schuller (ed.), *Politische Theorie und Praxis im Altertum*, Darmstadt, 122–33.

Moretti, L. (1958), 'Note egittologiche: A proposito di Neotera', *Aegyptus* 38, 199–209.

Mørkholm, O. (1966), *Antiochus IV of Syria*, Copenhagen.

Mpatziou-Efstathiou, A. (1991), *Excavation Reports about the Palace in Demetrias*, AD 46, Athens.

— (1996), *Excavation Reports about the Palace in Demetrias*, AD 51, Athens.

— (1997), *Excavation Reports about the Palace in Demetrias*, AD 46, Athens.

— (2008), 'Το ανάκτορο της Δημητριάδος', in *First International Congress on the History and Culture of Thessaly, 1–11 November 2006*, Athens, 259–65.

Muccioli, F. (1997), 'Seleuco III, i Tolemei e Seleucia di Pieria', *Simbolos* 2, 135–50.

— (2001), 'La scelta delle titolature dei Seleucidi: Il ruolo dei *philoi* e delle classi dirigenti cittadine', *Simbolos* 3, 295–318.

Mueller, K. (2006), *Settlements of the Ptolemies: City Foundations and New Settlement in the Hellenistic World*, Studia Hellenistica 43, Leuven.

Müller, D. (1989a), 'Levkadia', in S. Lauffer (ed.), *Griechenland: Lexikon der historischen Stätten*, Munich, 392.

— (1989b), 'Thessalonike', in S. Lauffer (ed.), *Griechenland: Lexikon der historischen Stätten*, Munich, 676–82.

Müller, O. (1973), *Antigonos Monophthalmos und das 'Jahr der Könige'*, Bonn.

Müller, S. (2003), *Maßnahmen der Herrschaftssicherung gegenüber der makedonischen Opposition bei Alexander dem Großen*, Frankfurt am Main.

Musti, D. (1984), 'Syria and the east', *CAH* 7.1, 175–220.

Narain, A. K. (1957), *The Indo-Greeks*, Oxford.

Nederlof, A. B. (1978), *Pyrrhus van Epirus*, Amsterdam.

Neils, J. (2001), 'Athena, alter ego of Zeus', in S. Deacy and A. Villing (eds), *Athena in the Classical World*, Leiden, 219–32.

Netz, R. (2004), *The Transformation of Mathematics in the Early Mediterranean World: From Problems to Equations*, Cambridge.

Netzer, E. (1999), *Die Paläste der Hasmonäer und Herodes' des Grossen*, Mainz am Rhein.

— (2008), *The Architecture of Herod, the Great Builder*, Grand Rapids.

Neuffer, E. (1929), *Das Kostüm Alexander des Grossen*, dissertation, Giessen.

Nevett, L. C. (1999), *House and Society in the Ancient Greek World*, Cambridge.

Nielsen, I. (1994), *Hellenistic Palaces: Tradition and Renewal*, Aarhus.

— (1996), 'Oriental models for Hellenistic palaces?', in G. Brands and W. Hoepfner (eds), *Basileia: Die Paläste der hellenistischen Könige, Internationales Symposion in Berlin vom 16.12.1992 bis 20.12.1992*, Mainz am Rhein, 209–12.

— (1998), 'Royal banquets: The development of royal banquets and banqueting halls from Alexander to the Tetrarchs', in H. S. Nielsen and I. Nielsen (eds), *Meals in a Social Context: Aspects of the Communal Meal in the Hellenistic and Roman World*, Aarhus and London, 102–33.

— (ed.) (2001), *The Royal Palace Institution in the First Millennium* BC, Monographs of the Danish Institute at Athens 4, Athens.

Nock, A. D. (1953), 'Neotera: Queen or goddess?', *Aegyptus* 33, 283–96.

Nourse, K. L. (2002), *Women and the Early Development of Royal Power in the Hellenistic East*, dissertation, University of Pennsylvania.

O'Brien, J. M. (1992), *Alexander the Great: The Invisible Enemy*, London and New York.

Oelsner, J. (1978), 'Kontinuität und Wandel im Gesellschaft und Kultur Babyloniens in hellenistischer Zeit', *Klio* 60, 101–16.

Ogden, D. (1999), *Polygamy, Prostitutes and Death: The Hellenistic Dynasties*, London.

— (ed.) (2002), *The Hellenistic World: New Perspectives*, London.

— (2011), 'How to marry a courtesan in the Macedonian courts', in A. Erskine and L. Llewellyn-Jones (eds), *Creating a Hellenistic World*, Swansea and Oxford, 221–46.

Olbrycht, M. J. (2010), 'Macedonia and Persia', in J. Roisman and I. Worthington (eds), *A Companion to Ancient Macedonia*, Malden, 342–69.

Olshausen, E. (1974), *Prospographie der hellenistischen Königsgesandten 1: Von Triparadeisos bis Pydna*, Leuven.

O'Neil, J. L. (2002), 'Iranian wives and their roles in Macedonian royal courts', *Prudentia* 34.2, 159–77.

— (2003), 'The ethnic origins of the friends of the Antigonid kings of Macedon', *CQ* 53, 510–22.

— (2006), 'Places of origin of the officials of Ptolemaic Egypt', *Historia* 55.1, 16–25.

Orth, W. (1977), *Königlicher Machtanspruch und städtische Freiheit: Untersuchungen zu den politischen Beziehungen zwischen den ersten Seleukidenherrschern (Seleukos I., Antiochos I., Antiochos II.) und den Städten des westlichen Kleinasien*, Munich.

Otto, W. (1927), 'Zum Hofzeremoniels des Hellenismus', in *Epitumbion H. Swoboda dargebracht*, Reichenberg, 194–200.

Palagia, O. (1998), 'Alexander the Great as lion hunter: The fresco of Vergina tomb II and the marble frieze of Messene in the Louvre', *Minerva* 9, 25–8.

— (2000), 'Hephaestion's pyre and the royal hunt of Alexander', in A. B. Bosworth and E. J. Baynham (eds), *Alexander the Great in Fact and Fiction*, Oxford, 167–206.

Paravicini, W. (2004), 'Der Fall des Günstlings: Hofparteien in Europa vom 13. bis zum 17. Jahrhundert', in J. Hirschbiegel and W. Paravicini (eds), *Der Fall des Günstlings: Hofparteien in Europa vom 13. bis zum 17. Jahrhundert*, Ostfildern, 13–20.

Parisinou, E. (2000), *The Light of the Gods: The Role of Light in Archaic and Classical Greek Cult*, London.

Parpola, S. (2004), 'The leftovers of god and king: On the distribution of meat at the Assyrian and Achaemenid imperial courts', in C. Grottanelli and L. Milano (eds), *Food and Identity in the Ancient World*, History of the Ancient Near East Studies 9, Padua, 281–312.

Parsons, T. (1968), *The Structure of Social Action* I, New York.

Paspalas, S. A. (2005), 'Philip Arrhidaios at court: An ill-advised Persianism? Macedonian royal display in the wake of Alexander', *Klio* 87, 72–101.

Paterson, J. (2007), 'Friends in high places: The creation of the court of the Roman emperor', in A. J. S. Spawforth (ed.), *The Court and Court Society* in *Ancient Monarchies*, Cambridge, 121–56.

Patterson, C. B. (1998), *The Family in Greek History*, Cambridge and London.

Pedersen, P. (1991), *The Mausolleion Terrace and Accessory Structures*, Aarhus.

Peremans, W., and Van 't Dack, E. (1968), *Prosopographia Ptolemaica. Volume VI: La cour, les relations internationales et les possessions extérieures, la vie culturelle, par W. Peremans, E. Van 't Dack, L. Mooren et W. Swinnen*, Studia Hellenistica 17, Leuven.

Petrie W. M. F., and Walker, J. H. (1909), *Memphis II: The Palace of Apries*, London.

Petsas, P. (1978), *Pella: Alexander the Great's Capital*, Thessaloniki.

Pfrommer, M. (1999), *Alexandria: Im Schatten der Pyramiden*, Mainz am Rhein.

— (2002), *Königinnen vom Nil*, Mainz am Rhein.

Picard, B. (ed.) (1969), *Sigmund von Herberstein: Description of Moscow and Muscovy*, London.

Piejko, F. (1990), 'Episodes from the Third Syrian War in a Gurob papyrus, 246 B.C.', *ArchPF* 36, 13–27.

Pollitt, J. J. (1986), *Art in the Hellenistic Age*, Cambridge.

Pomeroy, S. B. (1997), *Families in Classical and Hellenistic Greece: Representations and Realities*, Oxford.

Porteous, A. (1928), *Forest Folklore*, London.

Potts, D. T. (1999), *The Archaeology of Elam: Formation and Transformation of an Ancient Iranian State*, Cambridge.

Préaux, C. (1939), *L'économie royale des Lagides*, Brussels.

— (1978), *Le monde hellénistique: La Grèce et l'orient (323–146 av. J.C.)*, 2 vols, Paris.

Prestianni-Galliombardo, A. M. (1989), '*Kausia diadematophoros* in Macedon : Testimonianze misconosciute e nuove proposte', *Messana* n.s. 1, 1–13.

Pritchett, W. K. (1979) 'Military vows', in W. K. Pritchett, *The Greek State at War. Part III: Religion*, Berkeley, Los Angeles and London, 230–9.

Queyrel, F. (2005), *L'autel de Pergame: Images et pouvoir en Grèce d'Asie*, Antiqua 9, Paris.

Raaflaub, K. (2004), 'Aristocracy and freedom of speech in the Graeco-Roman world', in I. Sluiter and R. M. Rosen (eds), *Free Speech in Classical Antiquity*, Mnemosyne Supplement 254, Leiden, 41–61.

Radt, W. (1999), *Pergamon: Geschichte und Bauten einer antiken Metropole*, Darmstadt.

Ragotzky, H., and Wenzel, H., (eds) (1990), *Höfische Repräsentation: Das Zeremoniell und die Zeichen*, Tübingen.

Rappaport, R. A. (1979), *Ecology, Meaning and Religion*, Richmond.

Raup Johnson, S. (1993), 'Antiochus IV's procession at Daphne (166 B.C.)', *Journal of Associated Graduates in Near Eastern Studies* 4.1, 23–34.

Reinhold, M. (1969), 'On status symbols in the ancient world', *CJ* 64.7, 300–4.

— (1970), *History of Purple as a Status Symbol in Antiquity*, Brussels.

Rice, E. E. (1983), *The Grand Procession of Ptolemy Philadelphus*, Oxford.

Ritter, H. W. (1965), *Diadem und Königsherrschaft: Untersuchungen zu Zeremonien und Rechtsgrundlagen des Herrschaftsantritt bei den Persen, bei Alexander dem Grossen und im Hellenismus*, Munich and Berlin.

— (1984), 'Zum sogenannten Diadem des Philipsgrabes', *AA*, 105–11.

— (1987), 'Die Bedeutung des Diadems', *Historia* 36.3, 290–301.

Robert, L. (1984), 'Pline VI 49, Démodamas de Milet et la reine Apamè', *BCH* 108.1, 467–72.

Rodríquez-Salgado, M. J. (1991), 'The court of Philip II of Spain', in R. G. Asch and A. M. Birke (eds), *Princes, Patronage, and the Nobility: The Court at the Beginning of the Modern Age, c. 1450–1650*, London and Oxford, 206–44.

Roisman, J. (ed.) (2003), *Brill's Companion to Alexander the Great*, Leiden.

Rostovtzeff, M. (1928), 'Ptolemaic Egypt', in S. A. Cook, F. E. Adcock and M. P. Charlesworth (eds), *The Cambridge Ancient History. Volume 7: The Hellenistic Monarchies and the Rise of Rome*, Cambridge, 109–54.

— [1941] (1967), *The Social and Economic History of the Hellenistic World*, 3 vols, 5th edn, Oxford.

Roussel, P. (1934), 'Un règlement militaire de l'époque macédonienne', *RA* 6.3, 39–47.

Roy, J. (1998), 'The masculinity of the Hellenistic king', in L. Foxhall and J. Salmon (eds), *When Men Were Men: Masculinity, Power and Identity in Classical Antiquity*, London and New York, 111–35.

Rzepa, J. (2008), 'The units of Alexander's army and the district divisions of late Argead Macedonia', *GRBS* 48, 9–56.

Saatsoglou-Paliadeli, C. (1993), 'Aspects of ancient Macedonian costume', *JHS* 113, 122–47.

— (2000), 'Queenly appearances at Vergina-Aegae: Old and new epigraphic and literary evidence', *AA* 3, 387–403.

— (2001), 'The palace of Vergina-Aegae and its surroundings', in I. Nielsen (ed.), *The Royal Palace Institution in the First Millennium* BC, Athens, 201–13.

Said, E. W. (1978), *Orientalism: Western Conceptions of the Orient*, London.

Sakellariou, M. B. (1983), *Macedonia: 4000 Years of Greek History and Civilization*, Greek Lands in History 1, Athens.

Salmon, X. (1995), 'Des animaux exotiques chez le roi', in X. Salmon (ed.), *Les chasses exotiques de Louis XV*, Paris, 15–34.

Salzmann, D. (1995), 'Zu den Mosaiken in den Palästen IV und V von Pergamon', *Asia Minor Studien* 16, 101–12.

Sancisi-Weerdenburg, H. W. A. M. (1980), *Yauna en Persai: Grieken en Perzen in een ander perspectief*, Groningen.

— (1983), 'Exit Atossa: Images of women in Greek historiography on Persia', in A. Cameron and A. Kuhrt (eds), *Images of Women in Antiquity*, London and Canberra, 20–33.

— (1988), 'Περσικον δε καρτα ο οτρατος δωρον: A typically Persian gift (Hdt. IX 109)', *Historia* 37.3, 372–4.

— (1989), 'Gifts in the Persian empire', in P. Briant and C. Herrenschmidt (eds), *Le tribut dans l'empire perse*, Paris, 286–302.

Sancisi-Weerdenburg, H. W. A. M., and Henkelman, W. (1998), 'Crumbs from the royal table: Foodnotes on Briant', *Topoi Supplement* 1, 333–45.

Sanders, L. J. (1991), 'Dionysius of Syracuse and the origins of the ruler cult in the Greek world', *Historia* 40, 275–87.

Sartre, M. (2005), *The Middle East Under Rome*, Cambridge and London.

Saunders, N. J. (2006), *Alexander's Tomb: The Two Thousand Year Obsession to Find the Lost Conqueror*, New York.

Sauvaget, J. (1934), 'Le plan de Laodicée-sur-mer', *Bulletin d'Études Orientales* 4, 81–114.

Savalli-Lestrade, I. (1996), 'Courtisans et citoyens: Le cas des *philoi* attalides', *Chiron* 26, 149–81.

— (1998), *Les philoi royaux dans l'Asie hellénistique*, Études du Monde Gréco-Romain 25, Geneva.

Saxonhouse, A. W. (2006), *Free Speech and Democracy in Ancient Athens*, Cambridge.

Schachermeyr, F. (1970), *Alexander in Babylon und die Reichsordnung nach seinem Tode*, Vienna.

Schalles, H.-J. (1985), *Untersuchungen zur Kulturpolitik der pergamenischen Herrscher im dritten Jahr-hundert vor Christus*, Tübingen.

Schmitt Pantel, P., and Schnapp, A. (1982), 'Image et société en Grèce ancienne: Les représentations de la chasse et du banquet', *RA* 1, 57–74.

Schramm, P. E. (1954–6), *Herrschaftszeichen und Staatssymbolik*, 3 vols, Stuttgart.

Schrapel, T. (1996), *Das Reich der Kleopatra: Quellenkritische Untersuchungen zu den 'Landschenkungen' Mark Antons*, Trier.

Schwarz, A. (1979), 'Uncovering the secret vice: Toward an anthropology of clothing and adornment', in J. M. Cordwell and A. Schwarz (eds), *The Fabrics of Culture: The Anthropology of Clothing and Personal Adornment*, The Hague, Paris and New York, 23–46.

Schwinge, E.-R. (1986), *Künstlichkeit von Kunst: Zur Geschichtlichkeit der alexandrinischen Poesie*, Munich.

Scott, M. (1982), '*Philos, philotes* and *xenia*', *AC* 25, 1–19.

Segre, M. (1948), 'L'institution des Nikephoria de Pergame', in L. Robert (ed.), *Hellenica* V, Paris, 104–5.

Seyrig, H. (1970), 'Séleucos I et la fondation de la monarchie syrienne', *Syria* 47, 290–311.

— (1973), *Trésors du Levant, anciens et nouveaux: Trésors monétaires séleucides* 2, Paris.

Shayegan, M. R. (2011), *Arsacids and Sasanians: Political Ideology in Post-Hellenistic and Late Antique Persia*, Cambridge.

Shennon, J. H. (1974), *The Origins of the Modern European States, 1450–1725*, London.

Sherwin-White, S. M. (1983), 'Ritual for a Seleucid king at Babylon', *JHS* 103, 156–9.

— (1987), 'Seleucid Babylonia: A case study for the installation and development of Greek rule', in A. Kuhrt and S. M. Sherwin-White (eds), *Hellenism in the East*, London, 1–31.

Shils, E. (1975), *Center and Periphery: Essays in Macrosociology*, Chicago.

Shils, E., and Young, M. (1953), 'The meaning of the coronation', *Sociological Review* n.s. 1, 63–81.

Shipley, G. (2000), *The Greek World after Alexander, 232–30 BC*, London and New York.

Siganidou, M. (1996), 'Die *basileia* von Pella', in G. Brands and W. Hoepfner (eds), *Basileia: Die Paläste der hellenistischen Könige, Internationales Symposion in Berlin vom 16.12.1992 bis 20.12.1992*, Mainz am Rhein, 144–7.

Siganidou, M., and Lilimpaki-Akamati, M. (2003), *Pella: Capital of the Macedonians*, Athens.

Silverman, S. (1977), 'Patronage as myth', in E. Gellner and J. Waterbury (eds), *Patrons and Clients in Mediterranean Societies*, London, 7–19.

Simpson, R. S. (1996), *Demotic Grammar in the Ptolemaic Sacerdotal Decrees*, Oxford.

Sinopoli, C. M. (1994), 'The archaeology of empires', *Annual Review of Anthropology* 23, 159–80.

Sluiter, I., and Rosen, R. M. (eds) (2004), *Free Speech in Classical Antiquity*, Mnemosyne Supplement 254, Leiden.

Smith, R. (2007), 'The imperial court of the late Roman empire, c. AD 300–c. AD 450', in A. J. S. Spawforth (ed.), *The Court and Court Society in Ancient Monarchies*, Cambridge, 157–232.

Smith, R. R. R. (1988), *Hellenistic Royal Portraits*, Oxford.

Smith Pangle, L. (2002), *Aristotle and the Philosophy of Friendship*, Cambridge.

Śnieżewski, S. (1998), 'Divine connections of Marcus Antonius in the years 43–30 BC', *Grazer Beiträge* 22, 129–44.

Southern, P. (2000), *Cleopatra*, London.

Spawforth, A. J. S. (ed.) (2007a), *The Court and Court Society in Ancient Monarchies*, Cambridge.

— (2007b), 'The court of Alexander the Great between Europe and Asia', in A. J. S. Spawforth (ed.), *The Court and Court Society in Ancient Monarchies*, Cambridge, 82–120.

Spek, R. J. van der (1986), *Grondbezit in het Seleucidische Rijk*, Amsterdam.

— (1999), 'The *šatammus* of Esagila in the Seleucid and Parthian periods', in J. Marzahn and H. Neumann (eds), *Festschrift Joachim Oelsner*, Berlin, 437–46.

— (2005), 'Ethnic segregation in Hellenistic Babylonia', in W. H. van Soldt (ed.), *Ethnicity in Ancient Mesopotamia*, Leiden, 393–408.

Staal, F. (1975), 'The meaninglessness of ritual', *Numen* 26.1, 2–22.

Stähelin, F. (1924), *Das hellenistischen Thessalien: Landeskundliche und Geschichtliche Beschreibung Thessaliens in den hellenistischen und römischen Zeit*, Stuttgart.

Stähelin, F., Meyer, E., and Heidner, A. (1934), *Pagasai und Demetrias: Beschreibung der Reste und Stadtgeschichte*, Berlin and Leipzig.

Starkey, D. (1977), 'Representation through intimacy: A study in the symbolism of monarchy and court office in early modern England', in I. M. Lewis (ed.), *Symbols and Sentiments*, London and New York, 187–224.

— (1987), 'Court history in perspective', in D. Starkey, *The English Court: From the Wars of the Roses to the Civil War*, London, 1–24.

Stavrianopoulou, E. (ed.) (2013), *Shifting Social Imaginaries in the Hellenistic Period: Narrations, Practices, and Images*, Leiden and Boston.

Stewart, A. (2000), '*Pergamon ara marmorea magna*: On the date, reconstruction, and functions of the Great Altar of Pergamon', in N. De Grummond and S. Ridgway (eds), *From Pergamon to Sperlonga: Sculpture and Context*, Berkeley, 32–3.

— (2005), *Attalos, Athens, and the Akropolis: The Pergamene 'Little Barbarians' and their Roman and Renaissance Legacy*, Cambridge.

Stolper, M. W. (1985), *Entrepeneurs and Empire*, Istanbul.

Streck, M. (1917), 'Seleukia und Ktesiphon', *Der Alte Orient* 16, 1–64.

Strobel, K. (1994), 'Keltensieg und Galatersieger', in E. Schwertheim (ed.), *Forschungen in Galatien*, Bonn, 67–96.

Strootman, R. (1993), *Hof en heerser in de Hellenistische periode: De betekenis van het hof voor de legitimatie van absolute macht in de Hellenistische monarchieën, 323–30 v.Chr.*, MA dissertation, Leiden University.

— (2001), 'Mecenaat aan de hellenistische hoven', *Lampas* 34.3, 190–206.

— (2002), 'De vrouwelijke koning: Machtige vrouwen in de Hellenistische vorstendommen, 323–30 v.Chr.', *Groniek* 158–9, 45–62.

— (2005a), 'Kings against Celts: Deliverance from barbarians as a theme in Hellenistic royal propaganda', in K. A. E. Enenkel and I. L. Pfeijffer (eds), *The Manipulative Mode: Political Propaganda in Antiquity*, Leiden, 101–41.

— (2005b), 'De vrienden van de vorst: Het koninklijk hof in de Hellenistische periode', *Lampas* 38.3, 184–97.

— (2005c), 'Hellenistische Geschiedenis', *Lampas* 38.3, 280–5.

— (2006), 'Van wetsgetrouwen en afvalligen: Religieus geweld en culturele verandering in de tijd der Makkabeeën', in B. Becking and G. Rouwhorst (eds), *Religies in interactie: Jodendom en Christendom in de Oudheid*, Zoetermeer and Utrecht, 79–97.

— (2007), *The Hellenistic Royal Courts: Court Culture, Ceremonial and Ideology in Greece, Egypt and the Near East, 336–30 BCE*, PhD thesis, University of Utrecht.

— (2010a), 'Literature and the kings', in J. Clauss and M. Cuijpers (eds), *A Companion to Hellenistic Literature*, Malden and Oxford, 30–45.

— (2010b), 'Queen of kings: Cleopatra VII and the donations of Alexandria', in M. Facella and T. Kaizer (eds), *Kingdoms and Principalities in the Roman Near East*, Occidens et Oriens 19, Stuttgart, 140–57.

— (2011a), 'Hellenistic court society: The Seleukid imperial court under Antiochos the Great, 223–187 BCE', in J. Duindam, M. Kunt and T. Artan (eds), *Royal Courts in Dynastic States and Empires: A Global Perspective*, Rulers and Elites 1, Leiden, 63–89.

— (2011b), 'Kings and cities in the Hellenistic age', in R. Alston, O. van Nijf and C. Williamson (eds), *Political Culture in the Greek City after the Classical Age*, Groningen–Royal Holloway Studies on the Greek City after the Classical Age 2, Leuven, 141–53.

— (2012), 'The Seleukid empire between orientalism and Hellenocentrism: Writing the history of Iran in the third and second centuries BCE', *Nāme-ye Irān-e Bāstān: The International Journal of Ancient Iranian Studies*, 11.1–2, 17–35.

— (2013a), 'Dynastic courts of the Hellenistic empires', in H. Beck (ed.), *A Companion to Ancient Greek Government*, Malden and Oxford, 38–53.

— (2013b), 'Babylonian, Macedonian, king of the world: The Antiochos Cylinder from Borsippa and Seleukid imperial integration', in E. Stavrianopoulou (ed.), *Shifting Social Imaginaries in the Hellenistic Period: Narrations, Practices, and Images*, Leiden and Boston, 67–97.

— (2013c), 'Hellenistic imperialism and the ideal of world unity', in C. Rapp and H. Drake (eds), *City – Empire – Christendom: Changing Contexts of Power and Identity in Antiquity*, Cambridge.

— (forthcoming a), 'The dawning of a golden age: Images of peace and abundance in Alexandrian court poetry in relation to Ptolemaic imperial ideology', in M. A. Harder, R. F. Regtuit and G. C. Wakker (eds), *Hellenistic Poetry in Context*, Hellenistica Groningana 10, Leuven.

— (forthcoming b), 'Eunuchs, renegades and concubines: The "paradox of power" and the promotion of favourites in the Hellenistic empires', in A. Erskine and L. Llewellyn-Jones (eds), *The Hellenistic Royal Court*.

Stulz, H. (1990), *Die Farbe Purpur im frühen Griechentum: Beobachtet in der Literatur und in der bildenden Kunst*, Stuttgart.

Sullivan, R. D. (1990), *Near Eastern Royalty and Rome, 100–30 BC*, Toronto, Buffalo and London.

Tamm, B. (1968), '*Aula regia*, "*aulē*" und *aula*', in G. Säflund (ed.), *Opuscula Carolo Kerenyi Dedicata*, Stockholm, 135–242.

Tarn, W. W. (1913), *Antigonos Gonatas*, Oxford.

— (1930), *Hellenistic Military and Naval Developments*, Cambridge.

— [1938] (1951), *The Greeks in Bactria and India*, 2nd edn, Cambridge.

— (1948), *Alexander the Great*, 2 vols, Cambridge.

Tataki, A. B. (1998), *Macedonians Abroad: A Contribution to the Proso-pography of Ancient Macedonia*, Meletemata 26, Athens.

Tatum, W. J. (1996), 'The regal image in Plutarch's *Lives*', *JHS* 116, 135–51.

Thompson, D. B. (1963), *The Terracotta Figurines of the Hellenistic Period*, Princeton.

Thompson, D. J., Clarysse, W., and Quaegebeur, J. (eds) (1980), *Studies on Ptolemaic Memphis*, Studia Hellenistica 24, Leuven.

Thompson, D. J. (1980), 'Ptolemy, Ptah and Apis in Hellenistic Memphis', in D. J. Thompson, W. Clarysse and J. Quaegebeur (eds), *Studies on Ptolemaic Memphis*, Studia Hellenistica 24, Leuven, 1–42.

— (1988), *Memphis under the Ptolemies*, Princeton.

— (2000), 'Philadelphus' procession: Dynastic power in a Mediterranean context', in L. Mooren (ed.), *Politics, Administration and Society in the Hellenistic and Roman World*, Studia Hellenistica 36, Leuven, 365–88.

— (2001a), 'Athenaeus in his Egyptian context', in D. Braund and J. Wilkins (eds), *Athenaeus and his World: Reading Greek Culture in the Roman Empire*, Exeter, 77–86.

— (2001b), 'Hellenistic Hellenes: The case of Ptolemaic Egypt', in I. Malkin (ed.), *Ancient Perceptions of Greek Ethnicity*, Cambridge and London, 301–22.

— (2003), 'The Ptolemies and Egypt', in A. Erskine (ed.), *A Companion to the Hellenistic World*, Oxford, 105–20.

Thonemann, P. (2005), 'The tragic king: Demetrios Poliorketes and the city of Athens', in O. Hekster and R. Fowler (eds), *Imaginary Kings: Royal Images in the Ancient Near East, Greece and Rome*, Oriens et Occidens 11, Stuttgart, 63–86.

Tilg, S. (2010), *Chariton of Aphrodisias and the Invention of the Greek Love Novel*, Oxford and New York.

Tilly, C. (1990), *Coercion, Capital, and European States, AD 900–1990*, Cambridge and Oxford.

— (1994), 'Entanglements of European cities and states', in C. Tilly (ed.), *Cities and the Rise of States in Europe, A.D. 1000 to 1800*, Boulder, San Francisco and Oxford, 1–27.

Tomlison, R. A. (1983), 'Southern Greek influences on Macedonian architecture', in *Ancient Macedonia* 3, Thessaloniki, 285–9.

Tondriau, J. (1946), 'Le thiases dionysiaques royaux de la cour ptolé-maique', *CE* 41, 160–7

— (1948), 'Rois lagides comparés ou identifiés á des divinités', *CE* 45/6, 127–46.

— (1950), 'La dynastie ptolémaïque et la religion dionysiaque', *CE* 50, 282–316.

— (1953), 'Dionysos, dieu royale : Du Bacchos tauromorphe primitif aux souverains hellénistiques Neoi Dionysoi', in *Mélanges H. Grégoire*, Brussel, 441–66.

Tourraix, A. (1976), 'La femme et le pouvoir chez Hérodote : Essai d'histoire des mentalités antiques', *DHA* 2, 369–86.

Trell, B. L. [1988] (1989), 'The temple of Artemis at Ephesos', in P. A. Clayton and M. J. Price (eds), *The Seven Wonders of the Ancient World*, 2nd edn, London and New York, 78–99.

Trevor-Roper, H. (1976), *Princes and Patronage: Patronage and Ideology at Four Habsburg Courts, 1517–1633*, London.

Tripodi, B. (1992), 'Demetrio Poliorcete re-cacciatore', *Messana* 13, 123–42.

— (1998), *Cacce reali macedoni: Tra Alessandro I e Filippo V*, Messina.

Tuck, S. L. (2005), 'The origins of Roman imperial (lion) hunting imagery: Domitian and the redefinition of *virtus* under the Principate', *G&R* 52.2, 221–45.

Turner, E. G. (1984), 'Ptolemaic Egypt', in F. W. Walbank (ed.), *The Cambridge Ancient History. Volume 7.1: The Hellenistic World*, Cambridge, 118–74.

Van Wees, H. (1992), *Status Warriors: War, Violence and Society in Homer and History*, Amsterdam.

Versluys, M. J. (2002), *Aegyptiaca Romana: Nilotic Scenes and the Roman Views of Egypt*. Religions in the Graeco-Roman World 144, Leiden.

— (2010), 'Understanding Egypt in Egypt and beyond', in L. Bricault and M. J. Versluys (eds), *Isis on the Nile: Egyptian Gods in Hellenistic and Roman Egypt. Proceedings of the IVth International Conference of Isis Studies. Michel Malaise in Honorem*, Leiden, 7–36.

Versnel, H. S. (1970), *Triumphus: An Inquiry into the Origin, Development and Meaning of the Roman Triumph*, Leiden.

— (1974), 'Heersercultus in Griekenland: Het ontstaan van de heersercultus in Griekenland', *Lampas* 7.2, 129–63.

— (1978), *De tyrannie verdrijven? Een les in historische ambiguïteit*, Leiden.

— (1987), 'What did ancient man see when he saw a god? Some reflections on Greco-Roman epiphany', in D. van der Plas (ed.), *Effigies Dei: Essays on the History of Religions*, Numen Supplement 51, Leiden, 42–55.

— (1990), 'Isis, una quae es omnia. Tyrants against tyranny: Isis as a paradigm of Hellenistic rulership', in H. S. Versnel, *Ter Unus: Isis, Dionysos, Hermes. Three Studies in Henotheism*, Studies in Greek and Roman Religion 1, Leiden, 39–95.

— (1993), 'What is sauce for the goose is sauce for the gander: Myth and ritual, old and new', in H. S. Versnel, *Inconsistencies in Greek and Roman Religion II: Transition and Reversal in Myth and Ritual*, Studies in Greek and Roman Religion 6, Leiden, 16–88.

— (2011), *Coping with the Gods: Wayward Readings in Greek Theology*, Religions in the Graeco-Roman World 173, Leiden and Boston.

Vincient, J. (1992), 'Les artistes de cour aux temps d'Alexandre Ie Grand', *Revue Historique* 287, 3–9.

Virgilio, B. (1999), *Lancia, diadema e porpora: Il re e la régalità ellenistica*, Studi Ellenistici 11, Pisa and Rome.

Visser, C. E. (1938), *Götter und Kulte im ptolemäischen Alexandrien*, Amsterdam.

Volkmann, H. (1953), *Kleopatra: Politik und Propaganda*, Munich.

Vries, P. H. H. (1995), 'Clifford Geertz en de interpretatieve antropologie', in P. H. H. Vries, *Verhaal en Betoog: Geschiedbeoefening tussen postmoderne vertelling en sociaal-wetenschappelijke analyse*, Leiden, 121–34.

Wagner, J. (1976), *Seleukeia-am-Euphrat/Zeugma: Studien zur historischen Topographie und Geschichte*, Beihefte zum Tübinger Atlas des Vorderen Orients 10, Wiesbaden.

— (ed.) (2000), *Gottkönige am Euphrat: Neue Ausgrabungen und Forschungen in Kommagene*, Mainz.

Walbank, F. W. (1940), *Philip V of Macedon*, Cambridge.

— (1984a), 'Monarchies and monarchic ideas', *CAH* 7.1, 62–100.

— (1984b), 'Macedonia and Greece', *CAH* 7.1, 221–56.

— (1985), 'The problem of Greek nationality', in F. W. Walbank, *Selected Papers: Studies in Greek and Roman History and Historiography*, Cambridge, 1–19.

— (1996), 'Two Hellenistic processions: A matter of self-definition', *Scripta Classica Israelica* 15, 119–30.

Waterman, L. (1931), *Preliminary Report upon the Excavations at Tell Umar*, London.

— (1933), *Second Preliminary Report upon the Excavations at Tell Umar, Iraq*, London.

Waywell, G. B. (1988), 'The Mausoleum at Halicarnassus', in P. A. Clayton and M. J. Price (eds), *The Seven Wonders of the Ancient World*, London and New York, 100–23.

Weber, G. (1993), *Dichtung und höfische Gesellschaft: Die Rezeption von Zeitgeschichte am Hof der ersten drei Ptolemäer*, Stuttgart.

— (1995), 'Herrscher, Hof und Dichter: Aspekte der Legitimierung und Repräsentation hellenistischer Könige am Beispiel der ersten drei Antigoniden', *Historia* 44, 283–316.

— (1997), 'Interaktion, Repräsentation und Herrschaft: Der Königshof im Hellenismus', in A. Winterling (ed.), *Zwischen Haus und Staat*, Munich, 27–71.

— (1998/9), 'The Hellenistic rulers and their poets: Silencing dangerous critics?', *AncSoc* 29, 147–74.

— (2009), 'The court of Alexander the Great as social system', in W. Heckel and L.A. Tritle (eds), *Alexander the Great: A New History*, Malden, 83–98.

Weber, M. [1921–2] (1964), *Wirtschaft und Gesellschaft: Grundriss der verstehender Soziologie*, 5th rev. edn, Tübingen.

— (1968), 'Drei reinen Typen der legitimen Herrschaft', in M. Weber, *Methodologische Schriften*, Frankfurt am Main, 215–28.

Weill Goudchaux, G. (2001), 'Cleopatra's subtle religious strategy', in S. Walker and P. Higgs (eds), *Cleopatra of Egypt: From History to Myth*, Princeton, 128–41.

Weissert, E. (1997), 'Royal hunt and royal triumph in a prism fragment of Ashurbanipal', in S. Parpola and R. M. Whiting (eds), *Assyria 1995: Proceedings of the 10th Anniversary Symposium of the Neo-Assyrian Text Corpus Project, Helsinki, September 7–11, 1995*, Helsinki.

Welles, C. B. (1934), *Royal Correspondence in the Hellenistic Period: A Study in Greek Epigraphy*, 2nd edn, London.

— (1963), 'The reliability of Ptolemy as an historian', in *Miscellanea di studi alessandri in memoria di A. Rostagni*, Turin, 101–16.

Wenning, R. (1978), *Die Galateranatheme Attalos I: Eine Untersuchung zum Bestand und zur Nachwirkung pergamenischer Skulptur*, Berlin.

Wheatly, P.V. (2001), 'The Antigonid campaign in Cyprus, 306 BC', *AncSoc* 31, 133–56.

Whitehorne, J. (1994), *Cleopatras*, London and New York.

Wiemer, H. U. (2003), 'Vergangenheit und Gegenwart im "Antiochikos" des Libanios', *Klio* 85, 442–68.

Wijma, S. M. (2010), *Joining the Athenian Community: The Participation of Metics in Athenian Polis Religion in the Fifth and Fourth Centuries B.C.*, dissertation, Utrecht University.

Wikander, C. (1992), 'Pomp and circumstance: The procession of Ptolemy II', *Opuscula Atheniensia* 19.12, 143–50.

— (1996), 'Religion, political power and gender: The building of a cult image', in P. Hellström and B. Alroth (eds), *Religion and Power in the Ancient Greek World*, Uppsala, 183–8.

Wikander, M. H. (1993), *Princes to Act: Royal Audience and Royal Performance, 1578–1792*, Baltimore.

Wilentz, S. (1985), *Rites of Power*, Philadelphia.

Will, É. (1979), *Histoire politique du monde hellénistique (323–30 av. J.-C.). Tome I: De la mort d'Alexandre aux avènements d'Antiochos III et de Philippe V*, 2nd rev. edn, Nancy.

— (1990), 'La capitale des Séleucides', in *Akten des XIII. Internationalen Kongress für klassische Archäologie, Berlin 1988*, Mainz am Rhein, 259–65.

Willrich, H. (1909), 'Zum hellenistischen Titel- und Ordens-wesen', *Klio* 9, 416–21.

Winter, E. (2011), 'Formen ptolemäischer Präsenz in der Ägäis zwischen schriftlicher Überlieferung und archäologischem Befund', in E. Winte (ed.), *Militärsiedlungen und Territorialherrschaft in der Antike*, Topoi: Berlin Studies of the Ancient World 3, Berlin and New York.

Winter, F. E. (1971), *Greek Fortifications*, Toronto.

Winterling, A. (1986), *Der Hof der Kurfürsten von Köln 1688–1794: Eine*

Fallstudie zur Bedeutung 'absolutistischer' Hofhaltung, Bonn.

— (ed.) (1997), *Zwischen Haus und Staat: Antike Höfe im Vergleich*, Munich.

— (2004), '"Hof": Versuch einer idealtypischen Bestimmung anhand der mittelalterlichen und neufrühzeitlichen Geschichte' in R. Butz, J. Hirschbiegel and D. Willoweit (eds), *Hof und Theorie*, Cologne, Weimar and Vienna, 77–90.

Wolf, E. [1956] (1971), 'Aspects of group relations in a complex society', in T. Shanin (ed.), *Peasants and Peasant Societies*, Harmondsworth, 50–6.

Woodhead, A. G. (1981), 'Athens and Demetrius Poliorcetes at the end of the fourth century B.C.', in H. J. Dell (ed.), *Ancient Macedonian Studies in Honour of Charles F. Edson*, Thessaloniki, 357–67.

Woolf, G. (2001), 'Inventing empire in ancient Rome' in: S. E. Alcock, T. N. D'Altroy, K. D. Morrison and C. M. Sinopoli (eds), *Empires: Perspectives from Archaeology and History*, Cambridge, 311–22.

Wright, N. L. (2011), 'The iconography of succession under the late Seleukids', in N. L. Wright (ed.), *Coins from Asia Minor and the East: Selections from the Colin E. Pitchfork Collection*, Ancient Coins in Australian Collections 2, Sydney, 41–6.

Yoyotte, J. (1999), 'Alexandrie: La grande bataille de l'archéologie', *L'Histoire* 238, 50–4.

Zanker, G. (1987), *Realism in Alexandrian Poetry: A Literature and its Audience*, London.

Zorzi, E. G. (1986), 'Court spectacle', in S. Bertelli, F. Cardini and E. Garbero Zorzi (eds), *The Courts of the Italian Renaissance*, Milan, 127–87.

Zimmer, G. (1996), 'Prunkgeschirr hellenistischer Herrscher', in G. Brands and W. Hoepfner (eds), *Basileia: Die Paläste der hellenistischen Könige, Internationales Symposion in Berlin vom 16.12.1992 bis 20.12.1992*, Mainz am Rhein.

Index